PROFESSIONAL CONDUCT

PROFESSIONAL CONDUCT

Inns of Court School of Law

First published in Great Britain 1996 by Blackstone Press Limited,
Aldine Place, London W12 8AA. Telephone (020) 8740 2277
www.blackstonepress.com

© Inns of Court School of Law, 1996

First edition 1996
Second edition 1997
Third edition 1998
Fourth edition 1999

ISBN: 1 85431 956 6

British Library Cataloguing in Publication Data
A CIP catalogue record for this book is available from the British Library.

Typeset by Style Photosetting Ltd, Mayfield, East Sussex
Printed by Ashford Colour Press, Gosport, Hants

FOREWORD

These manuals are designed primarily to support training on the Bar Vocational Course, though they are also intended to provide a useful resource for legal practitioners and for anyone undertaking training in legal skills.

The Bar Vocational Course was designed by staff at the Inns of Court School of Law, where it was introduced in 1989. This course is intended to equip students with the practical skills and the procedural and evidential knowledge that they will need to start their legal professional careers. These manuals are written by staff at the Inns of Court School of Law who have helped to develop the course, and by a range of legal practitioners and others involved in legal skills training. The authors of the manuals are very well aware of the practical and professional approach that is central to the Bar Vocational Course.

The range and coverage of the manuals have grown steadily. All the manuals are updated annually, and regular reviews and revisions of the manuals are carried out to ensure that developments in legal skills training and the experience of our staff are fully reflected in them.

This updating and revision is a constant process and we very much value the comments of practitioners, staff and students. Legal vocational training is advancing rapidly, and it is important that all those concerned work together to achieve and maintain high standards. Please address any comments to the Bar Vocational Course Director at the Inns of Court School of Law.

With the validation of other providers for the Bar Vocational Course it is very much our intention that these manuals will be of equal value to all students wherever they take the course, and we would very much value comments from tutors and students at other validated institutions.

The enthusiasm of the staff at Blackstone Press Ltd and their efficiency in arranging production and publication of the manuals is much appreciated.

The Hon. Mr Justice Elias
Chairman of the Board of Governors
Inns of Court School of Law
September 1999

CONTENTS

CONTENTS

PREFACE

In its *First Report on Legal Education and Training* (April 1996), the Lord Chancellor's Advisory Committee on Legal Education and Conduct (ACLEC) begins by addressing the 'Changing Needs of Legal Practice in the 21st Century'. One of the foremost challenges to the future education and training of lawyers that the committee identified was 'the ethical challenge' (para. 1.21):

> From the earliest stages of education and training, intending lawyers should be imbued not only with the standards and codes of professional conduct, but also more generally with the obligations of lawyers to help protect individuals and groups from the abuse of public and private power.

In so far as the training and education of intending barristers is concerned, this Manual is a response to the ethical challenge.

Meeting the ethical challenge means first, that intending barristers learn the tenets of their Code of Conduct and are able to apply its letter and spirit in practice. The Manual includes the full text of the Code of Conduct of the Bar of England and Wales. In isolating, analysing and encouraging students to apply the provisions of the Code of Conduct, the Manual gives a grounding in what might be called 'traditional' or 'vocational' professional conduct.

The second part of the ethical challenge involves a broadening of perspectives and a greater consciousness of issues such as discrimination and harassment. In order to achieve this, the Manual includes two chapters which take students beyond the confines of the Code of Conduct.

In Chapter 3, The Ethical Challenge: the Equality Code, Harassment and Discrimination' we have included pieces from Lord Justice Brooke, the former chairman of the Ethnic Minority Advisory Committee of the Judicial Studies Board (EMAC), on 'Treating People Fairly'; Barbara Hewson on 'Harassment: Law and Professional Ethics', and Judicial Studies Board Papers on 'Ethnic Minorities: Appropriate Terminology', and 'Body Language and Cross-Cultural Communication'. It is only by confronting, understanding and learning to deal with issues such as discrimination and harassment that lawyers can fulfil the role ACLEC sees for them in protecting 'individuals and groups from the abuse of public and private power'.

In Chapter 4, 'The Ethical Challenge: Legal Ethics and Professional Responsibility', Professor Ross Cranston examines a range of broader ethical, political and economic issues which arise from a consideration of the barrister's professional responsibility beyond the confines of the Code of Conduct. The chapter raises wider ethical issues than may be apparent from a strict application of the provisions of the Code of Conduct.

In this Manual I have also tried to increase greatly the amount of practical advice and guidance from those at the 'coal-face' of practice at the Bar. In Chapter 2, 'Professional

Relationships' there are contributions from two senior solicitors (civil and criminal) on the 'Relationship with the Professional Client', a senior clerk writes on the 'Relationship between Barrister and Clerk', and the National Consumer Council has assisted with the section on the 'Relationship with the Lay Client'. There has also been invaluable input from members of the Bar and the Bar Council's professional conduct department. Key practical texts such as 'The Code For Crown Prosecutors' help to bring within one text the bulk of the materials on questions of conduct that the intending barrister needs.

The professional conduct of barristers will always be under scrutiny. The need to foster good practice and maintain the highest standards is an ongoing obligation for the profession. I hope that this Manual plays a part in honouring that obligation.

Clive Coleman,
Barrister,
Principal Lecturer in Law, ICSL

ONE

INTRODUCTION

Paragraph 201 of the Code of Conduct states that:

A barrister . . . must not:

(a) engage in conduct whether in pursuit of his profession or otherwise which is:

  (i) dishonest or otherwise discreditable to a barrister;

  (ii) prejudicial to the administration of justice; or

  (iii) likely to diminish public confidence in the legal profession or the administration of justice or otherwise bring the legal profession into disrepute.

There is nothing more important to practice at the Bar than the way in which barristers conduct themselves and the regard in which they are held by their peers, lay and professional clients and those holding judicial office before whom they appear. At a time when lawyers are under intense public scrutiny, any barrister who neglects to act at all times with integrity and strict compliance with professional standards does so at the peril of damaging both his or her own reputation and that of the profession. It is for these reasons that professional conduct is perhaps the single most important subject for the aspiring barrister to master, and the Code of Conduct, included in this Manual at **Appendix 1**, perhaps the most important single text to absorb and apply.

1.1 The Code of Conduct

The Code of Conduct contains the written standards of professional conduct to be observed by barristers, whether in employment or independent practice. Observance of the provisions of the Code is not confined to the inside of the courtroom. It extends to all aspects of the barrister's work, and in some respects to behaviour beyond work as a barrister. See, for instance, para. 201(b) which forbids a barrister to 'engage directly or indirectly in any occupation if his [or her] association with that occupation may adversely affect the reputation of the Bar or in the case of a practising barrister prejudice his [or her] ability to attend properly to the interests of his [or her] client'. Every student on a Bar Vocational Course, and every barrister should have a sound working knowledge of the main body of the Code of Conduct and be familiar with its annexes. Particular regard should be paid to Annexe F, entitled 'Written Standards for the Conduct of Professional Work' within which are contained both general standards and standards applicable to criminal cases.

It is important to realise that the Code of Conduct is not prescriptive. It sets out the main duties and obligations comprised in good professional conduct. It is somewhat akin to a set of principles and does not attempt to cover every situation and scenario in which a barrister will need to apply its provisions. The student on a Bar Vocational Course and the barrister in practice will encounter many professional conduct problems about which the Code of Conduct does not give specific advice or guidance. It is for that reason that students and barristers alike must become confident in applying the **spirit** of the Code where there is no **letter**. It goes without saying that it is only possible to apply the spirit of the Code properly if you are familiar with its main provisions.

No one has a monopoly of wisdom in coping with professional conduct problems. It is in recognition of this that there exists a genuine tradition of help and guidance amongst the Bar and judiciary. Senior colleagues in chambers, other counsel at court and the judge are all people from whom you can seek guidance in negotiating knotty professional conduct problems. Colleagues at the Bar will rarely, if ever, refuse to assist on a question of professional conduct. Barristers can also contact the Professional Conduct Committee of the Bar Council for guidance. A team of people in the professional conduct department takes calls from barristers at court or in chambers. If they are unable to assist with a particular problem then they will refer you on to a senior member of the Professional Conduct Committee, usually a QC, who will try to help. It is worth noting that a call to the professional conduct department can often be a sensible way of covering yourself when you are confronted with a tricky professional conduct problem. It shows that you have acted reasonably in trying to seek the best guidance before adopting a particular course of action.

1.2   The Consequences of Misconduct

Any breach of the Code of Conduct constitutes professional misconduct and will result in liability for disciplinary proceedings (see para. 802.1 of the Code of Conduct and **Chapter 6**). You could face being disbarred, suspended from practice, fined, ordered to forgo or repay fees, excluded from undertaking legal aid work, admonished or advised as to your future conduct. Disciplinary proceedings are the most obvious consequence of a violation of the ethics of the profession. They are not, however, the only one. If you gain a reputation as a 'sharp' practitioner, your life in practice will become very much more difficult. Other barristers will regard you with suspicion and each case you undertake will become much harder work than it need be. Trials rarely proceed in the precise way prescribed by the rules of court. Due to no fault of your own, time limits are missed, documents are served late and evidence which had been overlooked comes to light. To cope with this there needs to be a degree of mutual trust and respect between counsel. If you cannot command that degree of trust and respect from your opponents, you will experience a reluctance to accept late amendments to statements of case or late disclosure of documents. Settlement negotiations will ossify if your opponent does not believe that you are negotiating in good faith and to the acceptable standards (see further **Chapter 2**). He or she may be suspicious that you are failing to disclose material which would weaken your negotiating position. Barristers who do not trust their opponents tend to give them a very hard time. You do not want to be on the receiving end of such treatment each time you come into contact with counsel or indeed the solicitor for the other side.

It should also be noted that the Bar is still a small profession and as such it is an extremely effective 'grapevine'. A reputation for sharp practice will spread quickly and your future career could suffer significantly as a result. Sets of chambers sometimes split and the nature of your developing practice may prompt you to try to join another set in which your practice stands a better chance of prospering. Any application that you make during the course of your career as a barrister, whether it be for a tenancy in another set of chambers, for silk or a judicial office is likely to be blighted by a reputation for sharp or dishonest practice.

1.3   The Ethical Challenge

In its *First Report on Legal Education and Training* (April 1996), the Lord Chancellor's Advisory Committee on Legal Education and Conduct (ACLEC) begins by addressing the 'Changing Needs of Legal Practice in the 21st Century'. One of the foremost challenges to the future education and training of lawyers that the committee identified was the ethical challenge. ACLEC was concerned that 'teaching in ethical values should include more than a familiarisation with professional codes of conduct and the machinery for enforcing them' (p. 17). ACLEC sees it as crucial that trainee lawyers are made aware of their wider obligations to society and in particular the obligation to 'help protect individuals and groups from the abuse of private and public power'. This Manual aims to help intending barristers to meet that ethical challenge.

1.4 Behaviour and Discrimination

An integral part of good professional conduct is the attitude which you adopt and display towards the variety of people with whom you come into contact in your professional life. These range from colleagues in chambers, opponents, the judiciary, professional clients, lay clients, witnesses and court staff, to other professionals such as police officers, doctors and social workers. You will be dealing with people from every walk of life, every socio-economic group, with different mental abilities, customs and expectations. It is crucial that you treat people courteously and fairly and that you are scrupulous to avoid discriminating directly or indirectly against any person on grounds of 'race, colour, ethnic or national origin, nationality, citizenship, sex, sexual orientation, marital status, disability, religion or political persuasion' (see para. 204.1, Code of Conduct). Such discrimination is not only a breach of the Code of Conduct, it is also a breach of the Bar's Equality Code (see Annexe O of the Code of Conduct in **Appendix 1**). Your success at the Bar will depend more than anything upon the way that you treat other people. You will not like every client or person with whom you come into contact. There may be occasions when you dislike a client intensely, distrust the motives of another professional or become frustrated with the inaction of a solicitor. It is vital that, in addition to a commitment to courtesy, you heed the guidance and advice in **Chapter 3**. That chapter contains invaluable practical advice from Lord Justice Brooke, Barbara Hewson and guidance papers from the Judicial Studies Board. Preconceptions about different peoples, cultures and religions are dangerous and you must ensure that you are free of these. A lack of understanding of other cultures and religions will rarely, if ever, be acceptable as a way of excusing conduct which is insensitive to the point of being damaging.

1.5 Legal Ethics: a Broader View

Part of the job of meeting the ethical challenge involves an intellectual consideration of broader ethical issues than may be apparent from a strictly 'barrister's' reading of the Code of Conduct. In **Chapter 4** Professor Ross Cranston addresses some of the wider ethical issues that arise from a consideration of the barrister's professional responsibility. Barristers cannot afford to adopt a blinkered approach to ethical issues. A wider framework of ethical considerations should, to a degree, inform the way in which you negotiate professional conduct problems and consider your professional responsibilities.

1.6 Practical Advice and Key Texts

Because so much that is important in fostering good practice in professional conduct is learnt by experience, this Manual draws heavily upon the experience of barristers, solicitors, judges, clerks, the Bar Council and organizations to which lay clients turn, such as the National Consumer Council. See, in particular, **Chapter 2**. You will find contributions from those at the sharp end, those who have experience of good and bad professional conduct. Following the guidance and advice they give will put you well on the way to applying the letter and spirit of the Code of Conduct, and behaving towards others with the respect and sensitivity that the profession demands of its members.

A number of important texts have been gathered together in this volume. In addition to the Code of Conduct and the Equality Code, 'The Code for Crown Prosecutors', 'Crown Prosecution Service Standards' and Judicial Studies Board papers on, for instance, 'Body Language and Cross Cultural Communication', will provide the Bar Vocational course student and barrister alike with a thorough grounding in the standards, requirements and advice of those organizations who work with, instruct and observe barristers.

The emphasis upon the practical application of the principles of professional conduct is further illustrated by the threading of a series of problems through this Manual. The questions are designed to test your ability to apply the principles of professional conduct, and answers are contained in **Appendix 3**.

1.7   Content of the Course

The course is divided into a number of parts. There will be three lectures and three tutorials. An introductory lecture will be given by an eminent member of the profession, normally a member or former member of the Professional Conduct Committee of the Bar Council. Two further lectures will cover professional conduct on the Bar Vocational Course and in the early days of practice, and discrimination and the Equality Code.

Tutorials will be taken by senior practitioners. The problems for these tutorials can be found in **Chapter 7**. It is important that you come prepared in advance for these classes and be ready to discuss the way in which you would deal with each of the problems posed. You will be expected and encouraged to participate in seeking an appropriate solution to each question.

The practical training exercises in the skills subjects will incorporate and reinforce many aspects of professional conduct and you will be expected to recognize and deal with professional conduct problems as they occur. Some of the practical training exercises will be designed to highlight specific professional conduct issues in greater detail. It should be noted that professional conduct forms part of the assessment criteria in the skills subjects.

1.8   Professional Conduct and Pupillage

In 1994 Professor J Pottenger from Yale Law School conducted research on the professional conduct training that takes place during pupillage. He found that most (77%) of the pupils questioned had come across matters which they thought raised issues of professional conduct or etiquette. Nearly 60% had observed their pupil master or mistress 'dealing with an ethical dilemma'. These figures are indicative of the relevance of professional conduct issues in pupillage. Pupil masters and mistresses will expect, and pupils should possess, a sound knowledge and understanding of the principles and application of good professional conduct. It should also be noted that there is a professional conduct section to the pupillage check lists which pupil masters and mistresses supply to their pupils and which each pupil is required to satisfy.

1.9   Using this Manual as Your Code

This Manual reproduces the Code of Conduct in its exact form. The reason for this is to enable amendments to the Code to be added in. Students are advised to convert this Manual into loose leaf form and place it in a ring binder file. The binding and holes punched through the Manual make this possible. By so doing you will be able to insert amendments to the Code as and when they come out and are issued to you. It is hoped that you will take this Manual into practice with you. If you do, you will have the benefit of a large number of key professional conduct 'texts' and essays in one place. These will augment the Code of Conduct and assist you in dealing with the many professional conduct problems that you will encounter.

TWO

PROFESSIONAL RELATIONSHIPS

Whether instructed for the prosecution or defence, claimant or defendant, applicant or respondent, as counsel you must consider a number of responsibilities beyond those to your client. Of course everything possible must be done on behalf of the client, but counsel has a number of wider duties. Miscarriages of justice can and do occur when counsel forget or ignore their duties to the court, to their professional client and the Crown Prosecution Service, and to other members of the profession. There is even a duty to the Legal Aid Fund. A barrister should be concerned in the administration of justice, and **not** to win at all costs.

It is not uncommon for these duties to conflict, e.g., over the disclosure of some evidence or an authority harmful to your case. Frequently the question is not straightforward. It is important that from the earliest days you can at the very least recognise that there is a potential problem so that you can then take steps, e.g., discussion with a senior barrister or telephoning the Professional Conduct Committee, to ensure that the right answer is reached.

In this chapter we consider a number of ways in which the duty to one's client is, and must be, fettered, so that ultimately justice is achieved. More broadly we consider the range of professional relationships that the barrister will enter into in the course of practice and the duties and obligations that are owed in conducting each relationship successfully and to the appropriate ethical standard. In addition there is practical advice from some of those on the other side of the various relationships with counsel. Senior solicitors, a senior clerk and the National Consumer Council to whom dissatisfied lay clients can turn, all contribute practical guidance and advice which, if heeded, will provide you with a sense of how to make your professional relationships work effectively in day to-day practice.

2.1 Relationship with the Court

2.1.1 DUTIES AND RESPONSIBILITIES OWED TO THE COURT

Time and again, the judiciary have stressed the paramount duty of counsel to the court. In *Rondel* v *Worsley* [1969] 1 AC 191, 227 Lord Reid put it in this way:

> Every counsel has a duty to his client fearlessly to raise every issue, advance every argument, and ask every question, however distasteful, which he thinks will help his client's case. But, as an officer of the Court concerned in the administration of justice, he has an overriding duty to the Court, to the standards of his profession, and to the public, which may and often does lead to a conflict with his client's wishes or with what the client thinks are his personal interests.

In the same case, Lord Denning MR explained the nature of the duty to the Court in these terms:

> [Counsel] must accept the brief and do all he honourably can on behalf of his client. I say 'all he honourably can' because his duty is not only to his client. He has a duty

to the Court which is paramount. It is a mistake to suppose that he is the mouthpiece of his client to say what he wants: or his tool to do what he directs. He is none of these things. He owes allegiance to a higher cause. It is the cause of truth and justice. He must not consciously misstate the facts. He must not knowingly conceal the truth. He must not unjustly make a charge of fraud, that is, without evidence to support it. He must produce all the relevant authorities, even those that are against him. He must see that his client discloses, if ordered, the relevant documents, even those that are fatal to his case. He must disregard the most specific instructions of his client, if they conflict with his duty to the court. The code which requires a barrister to do all this is not a code of law. It is a code of honour. If he breaks it, he is offending against the rules of the profession and is subject to its discipline. But he cannot be sued in a Court of law. Such being his duty to the Court, the barrister must be able to do it fearlessly. He has time and time again to choose between his duty to his client and his duty to the Court. ([1966] 3 WLR 950, 962.)

2.1.1.1   Examples of duties and responsibilities

Your overriding duty to the court to ensure in the public interest that the proper and efficient administration of justice is achieved incorporates many separate responsibilities. These are set out in the Code of Conduct and include a duty:

(a) To assist the court in the fair administration of justice, and not to deceive or knowingly or recklessly mislead the court (para. 202). This would include, e.g., correcting any misleading information which is incorporated in your client's affidavit and which on your instructions, is inaccurate. In *Abraham* v *Justsun* [1963] 2 All ER 402, 404 Lord Denning MR explained this duty further:

> [It is an] advocate's duty to take any point which he believes to be fairly arguable on behalf of his client. An advocate is not to usurp the province of the judge. He is not to determine what shall be the effect of legal argument. He is not guilty of misconduct simply because he takes a point which the tribunal holds to be bad. He only becomes guilty of misconduct if he is dishonest. That is, if he knowingly takes a bad point and thereby deceives the court.

(b) To act with due courtesy to the court (Annexe F, General Standards, para. 5.5).

(c) To bring to the attention of the court all relevant decisions and legislative provisions of which you are aware, whether or not their effect is favourable to your case (para. 610(c)).

(d) To bring any procedural irregularity to the attention of the court during the trial (para. 610(c)).

(e) To advise that all relevant documents be disclosed and withdraw from the case if such advice is not followed (para. 506(f)).

(f) To record the proceedings. You have a duty to take a note of the judge's reasons for his decision and have it typed as soon as there is any question of an appeal (see *Letts* v *Letts*, *The Times*, 8 April 1987).

(g) Not to devise facts which will assist in advancing your lay client's case or settle a groundless statement of case (para. 606). In *Steamship Mutual Underwriting Association Ltd* v *Trollope & Colls Ltd*, *The Times*, 31 March 1986, May LJ put it in these terms:

> . . . To issue a writ when there was no evidential basis upon which a statement of claim could be founded and without any intention to serve one was an abuse of the process of the court.

(h) Not to allege fraud in any statement of case without clear instructions to do so and without reasonably credible material which establishes a prima facie case of fraud (para. 606(c)).

(i)   Not to assert a **personal** opinion of the facts or the law to the court unless invited to do so by the court (para. 610(b)).

(j)   Not to make statements or ask questions which are merely scandalous or intended or calculated only to vilify, insult or annoy either a witness or some other person (para. 610(e)).

2.1.1.2   Wasted costs orders: civil and criminal

The barrister is also under a duty to take all reasonable and practicable steps to avoid unnecessary expense or waste of the court's time (Annexe F, General Standards, para. 5.11); this includes a duty not to waste an appellate court's time. In *Ainsbury* v *Millington, The Times*, 13 March 1987, Lord Bridge stated that it was:

> the duty of counsel and solicitors in any pending appeal in publicly funded litigation whenever an event occurred which arguably disposed of the matter in contention, either to ensure that the appeal was withdrawn by consent or, in the absence of agreement, to bring the facts promptly to the attention of the appellate court and to seek directions.

Note that counsel could be made liable personally for costs thrown away (see Supreme Court Act 1981, s. 51(6) and CPR, Part 48, r. 48 and PD 48). Similar orders could follow under CPR, Part 44, r. 44 (assessment of costs). Section 19 of the Prosecution of Offences Act 1985, gave the magistrates' courts, the Crown Court and the Court of Appeal power, where satisfied that one party to criminal proceedings has incurred costs as a result of an unnecessary or improper act or omission by, or on behalf of, another party to the proceedings, to make an order as to the payment of those costs. Section 19A, which was inserted by the Courts and Legal Services Act 1990, gives similar powers to disallow or (as the case may be) order the legal or other representative concerned to meet the whole of any wasted costs or any part of them. 'Wasted costs' means any costs incurred by a party:

(a)   as a result of any improper, unreasonable or negligent act or omission on the part of any representative or any employee of a representative; or

(b)   which, in the light of any such act or omission occurring after they were incurred, the court considers it is unreasonable to expect that party to pay.

There have been a number of cases in which courts, including the Court of Appeal, have made wasted costs orders against barristers. In *Re A Barrister (Wasted Costs Order No. 1 of 1991)* [1992] 3 WLR 662, the Court of Appeal recommended a three-stage test:

(a)   Had there been an improper, unreasonable or negligent act or omission?

(b)   If so, had any costs been incurred by any party in consequence thereof?

(c)   If so, should the court exercise its discretion to disallow, or order the representative to meet, the whole of any part of the relevant costs and, if so, what specific sum was involved?

In the Court of Appeal case of *Ridehalgh* v *Horsefield* [1994] 3 WLR 462 Sir Thomas Bingham MR made it clear that the judgment was applicable to criminal as well as civil courts, and made the following points. This passage is taken from *Blackstone's Criminal Practice*, 1998.

(a)   'Improper' covered, but was not confined to, conduct which would ordinarily justify serious professional penalty. It was not limited to significant breach of the relevant code of professional conduct. It included conduct which was improper according to the consensus of professional, including judicial, opinion, whether it violated the letter of a professional code or not.

(b) 'Unreasonable' described conduct which was vexatious, i.e., designed to harass the other side rather than advance the resolution of the dispute. Conduct could not be described as unreasonable simply because it led to an unsuccessful result, or because other more cautious legal representatives would have acted differently. The acid test was whether the conduct permitted of a reasonable explanation. If it did, the course adopted might be regarded as optimistic and reflecting on a practitioner's judgment, but it was not unreasonable.

(c) 'Negligent' should be understood in an untechnical way to denote failure to act with the competence reasonably expected of ordinary members of the profession. It was not a term of art and did not necessarily involve an actionable breach of the legal representative's duty to his own client.

(d) A legal representative was not acting improperly, unreasonably or negligently simply because he acted for a party who pursued a claim or defence which was plainly doomed to fail.

(e) However, a legal representative could not lend his assistance to proceedings which were an abuse of process, and was not entitled to use litigious procedures for purposes for which they were not intended, e.g., by issuing proceedings for reasons unconnected with success in the action, pursuing a case which was known to be dishonest or knowingly conniving at incomplete disclosure of documents.

(f) Any judge considering making a wasted costs order must make full allowance for the fact that an advocate in court often had to make decisions quickly and under pressure.

(g) Legal professional privilege might be relevant. If so, the privilege was the client's which he alone could waive. Judges should make full allowance for the inability of respondent lawyers to tell the whole story. Where there was room for doubt, the respondent lawyers were entitled to the benefit of it. It was only when, with all allowance made, a lawyer's conduct of proceedings was quite plainly unjustifiable that it could be appropriate to make the order.

(h) When a solicitor sought the advice of counsel, he did not abdicate his own professional responsibility. He had to apply his mind to the advice received. But the more specialised the advice, the more reasonable it was likely to be for him to accept it.

(i) A threat to apply for a wasted costs order should not be used as a means of intimidation. However, if one side considered that the conduct of the other was improper, unreasonable or negligent and likely to cause a waste of costs, it was not objectionable to alert the other side to that view.

(j) In the ordinary way, such applications were best left until after the end of the trial.

(k) As to procedure, the respondent lawyer should be told very clearly what he was said to have done wrong. No formal process of discovery would be appropriate. Elaborate statements of case should in general be avoided. The court could not imagine circumstances in which the applicant could interrogate the respondent lawyer or vice versa. The legal representative must have opportunity to show cause why an order should not be made (Rules of the Supreme Court 1965, O. 62, r. 11(4)), but this did not mean that the burden was on the legal representative to exculpate himself. (Note that this extract was written before the introduction of the Civil Procedure Rules 1998.)

In *Re A Barrister (Wasted Costs Order No. 4 of 1992), The Times*, 15 March 1994, the Court of Appeal held that a barrister who practised at home without a clerk must not rely wholly on instructing solicitors to notify him of the dates and times of cases. He was responsible for keeping abreast of listing details and should have adopted a system which enabled him to do so.

In *Re A Barrister (Wasted Costs Order No. 4 of 1993)*, *The Times*, 21 April 1995, the Court of Appeal held that a judge should not impose such a Draconian penalty as a wasted costs order without taking into account the daily demands of practice and the difficulties associated with time estimates.

2.1.1.3 Contact with witnesses

The sixth amendment of the Code of Conduct changes considerably the rules governing a barrister's contact with witnesses.

Under the new rules certain key obligations remain. A practising barrister must not place a witness under any pressure to provide anything other than a truthful account of his or her evidence, and must not 'rehearse, practise or coach a witness in relation to his [or her] evidence or the way in which he [or she] should give it' (see para. 607 of the sixth amendment).

The major change arises in the amendment to paras. 6.1 to 6.2 of Annexe F. Under this amended section there is no longer any rule which prevents a barrister from having contact with any witness. In particular barristers are reminded that it is their responsibility to put nervous or vulnerable witnesses at ease by explaining unfamiliar court procedures. A distinction is drawn between contact with witnesses for the purpose of putting them at ease etc. and for the purpose of interviewing them or discussing the substance of their evidence. Contact for the latter purposes is now permissible but it is left to the barrister's discretion whether such contact is appropriate, bearing in mind, for example, that such discussions may lead to suspicions of coaching and tend to diminish the value of that witness's evidence. Further guidance on the exercise of this discretion is laid down in the sixth amendment.

Criminal cases in the Crown Court may expose barristers to special pressures and in such cases, with the exception of lay clients, character and expert witnesses, as a general principle, it is wholly inappropriate for a barrister to interview any potential witness. Interviewing includes discussing with any such witness the substance of his evidence or the evidence of other such witnesses. (See para. 6.3 of Annexe F in the sixth amendment for this and further guidance on contact with witnesses in Crown Court cases.)

2.1.1.4 Problems

(1)   In the course of legal argument, your opponent advances a proposition of law to the court in support of their client's case, but fails to produce a particular reported decision of which you are aware and which would plainly be of assistance. Without it you are likely to win; with it you may well fail. What do you do? Does your answer depend upon for whom you are acting and whether in civil or criminal proceedings?

(2)   Whilst sitting in court waiting for your case to be called, you listen to the previous case. Counsel for the claimant is seeking to persuade the judge that the maximum time that the judge can allow the defendant to vacate the claimant's premises is 14 days. The defendant is unrepresented. The judge is an assistant recorder with clearly little experience of landlord and tenant law. You are aware that the judge has a discretion to allow the defendant a maximum period of six weeks. Do you do anything?

(3)   You start to cross-examine a prosecution witness about matters which you consider to be vital to your client's case. The judge, having heard argument on the matter, disallows your line of questioning. You are convinced the judge is wrong and that your client will thereby be convicted. What, if anything, can you do?

2.1.2 SPECIFIC RESPONSIBILITIES OF PROSECUTING COUNSEL

(See also **2.3.3**.)

The role and responsibilities of prosecuting counsel are fully set out in Annexe F (Standards Applicable to Criminal Cases, para. 11) including guidance to counsel on the role of the prosecution in relation to the sentencing process. Although those provisions are not repeated here, it is important to be familiar with their content. The following paragraphs merely highlight some further aspects of those responsibilities, and are not a comprehensive guide in themselves.

2.1.2.1 The relationship between prosecuting counsel and the judge

This relationship was considered in the Farquharson Committee Report in 1986. The following passage is reproduced from Archbold's *Criminal Pleading, Evidence and Practice*, paras. 4–76 to 4–80, Vol 1, 1995 by kind permission of Sweet & Maxwell (an abbreviated version of this passage appears at 4–95 of the 1999 edition of *Archbold*). The committee stated:

> It is a matter of curiosity that the respective rights and duties of the Judge and Prosecution Counsel have never been clearly defined. The most likely explanation is that whenever a difference has arisen between the two as to which course to take in particular circumstances, it has usually been resolved by discussion. Such authority as there is suggests that there has been some change of view on the topic by the Court of Appeal over the last thirty years.

> In 1948 in the case of *Soanes* 32 Cr App R 136 Prosecution Counsel in an Indictment for murder agreed with defence Counsel to accept a plea of guilty to infanticide. The Judge, Singleton J refused to accept it on the grounds that there was nothing on the depositions which could justify such a course. As a matter of history the trial proceeded on the charge of murder and the jury convicted of infanticide. In the Court of Criminal Appeal Goddard LCJ said this:

>> '. . . it is impossible to lay down a hard and fast rule in any class of case in which a plea for a lesser offence should be accepted by counsel for the Crown — and it must always be in the discretion of the Judge whether he will allow it to be accepted — in the opinion of the Court, where nothing appears on the depositions which can be said to reduce the crime from the more serious offence charged to some lesser offence for which a verdict may be returned, the duty of Counsel for the Crown would be to present the offence charged in the Indictment . . . '

> In 1980 in *R v Coward* 70 Cr App R 70 at page 76 Lawton LJ said:

>> 'It is for Prosecuting Counsel to make up their own minds what pleas to accept. If the judge does not approve he can say so in open Court and then the Prosecution will have to decide what course to take.'

> We approach the problem by considering whether Counsel acting on behalf of the Prosecution may or should decide to offer no evidence on any particular count in an Indictment or on the Indictment itself, without the approval of the Judge. When taking such a decision it is usual for Counsel to explain his reasons for doing so to the Judge. It is open then to the Judge to express his own views and if he disapproves of the course taken by Counsel he will no doubt say so. In those circumstances, counsel is under an obligation to reconsider the matter, both personally and with his junior, if he has one, and his Instructing Solicitor. Whilst great weight should be given to the Judge's view, if Counsel still feels that the Prosecution's decision is the correct one then he must persist in the course he originally proposed. He will have much more information about the background and weight of the case than the Judge who will only have the depositions and exhibits. Counsel is therefore in the best position to make the decision and although one would expect that Counsel would rarely have to take the course of offering no evidence in defiance of the opinion of the Judge, in the final analysis the decision must be his.

> There is now no doubt that where Counsel for the Prosecution wishes to proceed on a properly laid Indictment the Judge cannot prevent him doing so because he is of the opinion that the evidence is too weak for the Prosecution to succeed. See *R v Chairman of London County Sessions, ex p. Downes*, 37 Cr App R 148. Nor may the judge refuse to allow the Prosecution to proceed on an Indictment on the grounds

that he disapproves of the course being taken unless it amounts to an abuse of the process of the Court. The explanation must be that Counsel for the Prosecution has the carriage of the proceedings and it is for him to decide in a particular case whether to proceed or not to proceed.

In accepting a plea of guilty to a lesser offence or offences Counsel for the Prosecution is in reality making a decision to offer no evidence on a particular charge. It follows in our opinion that if Counsel is entitled to decide whether he should offer no evidence on the Indictment as a whole, as we think he is, then correspondingly, it must be for him to decide whether or not to proceed on a particular count in an Indictment. This is subject to three important qualifications:

(a) It is sometimes the practice when Prosecution Counsel decides to accept a plea to a lesser count for him to invite the approval of the Judge. Counsel may feel it appropriate to do so in cases where it is desirable to reassure the public at large that the course proposed is being properly taken, or when he has been unable to reach agreement with his Instructing Solicitor.

As we have already said, Counsel is not bound to invite the Judge's approval but if he does so, then he must of course abide by the Judge's decision. 'When Counsel for the Crown invites the Judge to give approval to some course which he wishes to take the seeking of that approval is no idle formality. The Judge in such circumstances is not a rubber stamp to approve a decision by Counsel without further consideration, a decision which may or may not be right.' *R v Broad* 68 Cr App R 281, *per* Roskill LJ.

(b) While the Judge will not have all the information available to Counsel he will have derived considerable knowledge of the case from the depositions and exhibits; certainly enough to enable him to decide upon the right sentence after receiving the appropriate report and hearing any mitigation. There may well be cases where the Judge so disapproves of the decision taken by Prosecution Counsel to accept a plea to a lesser offence that he cannot consistently with his duty, as he sees it, proceed to sentence on that basis. The Judge may take the view that Counsel's decision proceeds from caprice or incompetence, or simply that he entirely disagrees with the decision however carefully Counsel has arrived at it. The Judge cannot in such circumstances be expected to lend himself to a process which in his judgment amounts to an abuse or to injustice. While for the reasons already given the Judge cannot insist on Prosecution Counsel proceeding on the major charge he may decline to proceed with the case without Counsel first consulting with the Director of Public Prosecutions, on whether he should proceed in the light of the comments the Judge will have made. In an extreme case he may think it right to invite Counsel to seek the advice of the Attorney-General. In the final analysis, when these steps have been taken, the Judge has no power to prevent Counsel proceeding. Indeed any attempt by him to do so would give the impression that he was stepping into the arena and pressing the Prosecution case. However, we are of the opinion that the occasions when counsel felt it right to resist the Judge's views would be rare.

These views are in accordance with the Guidelines to Prosecution Counsel given by the Bar Committee of the Senate of the Four Inns of Court and the Bar (dated 9 May, 1984) to the following effect:

'Counsel may in his discretion invite the trial Judge to assist him in his decision (whether to offer no evidence or to accept or to refuse pleas tendered by the accused) but he is never under a duty to do so nor should he do so as a means of avoiding his personal responsibility.' 'Counsel should in any case be ready to explain his decision in open Court and to reconsider it in the light of any observations made by the trial Judge.'

This guidance has recently received the approval of the Court of Appeal and must now be taken to be the proper approach for a Judge when he is informed by

Prosecuting Counsel that he does not intend to proceed. See *R* v *Jenkins* (1985) 83 Cr App R 152.

(c) Sometimes a decision has to be made to offer no evidence during the course of the trial; and similarly pleas of guilty may be tendered to lesser counts. While the Prosecution case is being presented the decision as to what course to take in these circumstances remains with Counsel.

After the prosecution case is completed, once the Judge has ruled that there is a case to answer or where he has not been invited to do so but the case is proceeding, then in our view the prosecution cannot be discontinued nor pleas of guilty to lesser charges be accepted without the consent of the Judge. *Ex hypothesi* there is at this stage a case to answer and it would, in our view, be an abuse of process for the Prosecution to discontinue without leave. In such a situation while the Judge may rule that the case shall proceed and be considered by the Jury it would not be the duty of Counsel to cross-examine the defence witnesses or address the Jury if he was of the view that it would not be proper to convict.

The only exception to this rule is when the Attorney-General enters a *nolle prosequi* which can be done at any stage of the proceedings.

4. Prosecuting counsel in the Court of Appeal

In the event of an Appeal against conviction or a reference by the Secretary of State Prosecution Counsel's view can be no more than persuasive. Section 2 of the Criminal Appeal Act 1968 expressly provides that:

'The Court of Appeal should allow an Appeal . . . if they think that . . .'

In other words by Statute the decision is vested exclusively in the Court of Appeal.

If Prosecution Counsel has formed the view that the Appeal should succeed he should acquaint the Court with the view and explain the reasons for it. If the Court disagrees with him Counsel is entitled to adhere to his view and is not obliged to conduct the Appeal in any way which conflicts with his own judgment. At the same time it remains Counsel's duty to give assistance to the Court if requested to do so.

5. In summary it is our opinion that:

(a) It is the duty of Prosecution Counsel to read the instructions delivered to him expeditiously and to advise or confer with those instructing him on all aspects of the case well before its commencement.

(b) A solicitor who has briefed Counsel to prosecute may withdraw his instructions before the commencement of the trial up to the point when it becomes impracticable to do so, if he disagrees with the advice given by Counsel or for any other proper professional reason.

(c) While he remains instructed it is for Counsel to take all necessary decisions in the presentation and general conduct of the prosecution.

(d) Where matters of policy fall to be decided after the point indicated in (b) above (including offering no evidence on the Indictment or on a particular count, or the acceptance of pleas to lesser counts) it is the duty of Counsel to consult his Instructing Solicitor/Crown Prosecutor whose views at this stage are of crucial importance.

(e) In the rare case where Counsel and his Instructing Solicitor are unable to agree on a matter of policy, it is, subject to (g) below, for Prosecution Counsel to make the necessary decisions.

(f) Where Counsel has taken a decision on a matter of policy with which his Instructing Solicitor has not agreed, then it would be appropriate for the Attorney-General to require Counsel to submit to him a written report of all the circumstances, including his reasons for disagreeing with those who instructed him.

(g) When Counsel has had the opportunity to prepare his brief and to confer with those instructing him, but at the last moment before trial unexpectedly advises that the case should not proceed or that pleas to lesser offences should be accepted, and his Instructing Solicitor does not accept such advice, Counsel should apply for an adjournment if instructed so to do.

(h) Subject to the above, it is for Prosecution Counsel to decide whether to offer no evidence on a particular count or on the Indictment as a whole and whether to accept pleas to a lesser count or counts.

(i) If Prosecution Counsel invites the Judge to approve the course he is proposing to take, then he must abide by the Judge's decision.

(j) If Prosecution Counsel does not invite the Judge's approval of his decision it is open to the Judge to express his dissent with the course proposed and to invite counsel to reconsider the matter with those instructing him, but having done so, the final decision remains with Counsel.

(k) In an extreme case where the Judge is of the opinion that the course proposed by Counsel would lead to serious injustice, he may decline to proceed with the case until Counsel has consulted with either the Director or the Attorney-General as may be appropriate.

2.1.3 FURTHER DUTIES

There are further duties of prosecuting counsel which are not included in the Code.

2.1.3.1 To inform the defence of any known previous convictions of any prosecution witness

See *R* v *Collister and Warhurst* (1955) 39 Cr App R 100. It should be noted that previous convictions include any disciplinary offences/findings and criminal cautions against police witnesses.

2.1.3.2 To call or tender witnesses at trial

The current scheme is governed by the Criminal Procedure and Investigations Act 1996. Under this Act committal proceedings are held without live witnesses. The court still decides whether there is a case to answer, with or without consideration of evidence. If with consideration of evidence, this will be written only.

By virtue of the 1996 Act, sch. 2, para. 1(2), a statement tendered at committal under s. 5B 'may without further proof be read as evidence on the trial of the accused' provided (para. 1(3)(c)) that the accused does not object. However, even if the accused does object, that objection may be overridden by the court of trial if that is in the interests of justice (sch. 2).

The exceptions to the general rule that the prosecution must call (or tender for cross-examination) all the witnesses whose evidence was used in the committal proceedings are those set out in the cases of *R* v *Russell-Jones* [1995] 3 All ER 230 and *R* v *Armstrong* [1995] 3 All ER 831:

(a) the defence has consented to the written statement of that witness being read to the court;

(b) counsel for the prosecution takes the view that the evidence of that witness is no longer credible; or

(c) counsel for the prosecution takes the view that the witness would so fundamentally contradict the prosecution case that it would make more sense for that person to be called as a witness for the defence.

There remains a limit to the prosecution's discretion, namely that it must be exercised in the interests of justice, so as to promote a fair trial.

2.1.3.3 To adduce all the evidence upon which you intend to rely to prove the defendant's guilt before the close of your case
This is provided that such evidence is then available.

2.1.3.4 To disclose not only all of the evidence that will be called at trial, but also information of which the defence may be unaware and which will not be part of the prosecution case
This duty is dealt with mainly in the Criminal Procedure and Investigations Act 1996. The statutory scheme is covered in the *Criminal Litigation and Sentencing Manual*.

In essence, there is a duty on the police officer investigating the offence to record and retain information and material gathered during the investigation. The prosecution must inform the defence of certain categories of that material that it does not intend to rely on at trial: 'primary disclosure by prosecutor'. The defence then has a duty to inform the prosecution of the case that it intends to present at trial. The prosecution then has a duty to present further material to the defence which might be reasonably expected to assist the accused's defence as disclosed by the defence: 'secondary disclosure by prosecutor'. After this, applications can be made to the court where there is a dispute as to whether the prosecution should disclose certain material. Where public interest immunity is involved, the 1996 Act expressly preserves the existing common law.

The prosecutor remains under a continuing duty to review questions of disclosure.

The prosecution's duty of primary disclosure applies to summary trial where the accused pleads not guilty. The defence may make voluntary disclosure. In such a case, the prosecution will be obliged to make secondary disclosure.

2.1.3.5 To consider whether witness statements need to be edited
See *Practice Direction* [1986] 2 All ER 511 for the relevant considerations and practice on editing witness statements.

2.1.3.6 To be familiar with the *Practice Direction: Crown Court (Plea and Directions Hearings)* [1995] 1 WLR 1318
The purpose of a Pleas and Directions Hearing (PDH) is to ensure that all necessary steps have been taken in preparation for trial and to provide sufficient information for a trial date to be arranged. The *Practice Direction* stresses that 'it is expected that the advocate briefed in the case will appear in the PDH wherever practicable'. With the demands of a busy practice this will not always be possible. Pupils and junior tenants should be very conscious of the fact that it is regarded as a serious dereliction of duty for counsel to turn up at a PDH and say 'Sorry, this isn't my brief and I can't provide the information required'. If you are going to appear at a PDH in the place of counsel who will be appearing in the case, go armed with all the relevant information, and there is a lot of it to gather together! Information required includes informing the court of the issues in the case, number of witnesses and the form their evidence will take, exhibits and schedules to be admitted at trial, points of law and admissibility of evidence that will arise at trial, applications for evidence to be given via television links etc., witness availability, length of witness testimony, counsel availability.

2.1.3.7 Problems
(1) You are instructed to prosecute a case in which the allegation is that the defendant and associates burst into the victim's flat intent on causing injury. The victim, seeing the group arrive, tried to escape by jumping off the fifth floor balcony. He fell and was seriously injured. The defendant was charged with causing grievous bodily harm with

intent. After the victim has given evidence, you are shown a note by the officer in the case which the officer says was written by the victim about ten days before these events. It shows that at that time the victim was threatening suicide. You do not think that that is the reason why he jumped that day and it certainly does not accord with the evidence the victim has just given. What do you do, if anything, about the note?

(2)   In the course of a ruling given following argument by counsel for both prosecution and defence, the judge gives reasons which are based on a case cited in argument. The ruling is favourable to you, the prosecution. It is, however, clear that the judge has misunderstood the passage quoted. What do you do?

(3)   You arrive in court to prosecute a defendant. You realise that the defendant was a client of a solicitor's firm for which you worked during the holidays. You learnt details about the defendant which might well help you in prosecuting the case. The defendant does not appear to recognise you. Do you do anything?

2.1.4 SPECIFIC RESPONSIBILITIES OF DEFENCE COUNSEL

You are referred to Annexe F, Standards Applicable to Criminal Cases, para. 12 (see **Appendix 1**) and to Guidance on Preparation of Defence Case Statements in Section 3 of the Code for a full consideration of these responsibilities. It is not proposed to repeat them here. The most common ethical problems associated with defending, other than those which involve a (potential) conflict of interest, tend to arise in the following circumstances where:

(a)   a client confesses his or her guilt. Coping in this situation is dealt with in para. 13 of Annexe F 'Confessions of Guilt';

(b)   a client changes his or her instructions;

(c)   a client insists upon you conducting the case in a manner which you consider detrimental to his or her interests, e.g., by calling unhelpful witnesses; or

(d)   you find yourself in the position of being a material witness.

These points will be considered in detail during the Professional Conduct Course tutorials (see **Chapter 7** for tutorial problems).

Although the primary responsibility of defence counsel in a criminal case is to endeavour to protect the client from conviction except by a competent tribunal and upon legally admissible evidence sufficient to support a conviction for the offence charged (para. 12.1 of Annexe F), this does not displace the overriding duty to the Court. It is important, however, to bear in mind the duty of confidentiality owed to the lay client which must not be breached (para. 603). As with prosecuting counsel, defence counsel should be familiar with the duties and obligations imposed by the *Practice Direction: Crown Court (Pleas and Directions Hearings)* [1995] 1 WLR 1318.

2.1.4.1 Problems

(1)   You represent a defendant in a trial at the Crown Court having advised and appeared (without your instructing solicitor having been present) at the magistrates' court. The defendant, having been given the new caution, did not answer any question in his or her police interview. During your client's cross-examination by the prosecution, it is suggested that the account he or she is giving has been thought up recently. You know that he or she gave that account to you on the first remand date. You were alone with him or her at the time. What should you do?

(2)   There is crucial prosecution evidence of your client's presence at the scene of the crime at a material time. Your instructions are that your client was present but merely an onlooker, not a participant in the crime. You conduct your cross-examination on that basis and do not challenge the evidence of your client's presence at the scene. When he or she gives evidence, the defendant denies his or her presence at the material

time by saying that he or she had just left the scene. The judge points out the difference and demands that you clarify the situation.

(3) Your client is pleading guilty in the magistrates' court. Your instructions are that he or she has a number of previous convictions. The police antecedents given to the court show him or her as a person of good character. How do you mitigate? Would your approach be different if the omitted previous conviction had involved the imposition of a suspended sentence of which the defendant was in breach by virtue of the instant conviction?

2.1.5 ACCESS TO THE JUDGE

2.1.5.1 *Turner* directions

The Court of Appeal has stressed the need for strict compliance with the directions given by that court in *R v Turner* [1970] 2 QB 321 on seeking guidance from the judge, in particular, upon the question of sentence. Those directions are now set out in full:

Before leaving this case, which has brought out into the open the vexed question of so-called 'plea-bargaining', the court would like to make some observations which may be of help to judges and to counsel and, indeed, solicitors. They are these:

1. Counsel must be completely free to do what is his duty, namely to give the accused the best advice he can and if need be advice in strong terms. This will often include advice that a plea of guilty, showing an element of remorse, is a mitigating factor which may well enable the court to give a lesser sentence than would otherwise be the case. Counsel of course will emphasise that the accused must not plead guilty unless he has committed the acts constituting the offence charged.

2. The accused, having considered counsel's advice, must have a complete freedom of choice whether to plead guilty or not guilty.

3. There must be freedom of access between counsel and judge. Any discussion, however, which takes place must be between the judge and both counsel for the defence and counsel for the prosecution. If a solicitor representing the accused is in the court he should be allowed to attend the discussion if he so desires. This freedom of access is important because there may be matters calling for communication or discussion, which are of such a nature that counsel cannot in the interests of his client mention them in open court. Purely by way of example, counsel for the defence may by way of mitigation wish to tell the judge that the accused has not long to live, is suffering maybe from cancer, of which he is and should remain ignorant. Again, counsel on both sides may wish to discuss with the judge whether it would be proper, in a particular case, for the prosecution to accept a plea to a lesser offence. It is of course imperative that so far as possible justice must be administered in open court. Counsel should, therefore, only ask to see the judge when it is felt to be really necessary, and the judge must be careful only to treat such communications as private where, in fairness to the accused person, this is necessary.

4. The judge should, subject to the one exception referred to hereafter, never indicate the sentence which he is minded to impose. A statement that on a plea of guilty he would impose one sentence but that on a conviction following a plea of not guilty he would impose a severer sentence is one which should never be made. This could be taken to be undue pressure on the accused, thus depriving him of that complete freedom of choice which is essential. Such cases, however, are in the experience of the court happily rare. What on occasions does appear to happen however is that a judge will tell counsel that, having read the depositions and the antecedents, he can safely say that on a plea of guilty he will for instance, make a probation order, something which may be helpful to counsel in advising the accused. The judge in such a case is no doubt careful not to mention what he would do if the accused were convicted following a plea of not guilty. Even so, the accused may well get the impression that the judge is intimating that in that event a severer sentence, maybe a custodial sentence would result, so that again he may feel under pressure. This accordingly must also not be done.

The only exception to this rule is that it should be permissible for a judge to say, if it be the case, that whatever happens, whether the accused pleads guilty or not guilty, the sentence will or will not take a particular form, e.g., a probation order or a fine, or a custodial sentence.

Finally, where any such discussion on sentence has taken place between judge and counsel, counsel for the defence should disclose this to the accused and inform him of what took place.

See also *Criminal Litigation and Sentencing Manual*.

2.1.5.2   A view for change

There is, however, a feeling among some senior members of the profession that these rules are unnecessarily restrictive and that while caution must be exercised, there are occasions when court time and costs could be saved by a more flexible and 'sensible approach'. This argument is supported by Robin Gray QC in the following paper. It is stressed that this is his personal view and not to be used as a justification for ignoring your duty to comply with the directions in *R* v *Turner*.

Seeing the Judge on Sentence: Should the Parameters be Extended?

For many years now, and more particularly since the case of *Turner* (1970) 54 Cr App R 352; [1970] 2 QB 321, counsel for defendants have been nervous about seeing the judge on sentence and judges themselves have been even more nervous in agreeing to a request to see them.

This seems to me to result from an unrealistic approach to the problem and an unreasonable fear of accusations of 'plea bargaining' putting unfair pressure on defendants. I believe this fear is unfounded and, if a sensible approach were adopted by the courts, a substantial shortening of trials would result and a considerable saving in cost. I doubt if it is an exaggeration to say that over 95 per cent of those charged with crime are guilty of some criminal offence, if not the precise offence with which they are charged.

It may well be for that reason that three questions are frequently asked in conference with counsel, although the client is protesting his innocence:

(1) What will I get if I'm convicted?; (2) Will I go to prison?; (3) How long will I get?

These are questions which counsel should be able to answer but can never give more than an educated guess, bearing in mind tariffs, precedents, etc.

When a person is arrested, no doubt the police officer will say 'you'd do better to put your hands up to this', the solicitor will say 'you'll get less on a plea', the barrister will say 'you appreciate that the judge is likely to feel more kindly disposed if you plead guilty', and yet the judge cannot say 'if you plead guilty, you'll get less or won't go inside', although everybody knows, and the client can and should be told, that all the authorities on sentencing enjoin the judges to give a reduction, sometimes substantial, for a plea of guilty.

So how do we answer the three questions posed above?

(1)   *What will I get if I'm convicted?*
In the last resort there is only one person who knows the sentence which is about to be passed and that is the trial judge himself, and indeed an honest answer to the question is 'it may depend on who the judge is'. Judges do not vary to any great degree in their sentencing, except in rare cases, but there is no doubt that some are more lenient than others and in borderline cases some will pass non-custodial and others custodial sentences.

Accordingly, there is only one way in which one can ever positively answer the client's question and that is by asking the judge at the trial. Unfortunately, since *Turner* (above), if the judge is prepared to discuss the matter with counsel at all, there are considerable limitations on what he or she can say. A judge has to be approached by counsel through the clerk of the court and very often the answer comes back: 'the judge will not see you on sentence'.

(2) *Will I go to prison?*

This question can only be answered if the judge is satisfied as to the nature of the sentence, whatever the plea. Waller LJ made this clear in *Ryan* (1977) 67 Cr App R 177, with these words:

> . . . the only permissible communication of intended sentence is that, whatever happens about the plea, the sentence will or will not take a particular form, and secondly, that the judge must not indicate what he will do on a plea of guilty and say nothing about a conviction after pleading not guilty.

Clearly, therefore, there is no problem if the judge decides that, whatever the plea, a non-custodial sentence will be imposed. He or she can say so. The difficulty arises in the borderline cases, where the judge feels that on a plea of guilty a non-custodial sentence can be imposed, but simply does not know how he or she would be minded at the end of a trial if the defendant were to plead not guilty. It would obviously be wrong for the judge ever to say 'if you plead you'll go free, but if you fight you'll go inside', as in *Bird* (1978) 67 Cr App R 203. That is putting obvious pressure on the defendant, and in any event a judge cannot know the final sentence in a case where a non-custodial sentence is a possibility until the end of the trial.

However, should it be wrong for a judge to say simply 'If you plead now, you'll go free' without any reference to what the situation would be after a fight? Waller LJ's dicta (above) clearly stated that it would be wrong. (See also *Atkinson* (1978) 67 Cr App R 201.)

However, there is a strong argument to say that the risk which the defendant chooses to take in those circumstances if he decides to plead not guilty is a no greater risk than he already appreciates he is taking, having been advised by competent counsel and solicitor that he runs a risk of a heavier sentence if he persists in fighting. Indeed the judge would not be going as far as that. He or she would simply be saying in effect: 'I can tell you that if you plead now, you won't go inside, but I'm afraid I simply can't say whether the position will remain the same by the end of the trial. It may be the same, it may not'; whereas counsel in any event, doing his duty, would already have said 'I can't tell you whether you'll go inside or not, but you certainly have a far better chance if you plead guilty'.

(3) *How long will I get?*

Waller LJ's dicta in *Ryan* (above) also allow a judge to indicate that the sentence will be custodial in any event, but that is not of any great assistance if it is not known how long the sentence will be. It is in this area that it may be that there is a stronger case than in any other situation for arguing that the rules of practice should be altered. There are very many serious cases in which the defendant's persistence in his innocence is simply brought about by the fact that he will on conviction, or so he believes, be sentenced to a far longer sentence than in fact the judge would have in mind, and counsel cannot disabuse him.

It seems to me that there should be nothing wrong in a judge telling counsel in *any* case that the *maximum* sentence will be 'so many' years of imprisonment, plea or fight. If the judge cannot give even a maximum indication at the outset of a trial, not yet being in possession of sufficient facts, he should be entitled to give such an indication *at any stage* of the trial. I believe this would lead to a substantial increase in pleas of guilty and an enormous saving of court time.

As an example, I defended a man charged with fraud, in 1987. The defence was one of 'subjective honesty', but I was told that he would take my advice whether to plead guilty or not on his version of events. He said that, if he were to receive no more than four years' imprisonment, he would think seriously of changing his plea. The judge, whom I approached through the clerk of the court, refused to see counsel on sentence at all. I could not, therefore, even know the *maximum* sentence. The trial lasted eight weeks, the defendant was convicted, and he was sentenced to four years' imprisonment. Eight weeks of public money was wasted.

Counsel can still attempt to approach the judge, whether or not their client has indicated an intention to plead, but more often than not, as the law stands at present, it comes to nothing.

2.1.5.3 Situations where it is permissible to see the judge

Although most judges will refuse to see counsel on a matter of sentence, there are a variety of other situations in which it is permissible and indeed advisable for counsel to ask to see the judge. These include:

(a) If your client is thinking of pleading guilty but, for instance, wants to discuss the matter with your instructing solicitor who is not present at court that day, counsel may see the judge and ask for an overnight adjournment. To mention that the client is thinking of pleading guilty in these circumstances is sensitive information that ought not to be mentioned in open court.

(b) If the defendant has given information or assistance to the police he or she may not wish details to be given to the judge in open court. His or her safety or that of his or her family may be at risk.

(c) Any matters that would be embarrassing to the defendant if mentioned in open court, for instance, if he or she is suffering from an illness that may make him or her appear drowsy or uninterested whilst in court.

(d) Any matters that are personal to counsel and would be embarrassing to mention in open court, e.g., illness, a bereavement necessitating an adjournment etc.

2.2 Relationship with the Lay Client

2.2.1 DUTIES AND RESPONSIBILITIES OWED TO THE LAY CLIENT

First and foremost, the profession requires strict observance of the 'cab-rank' rule: see para. 209 of the Code of Conduct. You must accept any instructions or brief to represent any client, at a proper professional fee (para. 502(b)), in the field(s) in which you profess to practise irrespective of the nature of the case or any belief or opinion which you may have formed as to the character, reputation, cause, conduct, guilt or innocence of that person. The cab-rank rule applies whether your client is paying privately or is legally aided or otherwise publicly funded.

Note that any brief or instructions in a legally aided matter is deemed to be at a proper and professional fee.

The duties and responsibilities you owe to the lay client are dealt with in the Code of Conduct. Before you accept any brief or instructions, you must satisfy yourself that you are competent and have adequate time to prepare and do the particular case (para. 501). You now have an added obligation to consider whether the best interests of the client would be served by instructing another member of the Bar or even the solicitor himself (see para. 504.1) to do the case and, if so, to advise the lay client accordingly (see para. 504.3). (See para. 504.2 for similar provisions where two counsel are instructed in the same matter.) If, however, the client insists that you do the case, you are bound by the 'cab-rank' rule subject to it being the sort of work you are competent to undertake. It is also obviously important to determine in any case whether a conflict of interest exists or arises which prevents you from acting/continuing to act for that client.

Your duties to the lay client include a responsibility:

(a)   To promote fearlessly and by all proper and lawful means your lay client's best interests and to do so without regard to your own interests or to any consequences to yourself or to any other person including your professional client (para. 203(a)).

(b)   To act towards your lay client at all times in good faith (para. 203(c)). As long ago as 1889, Lord Esher MR explained the extent of this duty in these words:

> A professional man, whether he were a solicitor or barrister, was bound to act with the utmost honour and fairness with regard to his client. He was bound to use his utmost skill for his client but neither a solicitor or barrister was bound to degrade himself for the purpose of winning his client's case. Neither of them ought to fight unfairly though both were bound to use every effort to bring their client's case to a successful issue. Neither had any right to set himself up as a judge of his client's case. They had no right to forsake their client on any mere suspicion of their own or on any view they might take as to the client's chances of ultimate success . . .

(c)   To preserve the confidentiality of your client's affairs (para. 603).

(d)   To act with reasonable competence and maintain professional independence.

(e)   To keep your lay client informed of the estimate and likely impact of costs. In *Singer (formerly Sharegin) v Sharegin* [1984] FLR 114, 119, Cumming-Bruce LJ expressed the duty in this way:

> I conclude by emphasising the immense importance of the obligation upon solicitors and counsel in all these cases (financial disputes) to form accurate estimates as to costs, to inform their lay client what the impact of costs is likely to be, to inform the lay client of the probable estimate of the totality of costs on both sides so that the lay client can fully understand the enormous financial risks they may incur if they insist on sticking to what they regard as their own sensible point of view and so refuse to make or accept an offer involving much compromise on both sides.

(f)   To advise your lay client, when a conflict of interest arises between your lay client and professional client, that it would be in his or her interests to instruct another professional adviser (para. 605).

(g)   To reconcile your duty to your lay client, in legally aided civil cases, with your duty to the Legal Aid Fund: see para. 203(b) and consider the following provisions of the Legal Aid (General) Regulations 1989:

> *Regulation 67*
> *(1)   Where an assisted person's solicitor or counsel has reason to believe that the assisted person has —*
> *(a)   required his case to be conducted unreasonably so as to incur an unjustifiable expense to the fund or has required unreasonably that the case be continued; or*
> *(b)   wilfully failed to comply with any regulation as to the information to be furnished by him or in furnishing such information has knowingly made a false statement or false representation,*
> *the solicitor or counsel shall forthwith report the fact to the area director.*
> *(2)   Where the solicitor or counsel is uncertain whether it would be reasonable for him to continue acting for the assisted person he shall report the circumstances to the area director.*

(h)   To advise your lay client (and professional client) where it becomes apparent that a legal aid certificate has been wrongly obtained by false or inaccurate information, and to withdraw from the case where action is not taken to remedy the situation immediately (para. 506(c)).

(i) Not to undertake any task which you do not have adequate time and opportunity to prepare for or perform (para. 501(b)).

In order to provide a practical and objective insight into the relationship between counsel and the lay client, the chairman of the National Consumer Council, David Hatch CBE, JP, and Marlene Winfield of the National Consumer Council, have written the following essay on barristers and their lay clients.

Barristers and their Lay Clients

We believe that the excellence of the Bar will not simply be judged by the quality of its advice and advocacy. The Bar, like other professions and businesses, needs to display a wider, more all-round excellence: value for money and good client communications are an essential part of the modern profession.
Report of the Bar Standards Review Body, September 1994

In future a solicitor will increasingly need to have a reason to instruct counsel rather than to do the work himself, or to refer it to his in-house advocacy department or to an agency solicitor. Moreover, he will need to have a reason which can be explained to the client.
The Work of the Young Bar, November 1993

A changing world
When today's fledgling barristers enter pupillage and practice, they will enter a world very different from that of their predecessors. The young barrister of today will face new types of work requiring different relationships with lay clients. Examples might include: providing or participating in alternative methods of dispute resolution such as mediation, arbitration and neutral case evaluation; coaching lay clients to be their own advocates; developing expertise in areas of social welfare law in order to take direct referrals from advice agencies operating under legal aid contracts.

Even in the traditional forms of work, things are changing. There is increasing specialisation by both barristers and solicitors. In areas such as personal injury and medical negligence, the harm that 'dabblers' can do is being recognised. Anecdotal evidence suggests that in all areas of the law lay clients are less content to take a passive role than they once were. Increasingly they want to be informed and consulted, to participate in decision-making. And they are more ready to complain if they feel they are not getting a good service.

Other changes to the nature of the traditional work of barristers are coming about as a result of the new Civil Procedure Rules 1998. New procedures have been introduced for dealing with multi-party actions, medical negligence, housing cases, and more generally with cases involving sums of money under £10,000. New procedures are streamlined, less adversarial and cheaper. A large share of the savings should be made on legal fees.

At the same time, competition is hotting up. Increased rights of audience and a desperate search for new sources of work, have driven solicitors into court in increasing numbers. Even that traditional training ground for new barristers, the magistrates' court, is equally likely these days to feature showdowns between salaried prosecutors and young solicitors.

Meanwhile, the size of the Bar has increased rapidly, by nearly a quarter in recent years. This means that more people are chasing fewer briefs. And as if that were not enough, the 1993 joint working party on the young Bar discovered other worrying trends: an apparent decline in levels of fees in the early years and increasing debt arising from barristers' training.

The many changes afoot pose threats, but they also offer opportunities for young barristers. What they all have in common is that they call for new ways of working with lay clients and their lay advisers. Those most likely to succeed in the brave new streamlined world of Woolf reforms and alternatives to trial will be those least afraid to explore new types of working relationships. It might be as well to start that exploration by learning from the mistakes of the past.

Working with lay clients

To a certain extent, barristers are shielded from the criticism of lay clients by solicitors. When something goes wrong, the solicitor is usually the first port of call. However, Action for Victims of Medical Accidents, AVMA, with over 19,000 medical negligence clients having passed through its doors, has experienced the highs and the lows of barristerial performance in an area of the law where sensitivity is perhaps most needed.

AVMA staff make the following observations about client care, based on their experience of accompanying lay clients on visits to counsel:

Inexperienced lay clients need to be adequately prepared by the solicitor for conferences with counsel. Clients need to know what to expect from the barrister and what the barrister expects from them. They also need to know what they are and are not allowed to do, for example, if they can speak directly to the barrister.

Lay clients need to be given a clear idea of who is making the decisions, the solicitor or barrister, and who is ultimately responsible for the conduct of the case.

Clients should be asked at an early stage what they hope to achieve by legal action. Thereafter, they should be asked their opinions.

It is essential that at the outset the client is given a clear idea about the difficulties of the case, the likely outcome and the potential costs.

Some clients are left feeling that their concerns were not addressed. If the client's concerns are not considered relevant, the reasons should be explained to them.

When a solicitor and barrister talk in legal jargon, it often excludes the client from the discussion.

If the solicitor and barrister wish to speak without the lay client being present, the purpose should be made clear.

Both solicitors and barristers should consider the client's needs as well as their own when determining the time and place of meetings. Factors such as ease of access for people with disabilities and availability of lavatories should be considered when fixing venues. Consideration should be given to where the client will feel most comfortable and thus best able to participate: chambers can be difficult to find and daunting places. Clients might prefer to meet in the solicitor's office, particularly if they have been there before. Wherever the meeting, clients should be given good directions.

When meetings are not well-organised or structured, clients can be left feeling that the barrister was not familiar with the case.

Simple kindnesses should not be forgotten. One AVMA staff member told of a stressful five hour conference during which the clients, who had travelled a long way and started very early in the morning, were not even offered a cup of coffee.

The above comments represent a mixture of good client care, common sense and basic courtesy. Lapses would be particularly out of place in medical accident cases, an area of the law where people can be extremely vulnerable. But, arguably, going to law for any reason is potentially stressful for lay clients, who will always benefit from sensitivity on the part of the barrister.

At a time of fierce and increasing competition between barristers, and between barristers and solicitors, those barristers – young and old – offering a high standard of client care will have a competitive edge

Owning up to complaints
There are occasions when the letter of the 'law' as embodied by the code of conduct is breached, or when lay clients think it has been. No look at the changing legal world would be complete without a word on dealing with complaints. Each year about 360 complaints are received by the Bar Council, of which about 70% are dismissed or have no further action taken. This compares with around 20,000 complaints a year made against solicitors. (Reasons for the disparity may have as much to do with the relative numbers in the professions and the relative accessibility of the two complaints procedures than with relative competence.) Of the complaints that reach the Bar Council, what are the most common?

According to Mark Stobbs of the Bar Council's Professional Standards Department, areas of the law which give rise to the most complaints are criminal matters (which account for about a quarter), family law and neighbour disputes. Lay clients complain most often about style in court, delay, rudeness, failure to advise properly about settlements, and misrepresentation. Looking at these things in a bit more detail:

- *Style in court* Complaints can be about overzealous representation (usually a complaint by a third party) or not being tough enough on the opponent. They usually arise from criminal and family matters and are only upheld when performance falls very seriously below that of a normal competent counsel, such as failing to put crucial points to a witness or inappropriately hostile questioning.

- *Delay* These complaints are more often upheld. They relate to failure to deal with paper work on time and late return of briefs. The latter commonly involves a barrister failing to warn the solicitor of a potential scheduling conflict in the vain hope that one or other case will settle. It can be a particular problem when clients have already had a conference with the barrister or have returned to someone they instructed before, and then at the eleventh hour are confronted by a hastily prepared stranger.

- *Rudeness* Common complaints are that the barrister didn't seem interested or was offhand or would not listen to the points the client was trying to make. This accords with AVMA's experience.

- *Failure to advise properly* Complaints in this category are of three types. The first are cases where people have second thoughts about what are deemed to be reasonable resolutions. These tend to be upheld only where there is evidence of rudeness or failure to listen to the client or to explain the consequences properly. In the second type, clients say they have been pressurised into agreeing unsatisfactory terms without having been advised of all the implications, particularly in family matters. These complaints are more often upheld than the former. The third type concerns failure to explain which of the parties' costs the client would be expected to pay.

- *Misrepresentation* Clients sometimes feel that counsel has misunderstood or misrepresented a particular issue, for example by failing to pursue a particular line of argument in court or by advising the Legal Aid Board that a case is without merit. These complaints are upheld if counsel has clearly misunderstood a crucial point or failed to act as competently as would be expected.

Looking to the future
The future is by no means all gloom and doom. The young Bar can look forward to new opportunities in areas such as alternative dispute resolution, new civil justice fast track procedures, social welfare law, and the burgeoning area of public policy. But if young barristers are to compete with the new generation of solicitors,

increasingly trained in both client care and advocacy skills, they too must adopt a more client-centred approach. A fine line has to be walked between providing good client care and retaining the objectivity that is the Bar's hallmark. The training of young barristers needs to grapple with how the changing expectations of lay clients can best be met within the Code of Conduct of the Bar and its working practices.

David Hatch CBE JP
Chairman
National Consumer Council
and
Marlene Winfield
National Consumer Council

2.2.1.1 Problems

(1)   Your client bombards you with instructions, both before and during the trial. He or she insists you put each one to the various witnesses, who are all children your client is said to have abused. Your client insists on giving evidence even though he or she has previous similar convictions. He or she is also adamant that you call a witness that you suspect will destroy his or her case. How do you conduct the trial?

(2)   Whilst discussing with your client his or her witness statement outside court, you query his or her explanation of a certain event. The client tells you that is not what really happened but 'it was what the solicitor told me to say'. The solicitor is not present but has sent an articled clerk. What, if anything, do you do?

(3)   Your client loses his claim for a residence order in respect of his children. Upon leaving court, he mumbles 'She'll be sorry, I'll make sure she doesn't live to enjoy them'. How do you react?

2.3   Relationship with the Professional Client

2.3.1   DUTIES AND RESPONSIBILITIES OWED TO THE PROFESSIONAL CLIENT

You may now accept instructions direct from members of approved professional bodies other than solicitors, for example, accountants and surveyors. In such cases, you must comply with the Direct Professional Access Rules reproduced in Annexe C of the Code of Conduct.

With regard to your relationship with instructing solicitors, problems can arise in circumstances where they seek to limit the way in which you present the case; where they take a different view of the lay client's prospects of success; where you consider they have been remiss/negligent in their handling of the client's affairs, or where they consider you have 'let them down' by not being available to do a case or have been guilty of delay. Many of these problems are due to poor communication, lack of control of your clerk or an unjustifiable attitude that you are somehow superior to the solicitor.

It is important that you foster good relations with the professional client, discuss any differences of opinion, and ensure that he or she is kept fully informed of any potential difficulties or conflicting dates in your diary. Your clerk should always inform any solicitor who seeks to instruct you on a case if there is likely to be a conflicting engagement. Watch the chambers diary yourself to ensure this is being enforced. Do not delay your paperwork. If some delay cannot be avoided due to other pressing work, telephone the solicitor and explain the position so that he or she is free to instruct other counsel.

Do not criticise your solicitor in front of the lay client without first discussing your view with the solicitor. Do not criticise your solicitor in court unless your solicitor agrees that some fault lies with him or her and he or she accepts that the court must be told to prevent the lay client suffering the consequences.

A further area in which the relationship with a solicitor may become problematical arises out of the growth of the number of solicitors with rights of audience in the higher courts. This can lead to a variety of difficulties — not least if you are co-defending with a solicitor whose firm is acting for your defendant too, and who may be more likely to go to him or her than you. Be tactful.

The Legal Services Committee of the Bar Council has provided guidance on the area of solicitors acting as juniors to silks, which it quaintly describe as 'mixed doubles'. The committee stressed the importance of ensuring that the right amount of advocacy expertise is properly used, and in particular:

(a) If a case requires both a leader and junior, it is inappropriate for a solicitor advocate to try to perform both roles.

(b) The junior in any case (whether he or she be a barrister or solicitor advocate) must have appropriate skills and experience for the roles he or she is to perform and must be competent and available to perform the junior work required by the leader including examination of witnesses, the preparation of skeleton arguments and chronologies, the drafting of pleadings etc. as the case may require.

(c) If a case is suitable for a silk to conduct alone, there should be no junior. But, if a junior is genuinely necessary, it would be manifestly inappropriate for a solicitor without rights of audience to seek to dispense with a junior on the basis that he or she will carry out the junior work, excluding advocacy, whilst also acting as a solicitor.

Guidance upon your main duties to the professional client can be found in paras. 203(c); 501; 508; 601(e); 605 and 608 of the Code. Remember that your primary duty is to the lay client (para. 203(b)). Note also Annexe B which covers the Terms of Work on which barristers offer their services to solicitors and the Withdrawal of Credit Scheme 1988.

2.3.1.1   Making the relationship work

A barrister's practice will depend largely upon the way in which he or she behaves towards and works with his or her instructing solicitors. The relationship requires counsel to understand clearly what it is that solicitors expect from them. It also requires counsel to understand what is likely to alienate a solicitor. In order to provide a practical insight into the relationship between solicitor and counsel, there follow two essays by senior solicitors on making the relationship work. The first is written from the perspective of civil work (specifically medical negligence), the second from that of criminal practice.

A Solicitor's View on the Barrister's Relationship with the Professional Client

Preface

The author specialises in claimant medical negligence litigation funded predominantly by legal aid. At the time of writing, he was a partner at Bolt Burdon, a firm that holds a legal aid franchise, and is in charge of supervising the firm's policy on the use of, 'approved sub-contractors', which includes barristers.

The starting premise for this article was the general myth that traditionally the relationship between solicitors and barristers has been an uneasy alliance. Do barristers really think that they are the intellectual superiors of solicitors, who are always having to look to counsel to sort out ill-prepared cases? Do solicitors really think that barristers are arrogant snobs who blame solicitors when well-prepared cases fall apart because they have not bothered to read the papers properly? The reality, I think, is that at the extremes both are true, but for most of the time barristers and solicitors work very well together, and lay clients benefit from the combination of skills.

Preparation for court

Competent solicitors will ensure that the case has been prepared thoroughly from the outset, and by the time of trial will normally have met with counsel and experts on two or three occasions. On each of those occasions counsel will have had very full instructions, and will have been encouraged to think forward to ensure that at the pre-trial conference there are no glaring omissions in the evidence. So, the first piece of advice is that you should always think ahead – both in practical terms and legal terms. On a number of occasions I have sat in conferences with counsel knowing that the papers have not been read properly, and with the sinking feeling that I will get poorly drafted statements of case that will need amendment, and that in the weeks before trial counsel will suddenly want information that he or she could have asked for at the first conference. This is very annoying and does little to inspire confidence in the lay client.

In the weeks leading up to a trial I expect to work fairly closely with counsel. Typically we arrange a pre-trial conference for two or three weeks before the trial, and even with the best prepared case there will always be further work to be done before the brief is delivered. I expect and welcome telephone conversations about particular aspects of the case, and I am always encouraged as the questions become more complex, as it indicates that counsel is making a proper analysis of the papers. If there are to be settlement negotiations I expect to conduct them, unless we are at court, and I would not expect counsel to speak with opposing counsel without first discussing the prospect with me. Generally I think settlement negotiations are better conducted by solicitors. It is difficult to rationalise why this is so, as it has to be acknowledged that counsel will have a better understanding of the law and evidential strengths and weaknesses of the case. I think that it is partly because the solicitor manages the case for a long time and should have a better 'feel' for the case and understanding of how the opposing legal team behave, and partly because solicitors are not constrained by the thought that they may have to present the case in court, which enables us to be tougher in negotiation.

I expect a barrister to have a thorough knowledge of matters of law and procedure. I will happily defer to counsel's views on these matters, but I expect a reasoned discussion of why a particular course of action is being taken. A competent solicitor will not be happy to spend three to four years preparing a case, only to abdicate responsibility for it when it comes to trial.

An uneasy alliance?

Most of the solicitors and barristers that I know are specialists in their fields. They are confident of their abilities, and do their respective jobs very well. For many it was not ever thus. I trained in a very general practice, where I was expected to carry out all types of contentious and non-contentious work. When working with counsel I invariably had only a very superficial understanding of the case. In some instances this did not really matter, because I was the clerk sent along to sit behind counsel at trial, and make no more contribution than to take notes. In other cases it did matter, because I was dealing with cases that were beyond my competence and experience. Mostly the barristers I worked with were very kind about this, but I would have forgiven any of them for thinking that he or she was the real lawyer, because on those occasions they undoubtedly were. I think much has changed in the training of solicitors since then and certainly in my firm we try to make sure that trainees have a proper and appropriate role to play in the preparation of cases.

When done properly, the solicitor's job is a complex and demanding one. We gather a great deal of information, narrow it down, and fashion it into a well-prepared and well-thought-out case that can then be finished off by counsel. Appropriate metaphors are elusive. Clients often ask if we are like GPs and barristers are like hospital specialists, but I think of the process more in terms of the case being a large cargo ship, perhaps an oil tanker, with the solicitor as its captain. As it approaches port a pilot comes on board to guide it through the treacherous rocks and shallows. The pilot is the barrister. Without him or her the ship will not get through the treacherous rocks and shallows, but he or she should still remember that the captain has managed to bring the vessel all the way from Africa. Which metaphor brings me rather neatly to my first anecdote which comes from the time when I was a shipping lawyer. I admit that I was not very interested in shipping law, and consequently was not a very good shipping lawyer. However, I was reasonably competent, and the barrister I was instructing, although very intelligent, was not much more experienced than me. He was a nice man, and during the conference he sympathised with me as he knew what it was like to be a solicitor 'standing at the photocopier all day'. Now I know that the mysteries of a solicitor's office can sometimes be difficult for counsel to understand, but to clear any doubt that is in your minds I can honestly say that the person who stands at a photocopier all day is a copying clerk, not a solicitor.

Returning to my main theme, I have no doubt that some solicitors still allow their cases to be 'counsel driven', but they are increasingly a thing of the past. It may interest you to know that there is a strong financial incentive for this. When my costs are taxed I can claim a higher hourly rate if I can show that as a specialist solicitor I was able to run the case with minimal use of counsel. As your career progresses, and you are able to move into a specialist area of law, you will start to get instructions from solicitors who also specialize, and when that happens the relationship can be a very good one.

So, I hope that I have now firmly established that solicitors are real lawyers, and that we have no doubts about the value of our work being equal to the value of the work performed by counsel. Now I will tell the truth, or at least the rest of the truth in so far as it applies to me, and, I suspect to quite a lot of solicitors. In a small corner of our minds we have a lingering jealousy of barristers – jealous because they spend more of their time thinking about interesting legal points, jealous because all of the drama attaches to the final days in court, rather than the three years of preparation, jealous because there are more television dramas about barristers than there are about solicitors, and jealous because barristers have more opportunity to dress up as eighteenth-century clergymen. Of course we are not jealous of the barrister's responsibility as the final presenter and advocate of the case, or jealous of the red eyes and tobacco-reeking breath that evidence the Sunday nights spent preparing for the Monday morning trial.

Ironically we still think that our job is harder. Your job may be intellectual and occasionally very stressful, but ours is continually stressful, often very frustrating, frequently intellectual, and above all never-ending. At the end of the conference or trial you give the papers back to us, but we have to carry on dealing with them, along with dozens of other cases. Too much drudgery and too little drama. Thus it was that I was very surprised to learn that barristers apparently think that they have the more difficult job. This revelation came to me only recently, when a very complicated medical negligence case settled just before trial. There was an enormous amount of paperwork, my expert witnesses were brilliant, but slightly eccentric, my client was nice, but near hysterical. My counsel was very able, but was delaying really getting to grips with the papers until the last possible moment. When the case settled, everyone concerned with it, including the defendant's lawyers, breathed a huge sigh of relief. When I spoke with counsel on the telephone, I was very surprised to find that he had anticipated that his task would be more difficult than mine. Did he not realise that all he had to do was turn up at court and present the case, whereas I had to orchestrate the whole thing, and make sure that papers and people (him included) were matched up and sent to the right place at the right time?

Behaviour towards the lay client
Most clients are scared of lawyers. It is scary for them to telephone a solicitor, and scary for them to walk into a solicitor's office for the first time. Happily most of them soon overcome that fear and build up a relationship of trust with their solicitor. However, the experience of litigation is still a stressful one, particularly when it involves professionals looking into very personal matters, as is often the case in a medical negligence claim.

Barristers are even scarier for the clients. The first meeting is usually a conference with counsel, and beforehand I reassure them that the purpose of the conference is to have a friendly, informal discussion about the case. Mostly the barristers I instruct never let me down. They are polite and do everything they can to put the clients at ease. One of the things I think about when selecting a barrister is how he or she will meet the needs of the case, and the client. If I have an exceptionally timid client I choose an exceptionally nice barrister. Occasionally I have very bullish clients who can be quite aggressive and difficult to control. In those circumstances I tend to choose a barrister who is more concerned with getting to the point than being charming. Having said that, on one notable occasion when I did that, within about 20 minutes the conference had turned into an all-out argument between the barrister and my client.

The only time when I have had cause to complain about a barrister arose out of a conference attended by my assistant. The client was a single woman in her late forties who had sustained gynaecological injuries as a result of medical negligence. The conference was with a male barrister, and was to be attended by two male medical experts. Inevitably it had to involve a detailed discussion of very intimate matters for my client, and as she was a rather shy woman, I knew she would be very apprehensive. I chose the barrister because he was recommended to me by some colleagues as being exceptionally intelligent, and very clear in his understanding of medical matters. I assumed that he would read the papers and realise that the client would have to be dealt with sensitively. He did just the opposite. First, he had a male pupil sitting in with him. Of course I have no objections to people training by observation, but it would have been courteous for him to ask my assistant, or indeed the client if she was happy to have yet another strange man discussing her very personal life. Secondly, he opened the conference not by talking about the weather, or the many general questions that had to be discussed, but by asking her if she was sexually active, and when was the last time that she had a sexual partner. Apparently the poor client tried her best to answer, but was clearly humiliated and uncomfortable.

I will never instruct that barrister again, although I should emphasise that it was an exceptional experience. Generally the barristers I use are very nice to my clients, and indeed that is one of the reasons why I use them. Perhaps I am in the fortunate position of using mostly very senior barristers who have had many years to practise their communication skills.

For any young professional starting out on his or her career, communicating with clients can be an area of weakness, and that is completely understandable. You will be working in a complicated field, uncertain about your ability to do the job, and the client may think that you look so young that you can't possibly be a properly qualified barrister. Therefore the temptation may be to prove that you are, by making everything sound so complicated that the client will think that you must be clever because he or she cannot understand a word you are saying.

Also, there is the all-embracing atmosphere of the legal profession, particularly in the Temple, where the centuries of wisdom will permeate your being, and you may find yourself acquiring the habits, dress and speech of a Chancery judge. That may make you seem and feel like a real barrister, and whilst to some extent we all have to act out our chosen role in order to placate our clients, remember that not all clients are stupid, and that solicitors in particular will not be terribly patient if very young barristers become too theatrical in presenting their professional selves.

Do you call your lay client/your solicitor by their first name, or address them formally? With lay clients you should always start by calling them Mr, Mrs or Ms. As you get to know them better you may move on to first name terms, but it is important to establish the professional relationship from the outset. It is always easy to get more friendly, but very difficult to withdraw from familiarity when, for example, you have to give unpalatable advice to an angry client. As for your instructing solicitors, I am sure that practice varies. I believe that it is probably sensible to address your instructing solicitors formally at first, particularly if they are older than you. If there is a substantial age difference you should continue to do so until invited to do otherwise. If there is not a big age difference I think you should move on to first name terms fairly soon, and in fact I find it rather odd when a barrister, particularly one of similar age to me, insists on calling me Mr Donovan. As far as I am concerned we are working in a team together, and it would concern me if I thought that my barrister would prefer to keep me at arm's distance – just like the potentially difficult lay client.

With all of this there is a substantial element of human nature, and ordinary social skills, and really the best person that you can be is yourself. (Although in saying that, I assume that you are intelligent, confident and charming. If you are not it will be necessary for you to act as much as possible, and it may even help to dye your hair grey!)

Behaviour at court

You now take centre stage. To a certain extent the case is yours, and it will sink or swim with you. However, do not forget that your lay client is the true owner, and that your solicitor has had custody of the case for much longer than you. You must involve the lay client, particularly if there is a possibility of settlement. Clients become very emotionally involved in their cases, and although many of them will be terrified on the day, and may just want you to sort it all out for them, I think it is much healthier for a client to be involved fully in the reasoning behind a settlement. That way when he or she goes home, and the fear disappears and friends and relatives start to give the client advice about the damages that they would have insisted upon, there is less scope for the client to feel cheated.

Many solicitors send a trainee clerk to court. This generally makes financial sense because a senior solicitor's costs will not be recoverable in full where counsel is instructed. Thus it is that sometimes the person sitting behind you will have only a superficial knowledge of the case. That will mean more work for you, but if that person is a trainee solicitor it presents a golden opportunity for you to make a friend and do some marketing. Solicitors, particularly junior solicitors, prefer to instruct barristers that they like.

Like barristers, solicitors have considerable egos, and it is important that you remember this if you wish to be instructed again. I recently had a very complicated case listed for a two week trial in the High Court. Half-way through, the defence began to collapse, and the judge rose to allow the three parties to negotiate a settlement. By that stage counsel for all sides had become deeply involved in the case. There was much debate about case law, and I was relying heavily upon the skills of my QC and junior counsel. However, having had conduct of the case for four years it was important that I be involved in discussions, both for the client's sense of security, and proper conduct of the case. Happily my own counsel appreciated that, but counsel for one of the defendants clearly did not. We were having one of those court corridor conversations where all of us were huddled into a close group. The defendant's barrister wanted to make a remark to one of my counsel, who was standing to one side of me. Instead of facing all three of us when speaking, he walked into the centre of the circle, stood with his back to me (the frayed tail of his wig was literally six inches away from my nose) and began discussing terms with my counsel. Possibly this was just bad manners, but such behaviour does perpetuate myths about barristers' views of the worth of solicitors, and once again, if you want to get instructions it is best to avoid doing things like that.

Delay and incompetence

Reading through the professional conduct rules of the Bar I find that paragraphs 501 and 601 stipulate that a barrister should not take on work if he or she does not expect to carry it out within a reasonable time, and that if he or she finds himself or herself too busy to complete work already taken on, he or she must inform the professional client.

I am sorry to say that in my experience these rules are continually flouted. With one or two exceptions, the barristers that I work with are all very pleasant and intelligent people who never let me down in conference or at court. However, time and again I have to wait and wait for written work. My reminder letters go unanswered, and my chasing telephone calls are met with promises that are made to be broken. My clients wonder why their cases stop, directions orders have to be ignored; experts do not get the draft statements of case that they really needed to read whilst the conversation from the conference was fresh in their mind, and defendants' solicitors apply to strike me out for want of prosecution. If you chose to take note of only one thing in this paper, let it be this. Solicitors are very busy people who have to juggle many things in order to keep their large case loads moving along. A slow barrister is just one more thing to worry about, and it is a bitter irony indeed when your own barrister's involvement in a case can cause more problems than the opposing solicitors.

On at least two occasions in the last year I have had good cases that have moved along very well until counsel was instructed. In each case the barristers were experienced people, chosen because of their many excellent qualities. The conferences went very well, and finished with promises that the draft statements of case would be with me within a week. The weeks and months then slipped by, and despite reminder letters, faxes and phone calls, the statements of case did not come. Eventually there were applications to strike out by the defendants. This involved me in a great deal of work, for which I will not be paid, and even threats of personal costs orders against my firm. In my clients' eyes I became incompetent, and the cases having come from important referral sources, the reputation of my firm suffered. Fortunately in each case we were able to salvage the situation, but had we not done I might also have been facing a professional negligence claim.

Quality standards applied by solicitors to barristers
My firm has a legal aid franchise. This means that we have to set quality standards for our clients, and ensure they are stuck to. As the partner in charge of the 'Register of Sub-Contractors' I am responsible for monitoring the performance of the other professionals that we use on behalf of our clients, most notably counsel. When staff in the firm have good or bad experiences with counsel, they send a note to me, and I report on those notes at our weekly fee earners' meetings. This is not a matter of choice. If we want to keep the legal aid franchise we have to show that the people that we instruct will do a good job. Thus it was that I recently had to send a fax to a barrister that I like very much, to say that six months was too long to wait for a written advice, and that if it was not supplied within two weeks, I would have to ask him to return the papers and no further instructions would be sent to him. I thought about adding that under his own rules of professional conduct he should probably have returned them a long time ago in any event, but decided that he should know that.

Quality control standards such as the legal aid franchise are part of modern business culture. The solicitors that instruct you have to be increasingly accountable to their clients; we in turn are your clients and it is much better for you to say that the papers will be with us in three months, and for us to know that that is true, rather than for you to say that the papers will be with us next week, when there is no real expectation that they will arrive before next year.

This is, of course, very tough on a young barrister who is trying to build up a following. When you eventually start to get some work you will not wish to turn cases away for fear of losing your professional clients, and indeed solicitors operate in exactly the same way. We might be too busy now, but we are worried about whether we will have enough work to do next year. Nevertheless, in my firm we have made a policy decision not to take on work if we cannot progress the work that we have reasonably quickly, and I would have no difficulty with a barrister saying that he or she is too busy to take on any work at present, but will be taking cases in two months' time. That would suggest to me that he or she is reliable and sensible, and I would at least have certainty when I did instruct him or her. You should also be working towards building up a long-term relationship with your instructing solicitor, and being honest about how busy you are will not harm that. In fact in some respects being busy can enhance your reputation, and I would be happy to say to a client that I am instructing a certain barrister because although he or she is busy now, he or she will give his or her whole attention to the work when the time comes.

Fees
As most of my work is legally aided it is seldom that I have to agree fees with counsel's clerk. However, when I do, I expect to be given an hourly rate for the barrister I want to instruct. Once again, I now work in an environment where I have to give very precise costs information to my clients, and thus I need counsel's chambers to operate in a similar way. I would not instruct a barrister on behalf of a private client on the basis of an old-fashioned style of valuation of the case by counsel's clerk upon receiving the papers. I need to be able to say to my clients that they can either have barrister X for £150, or barrister Y for £160.

The barrister's clerk
Much has been written recently about how barristers' chambers are acknowledging that they are modern businesses. This is all to the good. From the outside it seems that traditionally the clerks have observed a veneer of deference and respect towards barristers, whereas in reality they have controlled much of the power and of the wealth within chambers. A junior barrister is not a young aristocrat, and his or her clerk is not his or her trusty family retainer. They are both there to do a job in what should be a modern business environment, and I think it would be better for all concerned if that was acknowledged. In modern business good manners and respect are enough. Dickensian deference, particularly if it is false, can only breed resentment and poor working relationships.

It is difficult to give advice on how you can get the best out of your clerks, but from a solicitor's point of view the following points are helpful. Encourage them to adopt a professional attitude towards marketing. Obviously this will not be your decision as a pupil, or a new tenant, but every chambers should have a brochure giving details of its barristers, their experience and specialisation. The clerks should be ready to send that out very quickly. You should also try to ensure that they know where your areas of interest lie, so that if an opportunity does come up they will be able to mention your name. Some of the barristers that I use most regularly were originally introduced to me when a clerk suggested that they take over a case where my original choice had to drop out. Make sure that your clerk is rigorous about passing on telephone messages, and prompt in delivering fee notes. If he or she is not doing so, let your instructing solicitors know that the fault does not lie with you.

Getting work
Referring once more to my firm's policy on sub-contractors, part of our quality control system is only to use counsel that come recommended by a suitable source – for example, another solicitor who has worked with the barrister. Unfortunately specialist medical negligence solicitors are not a very good source of work for newly qualified barristers. We tend to use only very experienced counsel who have also taken the trouble to attend the same medical courses as we do in order to learn about medicine. Moreover, we do not have many hearings, and if you go into medical negligence work too early you will spend too much of your time drafting statements of case, and not enough time on your feet in court, and it seems to me that the best thing that a young barrister can do is to spend as much time in court as possible, learning how to be an effective advocate.

When you do start to specialise it will be a good idea to market yourself to the solicitors who have the work that you want. You do this partly by cross-referrals between solicitors, but also by turning up at places where they tend to congregate, and getting your face known. For example, if you were to specialise in medical negligence you would be able to meet the solicitors who control most of the work by attending medical courses run by AVMA (Action for Victims of Medical Accidents, the medico-legal charity) or any of the numerous medico-legal conferences that take place. Those courses are expensive, but in addition to showing that you are committed to the work, and that you are taking steps to acquire the necessary medical knowledge, you will also have the opportunity to meet the solicitors from whom you want instructions. However, if you have only just finished your pupillage, your efforts might be wasted, because most of those specialist solicitors will be dealing only with the more complex cases, and they will not wish to send them to a newly qualified barrister. In contrast, if you wait until you can display the scars and experience of a few years experience as an advocate, and no longer look like a school leaver, specialist solicitors will be more likely to consider instructing you when you show an interest in their field.

Summary
If my contribution had been limited to a few exhortations, which it probably should have been, they would be as follows. Make sure that you know the law. Read your papers very thoroughly. Be professional but be yourself. Work with your solicitor as a team. Be well-organised. Be well-organised. Be well-organised.

Postscript
The day after I wrote this article I had a meeting with a client. I was very pleased about her case, because she was a nice woman, and I had used all my skills and experience to help her get her claim off the ground. I believed in the case when no-one else would, and I guided her through the system, and even waited a very long time for her to pay my bills. The case is now looking very strong indeed, and she will soon get a fairly large award of damages. Counsel has been involved, but only very minimally. Thus at the end of the meeting I was sitting back, modestly thinking about how lucky she was to have a solicitor who was not only a wonderful human being, but also a very shrewd and experienced lawyer. And what did she say to me? She said, 'Wasn't our counsel good and will you go on to be a barrister?' I said, 'No, I wouldn't want to be away from my photocopying'.

Terence Donovan
Litigation Solicitor
Bindman & Partners

The Solicitor's Relationship with Members of the Criminal Bar

To the matters raised by Terence Donovan I would only add a few points, especially aimed at the criminal Bar.

A changing relationship
The relationship between solicitors and counsel over the last 30 years has changed in all forms of work, but perhaps in no area more than in the field of criminal law. As late as the 1960s, the criminal solicitor was regarded as being at the bottom end of the legal heap, as a sort of necessary evil who would bring in clients as fodder for the exhibition of advocacy skills at trial by skilled members of the Bar. The opinions of the solicitor were rarely sought and certainly views as to how the case should be conducted in court were not encouraged.

Social relationships were discouraged by professional rules, to such an extent that, during the luncheon adjournment, it was not regarded as proper for the barrister to share his meal with his instructing solicitor. In magistrates' courts separate sections of the courtroom were set aside for solicitor advocates and members of the Bar, the latter in Bow Street, for example, occupying a position several feet higher than that occupied by the solicitor and on a level with the magistrate.

A number of factors combined to change this somewhat awkward and archaic relationship.

First, solicitors changed the perception of the criminal lawyer and the criminal solicitor advocate. They appreciated that, if the vast majority of advocacy in the magistrates' court was carried out by solicitors, both in cities and certainly in the countryside, it must be carried out by persons who were competent to do it, by persons who were known to the courts and trusted by them as advocates and carried out with skills which were the equal, if not, in the case of older practitioners, greater than those of the newly qualified barrister.

Secondly, the standard of education and training for solicitors had to rival that provided for the Bar.

Thirdly, the requirements which solicitors made of the Bar became much more exigent and solicitors were not willing to accept that their contributions to and judgment in the conduct of a criminal case had any less weight than that of the Bar.

Fourthly, changes in social structures and the proliferation of legislation in many fields meant that criminal practice was no longer confined, in large measure, to the so-called criminal and/or working classes. Increasingly, members of the middle and upper classes were becoming embroiled in the criminal courts, particularly as a result of road traffic legislation.

Rights of audience
Happily, the need for a changing relationship was recognised by the best on both sides of the profession and if there is any real justification for a division into two branches, it is in the symbiotic and productive relationship which is now common-place. In the future, however, there is still unease because of the battle which has recently been fought over the rights of audience in the higher courts, but I have never understood why this created such alarm in the Bar because it was always apparent that, except in rare cases, solicitors would be unlikely to engage in the conduct of long cases, or indeed to cover all of the workload which is produced either in the magistrates' court or the Crown Court, and I do not see that the Bar, as a whole, has any cause to fear.

However, it may not be a Bar of the same size. There are now solicitor advocates in criminal law who, in major urban areas, may be offering agency facilities to other solicitors and this may reduce the amount of work available to the young Bar. One of the reasons for this is that the solicitor advocate acting as agent will often have a greater understanding of what is required by the solicitor with conduct of the case than counsel working within a 'chambers' system.

This often comes down to a question of access. It is easier, frequently, for a solicitor in one part of the city or in one part of the country to telephone another solicitor to explain what is required and to fax the requisite instructions and to agree a cost, than it is to go through the chambers system to obtain the services of counsel and to instruct him or her.

Independence
The Bar has always claimed that its strength depends upon its independence because it is not so closely connected to the client. As a result, it has been claimed it is able to exercise a more dispassionate judgment in giving advice and is better able, because of that distance, to give unpalatable advice to a client. Properly used, that distance can be very effective, but the rule is gradually being undermined because the Bar is now moving towards a situation of seeking to offer direct access, currently to certain other professionals, but financial considerations may in the future persuade the Bar to seek an extension of such access. The proposals for direct access from Citizens' Advice Bureaux is a particular example.

My personal belief is that it will not extend very greatly because one of the great advantages which access only through the solicitors' branch of the profession gives to counsel is that he or she does not to have to make himself or herself available on the telephone to the client. It is a gift to the Bar which they should not lightly throw away, or if they do they will have to bear the consequences. It may be pleasant to think that important clients such as accountants, stockbrokers etc. can telephone counsel for advice, but it is hard to see the propriety of the Bar imposing a rule that only those clients whom they choose should be allowed to have such access. I doubt if they want Bill the burglar or his like to have it. Selective access to counsel would fly in the face of the 'cab-rank' principle, which is availability to all if chosen. It is a rule which has great merit, but one which is, in criminal cases in particular, easily circumvented. All counsel has to do is to be unavailable through other commitments. **If you are going to do criminal work, you must be prepared to do it on a non-selective basis.**

The qualities solicitors look for
The standards of training and competence are often disputed between the two sides of the profession, but there are areas in which the Bar, in many ways, excels. Clearly, in the Crown Court the procedures and much of the intricate work in relation to indictments is, in the early stages, better taught to the Bar than to solicitors; greater emphasis is placed on the rules of evidence at the Bar; the young Bar seemed to have better training in research; and, until recently, the techniques of advocacy were better taught at the Bar than to the solicitors' profession.

Knowledge of the law and the rules of evidence, together with the ability to draft quickly and accurately are taken for granted. If any member of the Bar does not show that basic competence when first instructed, he or she is unlikely to build the reputation to establish his or her practice. What is looked for above and beyond that is common sense, judgment, courage, civility and co-operation.

Common sense
In criminal cases, what is wanted by both the lay client and the professional client is an appreciation of what the case is about, what its effect is upon the individual client, what the consequences of conviction are and what is practical by way of presentation of the defence.

Judgment
Judgment involves the accurate assessment of the strength of the case to be met and the effectiveness of lines of defence, together with an ability to carry out a comparative evaluation of their strengths and weaknesses. It also includes judgment of the defendant and his or her version of events and his or her strengths and weaknesses as a witness. Counsel is expected by solicitors to have the courage to tell the client unpalatable truths, but equally to have the courage to accept, whatever counsel's personal view, that his or her task is to represent the client's view and not to seek to superimpose the former upon the latter.

Courage
Courage is also required often to represent clients who are distasteful to the advocate, or to defend cases which may result in unpleasant comment. The greatest claim to glory of the advocate is to ensure that those who have been vilified in advance of the trial through social, political or other causes, receive the same full-hearted representation as those for whom the public or others may have sympathy. It is not always the public who are the problem, it may be friends and relatives who say, 'how could you represent that person?'. An eminent American defence lawyer said that telling your parents that you were going to become a criminal defence lawyer was like telling them that, not only were you going to become a doctor, but you were going to specialise in abortion. It also requires courage to withstand the sometimes unhelpful judge or magistrate.

Talk to the client after the case, especially if you have lost. Explain rights of appeal, chances of success and field any complaints. Do not rush away saying, 'my solicitor will explain'. Such behaviour is as cowardly as it is discourteous.

Courtesy
A busy solicitor needs to know what is happening. Telephone the solicitor or solicitor's office to let him or her know if bail has been granted, if the client has gone to prison, what is the next date of hearing. A busy office needs to know what is happening quickly to organise its workload. This also means that counsel must keep his or her word. If papers are promised, deliver them; if unavoidable delay occurs,

phone to explain; if part-heard and unable to appear as briefed, explain and ensure your clerk returns the brief to a suitable substitute. If you are the substitute, get in touch and reassure the solicitor that you have read the papers and discuss any points you are unsure of.

Courtesy especially applies to the practice of discussions on a counsel to counsel basis. It is discourteous not to inform your solicitor that such a discussion is proposed and discuss what you can do at it. Report back. Do not make agreements without consultation. Remember that you are 'instructed' by the solicitor, not given carte blanche to go off on a frolic of your own.

Co-operation

It is not necessary, as was often the case in the past, to treat solicitors and clients as necessary evils. All good criminal defence work involves teamwork. That involves, initially, reading the papers that are sent in advance of any conference or hearing. Nothing irritates a solicitor more than knowing that counsel has been recommended to a client or instructed on his or her behalf, only to get to the conference and find it is quite obvious that counsel has not read the papers. If counsel is unable to find the time, he or she should not be taking the case. The clearest giveaway is counsel saying to the client at the first meeting, 'Now, Mr X, I have of course studied the papers your solicitor has sent me, but I would just like to run through the facts with you for myself.'. Counsel is entitled in return to expect proper instructions and to complain if he or she does not get them.

Civility

Civility is not seeking to be good mates with a defendant. From time to time counsel is seen desperately seeking to use what he or she thinks is the appropriate slang with an East End villain because he or she thinks that that will impress the client. In fact, nothing is less likely to impress the client who expects his or her lawyer to be down to earth, know what life is like on the streets, but not to use words and references which are clearly alien to him or her, just to try to make an impression. The client expects counsel to be learned in the law and competent or better in courtroom techniques. He does not expect him or her to be an ersatz member of the criminal community.

Counsel may also find that outside court police officers may try to adopt a matey attitude to both solicitors and counsel. It is purely a technique to try to discomfit and to obtain a psychological advantage. Civility will overcome this ploy.

Remember – the client rules ok!

It is the task of defence lawyers to represent the client. Of course advise the client whether he or she should plead guilty in view of the case against him or her, advise whether he or she should give evidence; whether documents should be produced, witnesses called, but if the solicitor has taken a different view in advising, discuss it with him or her before you discuss it with the client. If you disagree in front of the client, he or she is faced with an unpalatable choice between the lawyers who are supposed to be representing him or her. This does not instil in the client confidence in either lawyer. If you win the public battle, you may lose the private war.

If a client insists on pleading not guilty or on giving evidence despite your advice, fight his or her case (within the rules) as he or she wants it. Many advocates have been astonished to win cases they thought were hopeless and had told the client just that.

Do not do a deal with the Prosecution without the client's consent – it is the client's case, the client's reputation and the client's penalty which are at stake. The client is entitled to make the decision whether he or she is legally aided or paying privately. Bear in mind that the legally aided client is as entitled to your best effort, as is the private client. Nothing so diminishes counsel in the eyes of the solicitor as the impression that a legal aid case is less worthy.

A special relationship

To summarise, the Bar claims special qualities. When a member of the Bar has those qualities, this evokes nothing but admiration from a solicitor who can recognise them from his or her own training and experience. Good criminal solicitors want the Bar to have those qualities, but they want them to have them as equals and any assumption of superiority by a barrister is likely to reduce the number of briefs received.

Bear in mind that you may learn much more by co-operation and consultation. You will also earn more.

John Clitheroe
Senior Partner
Kingsley Napley

2.3.1.2 Problems

(1) You are asked to advise on quantum in a personal injuries case where the defendants have offered to negotiate a settlement. It is clear that the claimant's general damages will be substantial but their assessment is not straightforward. In conference you state that in your opinion the case is worth £30,000 to £35,000 on full liability. Your solicitors (who value the case more highly) ask you for an opinion in writing that the bracket is £40,000–£45,000 in order to support their negotiations and to achieve a settlement at £35,000. What should you do?

(2) You act for the claimant in civil proceedings. Unlike your client, the defendant has the benefit of a full legal aid certificate. You arrive at court on the day fixed for the hearing to find that the defendant's solicitor has forgotten to warn any of his or her witnesses. The judge accedes to the defendant's request for an adjournment. The defendant's solicitor is in fact well known to you and briefs you on a regular basis. What application, if any, do you make for costs?

2.3.2 RELATIONSHIP WITH THE CROWN PROSECUTION SERVICE

In August 1994 the Crown Prosecution Service issued two Service Standards dealing with the delivery of instructions and pre-trial preparation. These are important, and are now reproduced:

Service Standard on Timely Delivery of Instructions to Counsel in the Crown Court

1 Introduction

1.1 It is essential that prosecuting Counsel is instructed as early as possible after committal or date of transfer.

1.2 Timely delivery of instructions will ensure early preparation of the case and will enable Counsel to consider CPS views on the acceptance of pleas or to seek timely formal admissions in contested cases.

1.3 Cases in which Counsel is required to give urgent advice, to settle the indictment or to attend a fixed date hearing will naturally assume priority.

1.4 Where Counsel is instructed to advise on evidence or to settle the indictment, a reply date should be clearly marked on the brief.

1.5 CPS Areas should be realistic when setting reply dates and allow Counsel adequate time in which to advise or to draft the indictment.

1.6 In many cases where Counsel is instructed to settle the indictment, it will be clear that an extension beyond the 28th day will be required. CPS Areas should be alert to this possibility and make the necessary application well before the 28th day.

2   Target dates

2.1   All CPS Areas should set target dates for the delivery of instructions to Counsel in Crown Court cases in accordance with the following timetable:

Type of case	Date of delivery after committal, transfer or receipt of notice of appeal
Trials up to 3 days Most pleas of guilty Committals for sentence Appeals against sentence Appeals against conviction (This covers all standard fee cases)	14 days
Trials lasting 3 days or more Pleas of guilty to serious offences	21 days

2.2   The target dates should be regarded as maxima and every effort made to improve upon them.

2.3   Preparation of the case pre-committal should ensure that Counsel can be fully instructed immediately after committal or transfer.

2.4   Delivery of instructions to Counsel should not be dependent upon the receipt of formal documentation from the Crown Court. If necessary, authenticating certificates and depositions can be dispatched to Counsel separately, after delivery of the instructions.

2.5   Within the above timetable, CPS Areas must give priority to custody cases, child abuse cases and other cases involving children or vulnerable witnesses.

Service Standard on Pre-trial Preparation by Counsel

1   Introduction

1.1   Prosecution decisions made by the CPS are governed by the Code for Crown Prosecutors issued under section 10 of the Prosecution of Offences Act, 1985. All Counsel instructed by the CPS must be familiar with the principles set out in the Code and must apply them at all stages throughout the life of the case.

1.2   The duties set out in this standard apply in all cases whether or not Counsel has been specifically instructed on the matters herein.

1.3   Where two or more Counsel are instructed to prosecute in the same case, it will be sufficient for one of them to carry out some of these duties provided that, where Junior Counsel gives advice, it is done with the knowledge and approval of Leading Counsel.

1.4   Upon receipt of instructions to prosecute on behalf of the CPS, Counsel will read the papers within the time scale appropriate to the case.

1.5   Having read and considered the papers, Counsel will, where necessary, advise in writing on any matter requiring such advice, and will indicate whether a conference is required.

1.6   Whether or not formal written advice has been given, when Counsel has read the papers within the time scale appropriate to the type of case, the CPS must be notified that this has been done.

2   The indictment

2.1   If instructed to do so, Counsel will settle the indictment within any time limit imposed.

2.2.   If the indictment is already settled, Counsel will check the indictment for both substance and form. If the indictment is defective in any way, Counsel will notify the CPS forthwith with advice on any proposed amendments.

3   The evidence

3.1   If, in Counsel's opinion, the evidence available does not support any count in the indictment to the standard required by the Code for Crown Prosecutors, Counsel will advise or confer on this aspect of the case, identifying the relevant evidential insufficiency.

3.2   Counsel will appreciate that there needs to be a realistic prospect of conviction against each defendant in respect of each count in the indictment. The evidential test to be applied under the Code is an objective test and means that a jury, properly directed in accordance with the law, is more likely than not to convict the defendant of the charge alleged.

3.3   If, having considered the evidence available to support the indictment, Counsel feels that further evidence is necessary, Counsel will provide written advice as to precisely what is required.

3.4   If, in Counsel's opinion, a plea of guilty to an offence other than that charged is or might be acceptable to the Crown, Counsel will confer with the CPS on the matter or will advise in writing giving reasons for the view taken.

3.5   Counsel will eliminate all unnecessary material in the case so as to ensure an efficient and fair trial and, in particular, will consider the need for certain witnesses and exhibits.

3.6   Counsel will consider both the order of witnesses to be called and the timing of their attendance and, in appropriate cases, will provide a list of witnesses in order and time of call.

4   Disclosure

4.1   Counsel will consider whether all witness statements, documents and other material listed on the schedules supplied by the police have been properly disclosed to the defence in accordance with the Attorney General's Guidelines and the authorities on disclosure.

5   Preparation of documents

5.1   Counsel will, in appropriate cases, draft a case summary for transmission to the court.

5.2   Counsel will consider the possibility of admissions and, in appropriate cases, draft such admissions for agreement by the defence.

5.3   Counsel will advise on the preparation of documents for the court and jury in good time before the hearing date.

6   Time scales

6.1   According to the type of case, Counsel will read the case papers and advise as necessary within the following time scale:

Type of case	Time scale by reference to date of delivery of instructions within which prosecuting Counsel should read brief
Trials up to 3 days Most pleas of guilty Committals for sentence Appeals against sentence Appeals against conviction (This covers all standard fee cases)	7 days
Trials lasting 3 days or more Pleas of guilty to serious offences	14 days
Cases of substantial complexity or gravity or those likely to last over 10 days	21 days

6.2 The target dates should be regarded as maxima and every effort made to improve upon them.

6.3 Conversely, it is acknowledged that there will always be exceptional cases in which the above target dates cannot be met. The CPS will identify these cases at the time the instructions are delivered and will consult Counsel with a view to agreeing a target date.

6.4 If Counsel is unable to meet the target date set out in the above time scale, the CPS must be notified so that a revised date can be agreed.

In addition reference should be made to Annexe F of the Code of Conduct (Standards Applicable to Criminal Cases) and **2.1.2**.

2.3.2.1 Code for Crown Prosecutors

The Phillips Royal Commission emphasised the need for those who prosecute to follow clear and consistent criteria when deciding whether or not to bring a prosecution. Since 1986 these have been set out in the Code for Crown Prosecutors issued pursuant to s. 10 of the Prosecution of Offences Act 1985. It is important for both prosecuting and defence counsel to ensure that they have an up-to-date Code, and to be familiar with it. It will be highly relevant to the decision not just of whether or not to carry on with a case, but also the acceptability or otherwise of proposed pleas. The Code is reproduced below.

The Code for Crown Prosecutors

1 Introduction
1.1   The decision to prosecute an individual is a serious step. Fair and effective prosecution is essential to the maintenance of law and order. But even in a small case, a prosecution has serious implications for all involved – the victim, a witness and a defendant. The Crown Prosecution Service applies the Code for Crown Prosecutors so that it can make fair and consistent decisions about prosecutions.
1.2   The Code contains information that is important to police officers, to others who work in the criminal justice system and to the general public. It helps the Crown Prosecution Service to play its part in making sure that justice is done.

2 General principles
2.1   Each case is unique and must be considered on its own, but there are general principles that apply in all cases.
2.2   The duty of the Crown Prosecution Service is to make sure that the right person is prosecuted for the right offence and that all relevant facts are given to the court.

2.3   Crown Prosecutors must be fair, independent and objective. They must not let their personal views of the ethnic or national origin, sex, religious beliefs, political views or sexual preference of the offender, victim or witness influence their decisions. They must also not be affected by improper or undue pressure from any source.

3   Review
3.1   Proceedings are usually started by the police. Sometimes they may consult the Crown Prosecution Service before charging a defendant. Each case that the police send to the Crown Prosecution Service is reviewed by a Crown Prosecutor to make sure that it meets the tests set out in this Code. Crown Prosecutors may decide to continue with the original charges, to change the charges or sometimes to stop the proceedings.
3.2   Review, however, is a continuing process so that Crown Prosecutors can take into account any change in circumstances. Wherever possible, they talk to the police first if they are thinking about changing the charges or stopping the proceedings. This gives the police the chance to provide more information that may affect the decision. The Crown Prosecution Service and the police work closely together to reach the right decision, but the final responsibility for the decision rests with the Crown Prosecution Service.

4   The code tests
4.1   There are two stages in the decision to prosecute. The first stage is **the evidential test**. If the case does not pass the evidential test, it must not go ahead, no matter how important or serious it may be. If the case does pass the evidential test, Crown Prosecutors must decide if a prosecution is needed in the public interest.
4.2   This second stage is **the public interest test**. The Crown Prosecution Service will only start or continue a prosecution when the case has passed both tests. The evidential test is explained in section 5 and the public interest test is explained in section 6.

5   The evidential test
5.1   Crown Prosecutors must be satisfied that there is enough evidence to provide a 'realistic prospect of conviction' against each defendant on each charge. They must consider what the defence case may be and how that is likely to affect the prosecution case.
5.2   A realistic prospect of conviction is an objective test. It means that a jury or bench of magistrates, properly directed in accordance with the law, is more likely than not to convict the defendant of the charge alleged.
5.3   When deciding whether there is enough evidence to prosecute, Crown Prosecutors must consider whether the evidence can be used and is reliable. There will be many cases in which the evidence does not give any cause for concern. But there will also be cases in which the evidence may not be as strong as it first appears. Crown Prosecutors must ask themselves the following questions:

Can the evidence be used in court?

(a)   Is it likely that the evidence will be excluded by the court? There are certain legal rules which might mean that evidence which seems relevant cannot be given at a trial. For example, is it likely that the evidence will be excluded because of the way in which it was gathered or because of the rule against using hearsay as evidence? If so, is there enough other evidence for a realistic prospect of conviction?

Is the evidence reliable?

(b)   Is it likely that a confession is unreliable, for example, because of the defendant's age, intelligence or lack of understanding?
(c)   Is the witness's background likely to weaken the prosecution case? For example, does the witness have any dubious motive that may affect his or her attitude to the case or a relevant previous conviction?
(d)   If the identity of the defendant is likely to be questioned, is the evidence about this strong enough?
5.4   Crown Prosecutors should not ignore evidence because they are not sure that it can be used or is reliable. But they should look closely at it when deciding if there is a realistic prospect of conviction.

6   The public interest test

6.1   In 1951, Lord Shawcross, who was Attorney-General, made the classic statement on public interest, which has been supported by Attorneys-General ever since: 'It has never been the rule in this country – I hope it never will be – that suspected criminal offences must automatically be the subject of prosecution'. (House of Commons Debates, Vol. 483, col. 681, 29 January 1951.)

6.2   The public interest must be considered in each case where there is enough evidence to provide a realistic prospect of conviction. In cases of any seriousness, a prosecution will usually take place unless there are public interest factors tending against prosecution which clearly outweigh those tending in favour. Although there may be public interest factors against prosecution in a particular case, often the prosecution should go ahead and those factors should be put to the court for consideration when sentence is being passed.

6.3   Crown Prosecutors must balance factors for and against prosecution carefully and fairly. Public interest factors that can affect the decision to prosecute usually depend on the seriousness of the offence or the circumstances of the offender. Some factors may increase the need to prosecute but others may suggest that another course of action would be better.

The following lists of some common public interest factors, both for and against prosecution, are not exhaustive. The factors that apply will depend on the facts in each case.

Some common public interest factors in favour of prosecution

6.4   The more serious the offence, the more likely it is that a prosecution will be needed in the public interest. A prosecution is likely to be needed if:

(a)   a conviction is likely to result in a significant sentence;

(b)   a weapon was used or violence was threatened during the commission of the offence;

(c)   the offence was committed against a person serving the public (for example, a police or prison officer, or a nurse);

(d)   the defendant was in a position of authority or trust;

(e)   the evidence shows that the defendant was a ringleader or an organiser of the offence;

(f)   there is evidence that the offence was premeditated;

(g)   there is evidence that the offence was carried out by a group;

(h)   the victim of the offence was vulnerable, has been put in considerable fear, or suffered personal attack, damage or disturbance;

(i)   the offence was motivated by any form of discrimination against the victim's ethnic or national origin, sex, religious beliefs, political views or sexual preference;

(j)   there is a marked difference between the actual or mental ages of the defendant and the victim, or if there is any element of corruption;

(k)   the defendant's previous convictions or cautions are relevant to the present offence;

(l)   the defendant is alleged to have committed the offence whilst under an order of the court;

(m) there are grounds for believing that the offence is likely to be continued or repeated, for example, by a history of recurring conduct; or

(n)   the offence, although not serious in itself, is widespread in the area where it was committed.

Some common public interest factors against prosecution

6.5   A prosecution is less likely to be needed if:

(a)   the court is likely to impose a very small or nominal penalty;

(b)   the offence was committed as a result of a genuine mistake or misunderstanding (these factors must be balanced against the seriousness of the offence);

(c)   the loss or harm can be described as minor and was the result of a single incident, particularly if it was caused by a misjudgment;

(d)   there has been a long delay between the offence taking place and the date of the trial, unless:

- the offence is serious;
- the delay has been caused in part by the defendant;
- the offence has only recently come to light; or

- the complexity of the offence has meant that there has been a long investigation;
(e) a prosecution is likely to have a very bad effect on the victim's physical or mental health, always bearing in mind the seriousness of the offence;
(f) the defendant is elderly or is, or was at the time of the offence, suffering from significant mental or physical ill health, unless the offence is serious or there is a real possibility that it may be repeated. The Crown Prosecution Service, where necessary, applies Home Office guidelines about how to deal with mentally disordered offenders. Crown Prosecutors must balance the desirability of diverting a defendant who is suffering from significant mental or physical ill health with the need to safeguard the general public;
(g) the defendant has put right the loss or harm that was caused (but defendants must not avoid prosecution simply because they can pay compensation); or
(h) details may be made public that could harm sources of information, international relations or national security.
6.6 Deciding on the public interest is not simply a matter of adding up the number of factors on each side. Crown Prosecutors must decide how important each factor is in the circumstances of each case and go on to make an overall assessment.

The relationship between the victim and the public interest
6.7 The Crown Prosecution Service acts in the public interest, not just in the interests of any one individual. But Crown Prosecutors must always think very carefully about the interests of the victim, which are an important factor, when deciding where the public interest lies.

Youth offenders
6.8 Crown Prosecutors must consider the interests of a youth when deciding whether it is in the public interest to prosecute. The stigma of a conviction can cause very serious harm to the prospects of a youth offender or a young adult. Young offenders can sometimes be dealt with without going to court. But Crown Prosecutors should not avoid prosecuting simply because of the defendant's age. The seriousness of the offence or the offender's past behaviour may make prosecution necessary.

Police cautions
6.9 The police make the decision to caution an offender in accordance with Home Office guidelines. If the defendant admits the offence, cautioning is the most common alternative to a court appearance. Crown Prosecutors, where necessary, apply the same guidelines and should look at the alternatives to prosecution when they consider the public interest. Crown Prosecutors should tell the police if they think that a caution would be more suitable than a prosecution.

7 Charges
7.1 Crown Prosecutors should select charges which:
(a) reflect the seriousness of the offending;
(b) give the court adequate sentencing powers; and
(c) enable the case to be presented in a clear and simple way.
This means that Crown Prosecutors may not always continue with the most serious charge where there is a choice. Further, Crown Prosecutors should not continue with more charges than are necessary.
7.2 Crown Prosecutors should never go ahead with more charges than are necessary just to encourage a defendant to plead guilty to a few. In the same way, they should never go ahead with a more serious charge just to encourage a defendant to plead guilty to a less serious one.
7.3 Crown Prosecutors should not change the charge simply because of the decision made by the court or the defendant about where the case will be heard.

8 Mode of trial
8.1 The Crown Prosecution Service applies the current guidelines for magistrates who have to decide whether cases should be tried in the Crown Court when the offence gives the option. (See the 'National Mode of Trial Guidelines' issued by the Lord Chief Justice.) Crown Prosecutors should recommend Crown Court trial when they are satisfied that the guidelines require them to do so.

8.2 Speed must never be the only reason for asking for a case to stay in the magistrates' courts. But Crown Prosecutors should consider the effect of any likely delay if they send a case to the Crown Court, and any possible stress on victims and witnesses if the case is delayed.

9 Accepting guilty pleas
9.1 Defendants may want to plead guilty to some, but not all, of the charges. Or they may want to plead guilty to a different, possibly less serious, charge because they are admitting only part of the crime. Crown Prosecutors should only accept the defendant's plea if they think the court is able to pass a sentence that matches the seriousness of the offending. Crown Prosecutors must never accept a guilty plea just because it is convenient.

10 Re-starting a prosecution
10.1 People should be able to rely on decisions taken by the Crown Prosecution Service. Normally, if the Crown Prosecution Service tells a suspect or defendant that there will not be a prosecution, or that the prosecution has been stopped, that is the end of the matter and the case will not start again. But occasionally there are special reasons why the Crown Prosecution Service will re-start the prosecution, particularly if the case is serious.
10.2 These reasons include:
(a) rare cases where a new look at the original decision shows that it was clearly wrong and should not be allowed to stand;
(b) cases which are stopped so that more evidence which is likely to become available in the fairly near future can be collected and prepared. In these cases, the Crown Prosecutor will tell the defendant that the prosecution may well start again;
(c) cases which are stopped because of a lack of evidence but where more significant evidence is discovered later.

11 Conclusion
11.1 The Crown Prosecution Service is a public service headed by the Director of Public Prosecutions. It is answerable to Parliament through the Attorney-General. The Code for Crown Prosecutors is issued under section 10 of the Prosecution of Offences Act 1985 and is a public document. This is the third edition and it replaces all earlier versions. Changes to the Code are made from time to time and these are also published.
11.2 The Code is designed to make sure that everyone knows the principles that the Crown Prosecution Service applies when carrying out its work. Police officers should take account of the principles of the Code when they are deciding whether to charge a defendant with an offence. By applying the same principles, everyone involved in the criminal justice system is helping the system to treat victims fairly, and to prosecute defendants fairly but effectively.

2.3.3 PROSECUTING COUNSEL AND THE CROWN PROSECUTION SERVICE

You may find, on occasion, that a dispute arises between you and your instructing solicitor as to whether or not to continue with a prosecution or whether to accept a proposed plea. This problem was addressed by the committee presided over by Farquharson J (May 1986) on the role of prosecuting counsel. The summary of the recommendations of the committee, set out in para. 11.6, Annexe F to the Code of Conduct, is adopted as part of the Code. The full text of the committee's Report is reprinted in *Archbold: Criminal Pleading, Evidence & Practice* 1995 Re-issue Volume 1 at paras 4-71–4-80. The 1999 edition of *Archbold* does not reproduce the full text of the committee's Report but does contain the committee's summary of its views. This can be found at para. 4-95. It is reproduced below in so far as it deals with the relationship between prosecuting counsel and his or her instructing solicitor.

2.3.3.1 The relationship between prosecution counsel and his instructing solicitor/the crown prosecutor

Generally speaking, a Prosecuting Solicitor is in the same position as any other Solicitor instructing Counsel. This will be the case when instructions are received from the Crown Prosecutor, acting as Instructing Solicitor. He will not brief counsel whose competence he doubts and in whose judgment he has no faith. Moreover, he has available the ultimate sanction of the Professional Client that, if he does not like the way his work is done, he can brief other Counsel thereafter. There will remain rare occasions when an experienced Prosecuting Solicitor is not prepared to accept the advice of Counsel upon whose judgment he would normally rely. If the difference of opinion is about an unimportant aspect of the prosecution, then it will be resolved by the usual give and take which informs discussion between members of the profession. Sometimes the difference is more fundamental as, for example, where there is a conflict between Prosecution Counsel, wishing to accept a manslaughter plea in a murder case, and his Instructing Solicitor who does not. In such circumstances, it is the view of the majority of us that the Prosecuting Solicitor/Crown Prosecutor should be in the same position as other Instructing Solicitors: if he feels it is necessary, he should be entitled to take a second Opinion, either by taking in a Leader, to advise or by withdrawing the instructions from Counsel originally briefed and instructing other Counsel. There will come a point before the commencement of the trial, however, when it will cease to be practicable for him to withdraw his instructions. It is fundamental to our thinking that, from this point, Prosecution Counsel must be accepted as being in control of the case. In the vast majority of trials, Prosecution Counsel will not normally be attended by an experienced Prosecuting Solicitor/Crown Prosecutor: he is more likely to be attended by an unqualified Clerk. The only other person in Court equipped to give an opinion on a matter requiring decision is likely to be the Police Officer in the case. Whilst it is proper for Counsel to seek and consider their views, there can be no substitute for the view of Counsel himself.

We have suggested that the moment from which Prosecution Counsel's control should start is the point, before the commencement of the trial, when it becomes impracticable for his instructions to be withdrawn. This seems to us to allow for the present common experience of pleas to different or lesser counts being offered by the defence and considered by Prosecution Counsel when the parties are at Court but before the trial has begun. There has been a measure of dissension in the committee about this with one view being advanced that Prosecution Counsel's authority to consider and accept pleas should run from the time that he receives his brief to prosecute. Whilst recognising both the force and the convenience of that view, the majority of the Committee has concluded that the Prosecuting Solicitor has authority to withdraw his instruction for proper cause up to the point which we have indicated. Once the case reaches Court, so that it becomes impracticable as well as undesirable for instructions to be withdrawn (other than in the extreme circumstances of Counsel being unable to continue for physical or mental reasons), it is for Counsel to make the necessary decisions on all matters relating to the general conduct of the trial. These will include, for example: what evidence should be called; which witnesses, in the event, are to be relied upon and which are to be abandoned; what submissions are appropriate to be made to the Judge on matters of law and/or to the Judge and jury on the existence and strength of the evidence required and available to prove the count(s) in the indictment.

We recognise that there is a significant distinction between decisions on matters of 'policy' and other decisions which have to be made. We refer to the latter hereafter as 'evidential' decisions. We do not regard any of the decisions referred to in the examples just given as being 'policy' decisions. In our view, 'policy' decisions should be understood as referring only to non-evidential decisions on the acceptance of pleas of guilty to lesser counts or groups of counts or available alternatives; offering no evidence on particular counts; and the withdrawal of the prosecution as a whole.

On 'policy' matters, we consider that the proper practice is and should continue to be that Prosecution Counsel should act contrary to his instructions only in circumstances which give him no alternative. Before reaching that stage, he will have to consider his duty to those for whom he acts, his duty to the Court and his duty to do only that which he considers to be proper. If those considerations lead him to a different view from that held by those who instruct him, he will have to act accordingly. Consideration of the views of the Prosecuting Solicitor/Crown Prosecutor, important at every stage when any kind of decision has to be taken, is crucially important with regard to 'policy' decisions.

It is our experience, as well as that of the Prosecuting Solicitors' Society, that differences of view between Prosecution Counsel and those instructing him, be they on evidential or 'policy' matters, are almost always resolved by discussions between them. There is no reason to and we do not expect this to change. Nonetheless, we have had to consider what should be the position if the very remote possibility of an unresolved conflict should occur in fact and in circumstances where it will not be possible or desirable to obtain an adjournment. The exigencies of trials usually require immediate and effective decisions by somebody. In our view, there is no alternative to the practical position that Prosecution Counsel must take those decisions and do what he conscientiously believes to be right.

The ultimate authority for any prosecution is and will be the Attorney-General, under whose superintendence the Crown Prosecution Service will be administered by the Director and to whom Prosecution Counsel are and always will be answerable. It would be impracticable, generally, to refer a dispute on a 'policy' matter to one of the Law Officers during the course of a case. Not only are they unlikely to be immediately available, but it would take time for a Law Officer to familiarise himself with the details of the particular case sufficiently to make an informed decision. Therefore, if Prosecution Counsel, in discharging his duty, has found it necessary to proceed with the case on the basis of his own view as to the correct decision with which the Prosecuting Solicitor/Crown Prosecutor has not agreed, it would be appropriate for the Attorney-General, *ex post facto,* to require Counsel to submit to him a written report of all the circumstances, including his reason for disagreeing with those who instructed him. We would expect the Attorney-General so to require when the disagreement has been about a 'policy' decision. We would welcome such a practice and rule.

We emphasise that it is Prosecution Counsel's duty to read the instructions delivered to him expeditiously and to confer with those instructing him well before the commencement of the trial, so that either the evidential and 'policy' decisions (where the need for them is identifiable) can be agreed or the opportunity will be available without adjourning the trial, to withdraw instructions or to take in a leader. The purpose is to ensure the early preparation of the case and to make timely contact with the defence, either informally or in the context of a Case Conference. For this purpose to be achieved, we recognise that both Prosecuting Solicitor/Crown Prosecutor and Defence Solicitors must deliver proper instructions as early as possible and that Defence Counsel will have to give as high a priority to early preparation as we suggest that Prosecution Counsel must give. We draw attention to rule 141 of the Code of Conduct for the Bar. (See now para. 601 of the Code.)

It would be unacceptable for Prosecution Counsel, who has had the opportunity to prepare his brief and to confer with those instructing him, to advise at the last moment before the trial begins that, for example, the case ought not to proceed or that pleas to lesser offences should be accepted. If such a situation should arise, the Instructing Solicitor must be consulted before his advice is put into effect, and if the Instructing Solicitor is unable to accept it, and instructs Counsel to apply for an adjournment, the application should be made. If an adjournment is granted it would provide an opportunity for the Director to be consulted before any decision is made as to the future conduct of the case.

After the introduction of the Crown Prosecution Service, there will remain a number of prosecutions which will be conducted independently of the Service: the most important will be those conducted by the Revenue, Customs and Excise and other government departments with their own legal sections. We suggest that the principles and the thinking underlying the practices which we have outlined above should apply to such prosecutions.

This Report contemplates the procedures of the Crown Court. Where in a Magistrates' Court, Counsel is not attended by a representative of the Prosecuting Solicitors different considerations will apply: Counsel should not act contrary to his instructions and should seek the authority of those instructing him before departing from them.

It is the minority view of one of our number that all policy decisions, as defined in this paragraph, should in the future be made by the Crown Prosecutors.

2.3.3.2 Problem

A jury fails to agree in a case in which you have prosecuted. Given the nature of the case and the evidence available to you, their inability to reach a verdict is wholly understandable. You take the view that on the customary retrial the prosecution is almost certain to fail. You also consider that a rehearing would cause considerable distress to the principal witness. You decide to offer no further evidence when the case is relisted. Your instructing solicitors do not agree. How do you deal with the situation?

2.4 Relationship with Other Members of the Profession

2.4.1 DUTIES AND RESPONSIBILITIES TO THE PROFESSION AS A WHOLE

The main obligations which you are bound to observe are set out in the Code of Conduct and include a duty:

(a) To uphold at all times the standards set out in the Code of Conduct and to comply with its provisions.

(b) Not to engage directly or indirectly in any other occupation if your association with that occupation may adversely affect the reputation of the Bar or prejudice your ability to attend properly to the interests of your clients (para. 201(b)).

(c) To ensure that you are insured with Bar Mutual Indemnity Fund Limited against claims for professional negligence (paras. 301(b); 302).

(d) To pay to the Bar Council at such time(s) as it shall become due, the subscription currently payable by a barrister of your seniority as prescribed from time to time by the Bar Council (para. 303).

(e) To act with reasonable competence in all your professional activities and to ensure your practice is efficiently and properly administered (para. 304).

(f) To exercise your own personal judgment in all your professional activities (para. 206).

(g) Not to permit your absolute independence and freedom from external pressures to be compromised or to compromise your professional standards in order to please your client, the court or a third party (para. 205).

(h) Not to solicit clients or engage in any advertising or promotion in connection with your practice other than as may be permitted by the provisions of the Code relating to advertising and publicity (paras. 308.1; 308.2).

(i) As a practising barrister, not to enter into a professional partnership with another barrister or to be a member of a firm whereby you directly or indirectly supply legal services to the public (para. 207(a) and (b)).

2.4.2 DUTIES AND RESPONSIBILITIES OWED TO OTHER MEMBERS OF THE PROFESSION

The most important aspect of your relationship with other members of the Bar is to ensure that you never knowingly mislead or deceive them. It is equally important to treat them with courtesy. Your other responsibilities include a duty:

(a)   To inform counsel previously instructed in the same matter that you have received a brief or set of instructions in place of that other barrister.

(b)   To return, unread, a document belonging to another party which has come into your possession other than by the normal and proper channels (para. 506(g); para. 7.2 to Annexe F of General Standards).

(c)   To pay, upon receipt of any fee in respect of work done by another barrister, the whole of that fee forthwith to the other barrister (para. 310.1).

(d)   To remunerate your pupil, or any pupil other than your own, for any work done for you which, because of its value to you, warrants payment (para. 701.2).

In the course of negotiating with a view to a compromise, your relationship with your opponent is of particular importance. The ethics of negotiation are dealt with in the **Negotiation Manual**. However, as many of the aspects of the proper conduct of negotiations are not directly covered in the Code itself, they are repeated here in so far as they relate to your dealings with an opponent:

(a)   Negotiations between counsel with a view to a compromise are impliedly made 'without prejudice'. Such discussions are in effect privileged and must not be repeated in court or in open correspondence. The exception to this rule is where an admission of fact, which should properly have been openly disclosed, is made in the course of negotiations. For example, 'my client admits he gave your client a gift of £500 although the rest of his claim for £2,000 was a loan'. The umbrella of 'without prejudice' does not protect such an admission. You may therefore use the admission if it is in your lay client's best interests to do so. You should, however, inform your opponent of your intention to do so. On the other hand 'my client is prepared to waive £500 of his claim provided your client pays him the balance of £1,500 within 28 days' is not an admission. It is a concession made 'without prejudice' in the context of an offer of compromise.

(b)   Frequently, counsel discuss a matter 'between counsel'. This is not the same as a discussion 'on instructions'. Such conversations usually relate to matters of a more personal or confidential nature, e.g., the fact that a client is far too upset at the moment to discuss a proposal of settlement on a rational basis. Such conversations are **not** to be repeated. The only exception to this is an admission of fact as in the example set out in (a) above. Here again, before using the admission, you should inform your opponent of your intention to do so.

(c)   Never deliberately deceive or mislead your opponent in order to secure a more favourable offer of compromise, for example, by pretending that you have a witness to support your client's account of the events when you do not. While it is acceptable to use bluff, there is a fine dividing line between bluff and deception. This will be considered in **Chapter 7, Tutorial 3**. Err on the side of caution and do seek guidance from other members of chambers when you are unsure of the distinction.

(d)   Do not knowingly conceal something which ought properly to have been disclosed, for example a document, in the hope of securing a more favourable offer of settlement.

(e)   Do not make an offer or commit your client to an agreement without instructions or authority to do so. Make it clear to your opponent when your proposal is subject to your lay client's agreement. For example, 'If my client were prepared to do xyz, would your client do abc?'

(f)   Do not go back on your word, or subsequently pretend you did not say something, in order to cover your own mistake or indiscretion. If you have made an error, admit it.

(g) Avoid bickering with your opponent. It does not do your client any good. Nor is it wise to lose your objectivity by taking on the persona of your client in the course of negotiations. For example, 'your client is totally dishonest, he has already stolen £2,000 from me'. This merely serves to antagonise.

(h) Never use threats to secure a favourable offer of compromise.

2.4.3 RELATIONSHIP WITH THE CLERKS

In the early days of practice, it is quite common for members of the Bar to shy away from ever challenging the authority of the clerks in chambers. Whilst it is important to recognise the position of the clerks and build up a good rapport, trust and working relationship with them, it is vital that you remember you are responsible for ensuring that your practice is properly and efficiently administered. If your clerk makes an error, you must take the blame. Remember that you employ the clerks, they do not employ you. On occasions it may be necessary to 'have words with' the clerks. Do so in a polite manner and on a one to one basis. Do not embarrass the clerks in front of each other or other members of chambers. If you do not succeed in obtaining the clerks' co-operation, consider speaking to your head of chambers.

The following short essay is by Martin Griffiths, the senior clerk in a large set of common law chambers, and it provides a practical insight into the relationship between barrister and clerk.

Relations between Barrister and Clerk

One of the most important people in the personal and professional life of a barrister is the barrister's clerk. The title 'clerk' does little justice to the role that the barrister's clerk plays. The popular image remains one of a slightly rough and ready 'wide boy' who exerts an inordinate amount of control and influence over his or her barristers and without whom solicitors can get nothing done. Unfortunately, this image is perpetuated by the caricatures that frequently appear in TV dramas.

The modern clerk, however, is an experienced and skilful manager at the helm of what is often a multi-million pound business. He or she does much to guide the careers of the barristers in chambers and is the link between the barristers who supply a service and the solicitors who are the customers.

The clerk's role is unusual. He or she is the agent and business manager of the barrister, the ultimate manager of the support team within chambers and the personal adviser to the barrister on all aspects of his or her professional life. Of necessity the barrister may share many problems, both professional and personal, with the clerk and a real friendship may develop between the two.

When the barrister first starts in chambers the senior clerk may appear a remote and forbidding individual. This may be particularly true in a large set of chambers where the principal point of contact between the barrister and the clerks' room is a more junior clerk. However, as manager of the clerking team, the senior clerk will always be monitoring the development and progress of the new barrister. Initially, the new barrister is dependent upon the clerk for providing him or her with work and giving him or her introductions to appropriate solicitors. In the early years the barrister will be very dependent upon this supply of work. As the barrister gains experience and establishes a reputation with solicitor clients, he or she will hopefully develop a practice of his or her own. During this period the clerk is likely to advise the barrister on how to conduct himself or herself and tell him or her what he or she should or should not do.

Whilst the new barrister should, of course, respect the experience of his or her clerk, the clerk should not be regarded as unapproachable. A relationship needs to develop between the two so that there is easy communication; the barrister must be able to feel free to seek advice and to be able to raise concerns or indeed complaints about the management of his or her practice; the clerk needs to understand the strengths, weaknesses and interests of the barrister in order to be able to direct his or her career appropriately.

Communication is probably one of the most important aspects of the smooth running of the barrister's life. Without information the clerk cannot clerk.

- Tell the clerks what you think will happen to cases that you are booked for. Is the case likely to settle, is it listed for trial and you expect it to plead, is the time estimate too short?

- Be punctual and consistent. If you usually arrive in chambers at 9.00 am but tomorrow do not expect to be in until 10.00 am, say so. It is no good if at 9.05 am the clerk needs to send somebody to court on an urgent matter and is waiting for you to walk through the door. Notify your clerk of any changes to your normal routine so that he or she can plan accordingly.

- Always ensure that you telephone chambers with a progress report from court. Ring to say that you are finished and are returning to chambers, ring at lunchtime to say that the case will finish today, or will not and will last until tomorrow lunchtime. The clerk cannot properly plan without adequate warning and up-to-date information.

- Provide prompt and accurate information regarding work done for the purposes of billing. Each chambers will have its own system of time sheets. Complete these and legal aid claim forms promptly on completing any piece of work. The sooner the bill is sent, the sooner you will get paid.

The level and collection of fees is often a subject of discussion between barrister and clerk. Some barristers have absolutely no idea of the fee that a particular case can command; some believe that the fee should be far higher than can realistically be obtained, others undervalue their services dramatically. With experience some have a good idea and can be of tremendous assistance to the clerk in assessing what a particular case is worth. It is important to tell your clerk what is involved in a particular matter for without this information he or she will be assessing or negotiating in the dark. If you have a problem with the level of fees that are being obtained for you, or with the speed with which the fees are being collected, discuss the situation with the clerk. You may have got hold of the wrong end of the stick and not understand the problem; alternatively, he or she may be unaware that a problem exists and only by discussing it can the situation be rectified. If you cannot resolve the difficulty, raise the matter with your pupil master or mistress, with whom you may still have a strong relationship even though you are well past pupillage, or raise it with the head of chambers who has a duty to ensure that the chambers are managed properly.

All chambers are different and will operate in a slightly different way. In some the members of chambers will always be addressed formally, e.g., Mr Smith, Miss Jones, Mrs Brown. In others the senior clerk will be on first name terms with the barristers but will expect his or her staff to address members of chambers formally, in other sets everyone may be on first name terms. Each chambers is different and I would advise that you err on the side of caution until you establish the house style. Having said that, I doubt if any senior clerk would these days expect to be addressed by anything other than his or her first name by the barristers.

As I have said, each chambers operates in a slightly different manner and hopefully when you start your second six months, or upon your arrival as a practising barrister, the senior clerk will run through how the chambers function. A few golden rules may well be as follows:

- Stay out of the clerks' room unless you have necessary business there. It is often a crowded and certainly a busy room and you gossiping to another member of chambers, or a clerk who has other duties, is not helpful.

- Keep personal telephone calls in chambers to a minimum. Do not expect the clerks to take telephone calls for you to organise your busy social life, sort out the cricket team fixtures or arrange a holiday for a dozen people.

- Let the clerk know when you are contemplating going on holiday before making the booking. It won't be very helpful suddenly to find that the five most junior members of chambers are all on holiday at the same time.

- Ensure that bills for chambers' expenses and clerk's fees are paid promptly.

- Feed back to your clerks news and views that you pick up from other barristers and your solicitors at court.

Remember that at all times your clerk is monitoring the work that you do and your progress. He or she will have views as to your future development and hopefully will wish to discuss these with you. Do not hesitate to share your views with him or her because at the end of the day the pair of you are a partnership.

2.4.3.1 Problems

(1) A colleague in chambers comes to your room to discuss with you a quantum in a case in which he or she is giving some preliminary advice. He or she gives you the outline of the medical report and after you have exchanged valuations of the level of general damages, leaves you with the words 'We have terrible problems on liability'. Some months later, you receive instructions to settle a defence and, having read the papers, you realise that it is the same case which you discussed with your colleague. Do you continue to deal with the papers?

(2) You have a row with your clerks. During the following week, one of the pupils in chambers asks your advice upon a brief he or she has been given for the next day. You realise it is a case you advised upon last year, yet the clerks have informed you that you have no work for the following day. What do you do?

THREE

THE ETHICAL CHALLENGE: THE EQUALITY CODE, HARASSMENT AND DISCRIMINATION

3.1   Introduction

> . . . discrimination by a barrister is professional misconduct and the Bar Council will take disciplinary action against any barrister or employee of the Bar Council found to have discriminated (Bar Council Equal Opportunities Policy Statement)

In its *First Report on Legal Education and Training* published in April 1996, the Lord Chancellor's Advisory Committee on Legal Education and Conduct (ACLEC) identified 'the ethical challenge' as one of the foremost challenges facing lawyers in the 21st century. In summarising the committee's concern the report states:

> From the earliest stages of legal education and training, intending lawyers should be imbued not only with the standards and codes of professional conduct, but also more generally with the obligations of lawyers to help protect individuals and groups from the abuse of public and private power.

How do barristers go about meeting the ethical challenge?

3.1.1   A TWIN TRACK APPROACH

In this chapter we concentrate on issues of discrimination, equal opportunities and harassment and suggest that there are two aspects to meeting the ethical challenge in these areas. First, barristers must ensure that, in addition to a sound knowledge of, and ability to apply, the letter and spirit of the Code of Conduct, they are able to identify and deal with issues of discrimination, equal opportunities and harassment arising from the guidelines laid down in the Equality Code for the Bar (the Equality Code). The Equality Code focuses largely on discrimination, equal opportunities and harassment within chambers. Whilst an understanding of, and ability to apply, the Code of Conduct and the Equality Code are of enormous importance, they alone are insufficient in meeting the ethical challenge. The second aspect of meeting the challenge involves a broader look at discrimination. In order to 'help protect individuals and groups from the abuse of public and private power', the modern barrister needs to have an understanding of the different groups that make up Britain's multi-cultural society. A knowledge of differences in customs, behaviour and language between a minority community and the majority community is essential if the barrister is to provide adequate representation to members of that minority community and treat them with sensitivity and fairness. This second aspect to meeting the ethical challenge is addressed in the essay by Lord Justice Brooke entitled *Treating People Fairly* and in the papers on *Ethnic Minorities: Appropriate Terminology* and *Body Language and Cross-Cultural Communication* reproduced by kind permission of the Judicial Studies Board.

3.1.2 THE CODE OF CONDUCT AND DISCRIMINATION

An act of direct discrimination by a barrister amounts to a breach of the Code of Conduct. Paragraph 204.1 of the Code of Conduct states:

> A practising barrister must not in relation to any other person (including a lay client or a professional client or another barrister or a pupil or a student member of an Inn of Court) discriminate directly or indirectly or victimise because of race, colour, ethnic or national origin, nationality, citizenship, sex, sexual orientation, marital status, disability, religion or political persuasion.

The breadth of this provision means that it covers the barrister's relationship with all of those people with whom he or she comes into contact in the course of carrying out professional practice and in chambers.

3.1.2.1 Fair representation: the 'cab-rank' rule

Fair treatment under para. 204 would include fair representation, though this concept is specifically enshrined in para. 209 of the Code of Conduct and is known as the 'cab-rank' rule.

> A barrister in independent practice must comply with the 'cab-rank rule' and accordingly except only as otherwise provided in paragraphs 501, 502, 503, 504 and 505, he must in any field in which he professes to practise in relation to work appropriate to his experience and seniority and irrespective of whether his client is paying privately or is legally aided or otherwise publicly funded:
>
> (a) accept any brief to appear before a court in which he professes to practise;
>
> (b) accept any instructions;
>
> (c) act for any person on whose behalf he is briefed or instructed;
>
> and do so irrespective of (i) the party on whose behalf he is briefed or instructed (ii) the nature of the case and (iii) any belief or opinion which he may have formed as to the character reputation cause conduct guilt or innocence of that person.

(See also paras. 102, 203 of the Code of Conduct and para. 2.2 of Annexe F.)

The only permissible exceptions to the 'cab-rank' rule are set out in paras. 501 to 506 of the Code of Conduct. The rule means that a barrister must accept a brief or instructions to represent a client no matter how repugnant the client is to the barrister on political, religious or moral grounds. Thus, you are obliged to represent a man charged with rape, a parent charged with child abuse, a landlord, a member of a Fascist group charged with an offence involving racial violence etc., even though your personal views would normally make you recoil from an association with such an individual. Your personal views are irrelevant and must not be a factor in the acceptance of professional work.

3.1.3 THE EQUALITY CODE

In September 1995 the Bar Council published the final version of The Equality Code for the Bar (the Equality Code). The Equality Code is described as 'a guide to good equal opportunities practice to which all barristers in independent practice must have regard'. A comprehensive summary of the Equality Code can be found at Annexe O of the Code of Conduct in **Appendix 1**.

3.1.3.1 Content

The Equality Code might be seen to have two main areas of concern. First, it covers the regulatory and legislative framework governing barristers in the field of discrimination and equal opportunities (chapter 1). In that connection it very helpfully defines unlawful and prohibited discrimination (chapter 2) and provides guidance on

THE ETHICAL CHALLENGE: THE EQUALITY CODE, HARASSMENT AND DISCRIMINATION

harassment (chapter 3). Secondly, it covers anti-discrimination and equal opportunities obligations and policies across a range of areas of chambers activity and management (chapters 4-7).

3.1.3.2 Status of the Equality Code

It is worth distinguishing between the status of the Code of Conduct and the Equality Code. Whilst it is the case that by virtue of para. 304 of the Code of Conduct a barrister must have regard to the provisions of the Equality Code, not every breach of the Equality Code will render a barrister automatically liable to disciplinary proceedings. Paragraph 204.1 of the Code of Conduct prohibits a barrister from any act of direct or indirect discrimination (see below) and para. 802.1 of the Code of Conduct states that a barrister's failure to comply with the provisions of the Code of Conduct 'shall constitute professional misconduct rendering him liable to disciplinary proceedings'. Thus, breaches of the Equality Code may well amount to professional misconduct under para. 204.1 of the Code of Conduct but will not always automatically do so. Under para. 204.2 acts of indirect discrimination will not amount to a breach of the Code of Conduct if they were committed without any intention of treating the claimant less favourably on any ground in para. 204.1 to which the complaint relates. In short, the Equality Code provides an evidential standard against which allegations of discrimination may be judged, and an invaluable guide to good practice which it would be foolish for individual barristers or sets of chambers to ignore.

3.1.3.3 Statutory obligations

Barristers and their clerks should remember that in addition to the provisions of the Code of Conduct and the Equality Code, they are subject to a number of statutory obligations. Section 26A of the Race Relations Act 1976 and s. 35A of the Sex Discrimination Act 1975, both enacted by s. 64 of the Courts and Legal Services Act 1990, effectively outlaw discrimination by barristers or their clerks on grounds of race or sex. The Disability Discrimination Act 1995 prohibits barristers from discriminating on grounds of disability. An individual alleging discrimination can bring proceedings against a barrister or set of chambers in a County Court within six months of the alleged act of discrimination.

3.1.3.4 Discrimination

Discrimination, both direct and indirect, is defined in chapter two of the Equality Code. Readers should familiarise themselves with the concept of direct discrimination centred around the idea of 'less favourable treatment', and indirect discrimination whereby a condition or requirement is applied equally to everyone, but some individuals or groups who are unable to comply, suffer a detriment as a result and the requirement cannot be shown to be objectively justifiable in spite of its discriminatory effect.

3.2 Harassment

Harassment is dealt with in chapter 3 of the Equality Code, Guidance on Harassment. In order to give fuller guidance on the legal background of this subject and the practicalities of dealing with it, there follows an essay by Barbara Hewson, Joint Vice President of the Association of Women Barristers 1996–8. (The matters contained in chapters 4 to 7 of the Equality Code will be covered in detail in lectures.)

Harassment: Law and Professional Ethics

Barbara Hewson

A barrister . . . must not:
    (a) engage in conduct . . . which is:
    . . . (iii) likely to diminish public confidence in the legal profession . . . or otherwise bring the legal profession into disrepute [201]

A practising barrister must not in relation to any other person . . . discriminate directly or indirectly or victimise because of race, colour, ethnic or national origin, nationality, citizenship, sex, sexual orientation, marital status, disability, religion or political persuasion. [204.1]

(Bar's Code of Conduct)

Introduction

The concept of harassment has been a relatively recent arrival in the field of discrimination law. However, it has proved an effective means of challenging various forms of abusive and oppressive behaviour, which can be shown to be sex- or race-related, in our courts. Other forms of harassment, for example based on sexual orientation, or disability, rely on the principles developed in sex and race discrimination cases. Much of the relevant case law concerns sexual harassment.

Whether the Bar's disciplinary processes can deal adequately with the problems posed by harassment remains a matter of some debate. In theory, harassment attracts disciplinary sanctions which are covered by both the sections of the Bar's Code of Conduct quoted above. Much work has been done by the Bar Council's Sex Discrimination Committee and its Equal Opportunities Officers, in particular, on this topic (see chapter 3 of the Bar's revised Equality Code).

At present, the level of complaints to the Bar Council's Professional Conduct Committee (PCC) does not appear to reflect the level of sexual harassment which recent studies suggest occurs at the Bar. It is hoped that a new protocol, recently agreed with the PCC for dealing with complaints of harassment, will inspire greater confidence.

Given the increasing public awareness of harassment, it is important for barristers, and prospective barristers, to appreciate that this type of misconduct, if proven, carries not only legal but also disciplinary penalties. Paragraph 204 of the Code of Conduct (quoted above) is drafted in very wide terms, and could encompass complaints of harassment against barristers by judges, court staff, lay and professional clients, temporary or permanent staff in chambers or another organisation, students, mini-pupils, pupils, squatters, and tenants.

At present, it is recognised that certain forms of harassment tend to be under-reported. Sexual harassment appears to pose special problems. The European Commission states in section 5 of its Code of Practice on measures to combat sexual harassment:

> A distinguishing characteristic of sexual harassment is that employees subjected to it often will be reluctant to complain. An absence of complaints about sexual harassment in a particular organization, therefore, does not necessarily mean an absence of sexual harassment. It may mean that recipients of sexual harassment think that there is no point in complaining because nothing will be done about it, or because it will be trivialized or the complainant subjected to ridicule, or because they fear reprisals.

The current trend is to encourage the development of proper equal opportunities policies and procedures, to enable people to raise legitimate concerns about harassment, and to enable effective action to be taken, without fear of victimisation: this trend is reflected in the Equality Code. Recent research also suggests that the most effective way of tackling harassment is by official complaints. The message is, **complaining works**. However, it should be remembered that much 'low level' harassment can be dealt with through informal procedures without resorting to formal disciplinary measures.

Before examining ways of tackling harassment, it is worth posing some preliminary questions. What is harassment? Why is it unlawful? How prevalent is harassment? If the Bar is to deal adequately with harassment at a disciplinary level, then it must have regard to the legal framework which has evolved so far.

Harassment is, in summary, a form of anti-competitive and discriminatory behaviour, whereby people are impeded in, or prevented from, carrying on their chosen trade, profession or employment. Lawyers should be concerned in principle about harassment for two reasons: first, since it entails a denial of equal treatment, it has implications in terms of fundamental human rights; secondly, as it is capable of distorting the labour market, it has implications in terms of economic rights. It may also arise in the sphere of provision of services (see the case concerning Nigel Hamilton QC mentioned below); in which case, it may be said to distort the market in services (albeit, one suspects, to a lesser degree).

What is harassment?
Neither the Sex Discrimination Act 1975 (SDA), nor the Race Relations Act 1976 (RRA), nor the Disability Discrimination Act 1995 (DDA), contain any reference to harassment as such. However, s. 1(1)(a), SDA prohibits direct discrimination, that is, less favourable treatment 'on the ground of' sex (see s. 1(1)(a), RRA: less favourable treatment 'on racial grounds').

In addition, s. 6(1), SDA prohibits discrimination against women applying for employment, and s. 6(2)(b), SDA prohibits discrimination against female employees by subjecting them to dismissal, or to 'any other detriment' (see s. 4(1), (2)(c), RRA; s. 4(2)(d), DDA). As for barristers, comparable provisions were inserted as s. 35A(1), (2)(d), SDA and s. 26A(1), (2)(d), RRA, as a result of the Courts and Legal Services Act 1990. However, it is worth noting that there is no reference in the DDA to barristers, and s. 7(1), DDA exempts small businesses which employ fewer than 20 employees: this would cover most if not all sets of chambers. The approach adopted by the courts to sexual harassment is of assistance in considering what types of conduct might constitute harassment on other grounds, e.g., disability, race or sexual orientation.

Defining sexual harassment: (i) the Porcelli case
In a landmark decision, *Stratholyde Regional Council* v *Porcelli* [1986] ICR 134, the Court of Session held that sexual harassment was a particularly degrading and unacceptable form of treatment which it must have been Parliament's intention to restrain.

In that case, Mrs Porcelli, who was employed as a school laboratory technician, suffered from a prolonged campaign of harassment from two male colleagues, which included making suggestive remarks, brushing against her, and subjecting her to intimidation. The purpose of the campaign was to force her to leave the school, which ultimately she did. The question of law was whether the treatment she received was less favourable treatment 'on the ground of her sex', contrary to s. 1(1)(a), SDA. The Court of Session held that it was. It found that the treatment complained of by Mrs Porcelli included conduct of a sexual nature, which would not have been meted out to a male employee who was disliked. It was 'a particular kind of weapon, based upon the sex of the victim'.

That case made it clear that sexual harassment encompasses not only physical contact of a sexual nature which is unwelcome to the recipient, but conduct falling short of such physical acts. In that case the employer conceded that Mrs Porcelli had suffered a detriment within the terms of s. 6(2)(b), SDA: 'detriment' in this context meaning no more than 'disadvantage'.

As a form of direct discrimination, therefore, it is also important to note that the absence of any *intention to discriminate* is no defence (*James* v *Eastleigh BC* [1990] 2 AC 751, HL). Thus a harasser who argues that he was just 'being friendly', for example, will find his behaviour being objectively analysed by a tribunal or County Court.

Defining sexual harassment: (ii) the European Commission's Code
Those who have studied EC law will be familiar with the protection afforded to men and women by Article 141 (ex Article 119) of the EC Treaty (the principle of equal pay for equal work); the Equal Treatment Directive (76/207/EEC), and the Equal

Treatment Directive for the Self-Employed (86/613/EEC). In addition, on 27 November 1991 the European Commission produced a Recommendation on the dignity of women and men at work, to which is annexed a Code of Practice ('the Code') on measures to combat sexual harassment (*OJ* L 49). This is non-binding, but is commonly referred to in employment tribunals.

Section 2 of the Code (Definitions) provides:

Sexual harassment means **unwanted conduct of a sexual nature, or other conduct based on sex affecting the dignity of women and men at work**. This can include unwelcome physical, verbal or non-verbal conduct.

Thus, **a range of behaviour** may be considered to constitute sexual harassment. It is unacceptable if the conduct is unwanted, unreasonable and offensive to the recipient; a person's rejection of or submission to such conduct on the part of employers or workers (including superiors or colleagues) is used explicitly or implicitly as a basis for a decision which affects that person's access to vocational training or to employment, continued employment, promotion, salary or any other employment decisions; and/or **such conduct creates an intimidating, hostile or humiliating working environment for the recipient**.

The essential characteristic of sexual harassment is that it is unwanted by the recipient, **that it is for each individual to determine what behaviour is acceptable to them and what they regard as offensive**. . . . It is the unwanted nature of the conduct which distinguishes sexual harassment from friendly behaviour, which is welcome and mutual. [emphasis supplied]

Expanding on these general definitions, harassment in all its forms can include the following types of conduct:

(a) verbal: turning discussions to sexual topics; asking about someone's sex life; stereotypical comments and generalisations; racial name-calling; use of offensive language; sexual innuendoes or taunts; derogatory remarks, e.g., about someone's sexuality; requests for dates;

(b) non-verbal: sexually suggestive gestures; excluding a person from normal workplace conversations; displaying offensive material (e.g., on computer displays);

(c) physical: uninvited touching, patting or other forms of physical contact; unwanted attention, e.g., letters.

The most serious forms of harassment include physical intimidation, assault or attempted assault; sexual assaults; and requests for sexual favours in exchange for promotion or advancement at work. Specific examples of harassment appear in chapter 3 of the Bar's Equality Code.

The prevalence of certain types of harassment
The Introduction to the Commission's Code states:

The expert report carried out on behalf of the Commission found that sexual harassment is a serious problem for many working women in the European Community and research in Member States has shown without doubt that sexual harassment is not an isolated phenomenon. On the contrary, it is clear that for millions of women in the European Community, sexual harassment is an unpleasant and unavoidable part of their working lives. Men too may suffer sexual harassment and should, of course, have the same rights as women to the protection of their dignity.

Some specific groups are particularly vulnerable to sexual harassment. Research in several Member States, which documents the link between the risk of sexual harassment and the recipient's perceived vulnerability, suggests that divorced and separated women, young women and new entrants to the labour market and those with irregular or precarious employment contracts, women in non-traditional jobs, women with disabilities, lesbians and women from racial minorities are disproportionately at risk. Gay men and young men are also vulnerable to harassment. It is undeniable that harassment on grounds of sexual orientation undermines the dignity at work of those affected and it is impossible to regard such harassment as appropriate workplace behaviour.

Sexual harassment pollutes the working environment and can have a devastating effect upon the health, confidence, morale and performance of those affected by it. The anxiety and stress produced by sexual harassment commonly leads to those subjected to it taking time off work due to sickness, being less efficient at work, or leaving their job to seek work elsewhere. . . .

In general terms, sexual harassment is an obstacle to the proper integration of women into the labour market and the Commission is committed to encouraging the development of comprehensive measures to improve such integration.

Research into sexual harassment at the Bar
A 1992 Report by TMS Management Consultants, *Without Prejudice? Sexual Equality at the Bar and the Judiciary*, was commissioned by the Bar Council and the Lord Chancellor's Department. This found that, although sexual harassment did not emerge as a major source of disadvantage in the statistical analysis of the survey, there was significant comment from respondents in the open-ended section of the survey. 18 respondents commented on inappropriate behaviour and 16 on belittling 'witticisms'. TMS commented (at para. 26i):

The survey comments suggested that sexual harassment was not always recognised as such and was treated as a joke by perpetrators and sometimes by the targets. As one woman QC put it, 'The Bar is male dominated and a woman will have a tough time if one is too sensitive to, for example, sex oriented jokes'.

While some senior women at the Bar may still espouse this 'stiff upper lip' approach, there is more recent evidence that younger women are less likely to be so dismissive of what they perceive as inappropriate behaviour. In 1995, a report by Professor Joanna Shapland and Angela Sorsby, *Starting Practice: Work and Training at the Junior Bar* found that 40% of women respondents said they had encountered sexual harassment while at the Bar. This suggests that there is no room for complacency. In 1994, an internal Bar Council working party on pupillage found evidence of misconduct by pupil masters which, it said, warranted the epithet 'disgraceful' (the Malins report).

The importance of proper procedures
The Commission's Code emphasises that policies to deal with harassment are likely to be most effective when linked to a broader policy to promote equal opportunities (s. 3). In its recommendations to employers, it sets out a comprehensive set of measures, and these can be adapted not only to encompass different forms of harassment, but also so as to apply to barristers in private practice. These recommendations form a yardstick against which any chambers, or organisation, needs to assess its own internal procedures. A short summary of its main recommendations is as follows:

(a) those in senior management positions should issue a policy statement on harassment which sets out what is and is not acceptable behaviour; which commits all members of the organisation to comply with the policy; and which explains the procedures to be adopted when complaints are made;

(b) employers should make it clear that harassment is a disciplinary offence and state clearly the penalties;

(c) employers should make it clear that victimisation of a complainant acting in good faith is a disciplinary offence;

(d) employers should communicate the policy effectively;

(e) employers should positively promote the policy, by explaining it to staff and junior members, and being responsive and supportive in the case of any complaints;

(f) employers should provide training for those in managerial and supervisory positions to ensure that harassment does not occur and that, if it does, it is resolved efficiently;

(g) employers should develop clear and precise procedures for dealing with harassment once it has occurred, which should draw attention to a complainant's legal rights, and which should:

    (i) provide an informal means of confronting the person engaging in the unwanted conduct and make it plain that the conduct must stop;

    (ii) designate someone to provide advice and assistance to complainants and provide that adviser with training and protection from victimisation;

    (iii) provide formal procedures which make it clear to whom a formal complaint must be made (preferably to someone of the complainant's own sex);

    (iv) enable internal investigations to be conducted with sensitivity **and with due respect for the rights of both the complainant and the alleged harasser, give both the complainant and the alleged harasser the right to be accompanied and/or represented, ensure that the alleged harasser has full details of the complaint and the opportunity to respond**; and maintain strict confidentiality throughout;

    (v) recognise that recounting the experience of harassment can be difficult and damaging to a complainant's dignity (which means that complainants should not be asked to recount their experience more than is strictly necessary);

    (vi) ensure that a complete record of all investigations is kept.

For a model harassment policy, see the policy at the end of this section (first published in 'Dealing with harassment: a Practical Guide', Laura Cox QC and Barbara Hewson, *Counsel*, May/June 1996).

The importance of having a proper complaints procedure is illustrated by the case of *Bracebridge Engineering* v *Darby* [1990] IRLR 3. There, a woman employee who was leaving work was ordered into a room by two senior male employees, ostensibly to discipline her for leaving early. She was lifted up, manhandled and sexually assaulted. When she complained, her assailants denied the incident and the employer concluded that no action should be taken. Mrs Darby resigned.

The EAT held that a single episode of harassment, if sufficiently serious (as plainly it was here) could constitute a detriment within s. 6(2)(b), SDA. It also found that the employer's failure to investigate the assaults properly entitled Mrs Darby to resign and claim constructive dismissal. It can therefore be said that a failure to have a proper complaints procedure, or to administer it properly, might found a complaint of misconduct.

Another important case is that of *Insitu Cleaning* v *Heads* [1995] IRLR 4. There an area manager at a meeting was addressed by a Mr Brown, the son of one of the company's directors, in the following terms, 'Hiya, big tits'. Although this remark was not heard by others present, Mrs Heads said that the remark made her eyes fill with tears and her face flush with embarrassment. She complained after the meeting. The tribunal was particularly influenced by Brown's aggressive stance when the complaint was reported to him, his continued denials, and his arrogant air at the hearing. (Moral, for those making offensive remarks: apologise!)

The EAT, upholding the tribunal, said that Mrs Heads had suffered a detriment as a result of the remark made to her: for a director's son to make a sexual remark, causing distress to a female employee nearly twice his age, was **a form of bullying and not acceptable in the workplace in any circumstances.** As the European Commission Code of Practice on measures to combat sexual harassment makes clear, such conduct is likely to create an intimidating, hostile and humiliating work environment for the victim. It also held that it was not perverse for the tribunal to conclude that the one incident was so serious that it could of itself constitute sexual harassment. The reference in the EC Code to 'unwanted conduct' was essentially the same as 'unwelcome' or 'uninvited': here, only a person used to indulging in loutish behaviour could think that the remark made to Mrs Heads was other than obviously unwanted.

To prevent the recurrence of such incidents, the lay members of the EAT advised employers:

(a) to adopt a separate procedure which deals exclusively with complaints of sexual harassment;

(b) such a procedure should contain an informal first step, which would enable complaints to be dealt with sympathetically, before matters got out of hand. Many women just want the harassment to stop and are not concerned to have the offender disciplined;

(c) to deal with any complaint from the perception of the person aggrieved.

These common-sense measures, which recognise the nature of harassment, are now being applied by tribunals to assess the adequacy of procedures used by employers to prevent harassment in the workplace. Many employers are now revising their procedures in the light of these recommendations, to cover all forms of harassment.

Steps taken by the Bar to prevent harassment
It can be seen from chapter 3 of the Bar's revised Equality Code that a raft of measures is being put in place to try to tackle the problem that harassment poses. It has yet to be seen how, for example, the Mediation Panel will work, but it is clear that complainants have a number of options, including legal action. Legal action poses real problems for those without private means: a Tribunal recently ruled that an applicant for pupillage was not entitled to proceed in the Tribunal under part II of the SDA/RRA (which has obvious attractions, in being quicker and cheaper, and without the sanction of costs if one loses), but instead had to bring a complaint in the County Court under part III of the SDA/RRA (*Al-Ani v Robertson & Ors*, 15 October 1996, unreported). The costs of the latter forum may be prohibitive unless one is eligible for legal aid. One option is to take advice from the Commission for Racial Equality or Equal Opportunities Commission, who will back 'test' cases; or to join an established trade union, which will provide free legal advice, representation and support to members.

It is vital that sets of chambers put proper policies and procedures in place, otherwise it seems likely that recipients of harassment will be reluctant to complain about what is happening to them, either within the chambers, or to the PCC. The more, of course, that intending practitioners are prepared to quiz chambers about their policies, the more pressure chambers will be under to meet such expectations.

What can you do to cope with harassment?
If you or one of your colleagues is unfortunate enough to have experienced harassment, here is some practical advice on how to cope.

(a) do not blame yourself: you are not the only person in the world to have had such an experience;

(b) if practicable, tell the person whose behaviour is upsetting you that you find the conduct offensive, and want it to stop. Explain how it makes you feel (e.g., 'When you say things like that, it makes me embarrassed, and I can't concentrate on my work'; 'I find those types of jokes offensive, and I would appreciate it if you didn't make them in front of me');

(c) find out if the harasser has been doing this to anyone else;

(d) keep a contemporaneous record of all the incidents: what happened, who was there, what was said;

(e) get hold of a copy of the chambers' equal opportunity policy and see what procedures are available to you, to raise the matter informally, or formally;

(f) if your chambers are enlightened enough to have a pupillage welfare officer, or an equal opportunities officer, speak to him/her in confidence, with a view to resolving the matter informally if possible: they should be able to offer you advice and support, and to raise your concerns with the harasser if you wish;

(g) if your chambers are not so enlightened, and do not have a proper policy, then the risk you face is that they may overreact, or respond inappropriately to your concerns. Ideally, you need a senior and sympathetic member of chambers, with some management role, who will take the matter up, either formally or informally, on your behalf and who will be able to stop matters getting out of hand;

(h) what you probably want, in cases of 'low level' harassment, is the chance to relay your concerns to the harasser, so that he/she has the chance to apologise, to say it won't happen again, and to give you an assurance that you will not be victimised in future for having raised such concerns. Some harassers may be deeply embarrassed and should be encouraged to sort the matter out with a quick apology and reassurance that they will not hold it against the complainant in future;

(i) you can seek help outside chambers: from the Bar Council's Equal Opportunities Officers (who have a confidential telephone line to deal with matters of harassment, 0171 242 0768); the Bar's Disability Panel; the Bar's Mediation Panel; the Commission for Racial Equality or the Equal Opportunities Commission; Women Against Sexual Harassment (WASH); or sympathetic Bar organisations such as the Society of Black Lawyers, Bar Lesbian and Gay Group or the Association of Women Barristers;

(j) decide what **you** want to achieve: remember that if you pursue a formal complaint, either within chambers or to the PCC, this may prove stressful; you will need moral and emotional support, so make sure you have a good network of friends.

Disciplinary action: how does it work?
In January 1995, a Bar disciplinary tribunal suspended Nigel Hamilton QC for three months, for various acts of harassment of a lay client, and a solicitors' clerk. However, that case took some two years to come to a hearing, and the respondent contested the case until the day of the hearing, when he pleaded guilty. In early 1998, newspapers carried reports of a barrister found to have harassed a pupil: however, he has exercised a right of appeal.

The Canadian experience suggests that it is possible for professional bodies to adopt a sensible, measured and effective approach to complaints of harassment. Admittedly, harassment raises human rights issues under the Canadian Charter, which may account for an enhanced appreciation of the problem there. But a disciplinary incident referred to the Law Society of British Columbia gives a practical indication of how a complaint at the less serious end of the spectrum might be dealt with appropriately.

A complaint was referred by a woman advocate, who while waiting outside court for a contested motion, along with other lawyers, asked her male opponent: 'What is your position in this matter?' he replied: 'I prefer the missionary position'. She was particularly embarrassed and annoyed at being spoken to in this fashion at court. She complained to him in writing afterwards, and received a letter saying, 'If I have offended you in any way, I apologise'. She then made a formal complaint which was referred to a panel for a conduct review. The male advocate again apologised, saying he had no intention of harassing the woman advocate, but recognised that his remark had been entirely inappropriate.

The panel had no hesitation in finding that his remark was a clear case of sexual harassment: note that his intention was irrelevant. The remark clearly sexualised his female opponent in a manner which was overtly offensive. However, it noted his apologetic demeanour, and decided to take no further action. This demonstrates that it is possible to deal with a range of professional complaints in a way which recognises the importance of the issues involved, but in a proportionate manner.

If you are accused of harassment, it is important to bear in mind the differing fates of that male advocate, and Mr Brown in the *Insitu* case, whose obduracy won him no friends in the tribunal, and who was described as a lout. You should stand a much better chance, before a disciplinary body, if you can show that you have made some genuine effort to make amends, promptly, when a complaint is made; or at least have adopted a reasonably conciliatory stance. Remember: the absence of any intention to discriminate on your part is irrelevant, so if you have given offence, a speedy apology should go a long way to alleviating your situation.

If you are a victim of harassment, and your chambers is willing to consider outside mediation, the Bar Council has a Mediation Panel which has been set up for this purpose (so far, it has never been used). If you wish to pursue a formal complaint to the PCC, remember that the PCC, to date, has little experience of dealing with matters of harassment. You need to ensure that you have assistance in drafting your complaint, and you need to make the complaint promptly, or have a reasonable excuse for any delay (such as trying to find new chambers).

The PCC is unlikely to recommend that complaints be taken forward to a full disciplinary tribunal, which involves a formal 'prosecution' of charges by the PCC against the alleged harasser, and is a lengthy and expensive procedure, save only in cases of serious harassment. If a case is referred to a disciplinary tribunal, remember that you will have to be prepared to give oral evidence, and be cross-examined.

If, however, the PCC considers that a *prima facie* case of misconduct has been made out, but that there are no disputes of fact which would warrant the matter being referred to a tribunal, and no charges which (if proved) would be likely to result in a sentence of disbarment, it can deal with the matter by way of a summary procedure. If it considers that a *prima facie* case has been made out, but considers that the case is not so serious as to warrant a summary procedure, it can convene an informal panel hearing.

There is also the Bar's new protocol for complaints of harassment, which is intended to ensure that a complainant has an adviser and is kept in touch with what is happening to his/her complaint. Complaints are confidential, and the PCC will treat it as a disciplinary matter if a barrister against whom a complaint is made publicises the identity of the complainant (save for the very limited extent that may be necessary in order to interview witnesses, and prepare his or her own defence). One practical problem which a formal complaint to the PCC may encounter is that, if the complainant is also litigating a claim of discrimination in the courts, the PCC will generally not pursue the matter, pending the outcome of the litigation.

In the case of what you may regard as a perverse decision by the PCC, you have the options of:

(a) complaining to the Legal Services Ombudsman;

(b) judicial review; or

(c) if you are a barrister, legal action against the Bar Council under the SDA or RRA.

It is to be hoped that you will never find yourself in such a situation!

(The writer was a member of the Bar Council's Sex Discrimination Committee 1992–5, and Professional Conduct Committee 1993–4. The views expressed are her own.)

Harassment Policy

Chambers of Smith QC

(We are indebted to the Law Society of Upper Canada's recommended Personnel Policy regarding Employment-related Harassment for Small Firms, August 1994; and to the European Commission's Code.)

Statement of principle
Smith Chambers are committed to providing a working environment in which all clerks, members of staff, trainees, mini-pupils, pupils, squatters, tenants, door or associate tenants, visitors and clients are treated with dignity.

Smith Chambers are committed to ensuring that para. 204.1 of the Bar's Code of Conduct is effective. This prohibits any form of discrimination whether direct, or indirect, or by way of victimisation, against any person on the grounds of *race, colour, ethnic or national origin, nationality, citizenship, sex, sexual orientation, marital status, disability, religion or political persuasion.*

Smith Chambers believe that harassment is unacceptable and are committed to taking all necessary steps to ensure that no one visiting or working in chambers is subject to harassment.

You have a right to complain about harassment if you encounter it in Smith Chambers. Your complaint will be treated seriously in accordance with the procedures set out in this policy.

Responsibilities
All clerks, members of staff, trainees, mini-pupils, pupils, squatters, tenants, door or associate tenants, visitors and clients have a personal responsibility to ensure that their behaviour is not contrary to this policy.

All clerks, members of staff, trainees, mini-pupils, pupils, squatters, tenants, door or associate tenants, visitors and clients are encouraged to ensure the maintenance of a work environment in Smith Chambers which is free from harassment.

Definitions
'Chambers' includes all premises where the business of chambers is conducted; all work-related activities at any other site (e.g. other sets of chambers; court); and any social, business or other functions which are work-related (e.g. parties for clients; circuit messes).

Harassment means unwelcome physical, verbal, or non-verbal conduct based on *race, colour, ethnic or national origin, nationality, citizenship, sex, sexual orientation, marital status, disability, religion or political persuasion* where either:

(a) such conduct is unwanted, unreasonable or offensive to the recipient; or

(b) the recipient's rejection of or submission to such conduct on the part of clerks, staff, tenants, door tenants, clients or visitors (including superiors or colleagues) is used explicitly or implicitly as a basis for a decision which affects the recipient's access to vocational training, employment, continued employment, promotion, salary, mini-pupillage, pupillage, tenancy, instructions or fees, or any other decisions related to employment, professional career, or the provision of professional services; or

(c) such conduct creates an intimidating, hostile or humiliating working environment for the recipient.

Examples of harassment are:

(a) verbal: asking about someone's sex life; requests for dates; intrusive questioning about someone's racial or ethnic origins, their culture or religion; racial name-calling; use of offensive language or stereotypes; sexual innuendoes, teasing or taunts; homophobic jokes; patronising or derogatory remarks (e.g. about someone's physical attributes, sexuality or disability);

(b) non-verbal: sexually suggestive gestures; excluding a person from normal workplace conversations or functions; displaying or circulating offensive material (e.g. on computer displays);

(c) physical: uninvited touching, patting, stroking, or other forms of unwelcome physical contact; unwanted attention, e.g. letters; assaults or intimidation.

Such behaviour may be unlawful and must be avoided. Smith Chambers will take appropriate disciplinary measures against those who engage in harassment, or those who victimise or retaliate against anyone complaining of harassment.

Smith Chambers will take appropriate disciplinary measures against anyone who seeks directly or indirectly to prejudice any decision affecting a complainant's access to vocational training, employment, continued employment, promotion, salary, mini-pupillage, pupillage, tenancy, instructions or fees, or any other decisions related to employment, professional career, or the provision of professional services, following any complaint.

Who oversees the policy?
The following members of Smith Chambers have management responsibilities:

(a)   Smith QC who is Head of Chambers

(b)   the Senior Clerk/ Practice manager

(c)   the Equal Opportunities Adviser/ Welfare Adviser

(d)   the members of the Management Committee who are [names].

(They have all received awareness/sensitivity training in understanding and dealing with problems of harassment, as have all pupil-masters/mistresses. We recognise that further guidance is necessary for chambers in relation to training and where to get it.)

Their tasks are:

(a)   to ensure that everyone appreciates the problem of harassment and their individual responsibility to prevent harassment occurring;

(b)   to discourage and prevent harassment, in particular by promoting awareness of this policy;

(c)   to investigate every formal written complaint of harassment;

    (d)   to take appropriate remedial measures to respond to any substantiated allegations of harassment.

What happens if harassment occurs?

Smith Chambers acknowledges that people may find it difficult to raise concerns about harassment, especially people in junior positions. Many people just want the harassment to stop, and an apology. Smith Chambers is committed to providing a supportive environment in which to resolve concerns about harassment fairly, promptly, with due regard for confidentiality, and without fear of victimisation or retaliation.

Informal procedure:

    (a)   When all incident of harassment occurs, communicate your disapproval and objections to the person causing the harassment immediately and request him/her to stop. Keep a note of what has happened and of any future incidents.

    (b)   If the harassment does not stop, or you do not feel able to speak to the person directly, contact the Equal Opportunities Adviser/Welfare Adviser or [named individual A [another person with management responsibilities]] ('the designated adviser'). The designated adviser will provide you with advice and support; will approach the person concerned on your behalf if you wish; and will undertake any investigation necessary to resolve the matter informally.

    (c)   All informal complaints will be promptly investigated. The designated adviser undertaking the investigation will not be connected with the allegation in any way.

    (d)   Confidentiality will be maintained and where it is necessary to interview witnesses the importance of confidentiality will be emphasised.

    (e)   Possible ways of resolving the matter informally can include: giving the person causing the harassment an opportunity to apologise to you, either orally or in writing, and to give you an assurance that the harassment will not happen again, and that you will not be victimised or penalised in any way as a result of raising your concerns.

Note: in cases of extremely serious harassment, you will be invited to use the formal procedure set out below.

Formal procedure:

    (a)   If the harassment continues, or you are not satisfied with the outcome of the informal option, or you wish to make a formal complaint, set out your concerns in writing and draw them to the attention of [X [and Y] of the Management Committee].

    (b)   In addition, the Equal Opportunities Adviser/Welfare Adviser or [named individual A] ('the designated adviser') will provide you with advice and support.

    (c)   All complaints will be promptly investigated. The person(s) carrying out the investigation will not be connected with the allegation in any way.

    (d)   Confidentiality will be maintained and where it is necessary to interview witnesses the importance of confidentiality will be emphasised.

    (e)   The person against whom the complaint is made shall be given a proper opportunity to respond to the complaint, to put his/her side of the story, and to make representations within [—] days. If he/she wishes, he/she may approach [named individual] for advice and support.

(f) If at the conclusion of an investigation (which shall be no later than [—] weeks from the making of the complaint) the complaint is found to be substantiated on the balance of probabilities (this is the standard used in discrimination proceedings and should be applied in internal disciplinary proceedings), appropriate action will be taken against the harasser.

(g) Such action may include:

   (i) requiring the harasser to make a formal apology;

   (ii) requiring the harasser to attend awareness training;

   (iii) giving the harasser a written warning;

   (iv) suspending the harasser from chambers;

   (v) dismissing or expelling the harasser from chambers;

   (vi) refusing to accept instructions from the harasser in future;

   (vii) reporting the harasser to their professional body for professional misconduct.

(h) If a complaint is not upheld, but nonetheless the parties concerned do not wish to continue working together, consideration will be given to alternative working arrangements, where this is practicable.

(i) It is recognised that the fact that a complaint is not upheld should not be taken to imply that you were lying or acted in bad faith. You will continue to receive such advice and support from the designated adviser as you need.

Records
Records will be kept of all informal and formal complaints and investigations. These will be kept confidential, save where disclosure is required for legal or disciplinary action.

Monitoring
The outcome of every informal and formal complaint will be reviewed annually by the Management Committee/Head of Chambers to ensure the continuing effectiveness of this policy.

Additional rights
If you wish to raise concerns of harassment with people outside Smith Chambers, you should contact the Bar Council's Equal Opportunities Officers Kathryn Hamylton or Pamela Bhalla (tel. 0171-242 0082), or Jenny Maclean of the Professional Conduct Committee Secretariat (tel. 0171-440 4000) who will offer you advice.

The Bar Council's confidential telephone line for concerns about sexual harassment is 0171-242 0768.

The Commission for Racial Equality can be contacted on 0171-828 7022. The Equal Opportunities Commission can be contacted on 0161-833 9244. WASH (Women Against Sexual Harassment) can be contacted on 0171-405 0340.

The time limit for bringing a complaint of race or sex discrimination (which includes harassment) under the Sex Discrimination Act 1975 or Race Relations Act 1976 to an Employment Tribunal is three months from the act complained of. The Tribunal may extend time where it is just and equitable to do so.

It should be noted that in *Al-Ani* v *Robertson & Ors*, 15 October 1996, unreported, a Tribunal ruled that an applicant for pupillage had to bring a complaint of discrimination in the County Court.

3.3   Discrimination, a Broader Perspective

The Equality Code importantly points out (at p. 6) that:

> Direct discrimination may frequently be subconscious, based on stereotypical assumptions about particular minority ethnic groups or about the difference in capabilities, characteristics, personalities and motivation between women and men.

In the following essay Brooke LJ, examines the nature of subconscious and stereotypical assumptions, and illustrates how damaging their effect can be upon the administration of justice in general and the fair and proper representation of lay clients by counsel in particular.

Treating People Fairly

by Lord Justice Brooke

When I was called to the Bar in 1963, female bar students found it difficult to secure places in chambers, and there were still very few women barristers about. When I asked why, I was given a number of different answers. All of them were defensive. It was always someone else's fault. 'Other members of chambers don't want them.' 'The clerks don't want them.' 'Chambers solicitors won't send them work.' 'Clients don't want a woman barrister.' Only very occasionally was the discrimination more blatant. A female pupil told me in the early 1970s that she had been offered a pupillage in another set of chambers, but her prospective pupil master told her that she must not hope for a tenancy there because it was chambers policy not to accept women.

I was invited to chair the Bar's Race Relations Committee soon after I became a judge in 1988, and I heard then more echoes of those distant voices: this time, however, they were directed towards black and Asian bar students and barristers. During the three years I held that post there was no doubt in my mind that able lawyers were being deprived of opportunities which they were well equipped to take because of their unfamiliar cultural origin or the colour of their skin. Sometimes, again, the discrimination was obvious. A barrister's clerk told me he received far more work for a tenant called Smith than for a tenant called Owusu (both names are fictitious: the underlying story is true), although both were black and Owusu was much more able. A head of chambers told me that after a very able second six-months Asian pupil had attended a magistrates' court on a returned brief, the solicitor rang him up and told him that if his chambers ever sent a 'coloured' barrister again, his firm would stop sending chambers any more work. Much more often the discrimination was of a more subtle variety.

In the autumn of 1993 I was asked to speak at a seminar attended by the Lord Chancellor, the Lord Chief Justice and about 40 of our most senior judges. The occasion was being held to launch a series of seminars on ethnic minority issues for the whole of the full-time and part-time judiciary. During the course of my address I told them something of what I had learned about the cruelty of racial discrimination by lawyers, people who pride themselves on being fair. I gave them two examples from the 1970s and then went on like this:

> If we dismiss that as all happening a long time ago, listen to a very able Asian woman barrister, who often appears in front of me now in the Crown Office list, speaking to the Press this year about the way she built up her immigration law practice in the 1980s:

I wouldn't say it was all plain sailing. I wasn't unaware that there were people at the Bar you have to prove yourself to. Clients are the least of your problems. There is more of a problem with solicitors and other barristers. It takes longer to obtain solicitors' trust and confidence. You have to work twice as hard as your white counterparts. Discrimination works at that more subtle level. It's surprising, because you'd think you had the language skills and the cultural experience. Those skills and strengths are now acknowledged by the people I work for, which is an advantage, but it doesn't make up for all the disadvantages. Perhaps another reason why I've been able to break into the immigration field is that a lot of my work comes from law centres, which are much more willing to accept an Asian woman.

I said that I had quoted this because it spoke volumes about what I described as a culture which was still pretty dominant among older members of the legal profession, including judges. And I added that her experience certainly wasn't unique.

I have always regarded it as a paradox that a profession of men and women (mostly men) who have always prided themselves on their fairness and on their ability to recognise unfairness in others, who can quote you cases galore which illustrate the principle of natural justice, or 'fair play in action', as developed by the judges over the years, have not been willing to make more strenuous efforts to understand what they need to do themselves in order to avoid or mitigate the incidence of the unfairnesses that still exist within their own profession.

My own experience, on which I will draw during the course of this essay, has been mainly concerned with issues connected with race relations and with the commonest causes of the misunderstandings and difficulties which crop up between people of different cultures.

Discrimination, however, means unfair or unequal treatment across the board, and in his remarkable 1990 Kapila lecture, *Equal Opportunities – An Idea Whose Time Has Come*, Jerome Mack, the black American who runs the police training courses near Bedford, said this:

And I say, if you are going to be [concerned] about discrimination, then you must say that any discrimination which is arbitrary is bad. Not just discrimination that talks to your issue. I find that a lot of people are advocating their own issues as a way forward, but when they come to other people's issues they have no understanding or clarity about them. I find ethnic minorities who are sexist and cannot begin to understand the ramifications of sexism, but they cry crocodile tears when it comes to racism. I find women who are emotive on the issue of sexism and have no understanding of racism or disability and do not care. I say then that you are talking about self-interest, you are not talking about discrimination. We are all ill at ease on this subject, except our own issue.

For five years between January 1987, when I was asked to chair the Bar's new Professional Standards Committee, and December 1991, when I left the Race Relations Committee, I was at the centre of the Bar Council's battle to persuade the Bar to treat black and Asian barristers and Bar students fairly. Over four years have passed since then, during which I have been addressing these issues on a wider stage, but when I recently read the new Equality Code for the Bar, which the Bar Council adopted in September 1995, I found myself back on very familiar territory.

I remember how we campaigned to ensure that the assessment of applications for pupillages and tenancies should be made against objective and explicit selection criteria (p. 17). I remember the distressing stories we heard about inept questions being put to women and ethnic minority candidates which would never have been put to white male candidates (p. 25). I recollect our concerns about stereotypical assumptions about appropriate areas of work for women and black and Asian tenants (p. 31). I remember how troubled we were that financial support for pupils was unfairly distributed (p. 39). I recall our concern about the powerful effect of networks (p. 51) and the astonishment which greeted our advice that a blanket ban on entrants from what were then polytechnics was unfairly discriminatory (p. 50). And I remember our worries about the absence of effective, confidential complaints procedures that could lead to wrongs being righted without the necessity for embarrassment or confrontation (p. 44).

At the heart of all these worries was the realisation that important decisions were being taken about people on the basis of inadequate information: and where information is not present, people's subconscious prejudices and cultural assumptions tend to take over.

What lies within the Equality Code is a set of rules, principles and guidance which it is very important for every barrister to understand. Peter Goldsmith explains in his Foreword that the Bar Council as a matter of policy has not confined its anti-discrimination measures to the statutory areas of sex, race and, now, disability: it includes discrimination on grounds of religion, politics and sexual orientation, thereby reflecting, he says, the Bar's historic character as a profession where ability and integrity alone matter.

He goes on to add, percipiently, that equality of opportunity is a lot easier to agree about than to deliver: the reason for this, he explains, is that a complex of inherited practices and assumptions repeatedly gets in the way. The Code deals only with the Bar's internal affairs, and in the rest of this essay I have been asked to paint a wider canvas, and show how from his or her very first day in court a barrister must constantly be aware of the dangers of getting things wrong, or treating people hurtfully or unfairly, through ignorance or inherited assumptions that get in the way of clear vision.

I welcome the fact that teaching about equal opportunities principles and practice is now treated as an integral and important part of the Bar Vocational Course. When I chaired EMAC (the Ethnic Minorities Advisory Committee of the Judicial Studies Board) I spoke at more than 50 seminars or conferences attended by judges or magistrates, and I was repeatedly told this:

> It is very valuable that you have told us all this, and we needed to know it if we are to do our jobs properly. But what steps are being taken to teach it to barristers and solicitors? After all, they play a much more prominent part in what is said and done in court than we do.

What did they mean by 'all this'? I need to return to my 1993 talk to the judges for part of the answer:

> I have learned, too, about the offence which is so regularly caused by fair-minded, very well-educated white people, through complete ignorance. Like calling people 'coloured' or 'half-caste' when it is now pretty well known that most young black and Asian people and people of mixed origin dislike these descriptions intensely. Or getting hopelessly mixed up over people's names because we're so used to Judaeo-Christian naming systems. Or not having a clue about the way that the oaths of other religions should be properly administered in court and about the hurt which is regularly caused by avoidable mistakes. Or refusing adjournments and compelling people to attend court on the holiest of their holy days when plenty of notice is given of the difficulty.

When EMAC first met in July 1991, its members, who included black and Asian men and women of great wisdom and experience in matters connected with race relations, all told me that there was no way in which they were going to go upfront straightaway to tell people who were doing a difficult job as judges and magistrates how to do their jobs better. They needed a long time in which to listen and read and understand better the nature of the job being done by those who sit on the bench before they could identify the ways in which they could be most helpful. Teaching about equal opportunities cannot be done effectively by an equal opportunities expert, however gifted, who arrives from nowhere and leaves after a brisk 45-minute talk. Nothing can be achieved, they all told me, except by patient attention to a few essential principles. The teaching must be done by practitioners in the same field as the students (judges learning from judges, barristers learning from barristers, and so on: 'we need to realise', not the didactic, 'you need to realise'). And nothing can be achieved unless the students, whether they are judges or embryo barristers, are aware why equal opportunities issues are relevant to the professional work they do.

And why are these issues relevant to practice at the Bar? Why isn't it sufficient to know all about *Donoghue* v *Stevenson* and *Rylands* v *Fletcher*, about *Ridge* v *Baldwin* and *O'Reilly* v *Mackman*, about the differences between subjective and Caldwellesque objective recklessness or between crimes of basic and specific intent and why these differences matter, or about the latest jurisprudence of the courts at Luxembourg or Strasbourg? The answer is that practice at the Bar is all about justice, and one can't achieve much in the way of justice without taking into consideration the human beings for whom one is trying to achieve justice. This involves a quite different type of learning from the learning most lawyers feel comfortable with.

I remember that when we were planning the seminars for the judiciary the advice came through to me loud and clear from my fellow-members of EMAC:

A single day, between 10 am and 4 pm, will not achieve what you are seeking to achieve. Judges are good at dealing with information and intellectual concepts: this isn't the problem. If time is at a premium, you must at all events let them assemble the night before. This will give us the opportunity of introducing them to people from the local minority communities in which their courts are situated. Then they will have the opportunity to think overnight about what they've been told, and use their knowledge in the discussions next day about the tricky issues they have to handle in court.

Because time was at such a premium we prepared a handbook, for circulation in advance, which contained specialist papers we had prepared for their use. These included advice on family patterns and religions, oaths and names, body language and cross-cultural communication, demographic information and a mixed bag of other bits of information we thought would be helpful. In my view, everyone who holds themselves out as qualified to practise as a barrister in multi-cultural Britain today ought to have access to a similar knowledge base if judges, juries or, indeed, their own clients are always to have proper confidence in their all-round professional competence.

For in my professional lifetime this country has become a multi-cultural society. The statistics I used to quote to judges and magistrates in the early 1990s must be a bit out of date now: 840,000 Indians, half a million Afro-Caribbeans, the same number of Pakistanis, 200,000 black Africans, 200,000 Chinese, 160,000 Bangladeshis, and many thousands more from many different cultures, including people of mixed origin, more than half of whom were born in Britain. According to the 1991 census, 5.3% of the population comes from ethnic minorities, and if present immigration controls are maintained I am told that this figure is likely to move up gradually to about 10% in 2030, when it will level off. And in some of our urban areas, of course, the proportion is much higher.

'Race' used to be the touchstone by which people of different origins were classified. It is now generally recognised that it is much more valuable to look at a person's culture, and of course in some countries, with their boundaries carved out by modern cartographers, people co-exist from many different cultures, as those who had personal experience of countries like Kenya or Nigeria often pointed out at my talks. On the world stage today it is the tensions between people from different cultures within the same country which are most often in the news: in Chechnya, in Bosnia, in Rwanda, in Israel or in Ulster. On our national stage, too, the confluence and congruence of people of different cultures, and, often the tensions between them, are going to play an increasingly prominent part in national and local life as second generation and third generation settlers take the place of the first generation settlers who established their homes here in the 35 years or so that followed the Second World War.

Why does it matter if a lawyer knows little or nothing about the cultural diversity of the people he or she is paid to represent? In my 1993 Kapila Lecture, 'The Administration of Justice in a Multi-Cultural Society', I tried to answer this question by telling a number of real life stories.

I told the story about a dispute over the care of a child. The child's black grand-mother told the court she would willingly come down and live in her daughter's home to look after her granddaughter if the court was worried about her daughter's ability to care for her child herself. To someone of that grandmother's culture it was the most natural thing in the world to treat her child's child as her own child, but she had to endure questioning from a white advocate to the effect that there must be something wrong with her own marriage for her to be willing to leave her husband in order to live with her grandchild for a while. I was told this story by a very experienced black woman barrister who has also told me how often over the years she has encountered complete ignorance from fellow members of the Bar as to what the extended family, so familiar in many cultures, is all about, and how much surprise and offence this often causes to lay people in court.

Religion plays an important part in the culture of many of the South Asian people who have made their homes here, and I also told the story of a Sikh defendant in the Crown Court who had been remanded in custody and was brought from prison to court for his trial. When it was his turn to give evidence, he asked if he might be allowed to wash before taking the oath on the Sikh holy book. His request was refused, and he had to take the oath with the holy book in his unwashed hand. In due course he was acquitted. I was told about him by prosecuting counsel in the case, who came to one of our seminars as a Crown Court recorder. He told me that the case against that defendant was so strong that the only reason he could think of why he was acquitted was that there was a Sikh member of the jury who felt the defendant simply had not had a fair trial after being treated in that way by the judge. When I tell this story to Sikhs, they are horrified that anything like that should have happened in an English court. But what was defence counsel thinking about?

Barristers should not hold themselves out as competent to act for people of different cultures from their own unless they are willing to take elementary steps to teach themselves the things that are important to their clients which may feature in the case. And taking the oath is the very first step of all.

I will stay with religion for a moment because it is so important to a lot of people. I might just as well have told the story of the application for the adjournment of a trial made on behalf of a Hindu defendant whose father had just died. To him, as the oldest son, it was a categorical imperative that he should attend the funeral to light the funeral pyre in order to free his father's soul from his body. It was not going to be much use to him to have a barrister who knew all about the hearsay rules and the Codes of Practice under PACE if he or she could not communicate clearly to the judge why it was so much more important to the defendant to attend that funeral than anything which might happen to him in court. Or I might have told of the worries often evinced to me by Muslims when bail decisions are made on terms that a young Muslim man may not go to the mosque in the evening with his parents to pray, where there is an equally powerful need for an advocate to be able to articulate clearly to the judge why this is so important. Knowledge of the provisions of the Bail Act is only one of the tools of the trade needed for such an application: a clear understanding of the dynamics of Muslim family life is another.

I also told the story of the white youth and the black youth who were in the dock of a magistrates' court together. They had committed the same offence together, and they had identical records, but they received different sentences. The reason for this was that the white youth looked the magistrates in the eye, while the black youth looked all over the court and seemed shifty and evasive and unapologetic for what he had done, and the magistrates believed that he needed to be taught a lesson.

I was told this story by one of the three magistrates when I was out on circuit in the Midlands for the last time before my three-year stint as chairman of the Law Commission. He is a black man who holds a responsible professional job and commands great respect in his local community, but he had found it quite imposs-ible to persuade his two white colleagues that they were condemning the black youth for something that was completely ingrained in his culture. He had been conditioned from birth not to look people in authority in the eye, because this would be seen as insolent, but to keep his eyes averted. But the two white magistrates simply did not believe this, and they overruled him two to one.

This was a story about body language, a very significant method of communication of whose potency we are often completely unaware. Whereas in England it is a sign of respect and integrity for a young person to look a person in authority in the eyes, in Afro-Caribbean culture it is likely to indicate impudence or insult, as that young black man would have known. Among South Asian cultures, too, a subordinate or young person tends to indicate deference and respect by looking away from authority figures rather than directly at them.

In the written advice we have given to judges we have included advice, for example, about the way people position their bodies in relation to others. We have told them that research has shown that there is a lot of variation between people of different cultures as to the degree of closeness and general demeanour that are acceptable. In every culture people wish to maintain a certain amount of space around themselves, and they feel uncomfortable if this space is invaded, so that if such an invasion occurs, or if it is threatened, they take steps to avoid it or to defend themselves against it. Within any given culture, rules of this kind are learned in childhood and people subsequently apply these rules quite unconsciously, but in a multi-cultural situation it is likely that these rules are not held in common. Different people observe different rules, and this can easily lead to conflict. It is now fairly well known in England that because the police have such an important role in dealing with people in tense public settings, they are particularly vulnerable to becoming involved in misunderstandings of this kind. A lot of incidents in which conflict has developed between police officers and members of ethnic minorities in English urban areas have started or been aggravated because of this.

In all the seminars and conferences I addressed there was always a small minority who thought the whole thing was a complete waste of time. One magistrate emerged from a training session recently in that frame of mind, only to be confronted very soon afterwards with a case which illustrated vividly the problems that arise through misunderstandings about body language between the police and a person they had decided to arrest. She was then the first to admit that she would never have spotted the real cause of the trouble in the street if she had not been tipped off to look out for the possibilities of misunderstandings of this type.

Another fertile source of unnecessary difficulty lies in the way we describe people. Most black and Asian people in this country who are under the age of 40 genuinely dislike being described as 'coloured', and the description 'half-caste' is even more violently disliked by nearly everybody of mixed origin. The move to make black people proud of being black was unquestionably political in its origin long ago, but the advice on this topic that I have given to judges and magistrates over and over again has very little to do with political correctness. It is just a question of showing respect to the way in which people like to hear themselves described.

In my Kapila lecture I added this:

> Sometimes this advice is greeted with genuine surprise. Recently a Crown Court recorder, who is a QC, told me that one of the defendants in a high profile trial conducted by a senior judge had been described as 'the halfcaste' throughout. I

asked him if anybody had asked this defendant if he disliked this description. He did not know. If the incredulity is maintained, I quote a recent survey conducted among over 200 black and Asian teenagers at different schools in Kirklees, West Yorkshire. There is not a hint in any of the answers that any of them wished to be described as 'coloured' or 'half-caste'.

When I was on circuit in the East Midlands in 1996 I heard how a Muslim juror had recently passed a message to the judge because she was so exasperated by the barristers in the case describing the witnesses as coloured. Sometimes, too, jurors can be seen laughing at members of the Bar when they are evidently out of touch with modern usage, and I have even heard of a case where a judge in the Crown Court had to engineer an excuse to invite both counsel into his room to explain to one of them that the expressions he was using were being regarded as absurdly out of date by more or less everyone in court, and that this was not helping his client.

Another story I told that evening was of the defendant in a magistrates' court who had all the trappings of a very strict orthodox Jew. When he went into the witness-box he was invited to take the oath and asked, very politely, if he could affirm instead. At the end of his evidence the magistrates did not believe him and they convicted him. A little later one of them told the story at a dinner party in the hearing of a Jewish Crown Court recorder: 'We didn't know whether to believe the police or not, but we looked at the defendant, and he seemed so religious, but when he didn't take the oath he was obviously such a hypocrite that we simply didn't believe him'. There was rather a hush at the dinner table when he was told that some very devout Jews wish not to take the oath for fear that they may say something on oath which is not true although they were not aware that it was untrue when they said it.

This story is getting quite near to the heart of a lot of the difficulties of which any barrister needs to be aware. So was another story I told, about an incident at a magistrates' training event in the late 1980s:

> The magistrates were asked to give their impressions of two people who came into the room and talked to them for a minute or two. The first was a white English undergraduate wearing a collar and tie. They all knew at once the sort of person he was and the social background and education he probably had, even down to the fact, as one headmaster JP put it, 'That young man hasn't looked as tidy as this for years'.

> With the other, they were all over the place. She was a middle-aged Asian woman wearing a baggy top and trousers in a very pretty Liberty cotton in soft colours. They did not know her age, where she came from, what sort of social background she had or what kind of job she might have. She was in fact a college lecturer who also served as a magistrate. Eventually they worked out between them that she must be a person of excellent taste and some wealth. At this description the other Asian woman JP in the room got the giggles and said that only a very eccentric Sikh woman would dress like this.

In the story about the orthodox Jew, the magistrates felt sure they were on safe territory when they formed the judgment they did because they were subconsciously interpreting the witness's conduct in terms of their own cultural framework: in their (necessarily limited) experience, people who are obviously religious don't refuse to take the oath if they intend to tell the truth. In the other story, most of the magistrates felt completely at home with the first person they saw, while with a single exception they were all at sea with the second.

A psychologist has said that when people are unable to perceive clearly, they tend to make inferences from their immediate perceptions by using their reason or their imagination. Inevitably the general cultural background which each of us possesses tends to colour the way in which we reach our conclusions, so that these conclusions, as in the story of the strict Jew declining to take the oath, may be quite disastrously wrong. Turning to another discipline, a behavioural scientist would use the word 'ethnocentrism' to describe the very natural phenomenon by which we all tend to interpret the behaviour of others through our own cultural framework with which, of course, we are very familiar.

For the reasons I gave at the start of this essay, in drawing this wider canvas I have concentrated on matters which are common causes of misunderstandings and difficulties between people of different cultures since this is the area of which I have had most experience. Even in this field one must always be aware that everyone is different and that there is no such person as a typical Hindu or a typical Afro-Caribbean, to take only two examples. But the need for professional lawyers to be alive to the dangers of treating people unfairly or unevenly is certainly not confined to the field of race relations, although the solutions to the difficulties are similar. I remember being a member of a panel which interviewed eight very experienced equal opportunities consultants in 1991 after the Bar Council had agreed to appoint a consultant to help it to draw up a modern guide to good equal opportunities practice, and they all told us that the underlying principles were exactly the same whether the specialist subject matter was race or gender or disability or sexual orientation, or whatever.

As the title of this essay indicates, this subject is all about treating people fairly, whether the people in question are fellow professionals or the clients or others one encounters during the course of a professional life. I have often heard it said: 'Why bother about all this? It's just creating a new self-perpetuating industry. We all know what it means to be fair'. And I have seen plenty of instances where zealotry, usually single-issue zealotry, has overstepped the mark and provoked a quite justified backlash of anger and resentment.

But I know from my own personal experience how essential it is for the relevant principles to be written down and understood; for the necessary advice to be written down and promulgated clearly; and for performance against reasonable targets to be monitored effectively. Every barrister, young or old, needs the assistance these measures provide to help them ensure that their treatment of clients, their professional colleagues and everyone else with whom they have dealings is always fair, and that they can identify and deal effectively with any unfair discrimination should they encounter it in practice.

(Lord Justice Brooke chaired the Professional Standards Committee of the Bar Council, which has overall responsibility for the Bar's race relations policies, between January 1987 and July 1988 (when he became a judge) and then chaired its Race Relations Committee between January 1989 and December 1991. He went on to chair the new Ethnic Minorities Advisory Committee of the Judicial Studies Board between March 1991 and September 1994. In 1993 he delivered the eighth Kapila Fellowship Lecture at the Inns of Court School of Law on *the Administration of Justice in a Multi-Cultural Society*.)

3.4 Guidance from the Judicial Studies Board and How to Use It

The Judicial Studies Board is the body responsible for training all those who sit in a judicial capacity in courts and tribunals. The following papers have been used in training members of the judiciary in ethnic minority issues. Although they are not specifically addressed to barristers, it is submitted that the guidance they contain is equally valuable to barristers and can easily be applied by them. A brief example illustrates the point.

In the paper on 'Body Language and Cross-Cultural Communication' it is pointed out that with regard to times of the day, concepts of afternoon and evening may vary considerably between different cultures. In Britain time is largely measured by the way in which the working day is organized. In other cultures time may be measured more in terms of the length of daylight. The notion of 'afternoon' may continue to be applied much later that its counterpart in Britain. Why is it important for counsel, as opposed to a judge, to be aware of this? The answer is obvious. If timing is a crucial issue in a case and a witness from a different culture is giving, unwittingly, a misleading and thus damaging impression of the time due purely to the way in which his or her culture customarily measures or describes the time, counsel **must** be in a position to put further questions to the witness which enables more accurate evidence of the time to be given. Failure to do this could result in the tribunal making a finding of fact on the issue of time that is incorrect. If you, counsel, are ignorant of the misleading impression your client is giving then you will not be in a position to facilitate a correction of the impression. If you fail in this way you will not have provided proper representation.

The principle to derive from this example is this: ignorance of the differences between the cultures that go to make up Britain's multi-cultural society could result in your client(s) suffering. For this reason it is strongly advised that, in addition to heeding the guidance of Lord Justice Brooke, you read the following papers with care.

Ethnic Minorities: Appropriate Terminology

People coming into contact with the courts may be offended or embarrassed if they are described or referred to in inappropriate ways. The best way to describe members of minority ethnic communities – or indeed any person – is, obviously, the way in which they prefer to be described. Individual preferences may of course vary, but this note aims to give some general guidance on this question of appropriate terminology.

Does terminology matter?
Before proceeding to consider particular terms, it is important to consider why terminology matters.

There are two main reasons. The first is that we all like to be recognised and appreciated for who we are, and we therefore like to be described accurately and to be addressed in a manner which implies respect. If we realise this, it is easier to understand why any failure to treat other people in the same way can give offence. (Etiquette, for example, helps us to ensure that respect is given.) And if we make errors through ignorance, we will wish to be corrected and told the appropriate words to use. When lay people come into contact with the judiciary for instance, they often find themselves going through this process in learning the correct way in which they should address a judge in court.

However, using words appropriately isn't only a matter of technical correctness or accuracy. Words also tend to express how we feel and think. Whether or not this is true in any particular case, those who are listening to us are likely to perceive it this way. Our choice of language therefore may be read by others as an indication of our attitudes, even though we never intended it that way. Hearers may perceive subtle meanings in the use of a word or phrase, of which we as speakers are unaware. In the case of racial and ethnic terminology, it is likely to be members of the minority communities who have the greater level of awareness on this score. Their own history and background have often sensitised them to notice how the use of some terms tends to be exclusionary or demeaning.

There may of course be differences of opinion over some terms, just as there are over many other issues in a complex society. Furthermore, the meanings of words change, and views may vary as between different parts of the country. Appropriate terminology is therefore a subject in which there are not always unambiguous 'right answers'. What follows is a guide to some of the terms most commonly encountered. Beyond this, one can only ask people by what terms they wish to be identified, and seek advice about acceptable usage, generally from members of minority communities in the local area.

Some particular terms

Black
The term 'black', which at one time in Britain was felt to be derogatory, acquired a positive meaning under American influence during the 1960s and 1970s. At first it was used quite widely as a term to bring together all those groups liable to differentiation and discrimination on racial grounds. Today, as in America, it tends to be restricted to those who are directly or indirectly of African origin.

In general, therefore, it is acceptable to describe people of Caribbean or African origin as 'black'. Some people from the Indian subcontinent also accept this designation; others, however, do not – and may, indeed, strongly object to it. It is therefore inadvisable to use the term 'black' to refer collectively to people from Asian as well as Caribbean and African origins. If necessary, it would be preferable to refer to 'black and Asian people'.

Coloured
The once commonly used term 'coloured people' is now generally disliked and felt to be offensive or patronising: it should therefore be avoided.

The expression 'people of colour', which is in currency in the United States, is used on occasion by some members of minority ethnic communities. However, it is not in common parlance, and its use – especially by white people – may be misunderstood or misinterpreted. At least for the present, therefore, it is best avoided.

The expression 'visible minorities' has gained ground in the last few years as an acceptable term whose scope is wider than 'black'.

West Indian/Afro-Caribbean/African
The term 'West Indian', although used in this country as a 'catch-all' phrase to describe the first generation of settlers, was not generally employed in the Caribbean, where island origin was and remains the criterion of identity. Members of the settler generation therefore still think of and often describe themselves (especially among friends) as 'Jamaicans', 'Barbadians', 'Guyanese' and so on. The term 'West Indian' may not necessarily give offence, but in most contexts (apart from cricket!) it is inappropriate. It may also be felt to carry a colonial overtone. For these reasons it is better avoided, unless people actually identify themselves in this way.

The term 'Afro-Caribbean' is much more widely used, especially in official and academic documents, to refer to black people of West Indian origin, although it is not generally used by black people amongst themselves. Where it is desirable to specify geographical origin, use of this term is both appropriate and acceptable. The term does not, however, refer to all people of West Indian origin, some of whom are white or of Asian extraction.

Likewise, the term 'African' is acceptable and may be used in self-identification, although many of those of African origin will refer to themselves in national terms such as 'Nigerian', 'Ghanaian', etc.

Young people born in Britain will probably not use any of these designations, and will simply refer to themselves as 'black'. If racial identity is relevant, it will therefore be appropriate to describe them by this term (rather than to describe them as Afro-Caribbean or West Indian). However, increased interest among young black people in African roots and cultural origins is resulting in greater assertion of the African aspect of their identity, and the term 'African-Caribbean' in now used in some circles.

Asian
People in the Indian subcontinent do not consider themselves to be 'Asians', this being a collective term which has been applied to them in Britain. People identify themselves rather in terms of one or more of the following: their national origin ('Indian', 'Pakistani', 'Bangladeshi'); their region of origin ('Gujerati', 'Punjabi',

'Bengali'); or their religion ('Muslim', 'Hindu', 'Sikh'). Where it is appropriate to the context, designation in these terms will be acceptable.

However, the term 'Asian' is acceptable where the exact ethnic origin of the person is not known, or as a collective reference to people from the Indian subcontinent. Strictly speaking, however, it would be more accurate to refer to such people as being of 'South Asian' origin, so as to distinguish them from those from South Eastern Asia (e.g., Malaysians and Vietnamese) and from the Far East (e.g., Hong Kong Chinese). The term 'Oriental' should be avoided as it is imprecise and may be found racist or offensive.

Young people of South Asian origin born in Britain often accept the same identities, and thus designations, as their parents. However, this is by no means always the case, and some may prefer to describe themselves as 'Black' or as 'British Asian'.

British
Care should be taken always to use the term 'British' in an inclusive sense, i.e., so that it includes all inhabitants or citizens of our multi-racial, multi-cultural society. Exclusionary use of the term as a synonym for 'white', 'English' or 'Christian' will not prove acceptable.

Mixed race/half-caste
The term 'half-caste' is generally found offensive and should be avoided.

The term 'mixed race' is widely used, and is the generally accepted alternative. However, it is not liked all that much and carries negative connotations, and it is preferable wherever possible to refer to a person as being 'of mixed parentage'. The term 'multi-racial' may also be preferable on occasion, e.g., in referring to a 'multi-racial household'.

Ethnic minorities
The term 'ethnic minority' is widely used and generally acceptable as the broadest term to encompass all those groups who see themselves to be distinct from the majority in terms of ethnic or cultural identity. This term is clearly broader than 'black' or 'visible minorities', and brings in such groups as Greek and Turkish Cypriots, and Chinese.

Some prefer to reverse the order of words and speak of 'minority ethnic communities'. This usage makes it clearer that it is not just the minorities, but also the majority that has an 'ethnic' identity. It is important to stress this point, and counter the idea that it is only the minorities who are 'ethnic' (i.e., that 'we' are normal while 'they' are different). This dangerously ethnocentric view is sometimes conveyed by reference to minority communities as 'ethnics', an exclusionary expression which should certainly be avoided.

The description of all people of minority ethnic origin as 'immigrants' is also highly inaccurate, exclusionary and liable to give offence. Except in reference to 'immigrants' in the strict, technical sense (and when referring to persons of any origin), this term too should be avoided.

Body Language and Cross-cultural Communication

1. Introduction
In his 1993 Kapila Lecture, Mr Justice Brooke (as he then was) relates the following story:

> A white youth and a black youth were in the dock of a magistrates' court together. They had committed the same offence together, and they had identical records. Yet they received different sentences. Why? Because the white youth looked the magistrates in the eye, while the black youth looked all over the court and seemed shifty and evasive and unapologetic for what he had done, and the magistrates believed he needed to be taught a lesson.

Mr Justice Brooke goes on to relate that the reason he knew this story was that one of the magistrates was black and shared the story with him. The black magistrate told him that he had tried to persuade his two white colleagues that they were condemning the youth for behaviour which was ingrained in his culture and which they were misinterpreting. He explained to them that he too had been conditioned from birth not to look those in authority in the eye, as this would be perceived as being insolent and disrespectful, and that instead he should keep his eyes averted. But the two white magistrates simply could not accept this, and they overruled him by two to one.

This story is an example of the significance of body language, an important form of communication of which most of the time we are completely unaware. It is also an example of how communication between people from different cultures can easily produce misunderstandings, which if not recognised and remedied may in turn give rise to the possibility of injustice in court.

This background paper deals not only with body language, but also with cross-cultural communication generally. It explains and illustrates why both verbal and non-verbal communication can give rise to difficulty when people of different cultural backgrounds come together, and provides some tips for avoiding the more obvious pitfalls. It also provides some brief advice on the use of interpreters.

2. Why cross-cultural communication can be difficult
Most of the time in our daily lives we experience no difficulty in communicating with others. We speak the same language, and feel we understand one another – at home and at work – pretty well. If something seems unclear or we want more information, all we have to do is ask. If no one does this, we assume we have been understood.

This assumption does not necessarily hold up where the two people communicating with one another come from different cultural backgrounds. It may of course be obvious to one or both parties that they have not understood. Quite often, however, this is not the case: they may **think** they have understood correctly, but in fact they have not done so. The message may have been read quite differently from how it was intended, as was the case in the example quoted above. People are likely to 'read' behaviour from the point of view of their own cultural group, without being aware of the possibly different meaning attributed to it in the culture of the other party. It is where this quite natural tendency towards 'ethnocentrism' creeps in – i.e., where parties interpret the behaviour in terms of their own cultural frameworks, and do so unconsciously – that the greatest danger of cross-cultural misunderstanding arises. In cross-cultural situations, culture – normally the **means** to successful communication – paradoxically can become the **barrier** to such success.

It is important to recognise that the condition for success in overcoming this problem does not consist solely in acquiring knowledge about the culture of the other group. It requires also a degree of knowledge and awareness of one's **own culture**, since whatever others may do or say, it is this which provides the spectacles though which each of us looks out on the world. Not only this, but we also tend to be strongly **attached** to our own culture: we have grown up with it, it has made us what we are, and we have confidence in the perceptions and judgments which it allows us to form. Notice that in Mr Justice Brooke's example the two white magistrates were given information – but despite this they did not feel able to change their view.

We should not, therefore, underestimate the influence of our cultural background on our unconscious perceptions and its potential influence in our working lives. There is nothing reprehensible about this: it is a normal situation in any society, and produces no difficulty to the extent that the society is culturally homogeneous. The challenge arises as most societies come to be increasingly multi-cultural in their make-up. It is a challenge which members of the minority communities, like the black magistrate in the example, have already had to meet simply as a condition for being able to operate successfully in the majority society in the course of their day-to-day lives. It is a skill which may come more slowly to members of the majority culture, who do not face the same challenge routinely. However – especially for those in public service in multi-cultural Britain – it is a skill which it is no less necessary that we possess.

3.   Verbal communication

The culture of the courts attaches exceptional importance to verbal communication. The law is a written body of rules and procedures; evidence is what is stated in court; the verbal skills of the barrister and judge are fundamental for successful perform-ance of their roles. Any failures of verbal communication arising from cross-cultural misunderstanding may therefore strike deeply at the effectiveness of the delivery of justice in the court system.

There are a number of ways in which communication problems may arise in court at the verbal level. The most obvious is the straightforward lack of competency of a witness in the English language. This calls for the use of an interpreter, a situation which is considered in a later section. The more common, and less obvious, problems arise where basic competency is present, but specific problems arise around the use of certain terms or phrases, or around the manner in which a person speaks. A number of examples of such problems are considered below.

Words for time and space

All cultures have words dealing with aspects of time and space. Concepts of time and space may differ, and words in the English language may not always be correctly understood. The meaning attached in different cultures to relative terms such as long, tall and short may obviously vary, but use of such terms should in practice cause no special difficulties since in any context they would need to be rendered more precise. The difficulty arises rather with the apparently more specific catego-ries, whose meaning would be normally assumed to be clear and understood.

For example, with regard to the time of day, concepts of afternoon and evening may vary considerably between different cultures. In England, these are not measured by light and dark, but more by the organisation of the working day. In other societies such as in Southern Europe or the Caribbean, the period of daylight may be longer and more regular, and the working day organised differently or less rigidly. Here the concept nearest to the 'afternoon' may continue to be applied much later through the day than its counterpart in Britain. Witnesses from minority communities originat-ing from these parts of the world may sometimes use the English words for times of the day in a slightly different manner than would be presumed by a native English speaker. Such instances have been noted on occasion in the courts, and judges and magistrates would do well to bear this possibility in mind when time of day may be an issue in a case.

Other examples of time-related words which can give rise to misunderstanding and confusion for members of minority ethnic communities are the English words for mealtimes, 'dinner' and 'tea'. Such confusion is hardly surprising since the words are often found confusing by the English themselves, due to different uses between social classes and between the north and the south of England.

Words for family relationships

Words referring to family relationships may also be a source of misunderstanding when speakers have different cultural backgrounds.

The word 'family' itself may possibly give rise to confusion. In Britain this word normally refers to the immediate or 'nuclear' family group of parents and children, rather than any notion of wider family or ancestry – although both these other meanings are possible. In many of the minority ethnic communities, by contrast, the use of the word 'family' is more likely to involve this broader meaning, due to the greater significance and involvement of wider family members in a person's affairs.

The use of English words for relationships outside the immediate family unit, such as 'uncle', 'aunt', and 'cousin' may also be a potential source of difficulty. In Britain, it is normally understood that the words 'uncle' and 'aunt' refer only to the siblings of one's mother or father. In cultures where wider family ties are of importance, these terms may be used to refer to any relative of the parents' generation, without differentiation as to the closeness of the genealogical connection. If any distinction is employed, then it is likely to identify whether the connection is on the father's or mother's side. This is because across most of the Asian and African continents, kinship is reckoned primarily in terms of the male or (less commonly) female line, rather than (as in Britain) on both sides more or less equally. Care may therefore need to be taken in court when members of South Asian, Chinese or African communities use the terms 'uncle' or 'aunt', to check that the actual relationship has been understood correctly. The possibility should also be borne in mind that the words 'uncle' and 'aunt' may on occasion be used metaphorically as respectful terms of address for unrelated adults of the parents' generation, in the same way as this may be done in white British culture. All of the same considerations arise, for the same reasons, with regard to the word 'cousin'.

Racial and ethnic terminology

Racial and ethnic terminology may on occasion be a further source of difficulty; inappropriate use of such terminology may also give rise to offence. Confusion, for example, may arise unless the meaning of racial and ethnic terms (e.g., 'Asian', 'black') is made clear, and their relevance specified. It should also be borne in mind that use of certain racial or ethnic terms (e.g., 'coloured', 'oriental', 'half-caste') in court is likely to give offence to those to whom they are applied. Fuller consideration of appropriate racial and ethnic terminology is given in the separate guidance note on this subject.

Inappropriate words and expressions

There is little need to rehearse the fact that in all cultures offensive terms exist to refer to members of other racial, ethnic or national groups. Were such terms to be used in court, other than in the reporting of evidence, their offensiveness would be clear and they would not of course be tolerated.

There are, however, words and expressions which may be used by some members of the majority society without their being aware of the negative impact these may have on members of minority ethnic communities. The word 'coloured', cited above, is an obvious example.

Often, however, it may be a case of how the word is being used, rather than the word itself. Still staying with racial and ethnic terminology, the use of the word 'ethnic' can illustrate the point. When reference is made to 'ethnic minorities' implying a contrast with an 'ethnic majority', the term 'ethnic' is being used in a purely descriptive sense. If the words 'ethnic minorities' are used implying that only the minorities are 'ethnic', a rather different message is conveyed. This is likely to be read by a person of ethnic minority origin as 'you are different, and we are normal'. This message is conveyed – even, it must be stressed, if not intended – rather more strongly when members of ethnic minorities are referred to as 'ethnics'. In both these instances, the message, as it is likely to be read, is at the least one which conveys the idea of exclusion; it may also be read as implying superiority and inferiority as well. Members of the majority group should not therefore be surprised if those from the minority communities express a preference for the word 'ethnic' not to be used in this way.

Turning to inappropriate expressions, here too there should be little need to draw attention to phrases or metaphors that are quite clearly offensive or even racist. (Though it is perhaps surprising how one may still hear from time to time the unwitting use of phrases such as 'working like a black' or 'the nigger in the woodpile'.) Once again, though, it is primarily the more subtle ways in which a message may be phrased which need to be focused on as unintended causes of offence. Over-generalisation e.g., by speaking of all Nigerians or Chinese as if they are the same, is one example. Another is conveying a patronising attitude, by using a phrase such as 'you people must realise', or referring to 'the way we do things in this country'. A third is by seeming to imply that certain ethnic groups have particular criminal characteristics, as through use of popular stereotypical phraseology such as 'black muggers' and 'black crime'.

Jargon, slang, metaphor

Those responsible for the conduct of court business should also bear in mind that jargon, slang and metaphorical expressions are usages which may give rise to difficulty for members of ethnic minorities in court. Technical and legal jargon may cause difficulty for many members of the public, but may do so particularly for members of ethnic minorities who may have even less familiarity with the courts and their work. Use of slang expressions which are familiar to those who have grown up in Britain with full exposure to the mass media may also exclude minority group members from following the meaning of what is said. Use of metaphors too may be especially confusing for members of ethnic minorities, not merely because of the likely difficulty of comprehending the meaning of the metaphor, but because in an unfamiliar linguistic context, it is direct meaning that one looks for and expects. Jokes, implicit assumptions and the typically British art of understatement might also be mentioned as being capable of giving rise to similar confusion and misunderstanding in the minds of members of minority communities. Judges, magistrates and court staff should therefore take care to express themselves in as direct and explicit a manner as possible when communicating with people from different cultural backgrounds.

Accent/mispronunciation

Non-native speakers of English may often have strong accents based on the speech patterns of their own languages, and they may also have difficulties with pronunciation as well. This is a situation which may arise in any multi-lingual or multi-cultural society, and calls for patience and tolerance on the part of all. If a speaker who has difficulty in being understood feels under pressure on this account, he or she may speed up rather than slow down, and the accent may become stronger. It is therefore extremely important that those responsible for the management of the court should do all they can to relax the situation, and provide the speaker with reassurance and support. When evidence is being given, it is also important to bear in mind the possibility that key words may be mispronounced and consequently misunderstood. Judges and magistrates should not avoid confronting possible problems of these kinds out of fear of embarrassment or of giving offence. Courteous checking that a common understanding has been reached, and that all are confident that this is so, may be essential in such situations. Members of minority communities are likely to appreciate, rather than be discomfited by, judges and magistrates taking the time and the care to check that they have understood what has been said, provided that this is done in a sensitive manner.

It is not only as speakers that difficulties may arise for members of minority ethnic communities. English is spoken with a wide range of regional accents on the part of native speakers, among whom for the most part these variants are normally easily understood. Members of minority ethnic communities often have much less experience of regional English accents, and when broad variants of these happen to be in use in court, the possibility of difficulty for members of ethnic minorities should not be overlooked.

Speech delivery

Although true for the wider public as well, many members of minority ethnic communities may feel extremely nervous and lacking in confidence when appearing in court. Particular difficulties faced by members of minority communities tend to be greater lack of familiarity with the court system, and lack of confidence in speaking English – especially in a formal, public domain. In addition, especially among communities of Asian origin, some women (especially among the older generation) may find speaking in court difficult or embarrassing as a result of cultural conditioning, and of persisting conventions about the need for modesty in demeanour and about women's role. This may be particularly the case when subjects of an intimate or personal nature are under discussion or the matter is felt to belong to the world not of women but of men.

All of these difficulties may be manifested by persons speaking very softly or having difficulty in projecting the voice; or by their not being very forthcoming generally. On the other hand, some young black people in particular may arrive in court feeling suspicious or angry on account of prior experiences or expectations of racism, and may sometimes express this in a forthright and apparently aggressive manner – occasionally even in an outburst of some kind. Once again, judges and magistrates need to be aware of the factors which may possibly affect the performance of members of ethnic minorities in court, and in case of difficulty provide reassurance personally and ensure that the environment is as supportive and free from pressure as possible. Reducing pressure by allowing extra time for witnesses to give evidence is often sufficient to overcome the kinds of difficulties that have been mentioned.

4. Body language

Body language, as has already been explained, demands our attention for two reasons. The first is that it is a powerful form of non-verbal communication, the use and effects of which we are normally unaware. The second is that forms of body language, like verbal languages, differ between cultures, and thus – especially on account of their unconscious operation – have considerable potential for causing misunderstanding in cross-cultural communication. At first sight, therefore, the solution would simply appear to be to develop a bank of knowledge about the typical body language of members of different cultures.

Two health warnings

Knowledge about body language can indeed be formulated, but it is important to issue two major 'health warnings' about such knowledge and how it should be used.

The first warning is to be careful about how a 'culture' is to be identified or constituted as a discrete entity. For example, although there may be much in common within such broad cultural groupings as 'Asians', 'Caribbeans' or Chinese', there may also be internal differences. This would be particularly true of 'Muslims' in so far as they share a religious culture based on the Koran. This religious culture, however, has been grafted onto many other regional or local cultures, and as with verbal language it would therefore be most inaccurate to assume that Muslim groups will necessarily have any body language in common.

The second warning is that it is dangerous to assume that all those who identify (or are identified) with a particular ethnic group will necessarily display the same body language. Not only may there be differences **within** the group such as by gender or social class, but there are likely to be differences simply **between individuals** also. (This is obvious when one considers the differences in style and temperament among one's friends within one's own cultural group.) There is therefore great danger in moving towards over-generalisation about body language – and of thus creating stereotypes about behaviour or members of particular cultural groups which could be as damaging as ignorance itself.

Knowledge about body language of different cultural groups should therefore take the form of **guidelines** as to what might possibly be expected by way of behaviour, but what should certainly not be presumed. This is especially the case in a country such as Britain, where most of the main minority communities have arrived recently as a result of migration. In this situation, there tends to be a process of cultural change occurring within the minority ethnic communities, especially among the young, and much diversity also between individuals. Provided that knowledge about body language of different groups includes a recognition that such diversity exists, and that there is a need for its validity or application to be checked in each case, then such knowledge will be useful knowledge. If it is not used in this cautious and conditional way, then such knowledge will be in danger of becoming another form of stereotyping.

Scope of body language

It is only when we reflect on the subject that we normally become aware of the large number of ways in which we may use the body as a means of non-verbal communication. Gestures involving the hands are those which we most often think of, and these are the more likely ones to be conscious and intended. In terms of their importance in the non-verbal part of the communication process, however, they undoubtedly fall into second place behind the face. Here a wide variety of uses of the eyes and mouth tend to be of fundamental expressive significance, providing a context for – as well as supplementing – the use of spoken language itself. The manner of delivery of the spoken work should also be included at this point. Then in addition to the uses of the face and arms there are a large number of aspects of the movement and positioning of other parts of the body and the demeanour of the body itself.

Eyes

In many cultures, the eyes are an extremely important means of communication. In modern European culture, the eyes speak above all about feelings and about sincerity. Eyes of course cry, they have character, they express many different looks – not the least of which (as is endlessly celebrated in poetry and song) is love. Closely linked to the ability to express such feelings is the perceived ability of the eyes to convey whether a person is (or is not) respectful and sincere.

The assumption that one can tell whether or not a person is being honest and sincere through sustaining a direct gaze into the other's eyes is an assumption that pervades the practical as well as the romantic sides of life. In relation to criminal justice, it may be widely used by detectives engaged in criminal investigation, as well as in assessing the veracity of witnesses in court.

Mr Justice Brooke's example, however, cited at the beginning of this paper, shows how misleading and dangerous such assumptions about body language can sometimes be, especially if they are drawn from one cultural context and uncritically applied in another. Whereas in English culture the maintenance of direct gaze gives the recipient confidence that a subordinate or equal is being sincere, in many other cultures this may be untrue or even the reverse. Whereas in England for a young person to look a person in authority in the eyes is to signal respect and integrity, in Afro-Caribbean culture it is likely to indicate impudence or insult. Among South Asian cultures, looking away from authority figures, rather than directly at them, tends to be how a subordinate or young person indicate deference and respect.

For these reasons the greatest care should be taken before allowing eye behaviour to be interpreted in any particular way when there is a cross-cultural context involved. In particular, care should be taken to avoid generalising about the eye behaviour of any ethnic group in Britain due to the element of cultural diversity and change commented upon earlier. Most important of all, perhaps, is not the need to have specific knowledge of what eye behaviour means in any other particular culture, but simply to be aware how easily one may unconsciously interpret such behaviour falsely in terms of one's own.

Tone of voice

Tone of voice is another aspect of body language which is frequently in danger of being misunderstood in cross-cultural contexts.

In English culture, raising the voice is associated with becoming angry and losing control, or with trying to impose oneself aggressively upon a conversation or other situation. Value tends to be placed upon keeping 'cool' and behaving 'rationally'.

In other cultures, volume, pitch and manner of delivery do not necessarily convey the same meaning, nor are they necessarily judged in the same way. Using a loud voice does not necessarily indicate loss of control, nor does it necessarily indicate hostility or an aggressive disposition. Treating people as if this is the case may often be experienced as patronising, with the result that they may then indeed become angry at the very least. In the same way, if police officers immediately interpret the loud talk and animation of black youngsters on the street as aggressive behaviour, they may through their own response induce the very behaviour their role is to prevent.

The manner of delivery may also give rise to cross-cultural misunderstanding. Many people who grew up in South Asia before migrating to Britain will have an accent when speaking English which can appear to English ears to be rather tense and staccato, and may be interpreted as aggressive in tone. At the least this is likely to be an exaggerated perception, and often it may be simply incorrect as it will be the person's normal mode of English speech. A similar misunderstanding can arise when native Chinese or Japanese speakers converse in English.

The body
Posture, positioning of the body, and body movement generally are further important ways in which non-verbal communication is carried out. Here too care must be taken before interpreting the behaviour of those of minority ethnic origin in terms of English cultural assumptions and standards.

Positioning of the body in relation to others, for example, has been shown by cross-national research to be very variable between cultures as to the degree of closeness and general demeanour that are acceptable. Once again, the relevance of this to the courts lies primarily in its implications for policing. In all cultures people desire to maintain a certain amount of space around themselves, and feel uncomfortable if this is invaded. When such invasion occurs or is threatened, avoidance or defensive action is initiated. Within any particular culture, rules of this kind are learned in childhood and subsequently applied unconsciously. In a multi-cultural situation, there may no longer be rules held in common, and misunderstandings and thus conflict can easily arise. Police officers, due to the nature of their role in dealing with people in tense and public settings, are particularly vulnerable to becoming involved in misunderstandings of this kind. Many incidents in which there has developed conflict between police officers and members of ethnic minorities have originated or been exacerbated in this way.

Body movement is also capable of creating considerable misunderstanding in cross-cultural contexts, not only where relations between the police and public are involved, but also in court situations as well. Particular care should be taken as to how activities such as animation or fidgeting should be interpreted – as well as apparent disinterest or repeated looking away. Generally speaking it should be presumed that to make any inferences from such behaviour about honesty or integrity when different cultures are involved would be dangerous and unreliable.

Judges and magistrates should themselves be aware of possible ways in which their own body language might possibly be misunderstood by ethnic minority witnesses or defendants. In particular they should take care to ensure that their body language does not unwittingly imply ridicule or contempt when ethnic minority perceptions or customs are being referred to in court, for example through raised eyebrows, exchanged glances, or signs of exasperation, impatience or incredulity. Such subtle or impromptu forms of bodily expression may be barely noticed by the person who gives such signals, but members of minority communities may over time have become much more alert to them.

5. *Using interpreters*
The points raised in section 3 of this paper deal with the circumstances in which basic competence in the English language is assumed, but where specific problems of verbal or non-verbal communication arise due to the fact that the parties to the communication derive from different cultural backgrounds. A more fundamental difficulty arises when a person of minority ethnic background does not possess adequate linguistic competence for participation in court, and an interpreter needs to be involved in the communication process.

When is an interpreter needed?
An interpreter is needed when effective communication through the medium of the English language, at a level adequate for the purposes of the court, cannot be achieved. In most cases, the need will be apparent to all concerned, and will have been identified in advance of the hearing. In some cases, however, the need may be

more difficult to determine, and may only become apparent in court. It may become clear that a witness's understanding has been much less than has been apparent from formal replies, such as a series of 'Yes' or 'No' answers. It may also become clear that what is said by the witness is sometimes not quite what is meant. It is of importance that those responsible for the business of the courts bear in mind that such situations can arise where witnesses are from minority ethnic communities, and are ready to take action to involve an interpreter if required.

The role of interpreter
The role of interpreter is primarily to provide a technically efficient and accurate translation of what has been said, and the first qualification required of an interpreter is that the person has the necessary skill and integrity for undertaking this task.

Effective performance of this role in court, however, places a wider range of demands on the interpreter. First, although the interpreter is a servant of the court, he or she will need to be able to establish a sympathetic and supportive relationship with the person concerned, who may well feel disadvantaged and embarrassed by the situation, and will need to develop confidence and trust. Secondly, the interpreter will need to understand the cultural context for the linguistic interpretation and will therefore need to be a member of, or fully familiar with, the minority person's cultural group. Thirdly, it is important that there are no differences of dialect (or any other sources of difficulty in communication) between the person and the interpreter, since these if present could compound the problem the interpretation is intended to overcome.

In general it is important that an interpreter has a good understanding about the workings of the court, and is fully clear about the role he or she is expected to play. The judge or magistrate should ensure that the interpreter feels at ease in the role and in the court, and feels able to bring forward any difficulties or problems should these arise.

All of this points to one important implication of the use of interpreters in court which is the need to allocate extra time. In order to check that a translation has been achieved clearly and accurately to everyone's satisfaction, it may be necessary to repeat or review questions several times, ensuring that all possible nuances have been covered. This may require a special effort of patience and empathy from the judge or magistrates, but it is essential in order to create confidence throughout the court and to avoid the risk of confusion and disruption later.

How to obtain interpreters
A number of professional interpreting agencies now exist, which can be relied upon to provide a generally competent service. It should be borne in mind, however, that these agencies may not be able to deal with particular languages or dialects, and their interpreters may have little knowledge about or experience of working in the courts.

Using non-professional interpreters, on the other hand, may give rise to considerable problems and involve considerable risk. The incompetence or bias of an interpreter may sometimes be obvious. Often, however, these tendencies are difficult to detect. They may involve what, by the interpreter's standards, are only minor shortcomings, but these could be of great significance in court. Whenever there are reasons to suspect there may be shortcomings in the interpretation that has been given, this should be rehearsed and checked until all parties feel satisfied with the result.

Postscript
The following information about the provision of interpreters in courts has kindly been provided by the Court Service Headquarters of the Lord Chancellor's Department.

Some magistrates' courts have organised training days on court procedure for interpreters. This helps not only to increase the knowledge of the interpreters but also increases staff awareness of the need for interpreters. The provision of interpreters at court in criminal proceedings is, at present, a matter for the parties and their legal advisers, although the courts can assist by providing the names of interpreters if they maintain a list.

The position with arranging interpreters in civil proceedings is largely the same as in criminal cases in that it is solely the responsibility of the parties and their legal advisers as to whether an interpreter is appointed and, if so, who they appoint. There is no involvement on the part of the court other than to provide details of suitable local interpreters if such are held. In practice this would be unlikely unless it were a combined court centre where a list may well be kept for use in criminal cases.

A national register of interpreters is already under consideration by the Nuffield Foundation. The Lord Chancellor's Department, the Home Office and the Crown Prosecution Service are all represented on the project's working party and support the project with funding. The register would provide a list of qualified interpreters and their geographical locations. It would be widely available and would be updated on a regular basis.

Cross-cultural Communication in Court: Some Do's and Don'ts

Don't assume that just because someone responds to questions in English in court that person necessarily understands fully what has been said.

Do be prepared to check out the precise meaning of words for family relationships (such as 'uncle', 'cousin' and 'aunt') when used by members of ethnic minorities in court.

Don't assume that words for the time of day (such as 'afternoon' and 'evening') necessarily have precisely the same meaning when used by members of minority ethnic communities.

Do avoid use of racial and ethnic terms (such as 'coloured', 'oriental' or 'half-caste') that are liable to give offence.

Don't make generalisations about the characteristics of particular groups, unless these are clearly qualified or based on evidence.

Don't use phrases such as 'black crime' and 'black muggers' that may be perceived to express a criminal stereotype of an ethnic or racial group.

Do be sensitive to the difficulties that may be caused for ethnic minorities by such usages as jargon, slang and metaphor in court.

Do take care to provide reassurance and support where difficulties may arise over ethnic minority accents and pronunciation in court.

Do be sensitive to the lack of confidence and sense of embarrassment that may affect the performance of some members of ethnic minorities in court.

Don't assume that looking away rather than maintaining eye contact is necessarily a sign of dishonesty or disrespect in members of ethnic minorities (it may be the opposite!)

Don't assume that when members of ethnic minorities raise their voice they are necessarily losing control or becoming aggressive.

Do appreciate how cultural differences in body language can contribute to misunderstandings and conflicts between members of ethnic minorities and police officers.

Do be careful not to develop stereotyped notions about the body language of particular cultures.

Don't underestimate the influence of your own cultural background on your unconscious perceptions and behaviours.

Do listen to the advice of ethnic minority colleagues as to how to deal with cross-cultural misunderstandings and communication.

FOUR

THE ETHICAL CHALLENGE: LEGAL ETHICS AND PROFESSIONAL RESPONSIBILITY

4.1 Introduction

This chapter, by Professor Ross Cranston, is drawn from the author's contribution to R. Cranston (ed.), *Legal Ethics and Professional Responsibility*, Oxford, Clarendon, 1996, to which further reference should be made.

4.2 The Bar Code of Conduct and Ethics

The Bar Code of Conduct is not like some ethical codes, which are purely exhortatory in character. It can lead to legally enforceable consequences, and ultimately disbarment of a barrister from practice. In some respects the Code of Conduct is simply restating and expanding the general law. It is not exhaustive of all the ethical problems which lawyers face. While the Code of Conduct surfaces in judicial decisions, it has a far more important, daily application in rulings by the profession's disciplinary bodies.

An important policy issue is the extent to which the Code of Conduct ought to be infused by wider ethical notions. There are two aspects to this. One is encapsulated in the question: 'Can a good lawyer be a bad person?'. In other words, are the standards in the Code of Conduct untenable when laid alongside ethical thought or common morality? The second aspect is that if there is a discrepancy between the Code of Conduct and secular ethical thought, what is special about barristers that exempts them from the precepts of the latter? To put it another way, how is it that barristers can decide ethically on a course of action for a client which is different from that which they would adopt for themselves?

While there is a certain force in these questions, it seems to me that those who might argue for the primacy of ethical considerations do not give enough attention to their contingency in real life. One person's immorality is another's standard practice. One response to this might be to try to give ethical values a greater objectivity in the legal context. For example, it might be said that in litigation the prime goal is seeking truth and that this is therefore the lodestar for lawyers engaged in it. Even if this were the case – which is doubtful – that still does not give sufficient guidance to the barrister wanting to know how to act ethically in particular situations. Ethical issues arise in specific contexts and we need detailed guidelines for resolving the practical problems which arise.

None of this is to advocate moral relativism. In many cases the rightness or wrongness of conduct can be identified and reflection on what ethical thought might demand should inform any discussion of professional responsibility. Barristers cannot remain free from moral responsibility simply by pointing to a provision in the Code of Conduct. Barristers are not simply technicians; they must not submerge their own moral standards to the pursuit of a client's interest irrespective of what that might be. In any event, there is high authority that they must also serve other interests such as those of third parties and, more generally, justice.

There are grave problems, then, in putting ethical thought to the fore, not least lawyers' own unfamiliarity with this field. That does not mean that it has no role to play, just that it cannot be determining. There is also another possibility. In important respects the present Code of Conduct is too vague. In some especially difficult areas barristers are given no guidance as to how they should act, although in a few they are told that they have a discretion to withdraw from providing further services to a particular client. While it is impossible for the Code of Conduct to be more specific in many areas, there seems to be more scope for standards such as reasonableness – familiar to barristers in other contexts – which would force barristers to confront more directly the creative aspect of professional judgment and require them to justify a particular course of action.

The further point to make is that many of the issues are as much political as ethical. This is apparent in matters such as *pro bono* work and the unmet need for legal services. But even with the Code of Conduct there is the obvious point that control over its content rests largely in the profession itself, the very group whose ethical behaviour is in issue. In this area self-regulation has many advantages, not least in identifying wrongdoing and fissures in the Code of Conduct. It is just plain wrong to characterise the Code of Conduct as wholly, or mainly, self-serving. Yet there are dangers in self-regulation here as elsewhere. One is cartelisation and another is that the Code of Conduct might not adopt a strict line if economic pressures push in the opposite direction. The obvious conclusion is that barristers should not have a completely free hand in writing the Code of Conduct: there must be some mechanism additional to the Lord Chancellor's Advisory Committee on Legal Education and Conduct for ensuring that what is contained is subject to public scrutiny and really is best for society as a whole.

4.3   Confidentiality

There is a general rule about preserving the confidentiality of a client's affairs in the Bar Code of Conduct. In accordance with the general law, the duty of confidentiality stated in the Code of Conduct continues after the lawyer/client relationship has ended. Apart from the general provision there are a limited number of specific rules in the Code of Conduct relating to confidentiality. For example, barristers must cease to act if having accepted a brief or instructions on behalf of more than one client there is or appears to be a risk of a breach of confidence, and the clients do not consent to the barrister continuing to act.

Under the general law *disclosure* in breach of confidence is permissible in some cases on grounds of public interest (*Attorney-General* v *Guardian Newspapers (No. 2)* [1990] 1 AC 109). The Bar Code of Conduct does not seem to acknowledge this public interest exception. It posits withdrawal from a case where, for example, the barrister has a duty of disclosure to the court and the client refuses to sanction it. The Law Society code is more in line with the general law. It says that a duty to keep a client's confidences can be overridden 'in certain exceptional circumstances'.

4.4   Devotion to the Client's Interests

The Bar has always put its claim to loyalty boldly in espousing the fearless promotion and protection of a lay client's best interests, without regard to the barrister's own interest or to any consequences which might befall. Lord Brougham's defence of Queen Caroline is portrayed as an exemplary example of barrister zeal. Brougham alluded in his defence of the Queen to evidence which might harm the King, but argued that no matter what the consequences, his duty as an advocate demanded that he take every step necessary to defend his client (Hansard, new ser, iii, 3 October 1820, 114):

> [A]n advocate, by the sacred duty of his connection with his client, knows, in the discharge of that office, but one person in the world, that client and none other. To save that client by all expedient means – to protect that client at all hazards and costs to all others, and among others to himself – is the highest and most unquestioned of his duties; and he must not regard the alarm, the suffering, the torment, the destruction, which he may bring upon any other; nay, separating, even the duties of a patriot from those of an advocate, he must go on reckless of the consequences, if his fate it should unhappily be, to involve his country in confusion for his client.

Advocates are constantly reminded that they must not act as judges. Rights, it is said, are determined by the courts and not by advocates. 'It is for want of remembering this that foolish people object to lawyers that they would advocate a case against their own opinions' (*Johnson* v *Emerson* (1871) LR 6 Ex 329, 367). It is also said that advocates often find that arguments which they do not think to be valid are accepted by the courts. Notwithstanding this lay people, perhaps foolishly, do not share the same confidence as advocates that the adversarial system always works.

What are the public interest limits on loyalty? There are few common law boundaries to advocate zeal. One is honesty; advocates must present their client's case to the best of their ability, without making themselves a judge of its correctness, but they must not be dishonest. Lord Denning MR, in his own inimitable way, summed up the boundaries for advocates as follows (*Rondel* v *Worsley* [1966] 3 WLR 950, 962):

> [An advocate] must accept the brief and do all he honourably can on behalf of his client. I say 'all he **honourably** can' because his duty is not only to his client. He has a duty to the court which is paramount. It is a mistake to suppose that he is the mouthpiece of his client to say what he wants: or his tool to do what he directs. He is none of these things. He owes allegiance to a higher cause. It is the cause of truth and justice. He must not consciously misstate the facts. He must not knowingly conceal the truth. He must not unjustly make a charge of fraud, that is, without evidence to support it. He must produce all the relevant authorities, even those that are against him. He must see that his client discloses, if ordered, the relevant documents, even those that are fatal to his case. He must disregard the most specific instructions of his client, if they conflict with his duty to the court.

In other words, advocates must not assert what they know to be a lie, nor must they connive at, much less attempt to substantiate, a fraud, but they are entitled to require the other side to prove its case. The adversary system is supposed to produce a just result based on laws fairly applied to accurate facts.

The Bar Code of Conduct contains injunctions similar to the common law against acting dishonestly, unlawfully, or in any way likely to diminish public confidence in the profession. The Code of Conduct also says that although there is a duty to advance a client's interests, this must not be so as to compromise professional standards.

Specific guidance on these limits is harder to come by. There is a well known limit, restated in the Code of Conduct that barristers must not deceive or mislead a court (See *R* v *Visitors to the Inns of Court, ex parte Calder* [1994] QB 1). Derived from the obligation not to deceive or mislead the court are the more specific duties not to coach witnesses, not to devise facts to assist a client, and to ensure that the court is informed of all relevant decisions and legislation, however unfavourable. A client's admission of perjury or of misleading a court, prior to or in the course of proceedings, obliges a barrister to decline to act further, unless the client agrees fully to disclose the matter. Presenting perjured evidence would, of course, constitute misleading the court.

These various aspects of the duty of honesty derive from the adversary system: courts must be able to rely on the honesty of opposing parties since there is no inquisitorial system whereby they can investigate facts, and the pressure of business and absence of law clerks mean that judges are reliant on the advocates to research the law fully. While placing obligations on advocates in this way compensates for certain features of the adversary system, it does not address other matters such as any inequality of legal representation.

4.5 Conflicts of Interest

Conflicts of interest are pervasive in legal practice; the problem is that they may be so common that lawyers do not recognise them as such. For this reason it is better to attack an undesirable practice directly instead of imposing on the barrister the obligation to take action if that practice gives rise to a 'conflict'. Take the basic potential conflict between a client and a lawyer – the lawyer is being paid, which, especially if at an hourly rate, creates a potential incentive to contrive to create work. For example, litigation which is better settled might be unnecessarily prolonged. (It is fair to add that with a test case a disincentive to settle might occur for non-economic reasons.) This basic conflict is dealt with in the Code of Conduct by general rules such as those relating to lawyers acting with reasonable skill, care and diligence. Would it not be better to tackle the problem with specific code provisions, say, against undertaking unnecessary work? Such a rule might also mitigate the tendency for 'legal advisers, pressed by their clients, to take every point conceivable and inconceivable without judgment or discrimination' (*Ashmore* v *Corporation of Lloyd's* [1992] 1 WLR 446, 453, *per* Lord Templeman).

4.6 Lawyer Control

Another aspect of the barrister's relationship with a client is the latter's vulnerability. The ordinary person might be relatively ignorant of and mystified by the law. However unconsciously, a barrister might impose his or her agenda on the relationship. In one sense barrister control is a corollary of the law's mystery: the barrister has a superior learning and knowledge of legal processes which clients cannot hope to acquire (without a substantial investment), even if they had the inclination. Barrister control has an additional, functional justification, in suppressing anti-social behaviour. To use a sociological term, lawyers are gatekeepers. They advise clients about how to behave lawfully, they screen out unjustified claims, they encourage the settlement of disputes and they damp down abuses of the legal process. Arguably the lawyer's role as gatekeeper should be enhanced.

Concern that the lawyer might take advantage of the client is evident in the Bar's standards applicable to criminal cases. Barristers should advise defendants about their plea ('he may, if necessary, express his advice in strong terms') but must make clear that the client has complete freedom of choice. They should advise clients about whether or not to give evidence in their own defence, but the decision should be taken by clients themselves. One of the criticisms of plea bargaining is that it can lead defence lawyers to substitute good relations with the prosecution authorities, and other interests, for a zealous defence.

4.7 Lawyer Zeal and Client Wrongdoing

It is as well to recall the origins of lawyer zeal. They lie in criminal defence, and there the justification is obvious. Zealousness guarantees a thorough preparation of the case, not simply by the defence lawyers. Without it, the police and prosecution authorities would not have the same incentive thoroughly to investigate a matter, for example by investigating any corroboration for the defendant's account. Recent miscarriages of justice underlie how much worse the situation would be in the absence of a zealous defence.

Putting that to one side, however, the crucial issue is that the approach with criminal defence work cannot automatically be extended to other cases, in particular the barrister giving advice to, or representing a client where no litigation is in contemplation. Here we are not concerned with the state operating against the individual or with the possibility that the client might be deprived of his or her liberty. For good reasons the zeal which we expect of a barrister in criminal defence is not necessarily appropriate in these other, more common, situations. Generally speaking, of course, the client will have no truck with illegality and will want to stay well within the four corners of the law. But sometimes clients will want to push the law to its limit and will expect their barrister to facilitate this.

Over the years the Bar has been able to refine its approach to a client's confession of wrongdoing. In 1915 the English Bar Council drew a sharp distinction between confessions which were made to counsel before the proceedings commenced and those which were made subsequently. If the former it was said to be most undesirable for an advocate to whom the confession had been made to undertake the defence, since he or she would most certainly be seriously embarrassed in the conduct of the case. In any event no harm could be done by requesting the accused to retain another advocate. Other considerations applied in cases in which the confession was made during the proceedings, or in circumstances where the advocate could not withdraw without seriously compromising the position of the accused. In addressing this the Bar Council said that it was essential to bear in mind that the issue in a criminal trial was always whether the accused was guilty of the offence charged, not whether the accused was innocent, and secondly that the burden rested on the prosecution to prove the case. Thus the advocate's duty was to protect a client as far as possible from being convicted, except by a competent tribunal and upon legal evidence sufficient to support a conviction, although in the event of a confession there were very strict limitations on how the defence was to be conducted since no advocate should assert what he or she knew to be a lie, nor connive at, much less attempt to substantiate a fraud. This approach is, in substance, contained in the current code.

Illustrative of the principle is the Australian decision, *Tuckiar* v *R* (1934) 52 CLR 335. The accused, a nomadic aboriginal, was charged with the murder of a police constable in the Northern Territory. During the trial counsel for the accused interviewed his client at the suggestion of the trial judge to ascertain whether he agreed with evidence given by a witness for the Crown of a confession alleged to have been made by the accused to the witness. After interviewing the accused his counsel said in open court that he was in a worse predicament than he had encountered in all his career. The implication was obvious, and the accused was found guilty of murder. In a joint judgment the High Court of Australia (Gavan Duffy CJ, (at p.346) Dixon J, Evatt J, McTiernan J) said of counsel (at p. 34):

> Why he should have conceived himself to have been in so great a predicament, it is not easy for those experienced in advocacy to understand. He had a plain duty, both to his client and to the Court, to press such rational considerations as the evidence fairly gave rise to in favour of complete acquittal or conviction of manslaughter only.

After the defendant was convicted his counsel made a public statement in court to the effect that the accused admitted that the evidence called by the Crown of a confession was correct. The High Court said that this was wholly indefensible; in the event it rendered a retrial impossible because that would have been known through the Territory.

Outside the law this approach has never been universally accepted. Jeremy Bentham regarded the lawyer assisting a guilty client to an acquittal to be an accessory after the fact of the offence. In any event, the approach addresses cases of unequivocal guilt, not those of doubtful guilt. In practice the former will be rare and the reality is of a 'confession' in relation to which the lawyer will rarely, if ever, be able to conclude certain guilt. No doubt there are other cases, falling outside the strict words of the code, which lawyers themselves would almost universally condemn as professional misconduct. A striking example is *R* v *Dean* (see C. K. Allen, *R* v *Dean* (1941) 57 *LQR* 85). Dean was tried for attempted murder of his wife and defended by Meagher. He was convicted and after the trial Dean confessed to Meagher that he was in fact guilty. (Clearly this does not fall within the words of the Code of Conduct since it was not a confession before or during the trial.) Knowing this, Meagher still agitated for a Royal Commission to reopen the case, and when one was ultimately appointed Dean received a pardon as a result of its recommendations. Afterwards he had to concede Dean's confession and was struck off for professional misconduct.

What of those instances which do not fall squarely within the words of the Code of Conduct, or clear cases such as *R* v *Dean*, where a lawyer knows, or more probably suspects, that he is assisting a client in wrongful conduct, wrongful in the sense that it will be a breach of the criminal or regulatory law, fraudulent, or (possibly also) an intentional or bad faith breach of contract? Consider these hypothetical examples.

(a) Solicitors have sought advice for a company on the application of the Environmental Protection Act to some of its intended activities. It is fairly obvious to the pupil barrister that the activities are in clear breach of the Act, but at the conference, the pupil master indicates to the client that the area is doubtful legally, and that in any event it is unlikely that the enforcement authorities will discover the breach. At the end of the conference the pupil is told by the pupil master to draft the advice along those lines.

(b) An employed barrister in a law centre is advising on welfare benefit. The barrister is unsure whether the client is telling the truth about not having worked in the relevant period, but on being assured that no work was done proceeds with the claim and as a result has been successful. A short time later the barrister discovers that the client was not telling the truth and had full time employment for the period for which benefit was, wrongfully, obtained.

One approach in addressing these hypothetical examples is to ask to what extent non-lawyers would be in breach of the criminal or civil law – whether as aider or abettor, conspirator, accessory and so on – were they to advise or assist the client. On this approach if a non-lawyer were to be liable, exceptional reasons would have to be adduced to exculpate a lawyer. However, we saw at the outset that in the realm of legal ethics and professional responsibility we are not simply concerned with breaches of the criminal or civil law but with those broader standards which in particular will maintain the public standing of the profession. Thus this approach, while fruitful, will be too narrow in a number of cases.

Another approach is to reason from the Code of Conduct and from other sources about professional misconduct. There is authority that a party asking for an injunction without notice must bring all material facts to the notice of the court; this principle could extend to other cases creating or confirming rights which otherwise would not exist. With the hypothetical examples we can draw on various principles. First, lawyers are under no duty to assist a crime or fraud, or to become party to an abuse of process. The duty of confidence is dissolved under the crime/fraud exception. Indeed there is even some older professional authority that, in the case of a serious crime, a lawyer has an **obligation** to convey the information to the relevant authorities – thus going beyond the crime/fraud exception – notwithstanding the duty of confidence. In terms of our hypothetical examples however, these existing principles are only a baseline to providing definite guidance on what are patently troubling cases.

Whatever approach is adopted, much depends on the knowledge of the barrister with respect to the wrong the client will effect and on what the lawyer actually does to achieve it. As to the first, culpable knowledge must extend beyond actual knowledge to encompass wilfully shutting one's eyes to the obvious and wilfully and recklessly failing to make the enquiries an honest and reasonable person would make. In practice it should not be forgotten that barristers by training should be able to make astute judgments as to their clients' purposes.

Measuring the second factor, the extent of the lawyer's activity in effecting the wrongdoing, is similarly difficult. Much will turn on the circumstances. Performing an act which substantially furthers the client's wrongdoing should give rise to culpability. If the principles applying to accessory liability are relevant, there seems no reason why in some circumstances, if the barrister knows what is going on, giving advice should not make the lawyer guilty of professional misconduct if it enables the client to pursue the unlawful conduct.

4.8   The Profession's Wider Responsibilities

So far the focus has been on the profession's responsibilities in relation to clients. Although only partly articulated and patchy, barristers have acknowledged wider responsibilities. One aspect is the recently assumed obligation not only to end racial and sexual discrimination in the profession, but positively to advance the position of minorities and women. Another aspect is the responsibility to the law itself, in ensuring its renewal and amendment in the light of changing social and economic circumstances. Then there is what could in broad terms be described as facilitating access to justice. In this regard the reduction in the number of persons qualifying for legal aid highlights the importance of new initiatives.

Access to justice has a number of strands. One is ensuring that persons are not handicapped from establishing the rightness of their position because they or their cause are unpopular. Representation of unpopular causes is an essential component of public confidence in the legitimacy of the legal system. The 'cab-rank' rule for the Bar demands that barristers accept any instructions or brief to represent any client at a proper professional fee in the fields in which they profess to practise, irrespective of the nature of the case or any belief or opinion which the barrister might have formed as to the character, reputation, cause, conduct, guilt or innocence of that person. Extravagant claims have sometimes been made for the 'cab-rank' rule, and in some cases unpopular clients have found that barristers of their first or even second choice have been unavailable because of 'prior commitments'. On the whole, however, the rule has worked remarkably well and unpopular clients have been better served in England than in the United States, where there is no equivalent obligation. Not only has the rule ensured representation for unpopular clients, but it has gone a considerable way to removing the stigma from those barristers who have stuck their neck out on a regular basis to represent unpopular causes.

Unlike the Bar, solicitors are free to decline instructions, although any refusal must not be based on racial, sexual or religious grounds. Solicitors can therefore refuse assistance to those to whom they have moral or political objections. By the same token if they accept a retainer they are bound to the duties of confidence, diligence and loyalty already examined, however morally or politically obnoxious they find their client's cause. (There is nothing equivalent for the profession here to the American ethical rule whereby a lawyer might explicitly base advice to a client on his or her personal views of morality and similar non-legal values.) Representation of a client by a solicitor does not constitute endorsement of that client's morals or politics. But since solicitors are free to choose their clients on such grounds, it follows that their decisions to do so may be criticised. A solicitor's choice of client or cause is a moral decision and the solicitor must be prepared to justify it along with other decisions.

4.9   Concluding Comments

While the ethical rules themselves have not attracted much public attention, there has been a quiet transformation in recent decades. From some rather general standards which it was thought all lawyers would know, there has evolved a more legalised system based on codes of conduct. One interpretation of this development is that it reflects both movements in the market for legal services and the transformation of the profession. A socially homogeneous, relatively cohesive profession, with shared understandings, has become a much larger and variegated one, with members playing a variety of new roles. There has been a consequent need for rules and a bureaucratic machinery to assimilate and discipline the profession's disparate parts. Moreover, greater attention has had to be given within the profession to ethical standards because in many ways they are symbolic of how the profession sees itself. Disputes about the rules are surrogates for disputes about the future of the profession.

The move to more definite rules is not only inevitable but also desirable. Intuition or appeals to secular or other morality are no substitute for a framework of rules. Not only is there no consensus over the former, but in some important respects the correct ethical position is not immediately apparent. Issues of legal ethics do not come labelled as such but arise in particular contexts of legal practice. Without definite rules it is difficult to see how professional behaviour will be constrained.

By the same token the existing codes of professional practice cannot simply be treated as a system of specific rules. If that were to be the case they would become like any other body of rules which lawyers manipulate, and if needs be seek to avoid. The ends lawyers are pursuing, the ethics of their clients, the standing of the profession and the wider interests of justice – these are just some of the matters which must also be considered in channelling and justifying professional behaviour. Moreover, the present professional Code of Conduct does not give specific guidance in important respects. To return to one of the hypothetical examples above: if breach of a regulatory law is tolerated by officials, should barristers counsel a client to disregard it?

An underlying theme of this discussion is that in important respects the current set of ethical rules is contestable. I have focused on the duty of loyalty which barristers are mandated to give to a client's interests. The linchpin of the present rules is that barristers need not be convinced of a client's case; that is for the courts. In single mindedly serving a client's interest, the assumption is that a barrister is serving justice. As a barrister one need not be primarily concerned with any wider interest.

This argument and its conclusion is still largely valid. But there are a number of difficulties. First, many matters never get to court and on the civil side involve effectively only one party. Secondly, there is the widespread public perception these days that the self-interest of lawyers is masquerading as a public service. The unequal access to legal services and the unequal matching of parties in particular cases undermine the validity of the model. Thirdly, we have seen that however unformulated or inadequate they might be, there are limits to the barrister acting as hired gun. For advocates, Lord Reid sums up the position this way (*Rondel* v *Worsley* [1969] 1 AC 191, 227):

> Every counsel has a duty to his client fearlessly to raise every issue, advance every argument, and ask every question, however distasteful, which he thinks will help his client's case. But, as an officer of the court concerned in the administration of justice, he has an overriding duty to the court, to the standards of his profession, and to the public, which may and often does lead to a conflict with his client's wishes or with what the client thinks are his personal wishes.

The corollary is that in some circumstances the law and the profession's ethical rules recognise that unquestioning zeal in a client's interest may cause social harm.

What is necessary in this area is a further refinement of the provisions in the Code of Conduct. When do the interests of others and the public interest trump devotion to the client's interest? When should a barrister question his or her client's intentions and activities and be justified by provisions in the Code of Conduct in doing so? When should a barrister cease to act for a particular client or indeed disclose suspected wrongdoing to the relevant regulatory agency? Such questions demand careful analysis. One difficulty is that the current rules were forged in the context of the criminal law where the notion of the fearless advocate, zealously defending the client, come what may, is more understandable. But extension of the arguments in the criminal context to other areas, in particular advice to clients, does not always make sense. The enormous legal resources which powerful economic interests can marshal – whatever the cause – might well be politically contentious, socially harmful and possibly morally objectionable. Ultimately this phenomenon might also undermine the standing of the legal profession and the legitimacy of the law.

Legal ethics have to be conceived of within the more general area of professional responsibility. The wider ethical issues of the operation of the legal profession as a whole are now firmly on the agenda. The obvious example is the unequal utilization of legal services and of access to them. The Bar supports the Free Representation Unit, a registered charity providing free advice and representation for those before tribunals. This wider conception links with the rules in the Code of Conduct, since many of these are based on the notion that clients will be competently and adequately represented. Another aspect of this wider topic is inequality of access to the profession itself. The Bar has taken this on board in the realisation that the profession is failing to tap vital resources and denying opportunities to, for example, a significant minority of young people with ethnic backgrounds.

FIVE

COURT ETIQUETTE

5.1   Introduction

Each time you appear in court you are on a public stage, in full view of the judge, the client and, usually, the public at large. How you appear and conduct yourself in front of that audience is of great importance if you are to do the job of a barrister properly. If you are discourteous, inappropriately dressed or do not behave in the way that you ought to, you risk alienating the tribunal you are seeking to persuade. Remember that as a barrister you are always appearing on behalf of someone other than yourself: unfavourable views formed about you by the tribunal because of an unprofessional manner may rebound onto your client. Some of the requirements of the etiquette that you must observe are to be found in written sources, such as the Code of Conduct, or the occasional Practice Direction (e.g, *Practice Direction (Court Dress) (No. 2)* [1995] 1 WLR 648), but others have been established through custom, tradition and common-sense.

5.2   Courtesy

It should go without saying that in every sphere of practice you ought to be courteous, and this is reinforced by the Code of Conduct, which states '[a] barrister must at all times be courteous to the Court and to all those with whom he has professional dealings' (Annexe F, para. 5.5). You are, of course, required by the Code of Conduct to '. . . promote and protect fearlessly and by all proper and lawful means [your] client's best interests and do so without regard to [your] own interests or to any consequences to [yourself] or to any other person . . .' (para. 203(a)), but this does not give you *carte blanche* to be as rude as you like to judges, witnesses or your opposing counsel. Ultimately, discourtesy by counsel in court could amount to a contempt.

5.3   Dress in Court

The Code of Conduct requires that '. . . a barrister's personal appearance should be decorous, and his dress, when robes are worn, should be compatible with them.' (Annexe F, para. 5.12). In practice, this means that you should dress conservatively. A courtroom is not the place to make an individual fashion statement: you may like wearing paisley waistcoats and bright orange socks, but save that for your own time. As a barrister you are a professional: dress like one. Dressing conservatively means, amongst other things:

(a)   Men should wear a suit (the traditional black jacket and grey striped trousers is an alternative, although less common now amongst younger members of the Bar). Do not wear blazers or linen jackets in court, even in hot weather. Either single or double breasted suits are acceptable, but a waistcoat should be worn if the former is chosen. Suits and dresses should be dark in colour, i.e., black, dark navy or grey, and of a traditional cut. In May 1995 the then Lord Chief Justice, Lord Taylor of Gosforth, decided that it was perfectly acceptable for women to wear trousers when appearing in court.

(b) Dresses or blouses should be long sleeved and high to the neck, even in warmer weather.

(c) Shirts or blouses should be predominantly white; collars should be white. For men (when robes are worn) a separate wing collar is the norm: avoid, as has been seen in court, a dress evening shirt.

(d) Shoes should be black; avoid wearing boots in court.

(e) Jewellery should be discreet: avoid studs and rings through places other than ears. Men should avoid wearing an ear-ring in court.

(f) When a wig is worn, wear it so that it covers your hair as far as possible; avoid fringes showing at the front, and keep long hair neatly tied back.

The Professional Conduct Committee of the Bar Council has been asked about the propriety of a barrister who customarily wears a turban to do so in place of a wig. The Committee was of the view that such matters were properly determined by the court concerned rather than the committee itself. However, it expressed the view that it is entirely reasonable for a barrister who customarily wears a turban to do so in court in place of a wig.

5.4 Robes

For counsel, being robed means wearing wig, gown, and bands. You will be robed when you appear in open court in County Courts, the Crown Court, the High Court, the Court of Appeal, and the House of Lords.

It is unnecessary to robe when you appear before a judge in private, or generally in chambers or before a magistrates' court, tribunal or arbitrators.

It is generally unnecessary to robe when you appear before a Master or district judge, whether sitting in open court or in private. If, however, the district judge is sitting in robes in open court it is desirable that you also appear robed. For this reason it is always advisable, though rather inconvenient, to take your robes to court in case the district judge before whom you are appearing on a private matter chooses to take the matter robed and in open court.

Always turn up to your chambers prepared to appear in court in robes, even if you were planning a day on papers, i.e., wear a suit, have your robes with you and a collarless shirt to hand. It is not at all unusual for you to arrive at chambers to be told by your clerk that you are in open court on an urgent matter, when you thought you were going to have a paperwork day!

5.5 Customs

Much of court etiquette is derived from custom. Some of the more common customs are:

(a) Do not move or speak whilst a witness is being sworn; you should stay completely still and silent whilst this is being done, even if you are not involved in the case.

(b) Do not enter or leave court whilst a verdict is being taken, or when a defendant is being sentenced.

(c) When the judge enters the courtroom you must stand; he or she will normally bow to counsel before being seated – you should return the bow. You should also bow to the judge when leaving court, and, if you have just come in to a court when the judge is already sitting, as you sit down.

(d) Do not stare (indeed try not to look) at members of a jury when they come into court to deliver their verdict. At this stage they have made their decision: you can no longer influence them one way or the other, and there is no reason why you should make them feel uncomfortable by trying to guess their verdict.

(e) You should not show your emotions at a verdict, or a judge's ruling.

(f) By convention, briefcases are not usually carried by counsel when robed. Do not take a bag into court (other than a handbag). If you have to, for whatever reason, ensure it is concealed as far as possible. Similarly, newspapers and other miscellaneous items should be kept from the view of the tribunal you are before.

(g) There is a courtesy known as 'dressing the judge' which should be observed. A judge in robes should never be left without a member of the Bar being in court, unless the judge has indicated that he or she can leave. If your case is over, and you are the only barrister in court, do not leave unless the judge has given such an indication. In virtually every case the judge will so indicate.

(h) If your opponent rises to object, sit down. Two barristers should never be on their feet at the same time unless being addressed directly by the judge.

(i) Sometimes you will go into court where leading counsel will be appearing; by convention junior barristers sit in the row behind leading counsel, rather than the same one. Constraints of space sometimes mean that this is not always observed.

In addition to the above customs there are also a number of less common situations where there is still an element of custom and etiquette, e.g., on the death of a judge, it will usually fall to the most senior member of the Bar present in the robing room that day to perform some form of valediction before the business of the court is resumed.

5.6 Modes of Address

Reference should be made to the **Advocacy Manual** at **5.1** which contains a guide to the appropriate modes of addressing the court and the use of the correct form of address.

5.7 Problems

(1) You are instructed to represent the defendant in a High Court case at 10.30 am, at the Royal Courts of Justice. You sleep through your alarm clock and, to your horror, wake up at 10 am. The Court is an hour's journey from your home. What do you do?

(2) You are the junior pupil in chambers. At 4.30 pm on Thursday your clerk tells you that you have two cases listed at Exeter Crown Court for the following day: one at 10 am in court one, and one at 10.30 am, in court two, and that no one else in chambers is available to do either of them. At 10.35 am you are still conducting the case in court one, when you are passed a note by the usher from court two that that court has convened and that the judge is waiting for you and furious to know that you are in a different court. What do you do?

SIX

PROFESSIONAL MISCONDUCT: THE COMPLAINTS PROCEDURE

6.1   General

The Bar Council introduced a new complaints procedure with effect from 14 April 1997. Its procedures are laid down, or repeated, in the Code of Conduct as follows:

(a)   The Complaints Rules – Annexe K.

(b)   Disciplinary Tribunal Regulations 1991 – Schedule A to the Constitution of the Council of the Inns of Court (repeated as Annexe L).

(c)   Hearings before the Visitors Rules 1997 (repeated as Annexe M).

(d)   Summary Procedure Rules – Annexe N.

(e)   Adjudication Panel and Appeals Rules – Annexe P.

The structure of the system is outlined in the diagram at **6.16** below. There are two important figures in the procedure: the Complaints Commissioner and the Professional Conduct and Complaints Committee (PCC).

6.2   The Complaints Commissioner

The Complaints Commissioner is responsible for overseeing the investigation of complaints against barristers. The Commissioner is neither a barrister, nor a solicitor and has power to dismiss complaints which are clearly unmeritorious without referring them to the PCC. In addition, the Commissioner advises the PCC about issues of inadequate professional services and compensation and plays an important role in presenting the lay client's perspective.

6.3   Professional Conduct and Complaint Committee (PCC)

Under the present system, the PCC reports to the Professional Standards Committee (PSC) of the Bar Council and comprises 13 members of the Bar Council, two lay members (chosen by rota from a panel of lay representatives appointed by the Complaints Commissioner), 30 or more additional members and the Chairman and Vice-Chairman of the PSC who are members ex-officio.

A quorum of the PCC is one quarter of its membership (not including the lay representative's panel) of whom one must be a silk and the two lay representatives attending.

Apart from dealing with complaints, the PCC also deals with applications and queries from members of the Bar concerning Code of Conduct matters, in so far as these concern the exercise of discretion or questions of interpretation. Matters of policy, however, are the prerogative of the PSC.

6.4   The Nature of Complaints

It is too early to say how the new complaints system will affect the number and nature of complaints. Under the present system, however, about 450 complaints are received each year from a wide variety of complainants including members of the lay public, prisoners, judges, solicitors and other members of the Bar. Of these, about 70% are dealt with by the PCC, either being dismissed or no further action being taken. Of the remainder, about half (15%) are dealt with informally in one way or another and the remainder are referred either to a summary hearing or to a disciplinary tribunal.

The nature of complaints can vary widely but the most common, in descending order of frequency, are probably as follows:

(a)   Dissatisfied lay clients (especially prisoners) alleging:

   (i)   incompetence and/or negligence;

   (ii)   undue pressure to accept a settlement or to plead guilty;

   (iii)   poor advocacy, style or tactics.

(b)   Misbehaviour in court, especially rudeness to other counsel or to the judge and failure to accept the latter's rulings.

(c)   Failure to pay debts. These are normally accepted as being within the Committee's jurisdiction only if use of the status of barrister or a degree of moral turpitude is involved.

(d)   Maladministration of, or misbehaviour in, chambers.

(e)   Reports of driving, public order or criminal convictions. The last of these almost invariably result in reference to a disciplinary tribunal, often with the most severe consequences.

6.5   Pre-complaint Procedures

Procedures before the decision to raise a formal complaint is taken are relatively informal and depend on circumstances and/or the method of approach adopted by the potential complainant. In outline:

(a)   If lay complainants write to the Bar Council, telephone or call in person, stating explicitly or otherwise that they wish to make a complaint, they are sent an appropriate letter, covering notes for guidance and a complaints form for completion and return. If they appear to be seeking comments or the Bar Council's intervention, typically about a case in which they are or have been involved, they are sent another letter, again with covering Notes for Guidance and a form, which states that the Bar Council is unable to help except in the context of a formal complaint. In all such cases, a formal complaint is initiated on receipt of a completed form.

(b)   If non-lay complainants, e.g., judges, solicitors etc. write to the Bar Council supplying sufficient detail, completion of a complaints form is often, but not always, dispensed with, a formal complaint being raised without further ado.

(c)   Finally, cases arise in which barristers' conduct gives grounds for concern but which may or may not result in a formal complaint being raised. Examples include barristers who have been found guilty of minor offences, e.g., drunken driving, and cases of bankruptcy, Individual Voluntary Arrangements (IVAs) and Directors Disqualification Orders, all of which barristers are required to report to the Bar Council. Cases where the PCC is asked to intervene without a formal complaint being raised, e.g., involving delay in dealing with papers or minor disputes within chambers, also arise and may subsequently give rise to formal complaints.

Perhaps 70% or more of approaches by lay complainants, i.e. (a) above, eventually result in formal complaints and, obviously, 100% of those in (b). A very much lower proportion of other cases ((c) above), however, give rise to complaints, perhaps as low as 1–2%. The complainant in the vast majority of such cases is normally the Bar Council of its own motion.

6.6   Present Complaints Procedure

When a complaint has been received (other than one made by the Bar Council of its own motion) it is referred to the Complaints Commissioner (currently Michael Scott CB CBE DSO) who will give initial instructions on how the complaint should be investigated. In a relatively small number of cases it is likely that it will be obvious that the complaint as it stands shows no evidence of misconduct or of inadequate professional service. In such cases the Commissioner is able to dismiss the complaint immediately. In other cases, the matter may be suitable for conciliation or should be adjourned (for example because an appeal is pending). In the majority of cases, however, the Commissioner will seek further information and at this stage the comments of the barrister concerned with the complaint will be sought.

It is likely that the Commissioner will also approach the instructing solicitor (if there is one) for comments, together with other relevant witnesses at the same time. The barrister's comments are then sent to the complainant for further comments. Once these have been received the papers are sent to the Commissioner for further consideration.

If, having considered the papers, the Commissioner is satisfied that there is no *prima facie* evidence of professional misconduct or of inadequate professional service on the barrister's part, the complaint may be dismissed. Otherwise, it will be referred to the Professional Conduct and Complaints Committee (PCC). A member of the PCC will be asked to examine the file and prepare a report on the complaint for the PCC to consider.

This will summarise the background, the detailed nature of the complaint and the arguments for and against, and recommending a decision. This is tabled at the first available Committee meeting which the Sponsor Member can attend when the complaint is discussed in full and a decision is reached.

The primary purpose of consideration by the PCC is to determine whether a *prima facie* case of misconduct or inadequate professional services has been disclosed. The Committee considers only documentary evidence and neither the barrister concerned, the complainant nor any witnesses attend. Having considered the evidence, the PCC may:

(a)   with the concurrence of both lay representatives attending, dismiss the complaint or determine that no further action should be taken; or,

(b)   adjourn the matter for further enquiries; or,

(c)   require counsel to attend on the Chairman of the PCC or other person to receive advice as to his future conduct or to advise the barrister in writing as to his future conduct (this does *not* amount to a finding of professional misconduct);

(d) find a *prima facie* case of inadequate professional service, in which case the matter will be referred to an adjudication panel;

(e) find a *prima facie* case of professional misconduct (whether with or without inadequate professional service) whereupon, depending upon the seriousness of the matter and whether there is a significant dispute as to facts, the PCC may refer the matter to one of an informal hearing, a summary procedure panel or a disciplinary tribunal.

The complainant is invariably informed of the Committee's decision and, if it is dismissed, if no further action is taken or if the matter is dealt with informally, is told the outline reasons for the Committee's decision and, if appropriate, the nature of the advice given.

6.7   Adjudication Panels

Adjudication Panels exist to consider complaints where the PCC has only found that there is a *prima facie* case of inadequate professional service. This is defined as

such conduct towards the lay client (or in the case of an employed barrister the person to whom he has supplied the professional service in question) or performance of professional service for that client which falls significantly short of that which is to be reasonably expected of a barrister in all the circumstances.

Their procedures are governed by the Adjudication Panel and Appeals Rules. The panel may:

(a) dismiss the complaint;

(b) require the barrister to apologise to the lay client;

(c) require the barrister to repay or reduce the fee;

(d) require the barrister to pay compensation up to £2,000 to the lay client.

A finding of inadequate professional service may only be made where the person making the complaint is the lay client or their representative. Compensation will only be payable where the lay client has suffered loss which could be recovered at law.

Adjudication Panels normally sit in private and reach their decisions on the papers in front of them. The complainant will have been invited to make further representations about the matter and, in particular, any loss that has been suffered. A barrister may attend the panel and/or be represented there if he or she wishes.

6.8   Informal Hearings

Where the PCC considers that there is a *prima facie* case of misconduct but that it is relatively trivial, it may refer the matter to a panel comprising three barrister members of the PCC (usually chaired by a QC). If the panel finds either misconduct or inadequate professional services to have been established, it may advise as to future conduct or informally admonish the barrister. A panel making a finding of inadequate professional service may order the same remedies as an Adjudication Panel.

6.9   Summary Hearings

Summary hearings are held under the authority of Summary Procedure Rules. Panels, each consisting of a silk as chairman, a lay representative and at least one, and up to three, further members, all of whom must be past or present members of the PCC or the PSC, are appointed afresh by the Chairman of the PCC on each occasion. Procedure is informal. Proceedings are based on an agreed statement of facts, although witnesses can, with the prior permission of the chairman of the panel, be heard. Hearings are held in private, both the defendant and the PCC can be represented by counsel (although the latter is unusual) and evidence, where applicable, is taken on oath.

6.10 Tribunals

Disciplinary tribunals are held under the authority, and under the arrangements, of the Council of the Inns of Court and consist of a Chairman (a High Court or Circuit judge) together with three practising members of the Bar and a lay representative. Both oral and documentary evidence is taken. Hearings are normally held in public. Both the defendant and the PCC (as prosecuting authority) are represented by counsel and evidence is taken, where appropriate, on oath.

6.11 Penalties

If charges of professional misconduct are found proved, a summary hearing or a tribunal may sentence a barrister to be:

(a) disbarred (disciplinary tribunals only);

(b) suspended from practice for a prescribed period, with or without conditions (for three months only in the case of a summary hearing);

(c) ordered to pay a fine to the Bar Council of up to £5,000 (£500 in the case of summary hearings);

(d) ordered to forgo or repay fees;

(e) reprimanded by the Treasurer of his or her Inn;

(f) permanently or temporarily excluded from undertaking legal aid work;

(g) admonished;

(h) advised as to his or her future conduct.

A barrister may be admonished or be given advice as to his or her future conduct by the tribunal or summary hearing panel itself, or by attendance on a nominated person.

Summary Hearings and Disciplinary Tribunals may also make findings of inadequate professional service and order the same remedies as an Adjudication Panel.

6.12 Appeals

Findings of professional misconduct and subsequent sentences by summary hearings and disciplinary tribunals are subject to appeal under the Hearings Before the Visitors Rules 1997. Findings of inadequate professional service may be appealed to an Appeals Panel under the Adjudication Panel and Appeal Rules.

6.13 Publication of Findings and Sentence

The proceedings of, and decisions by, the PCC, informal hearings or adjudication panels are not published unless the barrister concerned so requests. All other findings of professional misconduct are published unless the tribunal or summary hearing panel decides otherwise.

6.14 Conciliation

In some cases, where it is clear to the Commissioner that misconduct is not involved, the Commissioner may consider that it is most appropriate for the barrister to attempt some informal conciliation with the complainant. This may arise, for example, in cases where it is clear that the complainant simply has not understood what has gone on or where some minor problem has arisen over delay or confusion in clerking which is not serious enough to amount to misconduct. It is often most satisfactory if such difficulties can be resolved between the parties rather than by formal findings and an investigation. It should be stressed, however, that in suggesting this the Commissioner has not reached any formal view as to whether an issue of inadequate professional service is involved.

In these circumstances, the Commissioner will suggest that the barrister should approach the complainant to see whether it is possible to resolve the difficulties informally. It is up to the barrister to decide what response to this is appropriate. It may, for example, be reasonable to offer some sort of explanation or financial compensation or to refer the matter to a Chambers complaints procedure (if one exists). It is equally open to the barrister to make no response at all but if it is not possible to resolve the dispute, the complainant may return the matter to the Bar Council for a formal investigation.

6.15 Legal Services Ombudsman

The Legal Services Ombudsman, who is neither a barrister nor a solicitor, was appointed under the Courts and Legal Services Act 1990 to oversee the handling of complaints against members of the legal professions. If a complainant is dissatisfied with the way his or her complaint has been dealt with, he or she has the right to request the Ombudsman to examine the PCC's treatment of the complaint and decide whether it was investigated fully and fairly. If the complainant's grievance is within his powers, the Ombudsman then asks to see the PCC's file. If, after considering the matter, he thinks the complaint was not dealt with properly, he can recommend further action including, in certain circumstances, reconsideration of the matter by the PCC or the payment of compensation by the Bar Council and/or by the barrister(s) concerned.

Complaints have to be referred to the Legal Services Ombudsman within three months of the letter notifying him of the PCC's decision. The Ombudsman has no power to deal with complaints which concern a barrister's handling of a case in court i.e., so-called 'advocate's immunity'), that is being, or has been, decided by a court or by a disciplinary tribunal or where an appeal is being, or could still be, made against the PCC's decision. He will also not normally intervene while the PCC is still investigating the matter and will in fact only do so if there appears to have been unreasonable delay or if other strong reasons exist. In effect, therefore, decisions by the PCC, informal hearings, adjudication panels and summary hearings are reviewable by the Ombudsman; cases referred to and heard by a tribunal, whatever the result, are not.

6.16   Complaints System Structure

Changes to the existing procedure are in bold and underlined

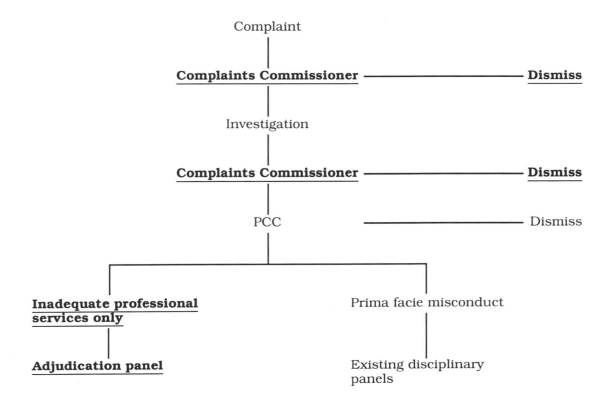

6.17 Advice to Counsel who are the Subject of a Complaint

The number of complaints received by the Bar Council from lay clients and others has increased steadily over the last six years and it is becoming increasingly likely that, at one stage or another, a barrister, particularly if he or she specialises in criminal or family work, will be required to respond to a complaint. Counsel will normally be informed of this in a letter from the Bar Council enclosing a copy of the material sent by the complainant to the Bar Council. That letter will indicate that counsel's comments are required within three weeks of its date.

It is worth making clear that, at this stage, the Bar Council or the Commissioner has not taken any view on the merits of the complaint. The majority of complaints are dismissed but in many cases the complainant will not have supplied sufficient information to allow the Commissioner to deal with the matter without seeking counsel's comments. The Legal Services Ombudsman oversees the working of the system and has power to refer matters back to the PCC for reconsideration. For this reason it is generally safer to seek counsel's comments where there may be any doubt about a particular complaint. Counsel should feel free to contact the Secretariat to discuss the handling of the complaint, the procedure generally or to seek advice. Clearly the Secretariat cannot advise on whether there is or is not a prima facie case of misconduct and cannot give a barrister advice on how to present his or her case. That said, the following questions arise frequently.

6.17.1 I AM IN A LONG CASE AND CANNOT PREPARE MY RESPONSE ADEQUATELY IN TIME

The Secretariat is usually able to agree reasonable extensions for good reasons over the telephone. Generally it is most important that a barrister should at least make contact with the Secretariat even if he or she is not able to produce a full response by the deadline. Barristers should make every effort to produce their response as soon as is reasonably possible. The PCC can and does take action against barristers who are unreasonably dilatory in preparing their replies.

6.17.2 THE COMPLAINT HAPPENED MANY MONTHS AGO AND I HAVE LITTLE RECOLLECTION OF THE CASE

There is no reason why counsel cannot approach his or her instructing solicitors for a copy of the original instructions in the case and such other details as he or she may need in order to refresh his or her memory. It is certainly open to him or her to seek an extension of time in order to obtain such documentation.

6.17.3 MAY I APPROACH SOLICITORS AND OTHER WITNESSES FOR THEIR VIEWS?

There is no reason why counsel should not approach instructing solicitors, judges, etc. to provide statements or other information in support of counsel.

6.17.4 THE CLIENT HAS ISSUED/IS LIKELY TO ISSUE PROCEEDINGS AGAINST ME IN NEGLIGENCE

Counsel should seek the advice of the BMIF on how to deal with the complaint. Normally consideration of such a complaint is adjourned until the matter has been considered by the civil courts. In any case if, on the advice of your insurers or for reasons of professional privilege, it is inappropriate for certain matters to be sent to the complainant which, nevertheless, it would be helpful for the Commissioner or the Committee to see, such material can be withheld from the complainant. If this is the case, counsel should make it clear which parts of the response should not be sent to the complainant.

6.17.5 WHAT SHOULD I SAY IN MY RESPONSE?

The content of the response to the complaint is very much a matter for the individual barrister to consider. There is nothing to stop him or her seeking advice from other colleagues or his or her head of chambers as to his or her reply. A good rule is to address specific allegations but not include comment or material 'just in case'. Simply refer to the further details or evidence which is available and can be supplied if required.

6.17.6 HOW WILL IT AFFECT MY APPLICATION FOR SILK OR JUDICIAL APPOINTMENT?

A complaint which has been dismissed is not at present required to be mentioned to the Lord Chancellor's Department in connection with any application for silk or judicial appointment and the Bar Council will not disclose such a complaint. The Bar Council will, however, disclose any finding of professional misconduct or any unresolved complaint. The exact effect of such disclosure is for the LCD to consider and will clearly depend on the circumstances of each case. It may be worth noting, however, that a finding of professional misconduct by one of the informal panels has not proved an insuperable barrier to preferment in the past.

6.17.7 SHOULD I BE REPRESENTED AT TRIBUNALS OR PANEL HEARINGS?

Barristers are almost invariably represented before disciplinary tribunals and may approach other counsel direct in order to be so represented. There is a long tradition at the Bar of very senior silks agreeing to act for no fee in such cases. It is, however, in each case, a matter for the individual concerned as to whom he or she seeks to approach and whether he or she needs to instruct solicitors on these matters. If a barrister has difficulty finding suitable counsel, then the Secretariat is usually able to assist. The individual should bear in mind that he or she will not always get his or her costs back even after a successful defence at a tribunal. Representation in front of panels and summary hearings is less common. There is, however, nothing to prevent a barrister from being represented if he or she wishes.

6.18 Legal Services Ombudsman: Recommendations for Compensation

As has been explained, the Ombudsman has power to consider the decisions of the Commissioner and the PCC and, on occasion, to recommend that the barrister concerned pay compensation direct to the lay client. The Bar Council is consulted about such recommendations but it is not its normal policy to make representations about the awards, unless those awards appear to it to be unreasonable. In dealing with the Ombudsman, barristers are recommended to contact the BMIF about any recommendations for compensation.

SEVEN

TUTORIAL PROBLEMS

7.1 Tutorial 1: Problems

(1) A solicitor seeks to instruct you to act for notoriously bad landlords in an action for possession of premises occupied by a highly regarded charitable organisation. The case is likely to draw adverse publicity. You hold yourself out to act in landlord and tenant cases, you have no connection with either party or with the premises, you have no conflicting professional commitment and the fee offered is a proper fee for you and for the case. Your clerk tells you that he or she wishes you to refuse the instructions because:

(a) it is chambers' policy not to act for landlords; and

(b) he or she fears that your normal professional clients will be reluctant to instruct you in future cases as their clients (tenants, consumers, etc.) would refuse to have as counsel one who had acted for these particular claimants.

(2) You act for a father whose former wife is now cohabiting with a black boyfriend. Your client instructs you to resist her application for contact with the parties' son on thinly veiled racist grounds. Can you refuse to put forward his instructions even if wrapped up as 'exposing his son to a cultural environment totally alien . . .'?

(3) You have successfully appeared for the claimants in an action where the unsuccessful defendants now wish to seek a Part 20 indemnity or contribution from a third party who was not a party to the original action. The defendants' solicitors were impressed with your performance and want you to be able to use your knowledge of the case against the third party. Do you accept the instructions?

(4) (a) You visit your client in the cells at the magistrates' court prior to a remand hearing. Your client is charged with threats to kill his wife. During the conference, he indicates that he does not intend to return to prison and has razor blades in his cell with him. What do you do about it when you leave the conference?
   (b) Following an unsuccessful bail application you go to see your client, an armed robber, in the cells. He is philosophical about his remand in custody but asks if you will take a message to his wife upstairs. You agree. The message is 'tell Shirley the gun is in the hi-fi'.

(5) A solicitor who regularly instructs you and your chambers, telephones you and instructs you to attend at a particular police station where a lay client is about to be interviewed in relation to a criminal matter. He or she asks you to be present throughout the interview and to advise the client as necessary. The solicitor undertakes to pay you a proper fee. If the matter leads to a charge or charges being preferred, the brief is likely to come into chambers for someone of your experience. Can you act? Would it make any difference if the brief would certainly be beyond your competence?

(6) You are prosecuting a plea of guilty where the defendant is unrepresented. It is a type of case in which the Court of Criminal Appeal has given sentencing guidelines.

The judge does not appear to be familiar with criminal work. You are aware from discussion with the officer in the case of a number of matters favourable to the defendant which he or she does not bring out when mitigating on his or her own behalf. What are your duties?

(7) You have received and accepted instructions to appear in case 'A' (a civil case fixed to be heard on 20 April). You have done a lot of preparatory work upon it and have seen the professional and lay clients in conference on a number of occasions. You have also accepted instructions to defend in a serious criminal case (case 'B') expected to be tried in the week beginning 1 April and to last for five days but which may well go longer. Before you have conferred with the client in case 'B' you learn that it will not be heard until the week beginning 15 April. Both solicitors assert priority and both clients are anxious to have your services. Which case do you do? Why?

(8) You have represented your client successfully in court. After the hearing, the client stuffs a £5 note in your pocket and tells you to enjoy a drink on him or her. Do you keep the money? Would it make any difference if your client instead sent you a bottle of whisky?

7.2   Tutorial 2: Problems

(1) (a) The defendant in a rape case instructs you that intercourse took place between him and the victim with her consent. At trial he tells you that he did not have intercourse with her and gives you the names of alibi witnesses.
    (b) You prepare the defence in a fraud case on the basis of your client's instructions that he is a man of impeccable reputation in the city and has no convictions at all. On the day of the trial you discover that he is a practised 'con-man' who has convictions for dishonesty.
    (c) Your client is mentally disturbed. His or her instructions differ each time you speak to him.

What should you do in these circumstances?

(2) You are prosecuting a case listed at the Crown Court for trial. Upon arriving you are informed by the officer that vital witnesses have disappeared, and that there is no prospect of tracing them. After considering the matter with the officer and a Senior Crown Prosecutor you all agree that the only course is to offer no evidence. You go to find defence counsel to tell him this. Before you can do so, he or she tells you that his or her client would be willing to plead to a lesser offence. What do you do?

(3) (a) You act for the claimant in civil proceedings. In the course of the claimant's evidence-in-chief, he produces several documents from his pocket which he alleges support his claim. You have never seen them before nor have they been disclosed to the defendants. What do you do?
    (b) What steps, if any, would you take if you were acting for the defendant in these circumstances?

(4) (a) You receive a set of instructions to advise and settle civil proceedings for a claimant from X and Co., a firm of solicitors who have instructed you on a number of occasions and are among your best clients. It is apparent that they have been negligent in handling the claimant's affairs. It appears to you that the claimant's chances have not been badly affected and he or she is likely to succeed in the litigation, but he or she has at least been prejudiced in the sense that, if the relevant matter 'surfaces' in the litigation, the defendants will be able to make use of it to reduce the damages or to obtain a better settlement than would otherwise have been open to them. What, if anything, should you do?
    (b) You are defending a trial at the Crown Court. In the course of giving his or her evidence the defendant makes an allegation which, although it is in your instructions, you had not put to the victim. It is apparent that it should have been, and the victim has gone on holiday and cannot be recalled. The judge is furious. What do you do?

(5) You advise the defendant, in conference, that he or she has no defence to the claimant's claim for possession of the premises where he or she is residing. The defendant tells you he or she understands that but believes if they hang on long enough the claimant will 'make it worth their while' to go. He or she instructs you to pursue 'a holding defence'. Do you do so? Would it make any difference to your response if the defendant were legally aided?

(6) You act for the claimant in a disputed claim for damages for breach of contract. At court, the defendant, who is unrepresented, asks you what he or she should do. To what extent do you discuss the case with him or her?

(7) You are appearing for a well known business man in his local magistrates' court on a charge of drink driving. After the hearing, you are approached by a reporter from the local newspaper who asks you for information about the client and the case. What should you do?

7.3   Tutorial 3: Problems

The following problems are set in a civil context and primarily concern the ethics of negotiation.

(1) You act for the defendant in civil proceedings in which the claimant is seeking liquidated damages in the sum of £6,000. Liability is in dispute. Just before the hearing is called on, your client instructs you to offer the claimant, on a 'without prejudice' basis, £5,000 plus costs to be paid within 28 days in full and final settlement of the claim. You relay this offer to your opponent. Your client then changes their mind and insists that the sum of £5,000 must include the claimant's costs. Before you can do anything, your opponent informs you that their client accepts the terms of your offer. How do you proceed?

(2) (a) You act for the husband in divorce proceedings. The wife has applied for periodical payments for herself and the children of the family. In the course of negotiations conducted 'without prejudice' outside court, your opponent lets slip that their client is working one night a week in her local pub. This is not disclosed in her statement of means. What use, if any, can you make of this information?

(b) Would your answer be different if the wife's application were adjourned and your opponent told you this 'off the record' during the train journey back to chambers?

(3) (a) You are asked to advise in conference upon the acceptability of an offer of £3,000 in settlement of your client's claim for damages in a personal injuries case. The latest medical report, which has been disclosed to the defence, is now three months old. In the course of the conference, your client informs you that the doctor's prognosis was unduly pessimistic and his condition has improved since the report was prepared. In the circumstances, the offer is generous and more than your client is likely to receive from the court. What advice do you give?

(b) Would it make any difference to your advice if your client was a minor?

(4) (a) You act for the wife in divorce proceedings. The husband has offered to pay her £80,000 in full and final settlement of all her claims for financial relief. This sum is sufficient to enable her to purchase alternative accommodation without the necessity of a mortgage and to meet her other needs. You see your client in conference to advise upon the acceptability of this proposal. You notice she is wearing an engagement ring. She tells you, in response to your query, that she has recently met a wealthy man and is proposing to re-marry in the near future. What advice do you give her?

(b) Would it make any difference to your advice if the man she was engaged to marry was a pauper?

(5) In the course of negotiations, the defendant makes a paltry offer in settlement of your client's claim. Your client is reluctant to pursue his or her case and states that he

or she wants to accept the offer. You believe he or she is likely to receive at least double this sum from the court. What do you do?

(6) You are instructed to represent the defendant in proceedings for damages for breach of contract. Upon your arrival at court, your instructing solicitor informs you that one of your witnesses has just telephoned the solicitor's office to say they are ill and cannot attend court to give evidence. That testimony is vital to the defendant's case. You have no option but to seek an adjournment. At that moment, your opponent approaches you and asks to have a word with you. Your opponent indicates that they have witness difficulties and invites you to agree an adjournment of the hearing for two weeks. In so doing:

(a) Do you inform your opponent and the court of your own witness difficulties?

(b) If not, do you make an application for the claimant to pay the defendant's costs thrown away by the adjournment?

(7) You represent the mother of two children who is responding to an application by their father for defined contact. Your client instructs you that she is agreeable to the children seeing their father every Saturday between 9 am and 6 pm. In the course of discussions outside court:

(a) Do you put forward a proposal in these terms or in lesser terms (e.g. every second Saturday)?

(b) If in lesser terms, do you inform your opponent that this is the most which your client is prepared to agree?

(c) If your opponent approaches you and proposes access every Saturday between the hours of 10 am and 5 pm, do you mention that your client is prepared to agree to more?

(d) Would your answers be any different if the issue involved was money rather than the future contact between two children and their non-custodial parent?

(8) You are a junior tenant and member of your chamber's pupillage selection committee. At the conclusion of an interview with a married black female candidate, one of the members of the committee says

(a) that he doesn't think the candidate will 'fit in'

(b) that he won't be party to selecting a married woman as a pupil, and that it would be different if it was a married man.

You had felt that the same member of the committee had been unduly antagonistic to the prospective pupil during the interview. What would you do?

APPENDICES

APPENDIX ONE

CODE OF CONDUCT OF THE BAR OF ENGLAND AND WALES

CODE OF CONDUCT

OF

THE BAR OF ENGLAND AND WALES

Adopted by the Bar Council 27 January 1990

Effective from 31 March 1990

Incorporating

Amendment No 1 effective from 22 October 1990

Amendment No 2 effective from 16 March 1991

Amendment No 3 effective from 1 October 1993

Amendment No 4 effective from 12 March 1994
(unless otherwise indicated)

Amendment No 5 effective from 14 April 1997
(unless otherwise indicated)

Amendment No 6 effective from 1 October 1998

The General Council of the Bar of England and Wales
3 Bedford Row
London WC1R 4DB

Amendment 6:1/10/98

SECTION 1

Table of contents

PART I - PRELIMINARY

101.1 This Code (which save as provided in paragraph 1001 replaces all earlier Codes) was adopted by the Bar Council on 26 September 1998 and came into force on 1 October 1998.

101.2 Amendments and additions to this Code may be made by Resolution of the Bar Council which shall be operative upon such date as the Resolution shall appoint. Amendments and additions will be published from time to time in such manner as the Bar Council may determine.

General purpose of the Code

102 The general purpose of this Code is to provide the standards of conduct on the part of barristers which are appropriate in the interests of justice in England and Wales (and so far as applicable elsewhere) and in particular:

(a) in relation to barristers in independent practice to provide common and enforceable requirements and prohibitions which together preserve and enhance the strength and competitiveness of the independent Bar as a whole in the public interest by requiring such barristers:

(i) to be completely independent in conduct and in professional standing as sole practitioners;

(ii) to act only as consultants instructed by solicitors and other approved professional persons;

(iii) to acknowledge a public obligation based on the paramount need for access to justice to act for any client (whether legally aided or not) in cases within his field of practice;

(b) in relation to employed barristers to make appropriately similar provision taking into account the fact that such barristers are employed to provide legal services to and may therefore act only on behalf of their employer.

Application of the Code

103.1 Save as otherwise provided this Code applies to all barristers whenever called to the Bar.

103.2 A barrister appearing in Court as a barrister outside the jurisdiction of the Courts of England and Wales or providing legal services as a barrister outside England and Wales shall whether he is practising there as an established lawyer or is providing occasional services:

(a)   remain subject to this Code;

(b)   also and without prejudice to his obligations as a barrister observe so far as is appropriate the rules of professional conduct of the place where he is providing the legal services.

103.3   In its application to employed barristers this Code shall apply mutatis mutandis as it applies to barristers in independent practice but with the substitution:

(a)   of references to the relevant employer or other person mentioned in paragraph 403.1 for references to the professional client or the lay client;

(b)   of references to the directions received in whatever form from the relevant employer or other person mentioned in paragraph 403.1 for references to a brief or instructions.

Waiver of the Code

104   The Bar Council shall have the power to waive the duty imposed on a barrister to comply with the provisions of this Code in such circumstances and to such extent as the Bar Council may think fit and either conditionally or unconditionally.

PART II – FUNDAMENTAL PRINCIPLES

Applicable to all barristers

201 A barrister must have regard to paragraph 102 and must not:

(a) engage in conduct whether in pursuit of his profession or otherwise which is:

(i) dishonest or otherwise discreditable to a barrister;

(ii) prejudicial to the administration of justice; or

(iii) likely to diminish public confidence in the legal profession or the administration of justice or otherwise bring the legal profession into disrepute;

(b) engage directly or indirectly in any occupation if his association with that occupation may adversely affect the reputation of the Bar or in the case of a practising barrister prejudice his ability to attend properly to the interests of his clients.

Applicable to practising barristers

202 A practising barrister has an overriding duty to the Court to ensure in the public interest that the proper and efficient administration of justice is achieved: he must assist the Court in the administration of justice and must not deceive or knowingly or recklessly mislead the Court.

203 A practising barrister:

(a) must promote and protect fearlessly and by all proper and lawful means his lay client's best interests and do so without regard to his own interests or to any consequences to himself or to any other person (including his professional client or fellow members of the legal profession);

(b) subject only to compliance with the specific provisions of Legal Aid Regulations owes his primary duty:

(i) as between his lay client and his professional client; and

(ii) as between the Legal Aid Fund and his lay client;

to his lay client and must not permit the Legal Aid Fund or his professional client to limit his discretion as to how the interests of his lay client can best be served;

(c)   must act towards his lay client and his professional client at all times in good faith.

204.1   A practising barrister must not in relation to any other person (including a lay client or a professional client or another barrister or a pupil or a student member of an Inn of Court) discriminate[1] directly or indirectly or victimise because of race, colour, ethnic or national origin, nationality, citizenship, sex, sexual orientation, marital status, disability, religion or political persuasion.

204.2   In respect of indirect discrimination, there is no breach of paragraph 204.1 if the barrister against whom the complaint is brought proves that the act of indirect discrimination was committed without any intention of treating the claimant unfavourably on any ground in that paragraph to which the complaint relates.

205   A practising barrister must not:

(a)   permit his absolute independence integrity and freedom from external pressures to be compromised;

(b)   do anything (for example accept a present) in such circumstances as may lead to any inference that his independence may be compromised;

(c)   compromise his professional standards in order to please his client the court or a third party.

206   A practising barrister is individually and personally responsible for his own conduct and for his professional work: he must exercise his own personal judgment in all his professional activities and must not if he is a barrister in independent practice delegate such responsibility to another barrister or agree to assume responsibility for the professional work of another barrister.

207   A practising barrister must not:

(a)   enter into a professional partnership with another barrister or enter into a professional partnership or any other form of unincorporated association (including in the case of a barrister in independent practice any arrangement which involves sharing the administration of his practice) with any person other than a barrister;

(b)   be a member of a firm or be employed or engaged by any person firm or company which is either wholly or in part a device whereby the barrister himself (with or without others) is intended directly or indirectly to supply legal services to the public or a section of the public;

---

[1] Discrimination is defined in the Sex Discrimination Act 1975 and the Race Relations Act 1976

(c)   have a seat in the office of any person (other than his employer in the case of an employed barrister) entitled to instruct him;

(d)   give a commission or present or lend any money for any professional purpose to or save as a fee in accordance with the provisions of this Code accept any money by way of loan or otherwise from any person (other than his employer in the case of an employed barrister) entitled to instruct him.

Applicable to barristers in independent practice

208   A barrister in independent practice must make his practice in England and Wales or in the Courts of the European Community his primary occupation and must hold himself out as being and must be willing at all times in return for the payment of fees to render legal services to the public generally in England and Wales.

209   A barrister in independent practice must comply with the 'Cab-rank rule' and accordingly except only as otherwise provided in paragraphs 501 502 503 504 and 505 he must in any field in which he professes to practise in relation to work appropriate to his experience and seniority and irrespective of whether his client is paying privately or is legally aided or otherwise publicly funded:

(a)   accept any brief to appear before a court in which he professes to practise;

(b)   accept any instructions;

(c)   act for any person on whose behalf he is briefed or instructed;

and do so irrespective of (i) the party on whose behalf he is briefed or instructed (ii) the nature of the case and (iii) any belief or opinion which he may have formed as to the character reputation cause conduct guilt or innocence of that person.

210   A barrister in independent practice whether or not he is acting for a fee:

(a)   may supply legal services only if he is briefed or instructed by a professional client;

(b)   must not when acting in a professional capacity enter into contractual relations relating to the services to be provided by him with any person other than his professional client;

provided that a barrister may without the intervention of a professional client accept a brief or instructions with or without fee directly from and represent another barrister on that other barrister's appeal as to his fees before a taxing master or in relation to an application for a wasted costs order against that other barrister.

Applicable to non-practising barristers

211 Not used pending approval.

212 A non-practising barrister:

(a) must not appear as counsel in any Court;

(b) must not supply legal services to the public or any section of the public unless:

(i) he is currently insured by insurers authorised to conduct such business against any and all claims in respect of civil liability for professional negligence arising out of or in connection with the supply of legal services for at least the first £250,000 of each and every claim, with an excess not exceeding £500.

(ii) he has delivered to the General Council of the Bar:

(a) Notification of his intention to supply legal services to the public, the nature of the service to be supplied and details of the current address(es) with telephone number from which such legal services will be supplied;

(b) A copy of the current insurance policy required under (i) or a current certificate of insurance issued by the insurer;

(iii) unless exempted by the Bar Council, he has paid to the Bar Council the subscription prescribed from time to time by the Bar Council for non-practising barristers supplying legal services.

(c) must not supply legal services in respect of any matter unless he has sufficient qualifications, competence and experience to handle the matter. Without prejudice to the foregoing, a non-practising barrister must not draw or prepare any instruments within section 22 of the Solicitors Act 1974 (save as permitted under sub-section 2A) or draw or prepare any papers for probate within section 23 of the said Act (save as permitted under sub-section 3) or act as a supervisor unless he has the qualifications, competence and experience to do so.

(d) must not in connection with the supply of legal services to the public or any section of the public hold or handle client money securities or other assets of whatsoever nature or description other than by receiving payment of his fees.

(e) must not in connection with the supply of legal services to the public or any section of the public describe himself or allow himself to be described as a barrister or Queen's Counsel as the case may be without qualifying that description by the addition of the words 'not practising' or 'non-practising'.

Without prejudice to paragraph 104, the Professional Standards Committee of the Bar Council may waive the requirement of (a) and/or (b)(i) and/or (ii) and/or (d) and/or (e) in whole or in part in respect of non-practising barristers working for solicitors, accountants or other professions, employers or organisations and/or outside England and Wales on such terms as the Committee thinks fit.

PART III – BARRISTERS IN INDEPENDENT PRACTICE

Prerequisites to independent practice

301   A barrister may supply legal services as a barrister in independent practice provided that:

(a)   he is qualified to practise and:

(i)   has unless exempted under Part IV of those Regulations complied with Regulations 54 and 55 of the Consolidated Regulations of the Inns of Court (reproduced in Section 4 of the Code);

(ii)   complies with any applicable requirement of the Rules of the Continuing Education Scheme (reproduced in Annexe Q);

(b)   he has paid the appropriate insurance premium to and is insured with BMIF against claims for professional negligence in accordance with paragraph 302;

(c)   he has unless exempted by the Bar Council paid to the Bar Council the subscription currently payable in accordance with paragraph 303;

(d)   in the case of a barrister who has engaged in independent practice for less than three years since the conclusion of twelve months' pupillage he does so from chambers of which he is not the sole member and of which at least one member has engaged in independent practice for not less than five years since the conclusion of twelve months' pupillage.

Insurance

302   Every barrister in or intending to engage in independent practice shall apply to be entered as a member with BMIF:

(a)   before he has completed his pupillage; or

(b)   if he is exempted from pupillage or does not intend to practise immediately upon completion of his pupillage before he commences to practise;

and every barrister entered as a member with BMIF shall:

(i)   pay immediately when due the appropriate insurance premium so as to be insured with BMIF against claims for professional negligence such insurance to provide cover of such amount and upon such terms as may be approved by the Bar Council from time to time;

(ii)   supply immediately upon being requested to do so such information as BMIF may from time to time require pursuant to its Rules.

Bar Council subscriptions

303   Every barrister in independent practice shall unless exempted by the Bar Council pay to the Bar Council at such time or times as it shall become due the subscription payable by a barrister in independent practice of his seniority as prescribed from time to time by the Bar Council.

Administration and conduct of independent practice

304   A barrister in independent practice:

(a)   must

(i)   prior to his commencing to practise notify the Bar Council of the address and telephone number of his chambers and of any change in the same;

(ii)   have or have ready access to library facilities which are adequate having regard to the nature of his practice;

(b)   must have regard to the published guidance as issued from time to time by the Bar Council as to:

(i)   the administration of chambers;

(ii)   pupillage (reproduced in Annexe A); and

(iii)   good equal opportunities practice in chambers in the form of the Equality Code for the Bar (as to which see Annexe O).

(c)   must take all steps which it is reasonable for him in the circumstances to take to ensure that:

(i)   his practice is efficiently and properly administered having regard to the nature of his practice;

(ii)   proper records are kept;

(iii)   he complies with the Terms of Work on which Barristers Offer their Services to Solicitors and the Withdrawal of Credit Scheme 1988 (reproduced in Annexe B) and with any Withdrawal of Credit Direction issued by the Chairman of the Bar pursuant thereto.

Heads of chambers

305   The head of chambers or if there is no head of chambers every member of chambers must take all steps which it is reasonable for him in the circumstances to take to ensure that:

(a)   his chambers are administered competently and efficiently and are properly staffed;

(b)   the affairs of his chambers are conducted in a manner which is fair and equitable for all barristers and pupils;

(c)   proper arrangements are made in his chambers for dealing with pupils and pupillage;

(d)   all barristers practising from his chambers (including 'squatters') are entered as members with BMIF and have effected insurance in accordance with paragraph 302;

(e)   all barristers practising from his chambers comply with paragraph 304(c)(iii);

(f)   all employees and staff in his chambers (i) carry out their duties in a correct and efficient manner and (ii) are made clearly aware of such provisions of this Code as may affect or be relevant to the performance of their duties;

(g)   fee notes in respect of all work undertaken by all members of chambers and pupils and (unless expressly agreed with the individual) former members and pupils of chambers are sent expeditiously to professional clients and in the event of non-payment within a reasonable time, pursued efficiently.

Direct Professional Access work

306.1   A barrister in independent practice must in every Direct Professional Access matter comply with the Direct Professional Access Rules (reproduced in Annexe E).

306.2   Save as otherwise provided by the Direct Professional Access Rules this Code applies to Direct Professional Access work as it applies to other work undertaken by a barrister in independent practice.

Overseas work

307.1   A barrister in independent practice must in every International matter comply with the International Practice Rules (reproduced in Annexe D).

307.2   Save as otherwise provided by the International Practice Rules this Code applies to International work as it applies to other work undertaken by a barrister in independent practice.

Advertising and Publicity

308.1   Subject to paragraph 308.2 a barrister in independent practice may engage in any advertising or promotion in connection with his practice which conforms to the British Codes of Advertising and Sales Promotion and such advertising or promotion may include:

(a)   photographs or other illustrations of the barrister;

(b)   statements of rates and methods of charging;

(c)   statements about the nature and extent of the barrister's services;

(d)(i)   the name of any case in which the barrister has appeared;

(ii)   the name of the professional or lay client for whom the barrister has acted;

where such information has already become publicly available or, where it has not already become publicly available, with the express prior written consent of the professional or lay client as appropriate.

308.2   Advertising or promotion must not:

(a)   be inaccurate or likely to mislead;

(b)   be likely to diminish public confidence in the legal profession or the administration of justice or otherwise bring the legal profession into disrepute;

(c)   make direct comparisons with or criticisms of other barristers or members of any other profession;

(d)   include statements about the barrister's success rate;

(e)   indicate or imply any willingness to accept a brief or instructions or any intention to restrict the persons from whom a brief or instructions may be accepted otherwise than in accordance with this Code;

Amended 27 March 1999

(f)   be so frequent or obtrusive as to cause annoyance to those to whom it is directed.

Fees and remuneration

309   Subject to paragraphs 205 and 207 a barrister in independent practice may charge for any work undertaken by him (whether or not it involves an appearance in court) on any basis or by any method he thinks fit provided that such basis or method:

(a)   is permitted by law;

(b)   does not involve the payment of a wage or salary.

310.1   A barrister in independent practice who receives fees in respect of work done by another barrister must himself and without delegating the responsibility to anyone else forthwith pay the whole of the fee in respect of that work to that other barrister.

310.2   A barrister in independent practice who arranges for another barrister to undertake work on his behalf (other than a person who has asked to do the work in order to increase his own skill or experience) must himself and without delegating the responsibility to anyone else:

(a)   pay proper financial remuneration for the work done;

(b)   make payment within a reasonable time and if possible within three months after the work has been done unless otherwise agreed in advance with the other barrister.

PART IV - EMPLOYED BARRISTERS

401   A barrister may supply legal services as an employed barrister provided that:

(a)   he is qualified to practise;

(b)   he has unless exempted by the Bar Council paid to the Bar Council the subscription currently payable in accordance with paragraph 402.

402   Every employed barrister shall:

(a) ·notify the Bar Council of the name address telephone number and nature of the business of his employer and of any change in the same;

(b)   unless exempted by the Bar Council pay to the Bar Council at such time or times as it shall become due the subscription payable by an employed barrister of his seniority as prescribed from time to time by the Bar Council.

403.1   An employed barrister so long as he does not himself supply legal services to the public or a section of the public may without being instructed by and without the intervention of a solicitor or other professional client (but only whilst acting in the course of his employment):

(a)   supply legal services to;

(b)   subject to compliance with the Conveyancing by Employed Barristers Rules (reproduced in Annexe E) undertake any form of conveyancing services on behalf of;

(c)   subject to paragraph 403.2 appear as counsel in any Court in circumstances where immediately before 7 December 1989 barristers in independent practice did not have an exclusive right of audience on behalf of;

(d)   unless rules of Court require the intervention of a solicitor or other profes-sional agent brief or instruct a barrister in independent practice in any contentious or non-contentious matter on behalf of

his employer or another employee of his employer or (if the barrister is employed by a trade association) an individual member of the association.

403.2   Unless exempted under Part IV of the Consolidated Regulations of the Inns of Court an employed barrister may act in pursuance of paragraph 403.1(c) only if:

(a)   he has completed a first six-months pupillage and is serving a further pupillage;

(b)   he has completed 12 months' pupillage; or

(c)   he became an employed barrister before 1 January 1989 and has been an employed barrister for a period or periods amounting to not less than five years

and he complies with any applicable requirements of the Rules of the Continuing Education Scheme;

403.3   An employed barrister who wishes to exercise rights of audience in pursuance of paragraph 403.1(c) shall notify the Bar Council accordingly and will become subject to the Rules of the Continuing Education Scheme from that date of that notice.

404   An employed barrister (other than a barrister in the Government Legal Service or employed by a local authority or any other public authority) who briefs or instructs a barrister in independent practice shall but only for the purposes of this Code be personally responsible for payment of the barrister's fees.

405   A barrister in the Government Legal Service may act on behalf of those Ministers or Officers of Crown organisations or public officers or servants for whom the Government Legal Service customarily acts and:

(a)   a barrister in the Government Legal Service or employed by a local authority or other prosecuting authority may brief or instruct a barrister in independent practice without the intervention of a solicitor in a prosecution by that service or authority;

(b)   any existing practice whereby barristers in the Government Legal Service or employed by public authorities brief or instruct barristers in independent practice without the intervention of a solicitor shall continue.

406   An employed barrister may (but only whilst acting in the course of his employment) do for his employer any excepted work not involving the receipt or handling of money not belonging to his employer.

PART V - BRIEFS AND INSTRUCTIONS
TO PRACTISING BARRISTERS

Acceptance of briefs and instructions and
application of the 'Cab-rank rule'

501   A practising barrister must not accept any brief or instructions if to do so would cause him to be professionally embarrassed and for this purpose a barrister will be professionally embarrassed:

(a)   if he lacks sufficient experience or competence to handle the matter;

(b)   if having regard to his other professional commitments he will be unable to do or will not have adequate time and opportunity to prepare that which he is required to do;

(c)   if the brief or instructions seek to limit the ordinary authority or discretion of a barrister in the conduct of proceedings in Court or to impose on a barrister an obligation to do any excepted work (except as permitted by the Overseas Practice Rules or in the case of an employed barrister by paragraph 406) or to act otherwise than in conformity with the provisions of this Code;

(d)   if the matter is one in which he has reason to believe that he is likely to be a witness or in which whether by reason of any connection of his with the client or with the Court or a member of it or otherwise it will be difficult for him to maintain professional independence or the administration of justice might be or appear to be prejudiced;

(e)   if there is or appears to be some conflict or a significant risk of some conflict either between the interests of the barrister and some other person or between the interests of any one or more of his clients;

(f)   if the matter is one in which there is a risk of a breach of confidences entrusted to him by another client or where the knowledge which he possesses of the affairs of another client would give an undue advantage to the new client;

(g)   if he is a barrister in independent practice in a privately funded matter if the brief or instructions are delivered by a solicitor or firm of solicitors in respect of whom a Withdrawal of Credit Direction has been issued by the Chairman of the Bar pursuant to the Terms of Work on which Barristers Offer their Services to Solicitors and the Withdrawal of Credit Scheme 1988 (reproduced in Annexe B) unless the brief or instructions are accompanied by payment of an agreed fee or the barrister agrees in advance to accept no fee for such work or has obtained the consent of the Chairman of the Bar;

(h)   if he is a barrister in independent practice in a Direct

Professional Access matter or an Overseas matter unless he has previously informed BMIF that he intends to accept Direct Professional Access work or Overseas work (as the case may be) and has paid the appropriate insurance premium.

502   A barrister in independent practice is not obliged to accept a brief or instructions:

(a)   requiring him to do anything other than during the course of his ordinary working year;

(b)   other than at a fee which is proper having regard to the complexity length and difficulty of the case and to his ability experience and seniority and any brief or instructions in a legally aided matter shall for this purpose unless the Bar Council or the Bar in general meeting otherwise determines (either in a particular case or in any class or classes of case or generally) be deemed to be at a proper professional fee;

(c)   if the expenses which will be incurred are likely to be unreasonably high in relation to the fee likely to be paid and are not to be paid additionally to such fee;

(d)   save in the case of legal aid work:

(i)   unless and until his fees are agreed;

(ii)   if having required his fees to be paid before he accepts the brief or instructions to which the fees relate those fees are not paid;

(e)   in a Direct Professional Access matter unless he has previously notified BMIF that he intends to accept Direct Professional Access work and has paid the appropriate insurance premium;

(f)   in an Overseas matter.

503   A Queen's Counsel in independent practice is not obliged to accept a brief or instructions:

(a)   to settle alone any document of a kind generally settled only by or in conjunction with a junior;

(b)   to act without a junior if he considers that the interests of the lay client require that a junior should also be instructed.

504.1   A practising barrister (whether he is instructed on his own or with another advocate) must in the case of each brief and if he is a barrister in independent practice also in the case of all instructions consider whether consistently with the proper and efficient administration of justice and having regard to:

(i) the circumstances (including in particular the gravity complexity and likely cost) of the case;

(ii) the nature of his practice;

(iii) his ability experience and seniority; and

(iv) his relationship with his client;

the best interests of the client would be served by instructing or continuing to instruct him in that matter.

504.2 Where more than one advocate is instructed in any matter each barrister must in particular consider whether the best interests of the client would be served by:

(a) his representing the client together with the other advocate or advocates; or

(b) his representing the client without the other advocate or advocates; or

(c) the client instructing only the other advocate or advocates; or

(d) the client instructing some other advocate.

504.3 Unless he considers that the best interests of the client would be served by his continuing to represent the client (together with any other advocate instructed with him) a barrister must immediately advise the client accordingly.

504.4 In cases involving several parties, a practising barrister must in the case of each brief and, if he is a barrister in independent practice, also in the case of all instructions, consider, on receipt of the brief or instructions and further in the event of any change of circumstances, whether, consistently with the proper and efficient administration of justice and having regard to all the circumstances and any actual or potential conflict of interest, his client needs to be separately represented or advised or whether he could properly be jointly represented or advised with another party or, where there is more than one client, whether it is in all their interests to be jointly represented or advised.

504.5 (a) If the barrister considers that the client could properly be jointly represented or advised with another party, he must immediately advise the client accordingly.

(b) If the barrister considers that it is not in the interests of all his clients that they should be jointly represented or advised, he must immediately advise the clients accordingly.

505 Not used pending approval.

Withdrawal from a case and return of brief or instructions

506   A practising barrister must cease to act and if he is a barrister in independent practice must return any brief or instructions:

(a)   if continuing to act would cause him to be professionally embarrassed within the meaning of paragraph 501 provided that if he would be professionally embarrassed only because it appears to him that he is likely to be a witness on a material question of fact he may retire or withdraw only if he can do so without jeopardising his client's interests;

(b)   if having accepted a brief or instructions on behalf of more than one client there is or appears to be:

(i)   a conflict or a significant risk of a conflict between the interests of any one or more of such clients; or

(ii)   risk of a breach of confidence;

and the clients do not all consent to him continuing to act;

(c)   if in any legally aided case (whether civil or criminal) it has become apparent to him that legal aid has been wrongly obtained by false or inaccurate information and action to remedy the situation is not immediately taken by his client;

(d)   if the circumstances set out in Regulation 67 of the Civil Legal Aid (General) Regulations 1989 arise at a time when it is impracticable for the Area Committee to meet in time to prevent an abuse of the Legal Aid Fund;

(e)   if the client refuses to authorise him to make some disclosure to the court which his duty to the court requires him to make;

(f)   if having become aware during the course of a case of the existence of a document which should have been but has not been disclosed on discovery the client fails forthwith to disclose it;

(g)   if having come into possession of a document belonging to another arty by some means other than the normal and proper channels and having read it before he realises that it ought to have been returned unread to the person entitled to possession of it he would thereby be embarrassed in the discharge of his duties by his knowledge of the contents of the document provided that he may retire or withdraw only if he can do so without jeopardising his client's interests.

507   Subject to paragraph 508 a practising barrister may withdraw from a case where he is satisfied that:

(a)   his brief or instructions have been withdrawn;

(b)   his professional conduct is being impugned; or

(c)   there is some other substantial reason for so doing.

508   A practising barrister must not:

(a)   cease to act or return a brief or instructions without having first explained to his professional client his reasons for doing so;

(b)   return a brief or instructions to another barrister without the consent of his professional client or his representative;

(c)   if he is a barrister in independent practice return a brief which he has accepted and for which a fixed date has been obtained or (except with the consent of his lay client and where appropriate the Court) break any other professional engagement so as to enable him to attend a social or non-professional engagement;

(d)   except as provided in paragraph 506 return any brief or instructions or withdraw from a case in such a way or in such circumstances that his client may be unable to find other legal assistance in time to prevent prejudice being suffered by the client.

PART VI - CONDUCT OF WORK BY PRACTISING BARRISTERS

General

601 A practising barrister:

(a) must in all his professional activities be courteous and act promptly conscientiously diligently and with reasonable competence and take all reasonable and practicable steps to avoid unnecessary expense or waste of the Court's time and to ensure that professional engagements are fulfilled;

(b) must not undertake any task which:

(i) he knows or ought to know he is not competent to handle;

(ii) he does not have adequate time and opportunity to prepare for or perform; or

(iii) he cannot discharge within a reasonable time having regard to the pressure of other work;

(c) must read all briefs and instructions delivered to him expeditiously;

(d) must have regard to the relevant Written Standards for the conduct of Professional Work (reproduced in Annexe F);

(e) must inform his professional client forthwith and subject to paragraph 508 return the instructions or the brief to the professional client or to another barrister acceptable to the professional client:

(i) if it becomes apparent to him that he will not be able to do the work within a reasonable time after receipt of instructions;

(ii) if there is an appreciable risk that he may not be able to undertake a brief or fulfil any other professional engagement which he has accepted.

Dual qualification

602 A practising barrister who is also qualified in some other system of law and practises concurrently in England and Wales and in a country or place outside England and Wales must comply with the Dual Qualification Rules (reproduced in Annexe G).

Confidentiality

603   Whether or not the relation of counsel and client continues a practising barrister must preserve the confidentiality of his lay client's affairs and must not without the prior consent of his lay client or as permitted by law lend or reveal the contents of the papers in any brief or instructions to or communicate to any third person (other than a devil his pupil or any of the staff of his chambers who need to know it for the performance of their duties) information which has been entrusted to him in confidence or use such information to his lay client's detriment or to his own or another client's advantage.

Media comment

604   A practising barrister must not in relation to any current matter:

      (i)   in which if he is a barrister in independent practice he is or has been briefed or instructed; or

      (ii)   in which if he is an employed barrister he is to appear or has appeared as an advocate;

comment to or in any news or current affairs media upon the facts of or the issues arising in that matter.

Conflicts between professional and lay clients

605   If a barrister in independent practice forms the view that there is a conflict of interest between his lay client and his professional client he must advise that it would be in the lay client's interest to instruct another professional adviser and such advice must be given either in writing or at a conference at which both the professional client and the lay client are present.

Drafting pleadings and other documents

606   A practising barrister must not devise facts which will assist in advancing his lay client's case and must not draft any originating process [statement of case] affidavit witness statement or notice of appeal containing:

      (a)   any statement of fact or contention (as the case may be) which is not supported by his lay client or by his brief or instructions;

      (b)   any contention which he does not consider to be properly arguable;

      (c)   any allegation of fraud unless he has clear instructions to make such allegation and has before him reasonably credible material which as it stands establishes a prima facie case of fraud;

(d)   in the case of an affidavit or witness statement any statement of fact other than the evidence which in substance according to his instructions the barrister reasonably believes the witness would give if the evidence contained in the affidavit or witness statement were being given viva voce;

provided that nothing in this paragraph shall prevent a barrister drafting a pleading affidavit or witness statement containing specific facts matters or contentions included by the barrister subject to the lay client's confirmation as to their accuracy.

Contact with witnesses

607   A practising barrister must not out of Court:

(a)   place a witness under any pressure to provide other than a truthful account of his evidence;

(b)   rehearse practise or coach a witness in relation to his evidence or the way in which he should give it.

Conduct at Court

608   Provided that he is satisfied that the interests of the lay client and the interests of justice will not be prejudiced a practising barrister to whom a brief has been delivered may agree with his professional client that attendance by the professional client and his representative may be dispensed with for all or part of any hearing

(a)   in a Magistrates' Court or a County Court;

(b)   provided that he has been supplied with any necessary proofs of evidence in any other Court.

609   Notwithstanding that neither his professional client nor his representative is present a practising barrister who has been briefed in a case may:

(a)   if the attendance of his professional client has been dispensed with pursuant to paragraph 608; or

(b)   if he arrives at Court and neither the professional client nor his representative is in attendance and there are no other grounds on which to request an adjournment and no practicable alternative

conduct the case on behalf of the lay client and if necessary interview witnesses and take proofs of evidence.

610   A practising barrister when conducting proceedings at Court:

(a)   is personally responsible for the conduct and presentation of his case and must exercise personal judgement upon the substance and purpose of statements made and questions asked;

(b)   must not unless invited to do so by the Court or when appearing before a tribunal where it is his duty to do so assert a personal opinion of the facts or the law;

(c)   must ensure that the Court is informed of all relevant decisions and legislative provisions of which he is aware whether the effect is favourable or unfavourable towards the contention for which he argues and must bring any procedural irregularity to the attention of the Court during the hearing and not reserve such matter to be raised on appeal;

(d)   must not adduce evidence obtained otherwise than from or through his professional client or devise facts which will assist in advancing his lay client's case;

(e)   must not make statements or ask questions which are merely scandalous or intended or calculated only to vilify insult or annoy either a witness or some other person;

(f)   must if possible avoid the naming in open Court of third parties whose character would thereby be impugned;

(g)   must not by assertion in a speech impugn a witness whom he has had an opportunity to cross-examine unless in cross-examination he has given the witness an opportunity to answer the allegation;

(h)   must not suggest that a victim, witness or other person is guilty of crime, fraud or misconduct or make any defamatory aspersion on the conduct of any other person or attribute to another person the crime or conduct of which his lay client is accused unless such allegations go to a matter in issue (including the credibility of the witness) which is material to his lay client's case and which appear to him to be supported by reasonable grounds.

PART VII - MISCELLANEOUS

Pupil-masters

701.1   A barrister who is a pupil-master must:

(a)   comply with Part V of the Consolidated Regulations of the Inns of Court (reproduced in Section 4 of the Code);

(b)   comply with the relevant requirements of paragraphs 304 and 305;

(c)   take all reasonable steps to provide his pupil with adequate tuition and experience.

701.2   Subject to paragraph 701.3 a barrister must remunerate any pupil (or in the case of an employed barrister ensure that a pupil is remunerated) for any work done for him which because of its value to him warrants payment.

701.3   Paragraph 701.2 shall not apply in the case of a pupil who is in receipt of an award which is paid by the chambers in which he is a pupil on terms that it is in lieu of remuneration which he might otherwise expect to receive from his pupil master or any other barrister.

Pupils

702   A barrister who is a pupil (whether in chambers or with an employed barrister) must:

(a)   comply with Part V of the Consolidated Regulations of the Inns of Court (reproduced in Section 4 of the Code);

(b)   apply himself full time to his pupillage save that a pupil may take part time employment which does not materially interfere with his pupillage;

(c)   preserve the confidentiality of every client's affairs and accordingly paragraph 603 applies to him as if the clients of his pupil master and of every barrister whom he accompanies to Court or whose papers he sees were his own clients.

Law Centres and Legal Advice Centres

703.1   A barrister providing legal services at a Law Centre or a Legal Advice Centre must comply with the Law Centres and Legal Advice Centres Rules (reproduced in Annexe H).

703.2   Save as otherwise provided by the Law Centres and Legal Advice

Centres Rules this Code applies to the provision of legal services at Law Centres and Legal Advice Centres as it applies to the provision of legal services by a barrister in independent practice.

Foreign lawyers

704.1   A barrister called to the Bar under Consolidated Regulation 40 (call to the Bar for temporary purposes only):

(a)   may not while in England or Wales conduct any litigation in England or Wales other than the case or cases specified in the Certificate referred to in Regulation 40(d);

(b)   may not at any time whether in England or elsewhere rely on the fact that he is or has been a member of the Bar for any purpose other than that of conducting such case or cases in England or Wales.

704.2   Subject to compliance with the Foreign Lawyers (Chambers) Rules (reproduced in Annex I) a foreign lawyer may have or be a member of chambers.

PART VIII – DISCIPLINARY PROCEEDINGS

801   A barrister must:

(a)   if he is a barrister in independent practice:

(i)   respond promptly to any requirement from the Bar Council for comments or information on or documents relating to the arrangements he has made for administering his practice and chambers whether or not any complaint has been received or raised arising out of those arrangements and in respect of any member of that barrister's chambers;

(ii)   permit the Bar Council or any agent appointed by it to inspect forthwith on request and at any time which is reasonable having regard to the circumstances and the urgency of the matter his chambers and the arrangements for administering and the records of his practice:

(b)   if he is a non-practising barrister supplying, or the Bar Council has reason to believe may be supplying, legal services to the public:

(i)   respond promptly to any requirement from the Bar Council for comments on or documents relating to the arrangements he has made for the purpose of supplying and administering the supply of legal services whether or not any complaint has been received or raised arising out of the supply by him of legal services:

(ii)   permit the Bar Council or any agent appointed by it to inspect forthwith and on request and at any time which is reasonable having regard to the circumstances and the urgency of the matter any premises from which he supplies or is believed to supply legal services, the arrangements he has made for the purpose of supplying legal services and administering the supply of legal services, and any records concerning such legal services.

(c)   report to the Bar Council if he is convicted of a criminal offence other than a minor Road Traffic offence;

(d)   report to the Bar Council if he is adjudicated bankrupt, if a Directors Disqualification Order is made against him or if he enters into an Individual Voluntary Arrangement with his creditors.

(e)   where a complaint has been made, or the Bar Council has reasonable grounds for believing that circumstances have arisen as a consequence of which a breach of this Code may have occurred or is about to occur, respond promptly to any requirement from the Bar Council for comments or information on a complaint or such circumstances as the case may be whether that complaint relates to him or to another barrister or such circumstances relate to his conduct or that of another barrister;

(f)   attend Disciplinary Tribunal, Summary Procedure, Adjudication Panel or Appeal Panel proceedings of the Professional Conduct and Complaints Committee when so required. in pursuance of the rules and procedures referred to in paragraph 802 or the Adjudication Panel and Appeals Rules (reproduced at Annexe P);

(g)   attend upon the Chairman of the Professional Conduct and Complaints Committee or other nominated person when so required in pursuance of the rules and procedures referred to in paragraph 802;

(h)   comply in due time with any direction of a Disciplinary Tribunal or of a Summary Procedure panel or of an Adjudication Panel or of an Appeal Panel or of the Professional Conduct and Complaints Committee which may be made against him in pursuance of the rules and procedures referred to in paragraph 802 or the Adjudication Panel and Appeals Rules;

provided for the avoidance of doubt that nothing in this paragraph shall require a barrister to disclose or produce any document or information protected by law or in circumstances to which paragraph 603 applies.

802.1   A barrister must comply so far as they are applicable to him with the provisions of the Act and of:

(a)   this Code;

(b)   such of the Consolidated Regulations of the Inns of Court as are referred to in this Code (reproduced in Section 4 of the Code);

(c)   the Code of Conduct for Lawyers in the European Community (reproduced in Annexe J);

(d)   the Legal Aid Act 1974 the Legal Aid Act 1988 or any regulations made for giving effect to or for preventing abuses of either of those Acts;

and any failure by a barrister to do so shall constitute professional misconduct rendering him liable to disciplinary proceedings in accordance with:

(i)   the Complaints Rules (reproduced in Annexe K);

(ii)   the Disciplinary Tribunals Regulations (reproduced in Annexe L);

(iii)   the Hearings before the Visitors Rules (reproduced in Annexe M);

(iv)   the Summary Procedure Rules (reproduced in Annexe N);

as approved from time to time.

802.2   If the declaration made by a barrister on call to the Bar is found to have been false in any material respect or if the barrister is found to have engaged prior to call in conduct which is dishonest or otherwise discreditable to a barrister and which was not, prior to call, fairly disclosed in writing to the Benchers of the Inn calling him or if any undertaking given by a barrister on call to the Bar is breached in any material respect that shall constitute professional misconduct.

PART IX - DEFINITIONS

901   In this Code except where otherwise indicated:

'the Act' means the Courts and Legal Services Act 1990 and where the context permits includes any orders or regulations made pursuant to powers conferred thereby;

'advocate' means an authorised advocate as defined in Section 119 of the Act and includes a barrister;

'authorised practitioner' means an authorised practitioner as defined in Section 119 of the Act;

'Bar' means the Bar of England and Wales;

'Bar Council' means The General Council of the Bar as constituted from time to time or a Committee thereof;

'barrister' means an individual who has been called to the Bar by one of the Inns of Court and who has not ceased to be a member of the Bar;

'barrister in independent practice' means a barrister who is both entitled to hold pursuant to paragraph 301 and does hold himself out to the public generally as willing in return for the payment of fees to render legal services in England and Wales or in or in relation to the Courts of the European Community to clients provided that:

(a)   a barrister who is a Law Officer of the Crown or who holds an appointment as standing Counsel to any Government Department or who is in full-time employment at a Law Centre or whose primary occupation is that of editor or reporter in England and Wales of any series of law reports shall be deemed to be a barrister in independent practice although he does not hold himself out to the public generally as willing to render legal services to clients;

(b)   a barrister who is a Member of Parliament or a Member of the European Parliament or an officer of or a teacher of law at an institution of higher or further education may be a barrister in independent practice notwithstanding the fact that his practice is not his primary occupation;

'BMIF' means Bar Mutual Indemnity Fund Limited;

'brief' means instructions delivered to a barrister in independent practice by a professional client whereby the barrister is retained on behalf of a client to appear at or before a Court;

'Centre' means a Law Centre or a Legal Advice Centre;

'chambers' means the principal place at or from which one or more barristers in independent practice carry on their practices and also refers where the context so requires to all the barristers who for the time being carry on their practices at or from that place;

'client' includes both professional client and lay client;

'Court' includes any court or tribunal or any other person or body whether sitting in public or in private before whom a barrister may appear as an advocate;

'Courts of the European Community' means any Court of the European Community not being a Court of a member of the European Community;

'Direct Professional Access work' means work undertaken by a barrister in independent practice pursuant to a brief or instructions delivered by a member of a recognised professional body in accordance with the Direct Professional Access Rules (reproduced in Annex C) and so that 'Direct Professional Access matter' shall have a corresponding meaning;

'employed barrister' means a barrister who in return for the payment of a salary is both entitled to be pursuant to paragraph 401 and is employed wholly or mainly for the purpose of providing legal services to his employer either under a contract of employment or by virtue of an office under the Crown or in the institutions of the European Communities;

'employer'

(a) where the employer is a company or other corporate body or firm shall include a holding subsidiary or associated company corporate body or firm of the employer;

(b) where the employer is a public authority (including a local authority) shall include:

(i) another public authority on behalf of which the employer has made arrangements under statute or otherwise to provide any legal services or to perform any of that other public authority's functions as agent or otherwise;

(ii) an employee of that other public authority in a case arising out of or in the course of such employee's employment;

(iii) another employee of the employer who has been appointed under any statute to institute proceedings in his own name by virtue of his appointment;

(iv) a company wholly or mainly owned by the employer;

(c) in relation to any justices' clerk or any employed barrister performing the functions of a justices' clerk includes the justices whom he serves;

'excepted work' means:

(a) the management administration or general conduct of a lay client's affairs;

(b) the management administration or general conduct of litigation or of inter-partes work (for example the conduct of correspondence with an opposite party); or

(c) the investigation or collection of evidence for use in any court;

(d) except as permitted by Paragraph 609, in any criminal case the taking of any proof of evidence; or

(e) the receipt or handling of clients' money;

(f) attendance at a police station without the presence of a solicitor to advise a suspect or interviewee as to the handling and conduct of police interviews.

'foreign lawyer' means a person who is qualified to practise and is practising as a foreign lawyer who is not a barrister or a solicitor of the Supreme Court of England and Wales;

'Government Legal Service' means those barristers advocates and solicitors qualified in any part of the United Kingdom who are employed or hold office as lawyers in any Government Department or other organisation listed in the Civil Service Year Book (or other publication for the time being fulfilling the same function) or in the Crown Prosecution Service the Serious Fraud Office or the British Council and includes any such person notwithstanding that he holds a rank in the unified Civil Service open structure;

'instructions' means instructions (other than a brief) delivered to a barrister in independent practice by a professional client whereby the barrister is retained on behalf of a client to provide legal services whether in a contentious or in a non-contentious matter;

'Law Centre' means a centre operated by a charitable or similar non-commercial organisation at which legal services are habitually provided to members of the public and which employs or has the services of one or more solicitors pursuant to paragraph 7(a) of the Employed Solicitors Code 1990 or for whom the Law Society has granted a waiver;

'lay client' means the person on whose behalf a barrister in independent practice is retained;

'Legal Advice Centre' means a centre (not being a Law Centre) at which legal services are habitually provided to members of the public without fee or for a nominal fee and which has been designated by the Bar Council as suitable for the employment of barristers;

'legal services' includes legal advice representation and drafting or settling any originating process pleading affidavit witness statement or other document but does not include:

(a)   lecturing teaching or the writing or editing of legal text books or of articles in newspapers or journals or giving advice on legal matters free to a friend or relative;

(b)   examining newspapers, periodicals, books, scripts and other publications for libel, breach of copyright, contempt of court and the like;

(c)   acting as unpaid or honorary legal adviser to any charitable benevolent or philanthropic institution;

(d)   the giving by a barrister who is a non-executive director of a company or a trustee or governor of a charitable benevolent or philanthropic institution or a trustee of any private trust to the other directors trustees or governors (as the case may be) of the benefit of his learning and experience on matters of general policy and of general legal principle applicable to the affairs of the company institution or trust;

'litigator' means an authorised litigator as defined in Section 119 of the Act;

'non-practising barrister' means a barrister who is neither a barrister in independent practice nor an employed barrister;

'Overseas work' means work undertaken by a barrister in independent practice pursuant to a brief or instructions delivered in accordance with the Overseas Practice Rules (reproduced in Annexe D) and so that 'Overseas matter' shall have a corresponding meaning;

'practising barrister' means a barrister who is either a barrister in independent practice or an employed barrister;

'professional client' means the solicitor or other proper professional person by whom a barrister in independent practice is instructed that is to say:

(a)   a solicitor litigator Parliamentary agent patent agent trade mark agent or London Notary;

(b)   a member of a recognised professional body in a matter of a kind which falls generally within the professional expertise of the members of the recognised professional body and in circumstances complying with the Direct Professional Access Rules (reproduced in Annexe C);

(c)   a Licensed Conveyancer or authorised practitioner in a matter in which the Licensed Conveyancer or authorised practitioner is providing conveyancing services;

(d)   the Government Legal Service;

(e)   the legal department of a local authority or other public authority if that department is headed by a barrister or a solicitor;

(f)   an employed barrister;

(g)   a barrister who is employed at a Law Centre or a Legal Advice Centre;

(h)   an arbitrator (including for these purposes an adjudicator under the Housing Grants Construction and Regeneration Act 1996) for the purpose of advising on any point of law practice or procedure arising in or connected with an arbitration in which he has been or may be appointed;

(i)   a person who has been appointed an Ombudsman and whose office as Ombudsman has been recognised by the Bar Council for the purpose of advising on any point of law practice or procedure arising in the course of the performance of his duties;

'recognised professional body' means a professional body which has been approved by the Bar Council for the purpose of Direct Professional Access work;

any reference to the masculine shall be deemed to include the feminine.

PART X - TRANSITIONAL PROVISIONS

1001   In respect of anything done or omitted to be done or otherwise arising before 1 October 1998:

(a)   this Code shall not apply;

(b)   the Code of Conduct in force at the relevant time shall notwithstanding paragraph 101.1 apply as if this Code had not been adopted by the Bar Council.

SECTION 2

Table of Annexes

A   Pupillage Guidelines

B   The Terms of Work on which Barristers Offer their Services to Solicitors and the Withdrawal of Credit Scheme 1988

C   The Direct Professional Access Rules

D   The Overseas Practice Rules

E   The Conveyancing by Employed Barristers Rules

F   Written Standards for the conduct of Professional Work

G   The Dual Qualification Rules

H   The Law Centres and Legal Advice Centres Rules

I   The Foreign Lawyers (Chambers) Rules

J   The Code of Conduct for Lawyers in the European Community

K   The Complaints Rules

L   The Disciplinary Tribunals Regulations

M   The Hearings before the Visitors Rules

N   The Summary Procedure Rules

O   Summary of the Equality Code for the Bar

P   The Adjudication Panel and Appeals Rules

Q   The Continuing Education Scheme Rules

ANNEXE A

PUPILLAGE GUIDELINES

PUPILLAGE GUIDELINES

PART I - Administration

A   Applications for pupillage and tenancies

1   General

(a)   All applications should be considered fairly.

(b)   When considering applications the desirability of proper representation within chambers of persons of different race ethnic origin sex religion or political persuasion should be borne in mind.

2   Advertisement of Vacancies

(a) Chambers should publicise vacancies for pupillage as widely as possible.

(b)   In particular

(i)   all pupillage vacancies should be advertised in the Bar Council's Chambers Pupillages and Awards booklet together with details of such awards or other financial arrangements as are made for pupils and should be advertised at each of the Inns of Court and at each of the Bar Vocational Course providers;

(ii)   all pupillage vacancies should also be notified to the Bar Council in such a way as to ensure that the information is at all times kept up to date.

(c)   Notices should state any minimum education or other qualification required.

3   Selection Procedures

(a)   Chambers should establish and follow selection procedures in order to ensure that applications are dealt with as fairly as possible.

(b)   In particular it is recommended that:

(i)   a decision to reject an applicant without an interview should where practicable be a decision taken or concurred in by more than one member of chambers;

(ii)   a decision to offer a place to an applicant or to refuse a place to an applicant who has been interviewed should always be a decision taken or concurred in by more than one member of chambers;

(iii)   applicants who are interviewed should at an early stage of the interview be informed of the chambers selection procedure;

(iv)   interviews should be conducted by as wide a cross-section of chambers as possible;

(v)   interviews should be conducted so as to avoid giving unnecessary offence.

B   Distribution of Work in Chambers

1   The distribution of briefs among working pupils should be carried out in a manner fair to all pupils.

2   Every set of chambers should where Court appearances by working pupils are a regular occurrence establish a system for the purpose of regulating the distribution of briefs or instructions among pupils. The system should be made known to pupils at the commencement of pupillage.

3   It is recognised that any system must allow for flexibility so as to enable the particular qualities and experience of particular pupils to be taken into account. But a brief or instructions which in accordance with the chambers system would normally have gone to a particular pupil should not unless it is unavoidable be diverted elsewhere except as a result of a decision made after discussion with the pupil master the member of chambers to whom responsibility for pupils has been delegated or the head of chambers.

4   In the event that a brief for a set of chambers has been diverted from the pupil to whom it would normally have gone the pupil master should (unless he or she knew of the decision) be informed as soon as possible. The pupil master should explain the position to the pupil.

5   No work should ever be diverted at the request of the professional client if it is believed by the person asked to make such a diversion that the request is the result of prejudice based on race, colour, ethnic or national origin, nationality, citizenship, sex, sexual orientation, marital status, disability, religion or political persuasion on the part of the professional or lay client in question.

6   Any request whether expressed or implied by a professional client that work be not given to a barrister on the grounds of — race, colour, ethnic or national origin, nationality, citizenship, sex, sexual orientation, marital status, disability, religion or political persuasion — should at once be reported to the head of chambers or senior member of chambers present at the time who shall forthwith report the matter to the Chairman of the Race Relations Committee of the Bar Council if it relates to race or ethnic origin and to the Chairman of the Professional Standards Committee of the Bar Council in any other case.

C   Documentation and Records

1   Every set of chambers taking pupils should prepare a document setting out generally its policies in relation to the choice and number of pupils the finance available to pupils the role and duties of pupils in those chambers the pattern of pupillage the check list used for pupillage and the general policy as to recruitment of tenants and in relation to pupils not taken on as tenants.

2   Records should be kept of all applicants for a period of two years in order to enable as a minimum the completion of the Bar Council's Race Relations Committee questionnaire.

3   Records should indicate the manner in which applications are disposed of and where discernible the race ethnic origin sex or religion of each applicant.

4   The check list referred to in paragraph C1 shall be in a form either generally or specially approved by the Education & Training Committee of the Bar Council or an appropriate specialist bar association.

5   Completed check lists shall be signed and dated by the pupil master and retained in chambers for a minimum period of three years. As part of monitoring of pupillage, check lists should be available on request for inspection by the Bar Council or a review panel.

PART II - Conduct of Pupillage

The general obligations and functions of a pupil master are as follows:

1   He should ensure that the pupil is well grounded in the rules of conduct and etiquette of the Bar.

2   He should ensure that his pupil is provided with and retains the check list referred to in Part I paragraphs C1 and C4 and completes it conscientiously and accurately.

3   He should require his pupil to read his papers and draft pleadings and other documents including opinions and should require his pupil to accompany him to court on sufficient occasions so that the pupil has the opportunity to do all such work and gain all such experience as is appropriate for a person commencing practice in the type of work done by the pupil master and in any event so as to enable the pupil to complete the check list.

4   He should take all reasonable steps to enable his pupil to see work done by junior members of chambers.

5   He should require his pupil to attend at least sufficient conferences to enable the pupil to obtain experience in how to conduct a conference.

6   In the second six months he should take a direct interest in and monitor all work his pupil does on his own. In particular he should in relation to court appearances by his pupil give assistance before he goes into court and the opportunity for discussion afterwards. He should however take all reasonable steps to ensure that his pupil does not do so much work of his own that his pupillage is impaired.

7   He should encourage a relationship between himself his chambers colleagues and his pupil whereby the pupil is encouraged to discuss problems and receive information on matters relating to practice and etiquette. He may and in appropriate circumstances should arrange for his pupil to spend time with and see the work of other members of chambers.

8   He must if it is proper for him to do so provide for his pupil the appropriate certificate required by the pupil pursuant to the Consolidated Regulations at the end of each relevant period of pupillage or take the necessary steps to ensure that some other person entitled by the Consolidated Regulations to sign such a certificate does so.

ANNEXE B

THE TERMS OF WORK ON WHICH BARRISTERS OFFER THEIR SERVICES TO SOLICITORS AND THE WITHDRAWAL OF CREDIT SCHEME 1988

THE TERMS OF WORK ON WHICH BARRISTERS OFFER THEIR SERVICES TO SOLICITORS AND THE WITHDRAWAL OF CREDIT SCHEME 1988

(As authorised by the General Council of the Bar on 16 July 1988 and amended by authority of the General Council of the Bar on 10 November 1990)

WHEREAS:

(1)   These Terms have been authorised by the General Council of the Bar and are intended to apply (save as hereinafter provided) in any case where a barrister is instructed by a solicitor;

(2)   Any solicitor who sends a brief or instructions to a barrister will be deemed to instruct that barrister on these Terms unless and to the extent that they have either in relation to the particular matter or generally been excluded or varied by agreement in writing between the barrister and the solicitor;

AND WHEREAS:

(3)   By the established custom of the profession a barrister looks for payment of his fees to the solicitor who instructs him and not to his lay client;

(4)   Except in legal aid cases a solicitor is personally liable as a matter of professional conduct for the payment of a barrister's proper fees whether or not he has been placed in funds by his lay client;

(5)   Where instructions have been given in the name of a firm all partners at that date incur personal liability and remain liable for the payment of counsel's fees incurred on behalf of the firm by a deceased bankrupt or otherwise defaulting former partner of the firm; and

(6)   The liability of a sole practitioner and of partners for the liabilities of their co-partners is a continuing one and is not cancelled or superseded by any transfer of the practice or dissolution of the partnership;

WITH EFFECT from 1 February 1991 the following will take effect:-

General

1   A solicitor may in his capacity as a director partner member employee consultant associate or other agent of a company firm or other body brief or instruct a barrister.

2   In any case where a barrister accepts a brief or instructions from a solicitor in his capacity as a director partner member employee consultant associate or agent of a company firm or other body:

      (a)   the solicitor warrants that he is authorised by his company firm or other body to instruct the barrister;

      (b)   the obligations of the solicitor under these Terms (including in particular his responsibility for the payment of the barrister's fees) shall be the joint and several obligations of him and that company firm or other body.

Instructions

3   A barrister has the duty or the right in certain circumstances set out in the Bar Code of Conduct to refuse to accept a brief or instruction and these Terms will apply only where the barrister has accepted the brief or instructions.

4   Notwithstanding that a brief or instructions have been delivered to a barrister the barrister shall not be deemed to have accepted that brief or those instructions until he has had a reasonable opportunity:

      (a)   to peruse them;

      (b)   in the case of a brief to agree a fee with the solicitor.

5   A barrister accepts a brief or instructions upon the understanding:

      (a)   that he must and will comply with the Bar Code of Conduct;

      (b)   that he will deal with instructions as soon as he reasonably can in the ordinary course of his work.

6   (1)   Where for any reason time is of the essence the solicitor must at the time when he delivers the brief or instructions but separately from the brief or instructions themselves inform the barrister of that fact and of the particular reason for urgency in order that the barrister may decide whether in those circumstances he can accept the brief or instructions. In addition the brief or instructions must be clearly marked 'Urgent.'

(2)   In the case of legal aid work the solicitor must at the time when he delivers the brief or instructions (or if any relevant certificate is not then available to him as soon as reasonably practicable thereafter) supply the barrister with copies of any relevant legal aid certificates.

Copies of Briefs and Instructions and Records of Advice

7   A barrister shall be entitled for the purposes of his records (but not otherwise) to retain his brief or instructions or any papers delivered therewith or (if the solicitor requires the return of such brief or instructions and papers) to take and retain a copy of such brief or instructions and papers and of any written advice PROVIDED that nothing shall entitle a barrister to exercise any lien over any brief instructions or papers.

Fees

8   Save in the case of legal aid work or in the case of a Notified Solicitor a barrister and solicitor may (subject to any rules regarding contingent fees) make such agreement or arrangement between them as to the time or times whether at the time of delivery of the brief or instructions or subsequently thereto or otherwise at which the barrister's fees shall be paid as they may think fit and the barrister's fees shall be paid by the solicitor accordingly PROVIDED that every such agreement or arrangement shall be recorded in writing.

9   Save in the case of legal aid work or in the case of work the fees for which are to be paid out of a fund but cannot be so paid without an order of the court a barrister may and in the case of fees payable by a Notified Solicitor a barrister (unless and except as otherwise previously authorised in writing by the Chairman) must require his fees to be agreed and paid before he accepts the brief or instructions to which the fees relate.

10   (1)   The barrister shall submit an itemised fee note not later than three months after the work to which the fee note relates has been done or at the conclusion of the matter in which the barrister is briefed or instructed whichever is the sooner.

(2)   The barrister shall as soon as reasonably practicable comply with a request by the solicitor for a fee note.

(3)   Every fee note shall include the solicitor's reference and (where appropriate) the barrister's case reference number the barrister's legal aid account number and any legal aid certificate number and date of issue.

(4) If any fees remain outstanding at the conclusion of a case the solicitor shall as soon as reasonably practicable inform the barrister that the case has concluded.

11   In the case of legal aid work:

(a) the solicitor and barrister shall respectively take such steps as may be open to each of them to take under the Legal Aid Regulations for the time being in force for the purpose of obtaining payment of the barrister's fees as soon as reasonably practicable;

(b) the solicitor shall as soon as reasonably practicable comply with a request by the barrister for information by (i) notifying the barrister of the date of issue and number and supplying the barrister with copies of any relevant legal aid certificates (ii) notifying the barrister of the date of any order for taxation or other event giving rise to a right to taxation (iii) informing the barrister of the steps taken by him pursuant to paragraph 11(a) hereof;

(c) the barrister unless such information and an explanation for non-payment satisfactory to him is thereupon received from the solicitor shall then report the facts to the Chairman.

12   In the case of work the fees for which are to be paid out of a fund but cannot be so paid without an order of the court:

(a) the solicitor shall use his best endeavours to obtain such order or orders as may be requisite to enable payment of the fees to be made as soon as reasonably practicable;

(b) the solicitor shall as soon as reasonably practicable comply with a request by the barrister for information by informing the barrister of the steps taken by him pursuant to paragraph 12(a) hereof;

(c) the barrister unless such information and an explanation for non-payment satisfactory to him is thereupon received from the solicitor shall then report the facts to the Chairman.

13   Save as aforesaid and subject to any such agreement or arrangement as is referred to in paragraph 8 hereof the barrister's fees if and to the extent that such fees have not been previously paid shall unless challenged by the solicitor as hereinafter provided be paid by the solicitor within three months after the fee note relating thereto has been sent to the solicitor whether or not the solicitor has been placed in funds by his client and whether or not the case is still continuing.

14   (1)   Any challenge by a solicitor to a barrister's fee (whether giving rise to an issue of competence or a dispute on quantum or otherwise) must be made by the solicitor in writing within three months after the first fee note relating to that fee has been sent to him or within one month after such letter relating to that fee as is referred to in paragraph 15(a) hereof has been sent to him whichever is the later.

(2)   No challenge to a barrister's fees will be accepted either by the barrister or in the case of a complaint by the barrister to the Bar Council of failure to pay those fees by the Bar Council unless:

(a)   the challenge was made in accordance with paragraph 14(1) hereof; and

(b)   the solicitor has within 14 days of being requested to do so either by the barrister or by the Bar Council agreed in writing (i) to submit the issue or dispute giving rise to the challenge to the decision of a Tribunal (ii) to abide by and forthwith give effect to the decision of the Tribunal.

15   Save as aforesaid and subject to any such agreement or arrangement as is referred to in paragraph 8 hereof the barrister if and to the extent that his fees have not been previously paid:

(a)   may at any time after the expiration of one month after the first fee note relating thereto has been sent send a reminder substantially in the form of the letter annexed hereto and marked 'A' or some reasonable adaptation thereof; and

(b)   unless an explanation for non-payment satisfactory to the barrister has been received shall at the expiration of three months after the first fee note relating thereto has been sent send a further reminder substantially in the form of the letter annexed hereto and marked 'B' or some reasonable adaptation thereof; and

(c)   unless an explanation for non-payment satisfactory to the barrister is thereupon received shall then report the facts to the Chairman.

Withdrawal of Credit

16   In any case where a barrister has made a report to the Chairman in accordance with paragraphs 11(c) 12(c) or 15(c) hereof and in any other case in which he is satisfied that it is appropriate to do so:

(a)   the Chairman may write a letter in the form of the letter annexed hereto and marked 'C' or some reasonable adaptation thereof; and

(b)   the Chairman shall report the facts to the Bureau unless within fourteen days after the letter referred to in paragraph 16(a) hereof has been sent either the fees referred to therein have been paid in full or an explanation for non-payment satisfactory to the Chairman has been received.

17   (1)   This paragraph applies where the following conditions are satisfied namely where:

(a)   such a letter as is referred to in paragraph 16(a) hereof has been sent and no explanation for non-payment satisfactory to the Chairman has been received; and

(b)   either (i) any fees referred to in such letter which are in the opinion of the Chairman properly payable remain unpaid or (ii) in the event that all such fees have been paid not more than twelve months have elapsed since payment or since the Chairman reported the facts to the Bureau (whichever is the later); and

(c)   circumstances have arisen in which the Chairman would otherwise have occasion to send to any person liable for the fees or to any connected person a further letter such as is referred to in paragraph 16(a) hereof.

(2)   In any case in which paragraph 17(1) hereof applies the Chairman shall write to such person or persons (as the case may be) to the effect that unless written representations received by him within 14 days after the date of such letter or within such extended period as he may allow justify an exceptional departure from the following course he will and unless persuaded by such representations not to do so the Chairman whether or not any fees remain unpaid shall:

(a)   issue a direction that no barrister may without the written consent of the Chairman (which consent may be sought urgently in exceptional cases) knowingly accept instructions in a privately funded case from any person or firm named in such direction or from any person who or firm which is or has at any time since the direction was issued been a connected person unless such instructions are accompanied by payment of an agreed fee for such work or unless he agrees in advance to accept no fee for such work; and

(b)   cause the names of the persons or firms named in such direction to be included in a list of persons and firms named in such directions to be circulated by pre-paid first-class post to all such persons and firms to all the Clerks and Heads of Chambers in England and Wales to the Master of the Rolls and to the President of the Law Society notifying them of such direction.

18   Notwithstanding anything to the contrary herein if in any case the Chairman is satisfied that it is appropriate to issue a direction such as is referred to in paragraph 17(2)(a) hereof in respect of any person or firm named in such direction and to circulate a list such as is referred to in paragraph 17(2)(b) hereof including the

names of the persons or firms named in such direction he may after giving such persons and firms due notice of why he considers it appropriate to take such course and after considering any written representations and after consultation with the Law Society issue a direction in respect of and cause the list to include the names of such persons and firms as may be appropriate.

19   The list referred to in paragraphs 17 and 18 hereof shall be circulated monthly unless there have been in the meantime no additions to or deletions from the list.

20   Any Notified Solicitor and any barrister may at any time after the expiration of six months after the name of any person or firm was first included in such a list seek the revocation of any relevant direction and the amendment of the list and the Chairman after considering any written representations and after consultation with the Law Society shall be empowered (but shall not be obliged) to accede to such application upon such terms as he considers appropriate.

Definitions and consequential provisions

21   For the purpose hereof:

  (i)   'Bar Code of Conduct' shall mean the Code of Conduct of the Bar of England and Wales for the time being in force;

  (ii)   'brief' 'instructions' and 'lay client' shall have the meanings assigned to them respectively in the Bar Code of Conduct;

  (iii) 'solicitor' shall where the context admits include any solicitor liable for the fees;

  (iv)   'person liable for the fees' shall mean any solicitor liable for the fees and any person company firm or other body responsible by virtue of paragraph 2(b) hereof for the payment of the fees;

  (v)   'connected person' shall mean any person who from time to time is either

    (a) a partner employee consultant or associate of any firm of which any person liable for the fees or any Notified Solicitor is a partner employee consultant or associate;

    (b) the employer of any person liable for the fees or of any Notified Solicitor;

    (c) an employee of any person liable for the fees or of any Notified Solicitor;

(d)   a firm of which any person liable for the fees or any Notified Solicitor is a partner employee consultant or associate;

(vi)   'Notified Solicitor' shall mean any person or firm whose name is for the time being included in the list referred to in paragraphs 17 and 18 hereof and any person who or firm which is or has at any time since the direction was issued been a connected person;

(vii)   'Tribunal' shall mean a Tribunal consisting of a barrister nominated by the Chairman and a solicitor nominated by the President of the Law Society;

(viii)   'the Chairman' shall mean the Chairman of the Bar Council and shall include any person including in particular the Vice Chairman of the Bar and the Chairman of the Legal Aid and Fees Committee to whom the Chairman may have delegated either the whole or any part of his responsibilities hereunder;

(ix)   'the Bureau' shall mean the Solicitors Complaints Bureau;

(x)   any letter written by the Chairman to any person pursuant to or which would otherwise have been effective for the purposes of either the Withdrawal of Credit Scheme which came into effect on 2 March 1987 or the Withdrawal of Credit Scheme 1988 as originally enacted shall in relation to such person be deemed to be such a letter as is referred to in paragraph 16(a) hereof.

22   Any fee note and any such letter as is referred to in paragraphs 15(a) 15(b) 16(a) 17(2) or 18 hereof may be sent and shall be treated as having been properly and sufficiently sent to each and every person liable for the fees and to each and every connected person (as the case may be) if posted by pre-paid first-class post or sent through any Document Exchange or by facsimile transmission addressed to:

(a)   any person liable for the fees; or

(b)   if any person liable for the fees is either a partner of or consultant to or associate of or employed by another or others to the person liable for the fees or to his employer or to his senior partner (as the case may be); or

(c)   if any such person practises (whether on his own or in partnership with others or otherwise) under a name other than his own to the firm under whose name he practises;

and addressed to any place at which such person or his employer or any partner of his carries on practice.

23   Any such letter as is referred to in paragraphs 17(2) or 18 hereof shall:

(a)   identify any earlier matters of complaint;

(b)   state the Chairman's proposed course of action; and

(c)   enclose a copy of this document provided that any accidental omission or failure to enclose such a copy may be remedied by the sending of a separate copy as soon as the Chairman is made aware of such omission or failure.

24   Any such direction as is referred to in paragraphs 17 or 18 hereof may contain or be amended so as to add or include any or all of the names and addresses:

(a)   of any person liable for the fees;

(b)   of any connected person; and

(c)   if any such person practises (whether on his own or in partnership with others or otherwise) under a name other than his own of the firm under whose name he practises.

Status of these Terms

25   Neither the General Council of the Bar in authorising these Terms nor a barrister in offering his services to a solicitor on these Terms has any intention to create legal relations or to enter into any contract or other obligation binding in law.

26   Neither the sending by a solicitor of a brief or instructions to a barrister nor the acceptance by a barrister of a brief or instructions nor anything done in connection therewith nor the arrangements relating thereto (whether mentioned in these Terms or in the Bar Code of Conduct or to be implied) nor these Terms or any agreement or transaction entered into or payment made by or under them shall be attended by or give rise to any contractual relationship rights duties or consequences whatsoever or be legally enforceable by or against or be the subject of litigation with either the barrister or the General Council of the Bar.

Exclusion or variation

27   The above Terms as to payment of fees and otherwise are the only terms on which barristers offer their services to solicitors. A solicitor who sends a brief or instructions to a barrister will be deemed to instruct that barrister on these Terms unless and to the extent that they have either in relation to the particular matter or generally been excluded or varied by agreement in writing between the barrister and the solicitor.

LETTER 'A'

(To be sent 1 month after fee note)

Privately funded cases

Dear Sir,

Re:_____

I refer to the Fee Note of [name of barrister] in respect of the above case which was sent to you on the [date].

My records indicate that this is a privately funded case and I would be grateful if you could make arrangements for these fees to be paid or let me know when payment may be expected.

Yours faithfully,

Clerk to [name of barrister]

Legal aid cases

Dear Sir,   [Legal Aid Certificate Number]
                                                                    [Date of issue]
Re:_____

I refer to the Fee Note of [name of barrister] in respect of the above case which was sent to you on the [date].

My records indicate that this is a legal aid case and I would be grateful if you could let me know when payment may be expected.

Yours faithfully,

Clerk to [name of barrister]

LETTER 'B'

(To be sent 3 months after fee note)

Privately funded cases

Dear Sir,

Re:_____

I have referred to [name of barrister] the letter I wrote to you concerning the fees in this matter. To date payment has not been made and no explanation for the non-payment has been forthcoming.

As you know Counsel is required as a matter of professional conduct to report to the Chairman of the General Council of the Bar the fact that these fees have been outstanding for more than three months without satisfactory explanation. Unless, therefore, I hear from you within the next 14 days I regret that Counsel will have no alternative other than to make such a report.

I sincerely trust that this will not be necessary and look forward to hearing from you in early course.

Yours faithfully,

Clerk to [name of barrister]

Legal aid cases

Dear Sir,   [Legal Aid Certificate Number]
                                                   [Date of issue]

Re:_____

I have referred to [name of barrister] the letter I wrote to you concerning the fees in this matter. To date payment has not been received.

My records indicate that this is a legal aid case. I must therefore ask you to notify me of:

(a) the date of issue and number of the relevant legal aid certificate(s);

(b) the date of any order for taxation or other event giving rise to a right to taxation; and

(c) the steps you have taken under the Legal Aid Regulations for the purpose of obtaining payment of Mr [name of barrister]'s fees.

Would you also supply me with copies of the relevant legal aid certificate(s).

As you know Counsel is required as a matter of professional conduct to report the matter to the Chairman of the General Council of the Bar unless he receives in response to this letter the information requested above and a satisfactory explanation for the fact that he has not yet been paid. Unless, therefore, I hear from you within the next 14 days I regret that Counsel will have no alternative other than to make such a report.

I sincerely trust that this will not be necessary and look forward to hearing from you in early course.

Yours faithfully,

Clerk to [name of barrister]

LETTER 'C'

(Chairman's First Letter)

Dear Sir,

I refer to Counsel's fees particulars of which are set out in the Schedule. Fee notes (attached) have been rendered and letters written regarding payment of these fees. Payment has not been received; consequently the matter has now, pursuant to the professional obligation to do so, been referred by Counsel to the General Council of the Bar.

[Complaints relating to or including privately funded cases: I would remind you again of your professional obligation to pay Counsel's fees in non legal aid matters irrespective of whether you have been placed in funds by your client.

Unless you challenged Counsel's fees in writing within 3 months after the first fee note was sent to you, I would ask you to pay Counsel within 14 days of the date of this letter. Failure to do so, or to supply a satisfactory explanation for non-payment, will mean, regrettably, that it will be necessary to refer these matters to the Solicitors Complaints Bureau.]

[Complaints relating to or including legal aid cases: Insofar as this complaint relates to a legal aid matter please within 14 days of the date of this letter:

(a) notify me of the date of issue and number and supply me with copies of any relevant legal aid certificates;

(b) notify me of the date of any order for taxation or other event giving rise to a right to taxation; and

(c) inform me of what steps you have taken under the Legal Aid Regulations for the purpose of obtaining payment of Counsel's fees.

Failure to do so, or to supply a satisfactory explanation for the fact that Counsel has not yet been paid, will [likewise OR regrettably] necessitate referral of the matter to the Solicitors Complaints Bureau.]

I am also enclosing for your attention a copy of The Terms of Work on which Barristers offer their services to Solicitors and the Withdrawal of Credit Scheme 1988 (as amended). You will appreciate from reading the text of the Scheme that its effect is such that if good grounds as specified above for withholding payment do not exist and the Chairman has occasion to write again in respect of other outstanding fees within the period referred to in paragraph 17(1)(b) of the Scheme, then the consequences spelt out in paragraph 17(2) of the Scheme will, save in the most exceptional circumstances, follow. In other words, credit will be withdrawn.

I hope that it will not be necessary to implement the Scheme in any case and that Counsel's fees will be paid promptly when due. However, should it be necessary to do so, I would want you to be fully informed in advance of the problems which would attend non-payment in due time of Counsel's fees.

It may be necessary to amend the Scheme from time to time and any such amendments will be drawn to your attention.

Yours faithfully,

[Name]
CHAIRMAN OF THE BAR

encls:

THE SCHEDULE

Name and address of Counsel   Fees in the matter of

[Here list name(s) and address(es) of Counsel and name(s) of case(s)]

THE DIRECT PROFESSIONAL ACCESS RULES

THE DIRECT PROFESSIONAL ACCESS RULES

1   A barrister must not accept any brief or instructions in a Direct Professional Access matter if he considers it in the interests of the lay client that a solicitor be instructed.

2   A barrister must decline to act further in a Direct Professional Access matter in which at any stage he considers it in the interests of the lay client that a solicitor be instructed.

3   A barrister must not accept any brief in a Direct Professional Access matter to appear in the Judicial Committee of the House of Lords the Privy Council the Supreme Court the Crown Court a County Court or the Employment Appeals Tribunal.

4   A barrister who accepts a brief or instructions in a Direct Professional Access matter must:

(a)   keep a case record (whether on card or computer) which sets out:

(i)   the date of receipt of the brief or instructions the name of the professional client the name of the case and any requirements of the professional client as to time limits;

(ii)   the date on which the brief or instructions were accepted;

(iii)   the terms on which the brief or instructions were accepted;

(iv)   the dates of subsequent instructions of the despatch of advices and other written work of conferences and of telephone conversations;

(v)   when agreed the fee;

(vi)   when made any promises or undertakings as to the completion of the work;

(vii)   as soon as they become apparent to the barrister any time limits;

(b)   retain:

(i)   copies of briefs and instructions (including supplemental instructions) save where and to the extent that the professional client has entered into an agreement to retain them on his behalf;

(ii)   copies of all advices given and documents drafted or approved;

(iii)   a list of all documents enclosed with any brief or instructions;

(iv)   notes of all conferences and of all advice given on the telephone; and

(c)   keep a forward diary (which may be kept on a chambers' basis or for each individual barrister provided that in either case it is easy to inspect and is regularly inspected) of all statutory or other time limits which are applicable to or which arise out of current Direct Professional Access matters.

ANNEXE D

THE OVERSEAS PRACTICE RULES

Amended 28 November 1998

THE OVERSEAS PRACTICE RULES

A barrister in independent practice may without prejudice to any other rules of conduct binding upon him but

(i)   subject so far as is appropriate to any requirements binding on him under local law or under rules which may be prescribed by national or local bars of the place where he is providing legal services; and

(ii)   provided that he does not accept the status of an employee or of a commercial or business agent; and

(iii)   provided that the work does not involve the performance in England and Wales of excepted work or the receipt or handling of clients' money in any jurisdiction;

do any of the following:

(1)   Accept instructions from any person qualified and practising as a foreign lawyer where all the following conditions are satisfied:

(a)   the work does not involve the barrister providing advocacy services before a court within the meaning of the Courts and Legal Services Act 1990, unless the foreign lawyer has a right to conduct litigation in that court pursuant to that Act or relevant provisions of Community law;

(b)   in respect of work before a court within the meaning of the Courts and Legal Services Act 1990, the work does not involve the barrister providing services other than advocacy services;

(c)   either the foreign lawyer is not a member of the barrister's chambers in England or Wales or the lay client carries on business or usually resides, and the instructions emanate from, outside England and Wales; and

(d)   the work is not conveyancing work or work falling within sections 22 or 23 of the Solicitors Act 1974 and usually performed by solicitors;

(2)   Accept instructions from any client:

(a)   for professional work relating to matters essentially arising taking place or contemplated outside the United Kingdom which is to be substantially performed outside the United Kingdom; or

(b)   for professional work (i) whether or not to be performed in the United Kingdom for the purpose of or in connection with litigation or arbitration or other proceedings outside the United Kingdom or (ii) which consists of giving advice incidental and subsidiary to work falling within paragraph (2)(a).

Amended 28 November 1998

(3)   Accept instructions from any client other than a foreign lawyer where the lay client carries on business outside England and Wales or usually resides outside England and Wales provided that:

(a)   the instructions emanate from outside the United Kingdom;

(b)   the work does not involve the barrister in providing advocacy services or conducting a litigation in a court within the meaning of the Courts and Legal Services Act 1990; and

(c)   the work is not conveyancing work or work falling within sections 22 and 23 of the Solicitors Act 1974 and usually performed by solicitors;

(4)   In relation to work failing within paragraphs (1) (2) or (3) accept (otherwise than as an employee) an annual fee or retainer a fixed fee or a conditional or contingent fee where this is permissible under the laws or rules of the place where the services are to be provided, and at his sole discretion agree any reduction in fees.

(5)   Employ outside the United Kingdom any person who is not a solicitor practising in England and Wales.

(6)   Enter into any association (including partnership) with any lawyer for the purpose of sharing any office or services outside the United Kingdom or doing or sharing fees relating to any work falling within paragraphs (1) (2) (3) or (4) provided that no such association shall be created or subsist with any solicitor practising in the United Kingdom or with any firm of solicitors so practising.

Amended 28 November 1998

THE CONVEYANCING BY EMPLOYED BARRISTERS RULES

THE CONVEYANCING BY EMPLOYED BARRISTERS RULES

1   An employed barrister who undertakes any form of conveyancing work must comply with these rules.

2   An employed barrister must not carry out conveyancing work unless:

(a)   he has submitted to the Bar Council such evidence as may reasonably be required as to his entitlement to exercise the right to carry out conveyancing; and

(b)   his name has been included in and remains in a Register maintained for that purpose by the Bar Council.

3   Application for entry on the Register must be made in the form set out in the Schedule to this Annex.

4   The Register will list the names of all barristers who have submitted applications and appear to be qualified. Entry on the Register is not be taken as a representation that any requirement as to insurance under paragraph 7 was or continues to be complied with.

5   An employed barrister will not be permitted to undertake conveyancing work unless:

(a)   he has passed the paper in Practical Conveyancing in the Bar Examination; or

(b)   he has passed at an approved standard such other examination in Practical Conveyancing as the Bar Council may from time to time approve;

and has in any case satisfied the Bar Council that he has had adequate working experience of practical conveyancing for at least two years provided that the Bar Council may in the case of a barrister called before 1st August 1980 grant exemption from the requirements set out at (a) and (b) above if the barrister has had adequate working experience of practical conveyancing for a substantially greater period.

6   The Bar Council may remove a barrister's name from the Register:

(a)   if he ceases to satisfy the requirements of these rules; or

(b)   if removal is ordered by a Disciplinary Tribunal.

7   An employed barrister undertaking conveyancing work:

(a)   must not do so unless there is in force a policy of insurance which complies with any requirement as to insurance covering the employer against liability to third parties occasioned by dishonesty misappropriation or similar conduct on the part of the barrister that may from time to time be made by the Bar Council;

(b)   must if required by the Bar Council (or a Committee acting on its behalf) when it thinks fit produce a certificate that such a policy of insurance is in force and the Bar Council may revoke the barrister's registration if such a certificate is not produced or is found inadequate;

(c)   must ensure that any sum of money due in respect of any conveyancing transaction carried out by him on behalf of his employer is not paid to himself and accordingly any contract to pay such a sum must not provide for payment to an employed barrister who is acting pursuant to these rules;

(d)   must comply with all aspects of the Code of Professional Conduct relating to conveyancing work and applying to solicitors as promulgated by the Council of The Law Society save those parts relating to the keeping of accounts;

(e)   shall be prima facie guilty of professional misconduct if he fails at any time to honour any undertaking given by him whether personally or on behalf of his employer in the course of carrying out his conveyancing work;

provided that paragraph 7(a) shall not apply to a barrister employed by the Government Legal Service a Local Authority or any other Public Authority.

The Schedule

APPLICATION TO THE BAR COUNCIL BY AN
EMPLOYED BARRISTER FOR ENTRY ON THE REGISTER
OF EMPLOYED BARRISTERS

1.   Name
Inn & Date of Call
Employer's Name
Employer's Address
Present Appointment

2.   I certify that I am employed:

(a)   wholly or primarily for the purpose of giving legal advice or performing legal services for my employer or for a holding subsidiary or associated company of my employer; and

(b)   by an organisation whose activities do not include the provision of legal advice or legal services (including conveyancing services) to the public or to the clients customers or members of the organisation connection with specific cases arising out of or in regard to their own affairs.

3.   I hereby apply for registration as entitled to do any form of Conveyancing work on behalf of my employer.

4.   * I have passed the paper in Practical Conveyancing in the Bar Examination.

* I have passed the examination in Practical Conveyancing detailed in the Schedule to this application.

* I claim exemption from the requirements set out in paragraphs 5(a) and (b) of Annex E of the Code of Conduct on the grounds set out in the Schedule to this application.

* (Delete as applicable).

5.   I have completed . . . . . . years . . . . . . months experience of Practical Conveyancing as detailed in the Schedule.

[NOTE: The Schedule should specify the part or parts of this experience which were completed under professional qualified supervision].

6.   I undertake not to do conveyancing work in pursuance of this application otherwise than for my employer (as defined in the Code of Conduct). I understand that this undertaking prevents me from doing conveyancing work for a fellow employee.

7.   I further undertake:

    (a)   not to carry out conveyancing work in pursuance of this application unless there is in force a policy of insurance which complies with any requirement as to insurance covering my employer against liability to third parties occasioned by dishonesty misappropriation or similar conduct on my part that may from time to time be made by the Bar Council. I will if so required by the Bar Council (or a Committee acting on its behalf) produce a certificate that such a policy of insurance is in force;

    (b)   to ensure that any sum of money due in respect of any conveyancing transaction carried out by me on behalf of my employer is not paid to me and that any contract to pay such a sum does not provide for payment to me.

[NOTE: Paragraph 7(a) does not apply to barristers employed by the Government Legal Service a Local Government Authority or any other Public Authority and should be deleted in an application by a barrister so employed]

8.   I understand that when acting in pursuance of this application:

    (a)   I shall be prima facie guilty of professional misconduct if I fail at any time to honour any undertaking given by me in the course of carrying out conveyancing work;

    (b)   I am required to comply with all aspects of the Code of Professional Conduct relating to Conveyancing work and applying to solicitors as promulgated by the Council of The Law Society save those parts relating to the keeping of accounts.

Date . . . .   Signature . . . .

[NOTES: 1. Two copies of this Application Form should be prepared. The original should be forwarded to the General Council of the Bar, 2/3 Cursitor Street, London

EC4A 1NE. The duplicate should be retained by the barrister.

2. This application is valid only for the employment stated on it. A barrister who changes his employment must make a fresh application for entry on the Register of Employed Barristers. It is not necessary to make fresh application in regard to a change of appointment within the same employment.

3. A Schedule setting out the matters referred to in paragraphs 4 and 5 should be attached to the completed Application Form.]

ANNEXE F

WRITTEN STANDARDS FOR THE CONDUCT OF PROFESSIONAL WORK

WRITTEN STANDARDS FOR THE CONDUCT OF PROFESSIONAL WORK

GENERAL STANDARDS

1   Introduction

1.1   These Standards are intended as a guide to the way in which a barrister should carry out his work. They consist in part of matters which are dealt with expressly in the Code of Conduct and in part of statements of good practice. They must therefore be read in conjunction with the Code of Conduct, and are to be taken into account in determining whether or not a barrister has committed a disciplinary offence. They apply to employed barristers as well as to barristers in independent practice, except where this would be inappropriate. In addition to these General Standards, there are Standards which apply specifically to the conduct of criminal cases.

2   General

2.1   The work which is within the ordinary scope of a barrister's practice consists of advocacy, drafting pleadings and other legal documents and advising on questions of law. A barrister acts only on the instructions of a professional client, and does not carry out any work by way of the management, administration or general conduct of a lay client's affairs, nor the management, administration or general conduct of litigation nor the receipt or handling of clients' money.

2.2   It is a fundamental principle which applies to all work undertaken by a barrister that a barrister is under a duty to act for any client (whether legally aided or not) in cases within his field of practice. The rules which embody this principle and the exceptions to it are set out in paragraphs 203 501 502 503 504 and 505 of the Code of Conduct.

3   Acceptance of Work

3.1   As soon as practicable after receipt of any brief or instructions a barrister should satisfy himself that there is no reason why he ought to decline to accept it.

3.2   A barrister is not considered to have accepted a brief or instructions unless he has had an opportunity to consider it and has expressly accepted it.

3.3   A barrister should always be alert to the possibility of a conflict of interests. If the conflict is between the interests of his lay client and his professional client, the conflict must be resolved in favour of the lay client. Where there is a conflict between the lay client and the Legal Aid Fund, the conflict must be resolved in favour of the lay client, subject only to compliance with the provisions of the Legal Aid Regulations.

3.4   If after a barrister has accepted a brief or instructions on behalf of more than one lay client, there is or appears to be a conflict or a significant risk of a conflict between the interests of any one or more of such clients, he must not continue to act for any client unless all such clients give their consent to his so acting.

3.5   Even if there is no conflict of interest, when a barrister has accepted a brief or instructions for any party in any proceedings, he should not accept a brief or instructions in respect of an appeal or further stage of the proceedings for any other party without obtaining the prior consent of the original client.

3.6   A barrister must not accept any brief or instructions if the matter is one in which he has reason to believe that he is likely to be a witness. If, however, having accepted a brief or instructions, it later appears that he is likely to be a witness in the case on a material question of fact, he may retire or withdraw only if he can do so without jeopardising his client's interests.

3.7   A barrister should not appear as a barrister:

         (a)   in any matter in which he is a party or has a significant pecuniary interest;

         (b)   either for or against any local authority, firm or organisation or which he is a member or in which he has directly or indirectly a significant pecuniary interest;

         (c)   either for or against any company of which he is a director, secretary or officer or in which he has directly or indirectly a significant pecuniary interest.

3.8   Apart from cases in which there is a conflict of interests, a barrister must not accept any brief or instructions if to do so would cause him to be otherwise professionally embarrassed: paragraph 501 of the Code of Conduct sets out the general principles applicable to such situations.

4   Withdrawal from a Case and Return of Brief or Instructions

4.1   When a barrister has accepted a brief for the defence of a person charged with a serious criminal offence, he should so far as reasonably practicable ensure that the risk of a conflicting professional engagement does not arise.

4.2   The circumstances in which a barrister must withdraw from a case or return his brief or instructions are set out in paragraph 506 of the Code of Conduct; the circumstances in which he is permitted to do so are set out in paragraph 507; the circumstances in which he must not do so are set out in paragraph 508.

5   Conduct of Work

5.1   A barrister must at all times promote and protect fearlessly and by all proper and lawful means his lay client's best interests.

5.2   A barrister must assist the Court in the administration of justice and, as part of this obligation and the obligation to use only proper and lawful means to promote and protect the interests of his client, must not deceive or knowingly or recklessly mislead the Court.

5.3   A barrister is at all times individually and personally responsible for his own conduct and for his professional work both in Court and out of Court.

5.4   A barrister must in all his professional activities act promptly, conscientiously, diligently and with reasonable competence and must take all reasonable and practicable steps to ensure that professional engagements are fulfilled. He must not undertake any task which:

    (a)   he knows or ought to know he is not competent to handle;

    (b)   he does not have adequate time and opportunity to prepare for or perform; or

    (c)   he cannot discharge within a reasonable time having regard to the pressure of other work.

5.5   A barrister must at all times be courteous to the Court and to all those with whom he has professional dealings.

5.6   In relation to instructions to advise or draft documents, a barrister should ensure that the advice or document is provided within such time as has been agreed with the professional client, or otherwise within a reasonable time after receipt of the relevant instructions. If it becomes apparent to the barrister that he will not be able to do the work within that time, he must inform his professional client forthwith.

5.7   Generally, a barrister should ensure that advice which he gives is practical, appropriate to the needs and circumstances of the particular client, and clearly and comprehensibly expressed.

5.8   A barrister must exercise his own personal judgment upon the substance and purpose of any advice he gives or any document he drafts. He must not devise facts which will assist in advancing his lay client's case and must not draft any originating process, statement of case, affidavit, witness statement or notice of appeal containing:

    (a)   any statement of fact or contention (as the case may be) which is not supported by his lay client or by his brief or instructions;

    (b)   any contention which he does not consider to be properly arguable;

    (c)   any allegation of fraud unless he has clear instructions to make such an allegation and has before him reasonably credible material which as it stands establishes a prima facia case of fraud; or

(d)   in the case of an affidavit or witness statement, any statement of fact other than the evidence which in substance according to his instructions, the barrister reasonably believes the witness would give if the evidence contained in the affidavit or witness statement were being given viva voce.

5.9   A barrister should be available on reasonable notice for a conference prior to the day of hearing of any case in which he is briefed; and if no such conference takes place then the barrister should be available for a conference on the day of the hearing. The venue of a conference is a matter for agreement between the barrister and his professional clients.

5.10   A barrister when conducting proceedings at Court:

(a)   is personally responsible for the conduct and presentation of his case and must exercise personal judgment upon the substance and purpose of statements made and questions asked;

(b)   must not, unless asked to do so by the Court or when appearing before a tribunal where it his duty to do so, assert a personal opinion of the facts or the law;

(c)   must ensure that the Court is informed of all relevant decisions and legislative provisions of which he is aware, whether the effect is favourable or unfavourable towards the contention for which he argues, and must bring any procedural irregularity to the attention of the Court during the hearing and not reserve such matter to be raised on appeal;

(d)   must not adduce evidence obtained otherwise than from or through his professional client or devise facts which will assist in advancing his lay client's case;

(e)   must not make statements or ask questions which are merely scandalous or intended or calculated only to vilify, insult or annoy either a witness or some other person;

(f)   must if possible avoid the naming in open Court of third parties whose character would thereby be impugned;

(g)   must not by assertion in a speech impugn a witness whom he has had an opportunity to cross-examine unless in cross-examination he has given the witness an opportunity to answer the allegation;

(h)   must not suggest that a victim, witness or other person is guilty of crime, fraud or misconduct or make any defamatory aspersion on the conduct of any other person or attribute to another person the crime or conduct of which his lay client is accused unless such allegations go to a matter in issue (including the credibility of the witness) which is material to his lay client's case, and which appear to him to be supported by reasonable grounds.

5.11 A barrister must take all reasonable and practicable steps to avoid unnecessary expense or waste of the Court's time. He should, when asked, inform the Court of the probable length of his case; and he should also inform the Court of any developments which affect information already provided.

5.12 In Court a barrister's personal appearance should be decorous, and his dress, when robes are worn, should be compatible with them.

6.1 Witnesses

6.1.1 The rules which define and regulate the barrister's functions in relation to the preparation of evidence and contact with witnesses are set out in paragraphs 501(c), 606, 607, 608, 609, and 901 of the Code of Conduct.

6.1.2 There is no longer any rule which prevents a barrister from having contact with any witness.

6.1.3 In particular, there is no longer any rule in any case (including contested cases in the Crown Court) which prevents a barrister from having contact with a witness whom he may expect to call and examine in chief, with a view to introducing himself to the witness, explaining the court's procedure (and in particular the procedure for giving evidence), and answering any questions on procedure which the witness may have.

6.1.4 It is a responsibility of a barrister, especially when the witness is nervous, vulnerable or apparently the victim of criminal or similar conduct, to ensure that those facing unfamiliar court procedures are put as much at ease as possible.

6.1.5 Unless otherwise directed by the Court or with the consent of the representative for the opposing side or of the Court, a barrister should not communicate directly or indirectly about the case with any witness, whether or not the witness is his lay client, once that witness has begun to give evidence until it has been concluded.

6.2 Discussing the Evidence with Witnesses

6.2.1 Different considerations apply in relation to contact with witnesses for the purpose of interviewing them or discussing with them (either individually or together) the substance of their evidence or the evidence of other witnesses.

6.2.2 Although there is no longer any rule which prevents a barrister from having contact with witnesses for such purposes a barrister should exercise his discretion and consider very carefully whether and to what extent such contact is appropriate, bearing in mind in particular that it is not the barrister's function (but that of his professional client) to investigate and collect evidence.

6.2.3 The guiding principle must be the obligation of counsel to promote and protect his lay client's best interests so far as that is consistent with the law and with counsel's overriding duty to the court (Code of Conduct paragraphs 202, 203).

6.2.4   A barrister should be alert to the risks that any discussion of the substance of a case with a witness may lead to suspicions of coaching, and thus tend to diminish the value of the witness's evidence in the eyes of the court, or may place the barrister in a position of professional embarrassment, for example if he thereby becomes himself a witness in the case. These dangers are most likely to occur if such discussion takes place:

(a)   before the barrister has been supplied with a proof of the witness's evidence; or

(b)   in the absence of the barrister's professional client or his representative.

A barrister should also be alert to the fact that, even in the absence of any wish or intention to do so, authority figures do subconsciously influence lay witnesses. Discussion of the substance of the case may unwittingly contaminate the witness's evidence.

6.2.5   There is particular danger where such discussions:

(a)   take place in the presence of more than one witness of fact; or

(b)   involve the disclosure to one witness of fact of the factual evidence of another witness.

These practices have been strongly deprecated by the courts as tending inevitably to encourage the rehearsal or coaching of witnesses and to increase the risk of fabrication or contamination of evidence: *R* v *Arif* (1993) May 26; *Smith New Court Securities Ltd* v *Scrimgeour Vickers (Asset Management) Ltd* [1992] BCLC 1104, [1994] 1 WLR 1271.

That is not to suggest that it is always inappropriate to disclose one witness' evidence to another. If the witness is one to be called by the other party, it is almost inevitable that a witness' attention must be drawn to discrepancies between the two statements. Discretion is, however, required, especially where the evidence of independent witnesses is involved.

6.2.6   Whilst there is no rule that any longer prevents a barrister from taking a witness statement in civil cases (for cases in the Crown Court see below), there is a distinction between the settling of a witness statement and taking a witness statement. Save in exceptional circumstances, it is not appropriate for a barrister who has taken witness statements, as opposed to settling witness statements prepared by others, to act as counsel in that case because it risks undermining the independence of the barrister as an advocate. The Cab-rank Rule does not require a barrister to agree to undertake the task of taking witness statements.

6.2.7   There is no rule which prevents a barrister from exchanging common courtesies with the other side's witnesses. However, a barrister should not discuss the substance of the case or any evidence with the other side's witnesses except in rare and exceptional circumstances and then only with the prior knowledge of his opponent.

6.3   Criminal Cases in the Crown Court

6.3.1   Contested criminal cases in the Crown Court present peculiar difficulties and may expose both barristers and witnesses to special pressures. As a general principle, therefore, with the exception of the lay client, character and expert witnesses, it is wholly inappropriate for a barrister in such a case to interview any potential witness. Interviewing includes discussing with any such witness the substance of his evidence or the evidence of other such witnesses.

6.3.2   As a general principle, prosecuting counsel should not confer with an investigator witness unless he has also discharged some supervisory responsibility in the investigation and should not confer with investigators or receive factual instructions directly from them on matters about which there is or may be a dispute.

6.3.3   There may be extraordinary circumstances in which a departure from the general principles set out in paragraphs 6.3.1 and 6.3.2 is unavoidable. An example of such circumstances is afforded by the decision in *Fergus* (1994) 98 Crim App R 313.

6.3.4   Where any barrister has interviewed any potential witness or any such witness has been interviewed by another barrister, that fact shall be disclosed to all other parties in the case before the witness is called. A written record must also be made of the substance of the interview and the reason for it.

7   Documents

7.1   A barrister should not obtain or seek to obtain a document, or knowledge of the contents of a document, belonging to another party other than by means of the normal and proper channels for obtaining such documents or such knowledge.

7.2   If a barrister comes into possession of a document belonging to another party by some means other than the normal and proper channels (for example, if the document has come into his possession in consequence of a mistake or inadvertence by another person or if the document appears to belong to another party, or to be a copy of such a document, and to be privileged from discovery or otherwise to be one which ought not to be in the possession of his professional or lay client) he should:

    (a)   where appropriate make enquiries of his professional client in order to ascertain the circumstances in which the document was obtained by his professional or lay client; and

    (b)   unless satisfied that the document has been properly obtained in the ordinary course of events at once return the document unread to the person entitled to possession of it.

7.3.1   If having come into possession of such a document the barrister reads it before he realises that he ought not to, and would be embarrassed in the discharge of his duties by his knowledge of the contents of the document, then provided he can do so without prejudice to his lay client he must return his brief or instructions and explain to his professional client why he has done so.

7.3.2   If, however, to return his brief or instructions would prejudice his lay client (for example, by reason of the proximity of the trial) he should not return his brief or instructions and should, unless the Court otherwise orders, make such use of the document as will be in his client's interests. He should inform his opponent of his knowledge of the document and of the circumstances, so far as known to him, in which the document was obtained and of his intention to use it. In the event of objection to the use of such document it is for the Court to determine what use, if any, may be made of it.

7.4   If during the course of a case a barrister becomes aware of the existence of a document which should have been but has not been disclosed on discovery he should advise his professional client to disclose it forthwith; and if it is not then disclosed, he must withdraw from the case.

8   Administration of Practice

8.1   A barrister must ensure that his practice is properly and efficiently administered in accordance with the provisions of paragraph 304 of the Code of Conduct.

8.2   A barrister should ensure that he is able to provide his professional client with full and proper details of and appropriate justification for fees which have been incurred, and a proper assessment of any work to be done, so that both the lay client and the professional client are able to determine the level of any financial commitment which has been incurred or may be incurred.

9   Not used.

STANDARDS APPLICABLE TO CRIMINAL CASES

10   Introduction

10.1   These standards are to be read together with the General Standards and the Code of Conduct. They are intended as a guide to those matters which specifically relate to practice in the criminal Courts. They are not an alternative to the General Standards, which apply to all work carried out by a barrister. Particular reference is made to those paragraphs in the General Standards relating to the general conduct of a case (5.8), conduct in Court (5.10), discussion with witnesses (6.1, 6.2) and the use of documents belonging to other parties (7.1, 7.2, 7.3), which are not repeated in these standards.

11   Responsibilities of Prosecuting Counsel

11.1   Prosecuting counsel should not attempt to obtain a conviction by all means at his command. He should not regard himself as appearing for a party. He should lay before the Court fairly and impartially the whole of the facts which comprise the case for the prosecution and should assist the Court on all matters of law applicable to the case.

11.2   Prosecuting counsel should bear in mind at all times whilst he is instructed that he is responsible for the presentation and general conduct of the case and that it is his duty to ensure that all relevant evidence is either presented by the prosecution or made available to the defence.

11.3   Prosecuting counsel should, when instructions are delivered to him, read them expeditiously and, where instructed to do so, advise or confer on all aspects of the case well before its commencement.

11.4   In relation to cases tried in the Crown Court, prosecuting counsel:

(a)   should ensure, if he is instructed to settle an indictment, that he does so promptly and within due time, and should bear in mind the desirability of not overloading an indictment with either too many defendants or too many counts, in order to present the prosecution case as simply and as concisely as possible;

(b)   should ask, if the indictment is being settled by some other person, to see a copy of the indictment and should then check it;

(c)   should decide whether any additional evidence is required and, if it is, should advise in writing and set out precisely what additional evidence is required with a view to serving it on the defence as soon as possible;

(d)   should consider whether all witness statements in the possession of the prosecution have been properly served on the defendant in accordance with the Attorney-General's Guidelines;

(e) should eliminate all unnecessary material in the case so as to ensure an efficient and fair trial, and in particular should consider the need for particular witnesses and exhibits and draft appropriate admissions for service on the defence;

(f) should in all Class 1 and Class 2 cases and in other cases of complexity draft a case summary for transmission to the Court.

11.5 Paragraphs 6 to 6.3.4 of the Written Standards for the Conduct of Professional Work refer.

11.6 Prosecuting counsel should at all times have regard to the report of Mr Justice Farquharson's Committee on the role of Prosecuting Counsel which is set out in full in volume 1 of Archbold. In particular, he should have regard to the following recommendations of the Farquharson Committee:

(a) Where counsel has taken a decision on a matter of policy with which his professional client has not agreed, it would be appropriate for him to submit to the Attorney-General a written report of all the circumstances, including his reasons for disagreeing with those who instructed him;

(b) When counsel has had an opportunity to prepare his brief and to confer with those instructing him, but at the last moment before trial unexpectedly advises that the case should not proceed or that pleas to lesser offences should be accepted, and his professional client does not accept such advice, counsel should apply for an adjournment if instructed to do so;

(c) Subject to the above, it is for prosecuting counsel to decide whether to offer no evidence on a particular count or on the indictment as a whole and whether to accept pleas to a lesser count or counts.

11.7 It is the duty of prosecuting counsel to assist the Court at the conclusion of the summing-up by drawing attention to any apparent errors or omissions of fact or law.

11.8 In relation to sentence, prosecuting counsel:

(a) should not attempt by advocacy to influence the Court with regard to sentence: if, however, a defendant is unrepresented it is proper to inform the Court of any mitigating circumstances about which counsel is instructed;

(b) should be in a position to assist the Court if requested as to any statutory provisions relevant to the offence or the offender and as to any relevant guidelines as to sentence laid down by the Court of Appeal;

(c) should bring any such matters as are referred to in (b) above to the attention of the Court if in the opinion of prosecuting counsel the Court has erred;

(d) should bring to the attention of the Court any appropriate compensation, forfeiture and restitution matters which may arise on conviction, for example pursuant to sections 35–42 of the Powers of Criminal Courts Act 1973 and the Drug Trafficking Offences Act 1986;

(e) should draw the attention of the defence to any assertion of material fact made in mitigation which the prosecution believes to be untrue: if the defence persist in that assertion, prosecuting counsel should invite the Court to consider requiring the issue to be determined by the calling of evidence in accordance with the decision of the Court of Appeal in R v Newton (1983) 77 Crim App R 13.

12   Responsibilities of Defence Counsel

12.1   When defending a client on a criminal charge, a barrister must endeavour to protect his client from conviction except by a competent tribunal and upon legally admissible evidence sufficient to support a conviction for the offence charged.

12.2   A barrister acting for the defence:

(a) should satisfy himself, if he is briefed to represent more than one defendant, that no conflict of interest is likely to arise;

(b) should arrange a conference and if necessary a series of conferences with his professional and lay clients;

(c) should consider whether any enquiries or further enquiries are necessary and, if so, should advise in writing as soon as possible;

(d) should consider whether any witnesses for the defence are required and, if so, which;

(e) should consider whether a Notice of Alibi is required and, if so, should draft an appropriate notice:

(f) should consider whether it would be appropriate to call expert evidence for the defence and, if so, have regard to the rules of the Crown Court in relation to notifying the prosecution of the contents of the evidence to be given;

(g) should ensure that he has sufficient instructions for the purpose of deciding which prosecution witnesses should be cross-examined, and should then ensure that no other witnesses remain fully bound at the request of the defendant and request his professional client to inform the Crown Prosecution Service of those who can be conditionally bound;

(h)   should consider whether any admissions can be made with a view to saving time and expense at trial, with the aim of admitting as much evidence as can properly be admitted in accordance with the barrister's duty to his client;

(i)   should consider what admissions can properly be requested from the prosecution;

(j)   should decide what exhibits, if any, which have not been or cannot be copied he wishes to examine, and should ensure that appropriate arrangements are made to examine them as promptly as possible so that there is no undue delay in the trial;

(k)   should as to anything which he is instructed to submit in mitigation which casts aspersions on the conduct or character of a victim or witness in the case, notify the prosecution in advance so as to give prosecuting Counsel sufficient opportunity to consider his position under paragraph 11.8(e).

12.3   A barrister acting for a defendant should advise his lay client generally about his plea. In doing so he may, if necessary, express his advice in strong terms. He must, however, make it clear that the client has complete freedom of choice and that the responsibility for the plea is the client's.

12.4   A barrister acting for a defendant should advise his client as to whether or not to give evidence in his own defence but the decision must be taken by the client himself.

12.5   Where a defendant tells his counsel that he did not commit the offence with which he is charged but nevertheless insists on pleading guilty to it for reasons of his own, counsel should:

(a)   advise the defendant that, if he is not guilty, he should plead not guilty but that the decision is one for the defendant; counsel must continue to represent him but only after he has advised what the consequences will be and that what can be submitted in mitigation can only be on the basis that the client is guilty.

(b)   explore with the defendant why he wishes to plead guilty to a charge which he says he did not commit and whether any steps could be taken which would enable him to enter a plea of not guilty in accordance with his profession of innocence.

12.5.2   If the client maintains his wish to plead guilty, he should be further advised:

(a)   what the consequences will be, in particular in gaining or adding to a criminal record and that it is unlikely that a conviction based on such a plea would be overturned on appeal;

(b)   that what can be submitted on his behalf in mitigation can only be on the basis that he is guilty and will otherwise be strictly limited so that, for instance, counsel will not be able to assert that the defendant has shown remorse through his guilty plea.

12.5.3   If, following all of the above advice, the defendant persists in his decision to plead guilty

(a)   counsel may continue to represent him if he is satisfied that it is proper to do so;

(b)   before a plea of guilty is entered counsel or a representative of his professional client who is present should record in writing the reasons for the plea;

(c)   the defendant should be invited to endorse a declaration that he has given unequivocal instructions of his own free will that he intends to plead guilty even though he maintains that he did not commit the offence(s) and that he understands the advice given by counsel and in particular the restrictions placed on counsel in mitigating and the consequences to himself; the defendant should also be advised that he is under no obligation to sign; and

(d)   if no such declaration is signed, counsel should make a contemporaneous note of his advice.

13   Confessions of Guilt

13.1   In considering the duty of counsel retained to defend a person charged with an offence who confesses to his counsel that he did commit the offence charged, it is essential to bear the following points clearly in mind:

(a)   that every punishable crime is a breach of common or statute law committed by a person of sound mind and understanding;

(b)   that the issue in a criminal trial is always whether the defendant is guilty of the offence charged, never whether he is innocent;

(c)   that the burden of proof rests on the prosecution.

13.2   It follows that the mere fact that a person charged with a crime has confessed to his counsel that he did commit the offence charged is no bar to that barrister appearing or continuing to appear in his defence, nor indeed does such a confession release the barrister from his imperative duty to do all that he honourably can for his client.

13.3   Such a confession, however, imposes very strict limitations on the conduct of the defence. A barrister must not assert as true that which he knows to be false. He must not connive at, much less attempt to substantiate, a fraud.

13.4   While, therefore, it would be right to take any objections to the competency of the Court, to the form of the indictment, to the admissibility of any evidence or to the evidence admitted, it would be wrong to suggest that some other person had committed the offence charged, or to call any evidence which the barrister must know to be false having regard to the confession, such, for instance, as evidence in support of an alibi. In other words, a barrister must not (whether by calling the defendant or otherwise) set up an affirmative case inconsistent with the confession made to him.

13.5   A more difficult question is within what limits may counsel attack the evidence for the prosecution either by cross-examination or in his speech to the tribunal charged with the decision of the facts. No clearer rule can be laid down than this, that he is entitled to test the evidence given by each individual witness and to argue that the evidence taken as a whole is insufficient to amount to proof that the defendant is guilty of the offence charged. Further than this he ought not to go.

13.6   The foregoing is based on the assumption that the defendant has made a clear confession that he did commit the offence charged, and does not profess to deal with the very difficult questions which may present themselves to a barrister when a series of inconsistent statements are made to him by the defendant before or during the proceedings; nor does it deal with the questions which may arise where statements are made by the defendant which point almost irresistibly to the conclusion that the defendant is guilty but do not amount to a clear confession. Statements of this kind may inhibit the defence, but questions arising on them can only be answered after careful consideration of the actual circumstances of the particular case.

14   General

14.1   Both prosecuting and defence counsel:

(a)   should ensure that the listing officer receives in good time their best estimate of the likely length of the trial (including whether or not there is to be a plea of guilty) and should ensure that the listing officer is given early notice of any change of such estimate or possible adjournment;

(b)   should take all reasonable and practicable steps to ensure that the case is properly prepared and ready for trial by the time that it is first listed;

(c)   should ensure that arrangements have been made in adequate time for witnesses to attend Court as and when required and should plan, so far as possible, for sufficient witnesses to be available to occupy the full Court day;

(d)   should, if a witness (for example a doctor) can only attend Court at a certain time during the trial without great inconvenience to himself, try to arrange for that witness to be accommodated by raising the matter with the trial Judge and with his opponent;

(e) should take all necessary steps to comply with the Practice Direction (Crime: Tape Recording of Police Interviews) [1989] 1 WLR 631.

14.2 If properly remunerated (paragraph 502 of the Code), the barrister originally briefed in a case should attend all plea and directions hearings. If this is not possible, he must take all reasonable steps to ensure that the barrister who does appear is conversant with the case and is prepared to make informed decisions affecting the trial.

15. Video Recordings

15.1 When a barrister instructed and acting for the prosecution or the defence of an accused has in his possession a copy of a video recording of a child witness which has been identified as having been prepared to be admitted in evidence at a criminal trial in accordance with Section 54 of the Criminal Justice Act 1991, he must have regard to the following duties and obligations:

(a) Upon receipt of the recording, a written record of the date and time and from whom the recording was received must be made and a receipt must be given.

(b) The recording and its contents must be used only for the proper preparation of the prosecution or defence case or of an appeal against conviction and/or sentence, as the case may be, and the barrister must not make or permit any disclosure of the recording or its contents to any person except when, in his opinion, it is in the interests of his proper preparation of that case.

(c) The barrister must not make or permit any other person to make a copy of the recording, nor release the recording to the accused, and must ensure that:

(i) when not in transit or in use, the recording is always kept in a locked or secure place, and:

(ii) when in transit, the recording is kept safe and secure at all times and is not left unattended, especially in vehicles or otherwise.

(d) Proper preparation of the case may involve viewing the recording in the presence of the accused. If this is the case, viewing should be done:

(i) if the accused is in custody, only in the prison or other custodial institution where he is being held, in the presence of the barrister and/or his instructing solicitor.

(ii) if the accused is on bail, at the solicitor's office or in counsel's chambers or elsewhere in the presence of the barrister and/or his instructing solicitor.

(e) The recording must be returned to the solicitor as soon as practicable after the conclusion of the barrister's role in the case. A written record of the date and time despatched and to whom the recording was delivered for despatch must be made.

16   Attendance of Counsel at Court

16.1   Prosecuting counsel should be present throughout the trial, including the summing-up and the return of the jury. He may not absent himself without leave of the Court; but, if two or more barristers appear for the prosecution, the attendance of one is sufficient.

16.2.1   Defence counsel should ensure that the defendant is never left unrepresented at any stage of his trial.

16.2.2   Where a defendant is represented by one barrister, that barrister should normally be present throughout the trial and should only absent himself in exceptional circumstances which he could not reasonably be expected to foresee and provided that:

(a) he has obtained the consent of the professional client (or his representative) and the lay client; and

(b) a competent deputy takes his place.

16.2.3   Where a defendant is represented by two barristers, neither may absent himself except for good reason and then only when the consent of the professional client (or his representative) and of the lay client has been obtained, or when the case is legally aided and the barrister thinks it necessary to do so in order to avoid unnecessary public expense.

16.2.4   These rules are subject to modification in respect of lengthy trials involving numerous defendants. In such trials, where after the conclusion of the opening speech by the prosecution defending counsel is satisfied that during a specific part of the trial there is no serious possibility that events will occur which will relate to his client, he may with the consent of the professional client (or his representative) and of the lay client absent himself for that part of the trial. He should also inform the judge. In this event it is his duty:

(a) to arrange for other defending counsel to guard the interests of his client;

(b) to keep himself informed throughout of the progress of the trial and in particular of any development which could affect his client; and

(c) not to accept any other commitment which would render it impracticable for him to make himself available at reasonable notice if the interests of his client so require.

16.3.1   If during the course of a criminal trial and prior to final sentence the defendant voluntarily absconds and the barrister's professional client, in accordance with the ruling of the Law

Society, withdraws from the case, then the barrister too should withdraw. If the trial judge requests the barrister to remain to assist the Court, the barrister has an absolute discretion whether to do so or not. If he does remain, he should act on the basis that his instructions are withdrawn and he will not be entitled to use any material contained in his brief save for such part as has already been established in evidence before the Court. He should request the trial judge to instruct the jury that this is the basis on which he is prepared to assist the Court.

16.3.2 If for any reason the barrister's professional client does not withdraw from the case, the barrister retains an absolute discretion whether to continue to act. If he does continue, he should conduct the case as if his client were still present in Court but had decided not to give evidence and on the basis of any instruction he has received. He will be free to use any material contained in his brief and may cross-examine witnesses called for the prosecution and call witnesses for the defence.

17 Appeals

17.1.1 Attention is drawn to the Guide to Proceedings in the Court of Appeal Criminal Division ('the Guide') which is set out in full its original form at (1983) 77 Crim App R 138 and is summarised in a version amended in April 1990 Volume 1 of Archbold at 7–173 to 7–184.

17.1.2 In particular when advising after a client pleads guilty or is convicted, defence counsel is encouraged to follow the procedures set out at paragraphs 1.2 and 1.4 of the Guide.

17.2 If his client pleads guilty or is convicted, defence counsel should see his client after he has been sentenced in the presence of his professional client or his representative. He should then proceed as follows:

(a) if he is satisfied that there are no reasonable grounds of appeal he should so advise orally and certify in writing. Counsel is encouraged to certify using the form set out in Appendix 1 to the Guide. No further advice is necessary unless it is reasonable for a written advice to be given because the client reasonably requires it or because it is necessary e.g. in the light of the circumstances of the conviction, any particular difficulties at trial, the length and nature of the sentence passed, the effect thereof on the defendant or the lack of impact which oral advice given immediately after the trial may have on the particular defendant's mind.

(b) if he is satisfied that there are more reasonable grounds of appeal or if his view is a provisional one or if he requires more time to consider the prospects of a successful appeal he should so advise orally and certify in writing. Counsel is encouraged to certify using the form set out in Appendix 1 to the Guide. Counsel should then furnish written advice to the professional client as soon as he can and in any event within 14 days.

17.3 Counsel should not settle grounds of appeal unless he considers that such grounds are properly arguable, and in that event he should provide a reasoned written opinion in support of such grounds.

17.4 In certain cases counsel may not be able to perfect grounds of appeal without a transcript or other further information. In this event the grounds of appeal should be accompanied by a note to the Registrar setting out the matters on which assistance is required. Once such transcript or other information is available, counsel should ensure that the grounds of appeal are perfected by the inclusion of all necessary references.

17.5 Grounds of Appeal must be settled with sufficient particularity to enable the Registrar and subsequently the Court to identify clearly the matters relied upon.

17.6 If at any stage counsel is of the view that the appeal should be abandoned, he should at once set out his reasons in writing and send them to his professional client.

THE DUAL QUALIFICATION RULES

THE DUAL QUALIFICATION RULES

1   A practising barrister who is also qualified in some other system of law and practises concurrently in England and Wales by virtue of that other qualification must:

    (a) in the course of his English practice observe the rules of conduct applicable to a practising barrister (including where relevant the Overseas Practice Rules); and

    (b) in the course of his foreign practice observe the Foreign Lawyers (Chambers) Rules (other than paragraph 2(a) thereof);

    (c) in any communication by him from his chambers in the course of his foreign practice indicate that he is acting by virtue of his foreign qualifications.

2   A barrister may as part of his foreign practice give advice on English law in circumstances where that advice is incidental and subsidiary to the conduct of his foreign practice in a particular case.

3   In England and Wales:

    (a) 'foreign practice' means advising on or drafting documents to be governed by that other system of law in which he is qualified and appearing before a tribunal whose constitution and procedure is governed by that system of law;

    (b) any other professional activity is English practice unless the Bar Council shall by prior dispensation have ruled that it may be considered foreign practice.

4   Whether any activity outside England and Wales is English practice or foreign practice depends on the circumstances of the particular case.

5   In paragraph 3(a) the expression 'system of law' in a case where the barrister is qualified in the law of one state or province of a federal constitution includes the law of every other state or province and the federal law of that constitution.

ANNEXE H

THE LAW CENTRES AND LEGAL ADVICE CENTRES RULES

THE LAW CENTRES AND LEGAL ADVICE CENTRES RULES

1   Subject to these rules a barrister may:

    (a)   accept employment either full-time or part-time at; or

    (b)   attend at (that is to say work voluntarily at);

a Law Centre or a Legal Advice Centre provided that a barrister must before accepting employment part-time at a Law Centre or Legal Advice Centre notify the Bar Council of the terms thereof and subsequently of any proposed variation thereof.

2   The remuneration of a barrister employed at a Law Centre or a Legal Advice Centre may only be by way of salary paid by the Centre. A barrister employed at a Law Centre must not in any circumstances receive a fee directly from a lay client.

3   Any fees accruing to a barrister employed at a Law Centre or a Legal Advice Centre as a result of work done by him in that employment must be paid over by him to the Centre.

4   Any fees accruing to a barrister attending at a Law Centre or a Legal Advice Centre as a result of work done by him in the course of that attendance must be paid over by him to the Centre.

5   A barrister who is employed at or attends at a Law Centre or a Legal Advice Centre may without the instructions of a solicitor:

    (a)   interview and take statements from clients and witnesses;

    (b)   write and sign letters on behalf of the Centre;

    (c)   carry on correspondence with third parties and negotiate settlements on behalf of clients of the Centre;

    (d)   permit himself to be described as a barrister on letter headings and other official publications used at or distributed by the Centre;

    (e)   draft letters on behalf of clients of the Centre for signature by them;

    (f)   draft (and in the case of a barrister employed by a Law Centre but not otherwise sign) pleadings on behalf of clients of the Centre.

6   A barrister who is employed at a Law Centre or Legal Advice Centre may without the instructions of a solicitor instruct Counsel.

7   A barrister who is employed at or attends at a Law Centre or a Legal Advice Centre must not:

    (a)   sue out any writ or process;

(b)   carry out conveyancing work.

8   A barrister who attends at a Law Centre or a Legal Advice Centre must not instruct Counsel.

9   A barrister in full-time employment at a Law Centre:

(a)   must not accept any brief other than a brief from a solicitor who is employed at the Centre;

(b)   may appear as an advocate in a Court for a client of the Centre provided that in cases in which a solicitor would have no right of audience he must not appear without a solicitor or other representative of the Centre in attendance.

10   A barrister in part-time employment at a Law Centre who is also a barrister in independent practice:

(a)   must not in the course of that employment:

(i)   accept any brief other than a brief from a solicitor who is employed at the Centre; or

(ii)   save as provided in paragraphs (b) and (c) appear as an advocate in a Court except upon the instructions of a solicitor who is employed at the Centre;

(b)   may appear as an advocate on the instructions of the Centre in courts in which a solicitor would have a right of audience;

(c)   may appear as an advocate on the instructions of the Centre in an application for bail to a Judge in chambers in the following circumstances:

(i)   when neither private finance nor legal aid is available to the client; or

(ii)   when no solicitor is prepared to accept the client's instructions; or

(iii)   in cases of real emergency the judge of which shall be the barrister concerned.

11   A barrister who is employed at a Law Centre:

(a)   may prepare his own brief;

(b)   must on each appearance as an advocate in the course of his employment at the Centre obtain a backsheet marked with:

(i)   the name of the case;

(ii)   the Court;

      (iii)   the name of the barrister;

      (iv)   the name of the Centre;

      (v)   the words 'Legal Aid' where appropriate;

and the decision of the Court must be recorded on the backsheet;

(c)   must at all Courts where Counsel normally appear robed wear robes when appearing as an advocate.

12   A barrister who attends at a Law Centre or who is employed at or attends at a Legal Advice Centre must not appear as an advocate in Court in the course of his work at the Centre.

13   A barrister in independent practice who is employed part-time at or attends at a Law Centre or Legal Advice Centre may in the course of his practice from chambers accept paid instructions in proceedings from a solicitor for a lay client from that Centre provided that he has not himself advised that client at a Centre in relation to those proceedings.

ANNEXE I

THE FOREIGN LAWYERS (CHAMBERS) RULES

THE FOREIGN LAWYERS (CHAMBERS) RULES

1   Subject to the conditions set out in paragraph 2 chambers may permit any person qualified to practise and practising as a foreign lawyer outside the United Kingdom to have his name shown at the chambers and to use chambers for professional purposes on such terms as may be agreed between them.

2   The conditions to be complied with are:

(a) The name of the foreign lawyer together with his professional title or qualifications and the country in which he is qualified to practise (either in full or in customary abbreviation) must be shown at the chambers in italics.

(b) The foreign lawyer must not have for professional purposes any office or address in the United Kingdom other than the above chambers.

(c) In all other respects the foreign lawyer will be subject to the same rules of practice as govern a barrister in independent practice practising in England and Wales except in so far as any such rules conflict with the ordinary or usual way in which the foreign lawyer properly conducts himself or his practice or with the rules of his own profession provided that the foreign lawyer must at all times in relation to his practice in the United Kingdom observe and where appropriate ensure that others with whom he might be connected abroad observe paragraphs 206 308 310 508(b) 603 604 and 701.2 of the Code of Conduct.

(d) Such conditions or modifications as the Bar Council in general or in a particular case may impose.

3   The head of chambers or if there is no head of chambers every member of chambers:

(a) before permitting a foreign lawyer to avail himself of paragraph 1 must ensure that such foreign lawyer signs an acceptance of the conditions in paragraph 2 and must inform the Bar Council thereof;

(b) in allowing a foreign lawyer to continue to avail himself of paragraph 1 must:

(i)   satisfy himself that the foreign lawyer complies with and continues to comply with the conditions of paragraph 2 and in particular the requirements of insurance;

(ii)   inform the Bar Council of any failure by the foreign lawyer to comply with the conditions of paragraph 2 which may be known to him.

ANNEXE J

THE CODE OF CONDUCT FOR LAWYERS IN THE EUROPEAN COMMUNITY

THE CODE OF CONDUCT FOR LAWYERS IN THE EUROPEAN COMMUNITY

1 PREAMBLE

1.1   The Function of the Lawyer in Society

In a society founded on respect for the rule of law the lawyer fulfils a special role. His duties do not begin and end with the faithful performance of what he is instructed to do so far as the law permits. A lawyer must serve the interests of justice as well as those whose rights and liberties he is trusted to assert and defend and it is his duty not only to plead his client's cause but to be his adviser.

A lawyer's function therefore lays on him a variety of legal and moral obligations (sometimes appearing to be in conflict with each other) towards:-

the client;

the courts and other authorities before whom the lawyer pleads his client's cause or acts on his behalf;

the legal profession in general and each fellow member of it in particular; and

the public for whom the existence of a free and independent profession, bound together by respect for rules made by the profession itself, is an essential means of safeguarding human rights in face of the power of the state and other interests in society.

1.2   The Nature of Rules of Professional Conduct

1.2.1   Rules of professional conduct are designed through their willing acceptance by those to whom they apply to ensure the proper performance by the lawyer of a function which is recognised as essential in all civilised societies. The failure of the lawyer to observe these rules must in the last resort result in a disciplinary sanction.

1.2.2   The particular rules of each Bar or Law Society arise from its own traditions. They are adapted to the organisation and sphere of activity of the profession in the Member State concerned and to its judicial and administrative procedures and to its national legislation. It is neither possible nor desirable that they should be taken out of their context nor that an attempt should be made to give general application to rules which are inherently incapable of such application.

The particular rules of each Bar and Law Society nevertheless are based on the same values and in most cases demonstrate a common foundation.

1.3   The Purpose of the Code

1.3.1   The continued integration of the European Community and the increasing frequency of the cross-border activities of lawyers within the Community have made necessary in the public interest the statement of common rules which apply to all lawyers from the Community whatever Bar or Law Society they belong to in relation to their cross-border practice. A particular purpose of the statement of those rules is to mitigate the difficulties which result from the application of 'double deontology' as set out in Article 4 of the EC Directive 77/249 of 22nd March 1977.

1.3.2   The organisations representing the legal profession through the CCBE propose that the rules codified in the following articles:-

- be recognised at the present time as the expression of a consensus of all the Bars and Law Societies of the European Union and European Economic Area;

- be adopted as enforceable rules as soon as possible in accordance with national or EEA procedures in relation to the cross-border activities of the lawyer in the European Union and European Economic Area;

- be taken into account in all revisions of national rules of deontology or professional practice with a view to their progressive harmonisation.

They further express the wish that the national rules of deontology or professional practice be interpreted and applied whenever possible in a way consistent with the rules in this Code.

After the rules in this Code have been adopted as enforceable rules in relation to his cross-border activities the lawyer will remain bound to observe the rules of the Bar or Law Society to which he belongs to the extent that they are consistent with the rules in this Code.

1.4   Field of Application Ratione Personae

The following rules shall apply to lawyers of the European Union and European Economic Area as they are defined by the Directive 77/249 of 22nd March 1977.

1.5   Field of Application Ratione Materiae

Without prejudice to the pursuit of a progressive harmonisation of rules of deontology or professional practice which apply only internally within a Member State, the following rules shall apply to the cross-border activities of the lawyer within the European Union and European Economic Area. Cross-border activities shall mean:

Amended 6 February 1999

(a)   all professional contacts with lawyers of Member States other than his own; and

(b)   the professional activities of the lawyer in a Member State other than his own, whether or not the lawyer is physically present in that Member State.

1.6   Definitions

In these rules:-

'Home Member State' means the Member State of the Bar or Law Society to which the lawyer belongs.

'Host Member State' means any other Member State where the lawyer carries on cross-border activities.

'Competent authority' means the professional organisation(s) or authority(ies) of the Member State concerned responsible for the laying down of rules of professional conduct and the administration of discipline of lawyers.

2   GENERAL PRINCIPLES

2.1   Independence

2.1.1   The many duties to which a lawyer is subject require his absolute independence, free from all other influence, especially such as may arise from his personal interests or external pressure. Such independence is as necessary to trust in the process of justice as the impartiality of the judge. A lawyer must therefore avoid any impairment of his independence and be careful not to compromise his professional standards in order to please his client, the court or third parties.

2.1.2   This independence is necessary in non-contentious matters as well as in litigation. Advice given by a lawyer to his client has no value if it is given only to ingratiate himself, to serve his personal interests or in response to outside pressure.

2.2   Trust and Personal Integrity

Relationships of trust can only exist if a lawyer's personal honour, honesty and integrity are beyond doubt. For the lawyer these traditional virtues are professional obligations.

2.3   Confidentiality

2.3.1   It is of the essence of a lawyer's function that he should be told by his client things which the client would not tell to others, and that he should be the recipient of other information on a basis of confidence. Without the certainty of confidentiality there cannot be trust. Confidentiality is therefore a primary and fundamental right and duty of the lawyer.

The lawyer's obligation of confidentiality serves the interest of the administration of justice as well as the interest of the client. It is therefore entitled to special protection by the State.

2.3.2   A lawyer shall respect the confidentiality of all information that becomes known to him in the course of his professional activity.

2.3.3   The obligation of confidentiality is not limited in time.

2.3.4   A lawyer shall require his associates and staff and anyone engaged by him in the course of providing professional services to observe the same obligation of confidentiality.

2.4   Respect for the Rules of Other Bars and Law Societies

Under the laws of the European Union and the European Economic Area a lawyer from another Member State may be bound to comply with the rules of the Bar or Law Society of the host Member State. Lawyers have a duty to inform themselves as to the rules which will affect them in the performance of any particular activity.

Members of organisations of CCBE are obliged to deposit their Code of Conduct at the Secretariat of CCBE so that any lawyer can get hold of the copy of the current Code from the Secretariat.

2.5   Incompatible Occupations

2.5.1   In order to perform his functions with due independence and in a manner which is consistent with his duty to participate in the administration of justice a lawyer is excluded from some occupations.

2.5.2   A lawyer who acts in the representation or the defence of a client in legal proceedings or before any public authorities in a host Member State shall there observe the rules regarding incompatible occupations as they are applied to lawyers of the host Member State.

2.5.3   A lawyer established in a host Member State in which he wishes to participate directly in commercial or other activities not connected with the practice of the law shall respect the rules regarding forbidden or incompatible occupations as they are applied to lawyers of that Member State.

2.6   Personal Publicity

2.6.1   A lawyer should not advertise or seek personal publicity where this is not permitted.

Amended 6 February 1999

In other cases a lawyer should only advertise or seek personal publicity to the extent and in the manner permitted by the rules to which he is subject.

2.6.2   Advertising and personal publicity shall be regarded as taking place where it is permitted, if the lawyer concerned shows that it was placed for the purpose of reaching clients or potential clients located where such advertising or personal publicity is permitted and its communication elsewhere is incidental.

2.7   The Client's Interests

Subject to due observance of all rules of law and professional conduct, a lawyer must always act in the best interests of his client and must put those interests before his own interests or those of fellow members of the legal profession.

2.8   Limitation of Lawyer's Liability towards his Client

To the extend permitted by the law of the Home member State and the host member State, the lawyer may limit his liabilities towards his client in accordance with rules of the Code of Conduct to which he is subject.

3   RELATIONS WITH CLIENTS

3.1   Acceptance and Termination of Instructions

3.1.1   A lawyer shall not handle a case for a party except on his instructions. He may, however, act in a case in which he has been instructed by another lawyer who himself acts for the party or where the case has been assigned to him by a competent body.

The lawyer should make reasonable efforts to ascertain the identity, competence and authority of the person or body who instructs him when the specific circumstances show that the identity, competence and authority are uncertain.

3.1.2   A lawyer shall advise and represent his client promptly conscientiously and diligently. He shall undertake personal responsibility for the discharge of the instructions given to him. He shall keep his client informed as to the progress of the matter entrusted to him.

3.1.3   A lawyer shall not handle a matter which he knows or ought to know he is not competent to handle, without co-operating with a lawyer who is competent to handle it.

A lawyer shall not accept instructions unless he can discharge those instructions promptly having regard to the pressure of other work.

3.1.4   A lawyer shall not be entitled to exercise his right to withdraw

Amended 6 February 1999

from a case in such a way or in such circumstances that the client may be unable to find other legal assistance in time to prevent prejudice being suffered by the client.

3.2   Conflict of Interest

3.2.1   A lawyer may not advise, represent or act on behalf of two or more clients in the same matter if there is a conflict, or a significant risk of a conflict, between the interests of those clients.

3.2.2   A lawyer must cease to act for both clients when a conflict of interests arises between those clients and also whenever there is a risk of a breach of confidence or where his independence may be impaired.

3.2.3   A lawyer must also refrain from acting for a new client if there is a risk of a breach of confidences entrusted to the lawyer by a former client or if the knowledge which the lawyer possesses of the affairs of the former client would give an undue advantage to the new client.

3.2.4   Where lawyers are practising in association, paragraphs 3.2.1 to 3.2.3 above shall apply to the association and all its members.

3.3   Pactum de Quota Litis

3.3.1   A lawyer shall not be entitled to make a pactum de quota litis.

3.3.2   By 'pactum de quota litis' is meant an agreement between a lawyer and his client entered into prior to the final conclusion of a matter to which the client is a party, by virtue of which the client undertakes to pay the lawyer a share of the result regardless of whether this is represented by a sum of money or by any other benefit achieved by the client upon the conclusion of the matter.

3.3.3   The pactum de quota litis does not include an agreement that fees be charged in proportion to the value of a matter handled by the lawyer if this is in accordance with an officially approved fee scale or under the control of the competent authority having jurisdiction over the lawyer.

3.4   Regulation of Fees

3.4.1   A fee charged by a lawyer shall be fully disclosed to his client and shall be fair and reasonable.

3.4.2   Subject to any proper agreement to the contrary between a lawyer and his client fees charged by a lawyer shall be subject to regulation in accordance with the rules applied to members of the Bar or Law Society to which he belongs. If he belongs to more than one Bar or Law Society the rules applied shall be those with the closest connection to the contract between the lawyer and his client.

3.5   Payment on Account

If a lawyer requires a payment on account of his fees and/or disbursements such payment should not exceed a reasonable estimate of the fees and probable disbursements involved.

Failing such payment, a lawyer may withdraw from the case or refuse to handle it, but subject always to paragraph 3.1.4 above.

3.6   Fee Sharing with Non-Lawyers

3.6.1   Subject as after-mentioned a lawyer may not share his fees with a person who is not a lawyer except where an association between the lawyer and the other person is permitted by the laws of the Member State to which the lawyer belongs.

3.6.2   The provisions of 6.1 above shall not preclude a lawyer from paying a fee, commission or other compensation to a deceased lawyer's heirs or to a retired lawyer in respect of taking over the deceased or retired lawyer's practice.

3.7   Cost Effective Resolution and Availability of Legal Aid

3.7.1   The lawyer should at all times strive to achieve the most cost effective resolution of the client's dispute and should advise the client at appropriate stages as to the desirability of attempting a settlement and/or a reference to alternative dispute resolution.

3.7.2   A lawyer shall inform his client of the availability of legal aid where applicable.

3.8   Clients Funds

3.8.1   When lawyers at any time in the course of their practice come into possession of funds on behalf of their clients or third parties (hereinafter called 'clients' funds') it shall be obligatory:

3.8.1.1   That clients' funds shall always be held in an account in a bank or similar institution subject to supervision of Public Authority and that all clients' funds received by a lawyer should be paid into such an account unless the client explicitly or by implication agrees that the funds should be dealt with otherwise.

3.8.1.2   That any account in which the clients' funds are held in the name of the lawyer should indicate in the title or designation that the funds are held on behalf of the client or clients of the lawyer.

3.8.1.3   That any account or accounts in which clients' funds are held in the name of the lawyer should at all times contain a sum which is not less than the total of the clients' funds held by the lawyer.

3.8.1.4   That all clients' funds should be available for payment to clients on demand or upon such conditions as the client may authorise.

Amended 6 February 1999

3.8.1.5   That payments made from clients' funds on behalf of a client to any other person including

      (a)   payments made to or for one client from funds held for another client and

      (b)   payment of the lawyer's fees,

be prohibited except to the extent that they are permitted by law or have the express or implied authority of the client for whom the payment is being made.

3.8.1.6   That the lawyer shall maintain full and accurate records, available to each client on request, showing all his dealings with his clients' funds and distinguishing clients' funds from other funds held by him.

3.8.1.7   That the competent authorities in all Member States should have powers to allow them to examine and investigate on a confidential basis the financial records of lawyers' clients' funds to ascertain whether or not the rules which they make are being complied with and to impose sanctions upon lawyers who fail to comply with those rules.

3.8.2   Subject as after-mentioned, and without prejudice to the rules set out in 3.8.1 above, a lawyer who holds clients' funds in the course of carrying on practice in any Member State must comply with the Rules relating to holding and accounting for clients' funds which are applied by the competent authorities of the Home Member State.

3.8.3   A lawyer who carries on practice or provides services in a Host Member State may with the agreement of the competent authorities of the Home and Host Member States concerned comply with the requirements of the Host Member State to the exclusion of the requirements of the Home Member State. In that event he shall take reasonable steps to inform his clients that he complies with the requirements in force in the Host Member State.

3.9   Professional Indemnity Insurance

3.9.1   Lawyers shall be insured at all times against claims based on professional negligence to an extent which is reasonable having regard to the nature and extent of the risks which each lawyer may incur in his practice.

3.9.2   When a lawyer provides services or carries out practice in a Host Member State, the following shall apply.

3.9.2.1   The lawyer must comply with any Rules relating to his obligation to insure against his professional liability as a lawyer which are in force in his Home Member State.

3.9.2.2   A lawyer who is obliged so to insure in his home Member State and who provides services or carries out practice in any Host

Amended 6 February 1999

Member State shall use his best endeavours to obtain insurance cover on the basis required in his home Member State extended to services which he provides or practice which he carries out in a Host Member State.

3.9.2.3   A lawyer who fails to obtain the extended insurance cover referred to in paragraph 3.9.2.2 above or who is not obliged so to insure in his home Member State and who provides services or carries out practice in a Host Member State shall in so far as possible obtain insurance cover against his professional liability as a lawyer whilst acting for clients in that Host Member State on at least an equivalent basis to that required of lawyers in the Host Member State.

3.9.2.4   To the extent that a lawyer is unable to obtain the insurance cover required by the foregoing rules, he shall inform such of his clients as might be affected.

3.9.2.5   A lawyer who carries out practice or provides services in a Host Member State may with the agreement of the competent authorities of the Home and Host Member States concerned comply with such insurance requirements as are in force in the Host Member State to the exclusion of the insurance requirements of the Home Member State. In this event he shall take reasonable steps to inform his clients that he is insured according to the requirements in force in the Host Member State.

4   RELATIONS WITH THE COURTS

4.1   Applicable Rules of Conduct in Court

A lawyer who appears, or takes part in a case, before a court or tribunal in a Member State must comply with the rules of conduct applied before that court or tribunal.

4.2   Fair Conduct of Proceedings

A lawyer must always have due regard for the fair conduct of proceedings. He must not, for example, make contact with the judge without first informing the lawyer acting for the opposing party or submit exhibits, notes or documents to the judge without communicating them in good time to the lawyer on the other side unless such steps are permitted under the relevant rules of procedure. To the extent not prohibited by law a lawyer must not divulge or submit to the court any proposals for settlement of the case made by the other party or its lawyers without the express consent by the other party's lawyer.

4.3   Demeanour in Court

A lawyer shall while maintaining due respect and courtesy towards the court defend the interest of his client honourably and fearlessly without regard to his own interests or to any consequences to himself or to any other person.

Amended 6 February 1999

4.4   False or Misleading Information

A lawyer shall never knowingly give false or misleading information to the court.

4.5   Extension to Arbitrators Etc

The rules governing a lawyer's relations with the courts apply also to his relations with arbitrators and any other persons exercising judicial or quasi-judicial functions, even on an occasional basis.

5   RELATIONS BETWEEN LAWYERS

5.1   Corporate Spirit of the Profession

5.1.1   The corporate spirit of the profession requires a relationship of trust and co-operation between lawyers for the benefit of their clients and in order to avoid unnecessary litigation and other behaviour harmful to the reputation of the profession. It can, however, never justify setting the interests of the profession against those of justice or the client.

5.1.2   A lawyer should recognise all other lawyers of Member States as professional colleagues and act fairly and courteously towards them.

5.2   Co-operation among Lawyers of Different Member States

5.2.1   It is the duty of a lawyer who is approached by a colleague from another Member State not to accept instructions in a matter which he is not competent to undertake. He should in such case be prepared to help his colleague to obtain the information necessary to enable him to instruct a lawyer who is capable of providing the service asked for.

5.2.2   Where a lawyer of a Member State co-operates with a lawyer from another Member State, both have a general duty to take into account the differences which may exist between their respective legal systems and the professional organisations competences and obligations of lawyers in the Member States concerned.

5.3   Correspondence Between Lawyers

5.3.1   If a lawyer sending a communication to a lawyer in another Member State wishes it to remain confidential or without prejudice he should clearly express this intention when communicating the document.

5.3.2   If the recipient of the communication is unable to ensure its status as confidential or without prejudice he should return it to the sender without revealing the contents to others.

Amended 6 February 1999

5.4   Referral Fees

5.4.1   A lawyer may not demand or accept from another lawyer or any other person a fee, commission or any other compensation for referring or recommending the lawyer to a client.

5.4.2   A lawyer may not pay anyone a fee, commission or any other compensation as a consideration for referring a client to himself.

5.5   Communication with Opposing Parties

A lawyer shall not communicate about a particular case or matter directly with any person whom he knows to be represented or advised in the case or matter by another lawyer, without the consent of that other lawyer (and shall keep the other lawyer informed of any such communications).

5.6   Change of Lawyer

5.6.1   A lawyer who is instructed to represent a client in substitution for another lawyer in relation to a particular matter should inform that other lawyer and, subject to 5.6.2 below, should not begin to act until he has ascertained that arrangements have been made for the settlement of the other lawyer's fees and disbursements. This duty does not, however, make the new lawyer personally responsible for the former lawyer's fees and disbursements.

5.6.2   If urgent steps have to be taken in the interests of the client before the conditions in 5.6.1 above can be complied with, the lawyer may take such steps provided he informs the other lawyer immediately.

5.7   Responsibility for Fees

In professional relations between members of Bars of different Member States, where a lawyer does not confine himself to recommending another lawyer or introducing him to the client but himself entrusts a correspondent with a particular matter or seeks his advice, he is personally bound, even if the client is insolvent, to pay the fees, costs and outlays which are due to the foreign correspondent. The lawyers concerned may, however, at the outset of the relationship between them make special arrangements on this matter. Further, the instructing lawyer may at any time limit his personal responsibility to the amount of the fees, costs and outlays incurred before intimation to the foreign lawyer of his disclaimer of responsibility for the future.

Amended 6 February 1999

5.8   Training Young Lawyers

In order to improve trust and co-operation amongst lawyers of different Member States for the clients' benefit there is a need to encourage a better knowledge of the laws and procedures in different Member States. Therefore when considering the need for the profession to give good training to young lawyers, lawyers should take into account the need to give training to young lawyers from other Member States.

5.9   Disputes Amongst Lawyers in Different Member States

5.9.1   If a lawyer considers that a colleague in another Member State has acted in breach of a rule of professional conduct he shall draw the matter to the attention of his colleague.

5.9.2   If any personal dispute of a professional nature arises amongst lawyers in different Member States they should if possible first try to settle it in a friendly way.

5.9.3   A lawyer shall not commence any form of proceedings against a colleague in another Member State on matters referred to in 5.9.1 or 5.9.2 above without first informing the Bars or Law Societies to which they both belong for the purpose of allowing both Bars or Law Societies concerned an opportunity to assist in reaching a settlement.

Amended 6 February 1999

ANNEXE K

THE COMPLAINTS RULES

THE COMPLAINTS RULES

Introduction

1   These Rules prescribe the manner in which all complaints about the conduct of or services provided by barristers shall be processed.

2   The membership of the Professional Conduct and Complaints Committee ('the Committee') shall be as prescribed by the Standing Orders of the Bar Council as amended from time to time.

3   Anything required by these Rules to be done or any discretion required to be exercised by, and any notice required to be given to, the Complaints Commissioner ('the Commissioner') or the Secretary of the Committee ('the Secretary'), may be done or exercised by, or given to, any person authorised by the Complaints Commissioner to act in his stead or by the Chief Executive of the Bar Council to act instead of the Secretary of the Committee (either prospectively or retrospectively and either generally or for a particular purpose).

Procedure for dealing with complaints

4   The Secretary shall take such steps as are reasonably practicable to inform the complainant of the progress and result of his complaint.

5   Any complaint other than a complaint raised by the Bar Council of its own motion shall be referred to and considered by the Commissioner before any further step is taken in accordance with these rules. The Commissioner's powers in relation to a complaint so considered by him shall be those set out in paragraph 8 *et seq.* below.

6   (a) If a complaint is not dismissed by the Commissioner following consideration as aforesaid, or is a complaint raised by the Bar Council, it shall be investigated by the Secretary of the Committee in the manner set out in paragraph 16 *et seq.* below.

         (b) Following such investigation, the Secretary shall refer the complaint back to the Commissioner together with the results of such investigation and the Commissioner shall reconsider the complaint and the results and shall exercise the powers given to him by paragraph 21 *et seq.* below in respect of the complaint.

7   If the Commissioner does not dismiss the complaint following reconsideration under paragraph 6(b) above, he shall refer the complaint to the Committee for consideration with his observations on it, if any. The Committee's powers in relation to such a complaint shall be those set out in paragraph 26 *et seq.* below.

Commissioner's powers under paragraph 5

8   The powers of the Commissioner shall be to consider complaints made by outside persons and to-determine whether in his view such a complaint discloses a *prima facie* case of professional misconduct or inadequate professional service and is apt for consideration by the Committee. In the exercise of that power he shall observe the following provisions.

9   If it appears to him that the complaint relates to a matter within the domestic jurisdiction of an Inn or a Circuit, he may refer the complaint without further consideration to the Treasurer of the Inn or the Leader of the Circuit concerned and notify the complainant of his decision.

10   (a)   If it appears to the Commissioner that the complaint arises out of a barrister's actions in a part-time or temporary judicial or quasi-judicial capacity, he shall act as follows:

(i)   If it appears to him that the complaint would otherwise fall to be dismissed under these provisions, he shall so dismiss it.

(ii)   If it appears to him that the complaint would otherwise not fall to be dismissed, the Commissioner shall refer the complaint without further consideration to the person responsible for the appointment of the barrister to the judicial or quasi-judicial office concerned (whether the Lord Chancellor, a Minister of the Crown or other person as appropriate), requesting him to notify the Commissioner when the complaint has been dealt with and of any action taken, and the Commissioner shall notify the complainant of his decision so to refer it. Where the Commissioner considers it inappropriate to refer the complaint to a person other than the Lord Chancellor or a Minister of the Crown or where that other person refuses to deal with a complaint, he shall consider the complaint and, subject to (iv) below, direct it to be proceeded with in accordance with paragraph 16 et seq below.

(iii)   If the Lord Chancellor, Minister of the Crown, or other person responsible for the appointment, having dealt with a complaint, believes that it may be appropriate for further consideration by the Bar Council, he may, subject to (iv) below, refer the matter to the Commissioner who may reconsider the complaint and may, if he sees fit, direct it to be proceeded with in accordance with paragraph 16 et seq below.

(iv)   No such reference to the Commissioner as is mentioned in (iii) above by the Lord Chancellor, Minister of the Crown, or other person responsible for the appointment shall be acted upon by the

Commissioner, nor shall the Commissioner exercise the powers under the last sentence of paragraph (ii) above in respect of any part of the complaint relating to anything said or done by the barrister in the exercise of his judicial functions or affecting the independence of the barrister in his judicial or quasi-judicial capacity.

(b) If it appears to the Commissioner that the complaint relates to the conduct of or professional services provided by a barrister who, since the events giving rise to the complaint took place, has been appointed to and continues to hold full-time judicial office and has ceased practice, the Commissioner shall not consider the complaint further and shall inform the complainant that his complaint should be directed to the Lord Chancellor.

11   If he has not disposed of any complaint under paragraph 9 or 10 above, he shall consider whether it fails to disclose a prima facie case of professional misconduct or inadequate professional service, is trivial, obviously lacks validity or for any other reason ought to be dismissed summarily. In order to decide this question, he may seek information or assistance, orally or in writing, as he thinks fit, from the complainant, any potential witness, any member of the Committee, the Secretary or the Equal Opportunities Officers of the Bar Council.

12   If he considers that it should be dismissed on any of the grounds set out in paragraph 11 above, he shall so dismiss it, and shall notify the complainant of his decision and of his reasons for it.

13   If in considering whether a complaint should be dismissed summarily the Commissioner decides that the complaint does not disclose any evidence of professional misconduct, and it appears to him that the complaint might be capable of resolution by agreement, he may invite the complainant and the barrister concerned to attempt to conciliate their differences.

14   The Commissioner may at any time adjourn consideration of a complaint for such period as he thinks fit, whether while the complainant and the barrister attempt conciliation, during the currency of related legal proceedings or for any other reason.

15   The Commissioner may reopen or reconsider a complaint which has been disposed of under paragraphs 9 10 or 12 above:

(a)   following a recommendation of the Legal Services Ombudsman that he do so, or

(b)   where new evidence becomes available to him which leads him to conclude that he should do so, or

(c)   for some other good reason.

Following such reconsideration he may take such further or different action as he thinks fit, as if the former decision had not been made.

Investigation of complaints by the Secretary

16   The investigation of complaints shall be carried out by the Secretary under the direction of the Commissioner or the Committee in such manner as they or either of them think fit. In directing the carrying out of such investigation, the Committee and the Commissioner shall have regard to the following provisions.

17   The complaint shall be sent to the barrister concerned together with a letter requiring him to comment in writing on the complaint and to make any written representations he sees fit as to his conduct or the services he has provided to the complainant. That letter shall be sent to the address notified by the barrister pursuant to paragraphs 304(a)(i) or 402(a) of the Code of Conduct.

      If no response is received within 28 days of the date of posting of such letter, the Secretary may proceed as if the barrister's response had been to deny the allegations made in the complaint in their entirety.

18   The complaint should normally also be sent to any solicitor or solicitor's agent named on the form of complaint as having instructed the barrister, and if the Commissioner directs to any other person whose name and address is provided by the complainant as a person able to assist the Committee together with a letter seeking their comments upon the complaint.

19   Any comments received by the Secretary from the barrister concerned in answer to the complaint should normally be sent to the complainant, under cover of a letter seeking his response to the barrister's comments, but the Commissioner may at his discretion direct that this step be omitted if, for example, issues of privilege or confidentiality make it inappropriate.

20   The Secretary may enter into further correspondence with any of the parties whose comments have been sought, or any other party who the Secretary, the Commissioner or the Committee think capable of affording further assistance.

Commissioners powers under paragraph 6(b)

21   When a complaint is referred to the Commissioner following investigation, as set out in paragraph 6(b) above, the Commissioner shall consider whether, on the information now available to him, it discloses a *prima facie* case of professional misconduct or inadequate professional service.

22   In order to decide this question, he may direct any further investigations to be made that he sees fit, and may seek further information or assistance from any other person whom he considers may be capable of affording it.

23   The Commissioner may at any time adjourn consideration of a complaint for such period as he thinks fit, whether during the currency of related legal proceedings or for any other reason.

24   If the Commissioner decides that a *prima facie* case of professional misconduct or inadequate professional service is not shown, he shall dismiss the complaint, and shall notify the complainant and the barrister complained against of his decision and of his reasons for it.

25   The Commissioner may reopen or reconsider a complaint which has been disposed of under paragraph 24 above:

(a) following a recommendation of the Legal Services Ombudsman that he do so, or

(b) where new evidence becomes available to him which leads him to conclude that he should do so, or

(c) for some other good reason.

Following such reconsideration he may take such further or different action as he thinks fit, as if the former decision had not been made.

Powers and functions of the Committee

26   The powers of the Committee shall be as follows:

(a) to determine whether any complaint discloses a *prima facie* case of professional misconduct, and if so to deal with it in accordance with these Rules.

(b) if it determines that no such *prima facie* case is disclosed, to determine whether the complaint discloses a *prima facie* case of inadequate professional service by the barrister concerned and if so to deal with it in accordance with these Rules.

(c) to prefer charges of professional misconduct before Disciplinary Tribunals (as provided by the Disciplinary Tribunals Regulations appended as Schedule A, as amended from time to time, to the Constitution of the Council of the Inns of Court), to refer to such tribunals any legal aid complaint relating to the conduct of a barrister and to be responsible for prosecuting any such charges or legal aid complaints before such Tribunals.

(d) to prefer and deal summarily with charges of professional misconduct in accordance with the Summary Procedure Rules forming Annexe N to the Code of Conduct.

(e) to take such other actions in relation to complaints as are permitted by these Rules.

(f) to make recommendations on matters of professional conduct to the Professional Standards Committee, as the Committee may think appropriate.

(g) to make rulings on matters of professional conduct when the Committee considers it appropriate to do so.

(h) to exercise the power of the Bar Council under paragraph 104 of the Code of Conduct to grant waivers of the provisions of that Code either generally or in particular cases.

(i) to exercise the power of the Bar Council to designate Legal Advice Centres for the purposes of Annexe H of the Code of Conduct.

27 The Committee shall consider complaints and the results of investigations thereof referred to it by the Commissioner pursuant to paragraph 7 above, together with the Commissioner's comments thereon, in such manner as it shall see fit.

28 Upon considering any complaint, the Committee may:

(a) dismiss the complaint provided that each of the Lay Members present at the meeting consents to such dismissal, whereupon the Secretary shall notify the complainant and the barrister complained against of the dismissal and the reasons for it.

(b) determine that no further action shall be taken on the complaint.

(c) at any time postpone consideration of the complaint, whether to permit further investigation of the complaint to be made, or during the currency of related legal proceedings or for any other reason it sees fit.

(d) if the complaint does not disclose a *prima facie* case of professional misconduct (whether with or without inadequate professional service) but the barrister's conduct is nevertheless such as to give cause for concern, draw it to his attention in writing. The Committee may in those circumstances advise him as to his future conduct either in writing or by directing him to attend on the Chairman of the Committee or some other person nominated by the Committee to receive such advice, and may thereafter exercise the powers given to it by paragraph (e) below, or dismiss the complaint. If the Committee considers that the circumstances of the complaint are relevant to the barrister's position as a pupilmaster, it may notify the barrister's Inn of its concern in such manner as it sees fit. If the complaint is dismissed the Secretary shall notify the complainant of the dismissal and the reasons for it.

(e) if the complaint does not disclose a *prima facie* case of professional misconduct but does disclose a *prima facie* case of inadequate professional service, the Committee shall consider whether the following conditions are satisfied:

(i) the complainant is the barrister's lay client or his duly authorised representative or in the case of an employed barrister the person to whom he has supplied the professional service in question, and

(ii)   the subject-matter of the complaint is something in respect of which the barrister would be not be entitled to immunity from suit as an advocate in civil law.

If the Committee considers that the above conditions are satisfied, it may direct that the complaint be referred to an Adjudication Panel to be dealt with in accordance with the Adjudication Panel Rules (Annexe P to the Code of Conduct). If the Committee considers that either of the above conditions are not satisfied, it may dismiss the complaint whereupon the Secretary shall notify the complainant and the barrister of the dismissal and the reasons for it.

(f)   if a *prima facie* case of professional misconduct (whether with or without inadequate professional service) is disclosed but in the opinion of the Committee the matter is not serious enough to warrant treatment under sub-paragraphs (g) or (h) below, direct that the complaint be dealt with by informal attendance by the barrister to explain his conduct following the procedure set out in paragraphs 39 *et seq.* below.

(g)   if a *prima facie* case of professional misconduct (whether with or without inadequate professional service) is disclosed but in the opinion of the Committee there are no disputes of fact which cannot fairly be resolved by a summary procedure, and no charge arising out of the complaint which, if proved or admitted before a Disciplinary Tribunal, would be likely to result in a sentence of disbarment, deal with the matter summarily in accordance with the Summary Procedure Rules (Annexe N to the Code of Conduct).

(h)   if a *prima facie* case of professional misconduct (whether with or without inadequate professional service) is disclosed in circumstances where in the opinion of the Committee paragraph (g) above does not apply, direct that the complaint should form the subject-matter of a charge before a Disciplinary Tribunal.

29   The Committee may reopen or reconsider a complaint which has been disposed of under paragraph 28 above:

(a)   following a recommendation of the Legal Services Ombudsman that they do so, or

(b)   where new evidence becomes available to the Committee which leads them to conclude that they should do so, or

(c)   for some other good reason.

30   Following such reopening or reconsideration, the Committee may take any further or different action it thinks fit, as if the former decision had not been made, provided that if a direction under

paragraph 28(h) above has been given, and charges have been forwarded to the Clerk and served on the Defendant, the Committee's actions shall be confined to instructing counsel for the Committee to

(a)   offer no evidence on a charge, or

(b)   apply to the Directions Judge for the making of additions to or amendments of a charge.

Disciplinary charges

31   If the Committee directs under paragraph 28(h) above that a complaint shall form the subject matter of a charge before a Disciplinary Tribunal, the following paragraphs shall have effect.

32   The Committee shall nominate one of its members ('the PCC Representative') to be responsible for the conduct of the proceedings on its behalf. If for any reason he is unable to act at any time, the Chairman of the Committee may nominate another member to act in his place. Where no further investigation is required, the PCC representative shall settle the charge having regard to the provisions of paragraph 34 below.

33   Save in cases where the charges have been settled by the PCC Representative, the Secretary or investigations officer shall arrange for the appointment of counsel to settle the charge and to present the case before the Tribunal, and may arrange for the appointment of a solicitor or such other person as may be necessary to assist counsel and prepare the case.

34   Save in cases where the charges have been settled by the PCC Representative, counsel shall settle such charges as he considers appropriate founded upon the facts or evidence from which the complaint arose and any further or other matters which have been revealed by investigations directed by either counsel, the PCC Representative or the Committee. Such charges may be of professional misconduct and, where appropriate, of inadequate professional service, save that no charges of inadequate professional service shall be settled unless:

(i)   the complainant is the barrister's lay client or his duly authorised representative or in the case of an employed barrister the person to whom he has supplied the professional service in question, and

(ii)   the subject-matter of the complaint is something in respect of which the barrister would be not be entitled to immunity from suit as an advocate in civil law.

35   It shall be the responsibility of the investigations officer at the Bar Council, subject to the supervision of the PCC Representative and/or the Committee:

(a)   to forward the charge to the Clerk to the Tribunal, as required by Regulation 5 of the Disciplinary Tribunal

Regulations, together with the other documents specified therein, and

    (b)   to make any necessary administrative arrangements for the summoning of witnesses, the production of documents, and generally for the proper presentation of the case on behalf of the PCC Representative before the Tribunal.

36   Enquiries shall be made of the Under- or Sub-Treasurer of the barrister's Inn and of the Bar Council concerning any previous findings of misconduct against him, so that this information may be available to be placed before the Tribunal if any charge against him is found to have been proved.

37   If a barrister is a member of more than one Inn, references in these Rules to his Inn shall mean the Inn by which he was called, unless he is a Bencher in which case his Inn shall mean the Inn of which he is a Bencher.

38   The Committee may, with the approval of the Finance and the Professional Standards Committees, authorise the Secretary in an appropriate case to arrange that Counsel, or any other person appointed pursuant to paragraph 33 above, be paid reasonable remuneration for work done on the Committee's behalf. The cost of such remuneration shall be borne by the Bar Council.

Informal Hearings

39   Where the Committee decides under paragraph 28(f) above that a complaint should be dealt with informally it shall direct that the barrister attend upon a panel consisting of not less than two nor more than three barrister members of the Committee and one lay member, who may be the Commissioner. When the Committee directs such attendance it shall specify

    (a)   what, in summary form, are the matters upon which the Committee has found a *prima facie* case of misconduct to be disclosed and on which the barrister's explanation of his conduct is required, and

    (b)   whether, on the information available to them, the Committee also regard a *prima facie* case of inadequate professional service as having been disclosed, and if so what, in summary form, are the matters arising in that regard which the barrister will also be asked to explain.

40   Where the Committee has specified any matters under paragraph 39(b), the Secretary shall make such enquiries as he sees fit, or as are directed by the Commissioner or the Committee, to establish whether the complainant claims to have suffered financial loss as a result of the conduct complained of, and if so the exact nature and amount of that claimed loss and the evidence available to support the claim, and to establish from the barrister the nature of the work he carried out for the complainant out of which the complaint arose, the fee rendered for such work, and whether or not such fee has been paid.

41   At the hearing the panel and the barrister shall have available a bundle of the documents relevant to the complaint, which shall include, in the case of a complaint where any matter under paragraph 39(b) has been specified, such information as the Secretary has obtained under paragraph 40 above.

42   The barrister shall attend on the panel at the day and time arranged, and shall provide to the panel such information as he wishes to put before them in connection with his conduct in relation to the matters specified, and shall answer so far as he is able such further questions as the panel may put to him which may relate to any aspects of the conduct complained of.

43   Following such hearing, the panel may reach the following decisions

   (a) It may conclude that the barrister's explanation of his professional conduct has been satisfactory, whereupon it shall dismiss the complaint.

   (b) It may conclude that no further action shall be taken on the complaint.

   (c) It may conclude that the barrister's explanation of his professional conduct has not been satisfactory, whereupon it may

      (i)   give him advice as to his future conduct, or

      (ii) admonish him

      and such advice or admonishment may be delivered orally or in writing.

   (d) Regardless of the conclusion reached in relation to the barrister's professional conduct, the panel may conclude that a barrister has provided inadequate professional service in respect of the subject-matter of the complaint, provided the following conditions are satisfied:

      (i)   the complainant is the barrister's lay client or his duly authorised representative or in the case of an employed barrister the person to whom he has supplied the professional service in question, and

      (ii) the subject-matter of the complaint is not something in respect of which the barrister would be entitled to immunity from suit as an advocate in civil law.

44   If the panel is not unanimous on any issue, the finding made shall be that of the majority of them. If the panel is equally divided, the burden of proof being on the complainant, the finding made shall be that most favourable to the barrister.

45   If a finding of inadequate professional service is made under paragraph 43(d), the panel shall consider what remedy should be

granted to the complainant in respect of such inadequate service. The panel may:

(a) determine that it is not appropriate to take any action in respect of the complaint,

(b) adjourn consideration of the remedy to permit investigation or further investigation of the consequences of the inadequate professional service for the complainant and reconvene the panel when the results of such investigations are known,

(c) direct the barrister to make a formal apology to the complainant for the conduct complained of,

(d) direct the barrister to repay or remit all or part of any fee rendered in respect of the inadequate service,

(e) direct the barrister to pay compensation to the complainant in such sum as the panel shall direct not exceeding £2,000.

Save that no order under paragraph (e) shall be made unless the panel are satisfied that the complainant has established on the balance of probabilities that he has suffered loss recoverable at law caused by the inadequate professional service and further that the panel are satisfied that no issue of law or fact arises in relation to such loss which cannot fairly be resolved on the material then before them. If the panel is so satisfied, it may direct payment of such sum by way of compensation as it sees fit up to the amount of such loss or £2,000, whichever is the less. Further in determining whether any sum is to be paid under paragraph (e) hereof, or in fixing the amount of such sum, the panel shall in particular have regard to the availability to the complainant of other forms of redress, to the gravity of the conduct complained of, and to the fee claimed by the barrister for the inadequate service.

46   An appeal shall lie at the instance of the barrister from any decision of a panel that a barrister has provided inadequate professional service, and against any decision as to the remedy to be granted to the complainant for such service in the same manner as an appeal lies from a decision of an Adjudication Panel in respect of the same matters.

47   No finding by a panel under this procedure shall be publishable, save that if the panel considers that the circumstances of the complaint are relevant to the barrister's position as a pupilmaster, it may notify the barrister's Inn of its concerns in such manner as it sees fit.

Definitions

48   In these Rules unless the context otherwise requires

(a) Any term defined in the Code of Conduct shall carry the same meaning as it does in the Code of Conduct.

(b) Any reference to a person includes any natural person, legal person and/or firm. Any reference to the masculine gender includes the feminine and the neuter, and any reference to the singular includes the plural, and in each case *vice versa*.

(c) 'professional misconduct' shall bear the same meaning in these Rules as in paragraph 802 of the Code of Conduct.

(d) 'inadequate professional service' means such conduct towards the lay client (or in the case of an employed barrister the person to whom he has supplied the professional service in question) or performance of professional services for that client which falls significantly short of that which is to be reasonably expected of a barrister in all the circumstances.

(e) 'a complaint' means an allegation by any person or by the Bar Council of its own motion, of professional misconduct as defined in paragraph 802.1 of the Code of Conduct or of inadequate professional service.

(f) 'a legal aid complaint' shall mean a complaint so described in s. 40 of the Administration of Justice Act 1985 as amended by the Legal Aid Act 1988, and references to 'a complaint' include a legal aid complaint.

Commencement and Transitional Provisions

49   In relation to any complaint which had been raised in the records of the Professional Conduct Committee before the date fixed by the Bar Council for these Rules to come into effect ('the Commencement Date'), these Rules shall not apply but the Professional Conduct Committee Rules in force immediately before that date shall apply to that complaint. In relation to complaints raised after the Commencement Date, the procedure set out in these Rules shall apply, save that no finding of inadequate professional service may be made against a barrister in respect of any conduct of his which took place before 13th July 1996.

ANNEXE L

THE DISCIPLINARY TRIBUNALS REGULATIONS

THE DISCIPLINARY TRIBUNALS REGULATIONS 1996

Arrangement of Regulations

1   Definitions

In these regulations:

(a)   'The PCC' shall mean the Professional Conduct and Complaints Committee that is to say the committee or sub-committee (however named) of the Bar Council to which is assigned the duty of preferring charges of professional misconduct (with or without charges of inadequate professional service) or charges consisting of legal aid complaints against barristers before Disciplinary Tribunals.

(b)   'The relevant procedure' shall mean the procedure adopted by the PCC from time to time for preferring such charges.

(c)   Any reference to the Inns' Council or to the members thereof shall be a reference to the Inns' Council or the members thereof other than the Officers and the Chairman of the Council of Legal Education.

(d)   Other expressions shall have the meanings respectively assigned to them by Paragraph 1 of the Introduction to the Constitutions of the General Council of the Bar, the Council of the Inns of Court and the Council of Legal Education, or by the Code of Conduct of the Bar Council.

(e)   'The Act of 1985' means the Administration of Justice Act 1985 as amended by the Legal Aid Act 1988.

(f)   'Legal aid complaint' has the meaning ascribed to it by Section 40 of the Act of 1985.

(g)   'Lay Representative' means one of the lay persons appointed by the Bar Council to serve on Disciplinary Tribunals.

(h)   'Inadequate professional service' shall have the meaning ascribed to it in Annex K of the Code of Conduct of the Bar of England and Wales.

2   Composition of Disciplinary Tribunals

(1)   A Disciplinary Tribunal shall consist of the following five persons nominated by the President:

(a)   a Judge

(b)   a Lay Representative

(c)   three Barristers in independent practice of not less than five years standing and not more than 70 years of age.

Provided that:-

(i)   if the Barrister charged is an Employed or Non-Practising Barrister, at least one of the barristers nominated should normally be Employed or Non-Practising;

(ii)   no Barrister or Lay Representative shall be nominated to serve on a Tribunal which is to consider a charge arising in respect of any matter considered at any meeting of the PCC which he attended.

(2)   The President shall select another member of the relevant class to fill any vacancy in the Disciplinary Tribunal membership that has arisen prior to the substantive hearing of the charge.

(3)   At any time before the commencement of the substantive hearing of the charge, the President may cancel any or all of the nominations made pursuant to this regulation, and make such alternative nominations as in the exercise of his discretion he deems to be expedient.

(4)   The proceedings of a Disciplinary Tribunal shall be valid notwithstanding that one or more of the members other than the Chairman or the Lay Representative becomes unable to continue to act or disqualified from continuing to act, so long as the number of members present throughout the substantive hearing of the charge is not reduced below three and continues to include the Chairman and the Lay Representative.

(5)   A member of a Disciplinary Tribunal who has been absent for any time during a sitting shall take no further part in the proceedings.

3   Sittings of Disciplinary Tribunals

The President shall appoint Disciplinary Tribunals to sit at such times as are necessary for the prompt and expeditious determination of charges preferred against barristers in accordance with the provisions of these Regulations.

4   Clerks

The President shall appoint a person or persons to act as Clerk or Clerks to the Disciplinary Tribunals to perform the functions specified in these Regulations and such other functions as the President or the Chairman of any Tribunal may direct. No person who has been engaged in the investigation of a complaint against a barrister in accordance with the relevant procedure or otherwise shall act as Clerk in relation to disciplinary proceedings arising out of that complaint.

5   Service of Charges

(1)   Following the formulation of the charge or charges by counsel appointed by the PCC Representative in accordance with the relevant procedure, the PCC Representative shall cause a copy thereof to be served on the barrister concerned ('the defendant'), together with a copy of these Regulations.

(2)   The PCC Representative shall at the same time cause copies of the charge or charges to be supplied to the President.

6   Representation of complainant's interests

It shall be the responsibility of the PCC Representative and counsel appointed by the PCC Representative to represent the interests of the complainant in relation to any charge of inadequate professional service.

7   Convening Orders

(1)   After receipt of the copy charge or charges supplied pursuant to Regulation 5, and in any case not less than 14 days

before the substantive hearing, the President shall issue an Order ('the Convening Order') specifying

    (a)   the date of the sitting of the Disciplinary Tribunal at which it is proposed the charge or charges should be heard

    (b)   the identities of those persons who it is proposed should constitute the Disciplinary Tribunal to hear his case

    (c)   the identity of the Clerk.

(2)   The President shall arrange for the service of the Convening Order on the defendant, and for copies thereof to be supplied to the nominated members of the Disciplinary Tribunal and the Clerk. In the order the defendant's attention will be drawn to:

    (a)   his right to represent himself or be represented by counsel, with or without instructing a solicitor, as he shall think fit

    (b)   his right to inspect and be given copies of documents referred to in the List served pursuant to Regulation 7 below

    (c)   his right (without prejudice to his right to appear and take part in the proceedings) to deliver a written answer to the charge or charges if he thinks fit.

(3)   The defendant shall have the right upon receipt of the Convening Order to give notice to the President objecting to any one or more of the proposed members of the Disciplinary Tribunal. Such notice shall specify the ground of objection.

(4)   Upon receipt of such objection, the President shall, if satisfied that it is properly made (but subject to Paragraph (5) of this Regulation) exercise the power conferred on him by Paragraph (3) of Regulation 2 to nominate a substitute Member or Members of the Tribunal, and notify the defendant accordingly. Upon receipt of such notification, the defendant shall have _mutatis mutandis_ in relation to such substitute Member or Members the like right of objection as is conferred by Paragraph (3) of this Regulation.

(5)   No objection to any Member of the Tribunal shall be valid on the ground that he has or may have had knowledge of a previous charge of professional misconduct or breach of proper professional standards or a charge consisting of a legal aid complaint against the defendant or any finding on any such charge, or of any sentence imposed on the defendant in connection therewith.

(6)   The Convening Order shall contain words drawing the attention of the defendant to the rights conferred by Paragraphs (2)–(5) of this Regulation.

8   Documents to be Served

(1)   A barrister who is to be charged before a Disciplinary Tribunal shall, as soon as practicable (but in any event not later than 10 days before the date of the Preliminary Hearing) be supplied with:

(a)   a copy of the statement of the evidence of each witness intended to be called in support of the charge or charges

(b)   a list of the documents intended to be relied on by the PCC Representative.

(2)   Nothing in this Regulation shall preclude the reception by a Disciplinary Tribunal of the evidence of a witness a copy of whose statement has not been served on the defendant (within the time specified aforesaid, or at all), or of a document not included in the List of Documents, provided the Tribunal is of opinion that the defendant is not materially prejudiced thereby, or on such terms as are necessary to ensure that no such prejudice arises.

9   Preliminary Hearings; Directions Judge; Powers of Chairman etc

(1)   The President shall designate a judge or judges ('the Directions Judge(s)') to exercise the powers and functions specified in this Regulation.

(2)   Before the sitting of the Disciplinary Tribunal at which the charges are to be heard, the Directions Judge shall (subject to Paragraph (7) of this Regulation) hold a Preliminary Hearing for the purpose of giving directions and of taking such other steps as he considers suitable for the clarification of the issues before the tribunal and generally for the just and expeditious handling of the proceedings.

(3)   The directions to be given and steps taken by the Directions Judge may concern, but shall not be limited to, the following matters:

(a)   whether the hearing should not be held in public

(b)   applications for separate hearings

(c)   applications to sever charges

(d)   applications to strike out charges

(e)   attendance of witnesses

(f)   a requirement that the parties provide each other with the names of all witnesses to be called at the hearing within a specified time limit

(g)   admission of documents, including any documents intended to be relied upon by the PCC Representative in relation to charges of inadequate professional service

(h)   admission of facts, in accordance with the procedure set out at Paragraph (4) of this Regulation

(i) the estimated duration of the substantive hearing

(j) such other matters as he deems expedient for the efficient conduct of the hearing

(k) consideration of any application under Regulation 21(12)(ii) .

(4) (a) The Directions Judge may, if he thinks fit, request the defendant or his representative to state (either forthwith or in writing within such time as may be specified) whether any and if so which of such of the facts relied on in support of the charges as may be specified is disputed, and/or the grounds on which such fact is disputed.

(b) The Clerk shall cause a record to be made of the making of such a request as aforesaid, and of the defendants's response thereto, and the same shall be drawn to the attention of the Disciplinary Tribunal at the conclusion of the substantive hearing, if relevant, on the question of costs.

(5) The powers and functions specified in this Regulation may be exercised by a Judge nominated by the President other than the Directions Judge, including the Judge designated in the Convening Order as Chairman of the Tribunal appointed to hear and determine the charge or charges against the defendant.

(6) The Clerk shall take a note of the proceedings at a Preliminary Hearing and shall cause a record to be drawn up and served on the parties setting out the directions given or admissions made at the Preliminary Hearing, including, without prejudice to the generality of the directions given, a record of any directions which relate to any of the matters specifically set out under Paragraph (3) of this Regulation.

(7) A defendant aggrieved by a direction given or other step taken pursuant to this Regulation may, provided that he acts promptly following the service on him of the record of any directions, give notice to the Clerk of his intention to apply for a review of such direction or step; such review will be conducted by the Chairman of the Tribunal sitting with a Lay Representative, who shall, on such application being made, give such directions or take such other steps as they see fit.

(8) The PCC Representative and the defendant or his representative may, in advance of the date fixed for the Preliminary Hearing, agree upon the directions to be made and/or steps to be taken thereat, or that no such directions or steps are required and shall notify the Clerk in writing of such agreement; following such notification the Directions Judge may, if he thinks fit, make directions in the terms agreed and/or direct that no Preliminary Hearing is required.

(9) For the avoidance of doubt the Directions Judge, or the Chairman of the Disciplinary Tribunal designated in the

Convening Order (or failing the Directions Judge or the Chairman, any other Judge nominated by the President) may

(a)   upon the application of either party at any time extend or abridge any time limit governing the disciplinary procedures on such terms as he thinks just

(b)   upon the application of either party, or of his own motion, hold further preliminary hearings for the purpose of giving any further directions or taking any other steps which he considers necessary for the proper conduct of the proceedings

(c)   adjourn the preliminary hearing from time to time as he considers appropriate.

10   Provision of Documents

There shall be provided to each member of the Disciplinary Tribunal prior to the commencement of the substantive hearing copies of the following documents:

(a)   the Order of the President constituting the Tribunal

(b)   the Charges and any particulars thereof

(c)   any documents proposed to be relied on by the PCC Representative or by the defendant, unless a direction has been made at the Preliminary Hearing or otherwise, that copies of such documents be withheld

(d)   any written answer to the charges submitted by or on behalf of the defendant

(e)   such other documents (which may include copies of witness statements) as at the Preliminary Hearing or otherwise have been directed to be or the PCC Representative and the defendant or his representative have agreed, should be laid before the Tribunal prior to the start of the hearing

(f)   the record of directions given at each preliminary hearing which has been drawn up and served on the parties pursuant to Regulation 9(6).

11   Procedure At The Hearing

The Proceedings of a Disciplinary Tribunal shall be governed by the rules of natural justice, subject to which the tribunal may

(a)   admit any evidence, whether oral or written, whether direct or hearsay, and whether or not the same would be admissible in a court of law

(b)   give such directions with regard to the conduct of and procedure at the hearing, and with regard to the admission of evidence thereat, as it considers appropriate for securing that the defendant has a proper opportunity of answering the charge or otherwise as shall be just

(c)   exclude any hearsay evidence if it is not satisfied that reasonable steps have been taken to obtain direct evidence of the facts sought to be proved by the hearsay evidence.

The tribunal shall apply the criminal standard of proof when adjudicating upon charges of professional misconduct, and the civil standard of proof when adjudicating upon charges of inadequate professional service, if any.

12   Hearing in Private

The hearing before a Disciplinary Tribunal shall be in public unless at a Preliminary Hearing or otherwise it has been directed that it shall not be held in public, and this direction has not been over-ruled by the Tribunal.

13   Decision of a Court or Tribunal

(1)   In proceedings before a Disciplinary Tribunal which involve the decision of a court or tribunal, the following rules of evidence shall apply provided that it is proved in each case that the decision relates to the defendant:

(a)   the fact that the defendant has been convicted of a criminal offence may be proved by producing a certified copy of the certificate of conviction relating to the offence; proof of a conviction in this matter shall constitute prima facie evidence that the defendant was guilty of the offence the subject thereof.

(b)   the finding and sentence of any tribunal in or outside England and Wales exercising a professional disciplinary jurisdiction may be proved by producing a certified copy of the finding and sentence.

(c)   the judgment of any civil court may be proved by producing a certified copy of the judgment.

(2)   In any case set out in Paragraph (1) of this Regulation, the findings of fact by the court or tribunal upon which the conviction, finding, sentence or judgment is based shall be admissible as prima facie proof of those facts.

14   Absence of Defendant

(1)   If a Disciplinary Tribunal is satisfied that the relevant procedure has been complied with and the defendant has been duly served (in accordance with Regulation 29 of these Regulations) with the documents required by Regulations 5, 7 and 8 and the defendant has not attended at the time and place appointed for the hearing, the tribunal may nevertheless proceed

to hear and determine the charge or charges, subject to compliance with Paragraph (12)(i) of Regulation 21 in the event of any charge being found proved.

(2)   If a Disciplinary Tribunal is satisfied that it has not been practicable to comply with the relevant procedure, the Tribunal shall hear and determine the charge or charges in the absence of the defendant subject to compliance with Paragraph (12)(ii) of Regulation 21 in the event of any charge being found proved.

15   Recording of Proceedings

The Clerk shall arrange for a record of the proceedings before a Disciplinary Tribunal to be made by the employment of a shorthand writer or the use of a recording machine.

16   Amendment of Charges

A Disciplinary Tribunal may at any time before or during the hearing direct that the charge or charges shall be amended provided always:

(a)   that the Tribunal is satisfied that the defendant will not by reason of such an amendment suffer any substantial prejudice in the conduct of his defence,

(b)   that the Tribunal shall, if so requested by the defendant, adjourn for such time as is reasonably necessary to enable him to meet the charge or charges as so amended,

(c)   that the Tribunal shall make such Order as to the costs of or occasioned by the amendment, or of any consequential adjournment of the proceedings, as it considers appropriate.

17   Adjournment

(1)   Subject to the provisions of the following Paragraph, the Disciplinary Tribunal shall sit from day to day until it has arrived at a finding and if any charge has been found proved until sentence is pronounced.

(2)   Notwithstanding the provisions of Paragraph (1) of this Regulation, a Disciplinary Tribunal may, if the Tribunal decides an adjournment is necessary for any reason, adjourn the hearing for such period as it may decide. In particular, if a finding of inadequate professional service is made and the Tribunal considers that an award of compensation to the complainant may be appropriate, it may adjourn to enable further investigation of that question to take place, if it does not already have the necessary material before it.

18   The Finding

At the conclusion of the hearing, the finding of the Disciplinary Tribunal on each charge shall be set down in writing and signed by the chairman and all members of the Tribunal. If the members of the Tribunal are not unanimous as to the finding on any charge, the finding to be recorded on that charge shall be that of the majority. If the members of the Tribunal are equally divided as to the finding on any charge, then, the burden of proof being on the PCC Representative, the finding to be recorded on that charge shall be that which is the most favourable to the defendant. The chairman of the Tribunal shall then announce the Tribunal's finding on the charge or charges.

19   The Sentence

(1)   If the Disciplinary Tribunal shall have found the charge or any of the charges proved, evidence may be given of any previous finding of professional misconduct or of breach of proper professional standards or of inadequate professional service or any finding on a charge consisting of a legal aid complaint against the defendant. After hearing any representations by or on behalf of the defendant the Tribunal shall set down in writing its decision as to the sentence. If the members of the tribunal are not unanimous as to the sentence, the sentence to be recorded shall be that decided by the majority. If the members of the Tribunal are equally divided as to the sentence, the sentence to be recorded shall be that which is the most favourable to the defendant. The chairman of the Tribunal shall then announce the Tribunal's decision as to sentence.

(2)   (a)   A barrister against whom a charge of professional misconduct has been found proved may be sentenced by the Disciplinary Tribunal to be:

> (i)   disbarred;
>
> (ii)   suspended for a prescribed period (either unconditionally or subject to conditions);
>
> (iii)   ordered to pay a fine of up to £5,000 to the Bar Council;
>
> (iv)   ordered to repay or forego fees;
>
> (v)   reprimanded by the Treasurer of his Inn;
>
> (vi)   admonished by the Tribunal; or
>
> (vii)   given advice by the Tribunal as to his future conduct; or
>
> (viii) ordered by the Tribunal to attend on a nominated person to be admonished; or
>
> (ix)   ordered by the Tribunal to attend on a nominated person to be given advice as to his future conduct.

(b)   A barrister against whom a charge of inadequate professional service has been found proved may be

> (i)   directed to make a formal apology to the complainant for the conduct in relation to which the finding was made;

> (ii)   directed to repay or remit all or part of any fee rendered in respect of the inadequate service; or

> (iii)   directed to pay compensation to the complainant in such sum as the Tribunal shall direct not exceeding £2,000.

Save that no order under paragraph (iii) shall be made unless the Tribunal is satisfied that the complainant has established on the balance of probabilities that he has suffered loss recoverable at law caused by the inadequate professional service and further the Tribunal is satisfied that no issue of law or fact arises in relation to such loss which cannot fairly be resolved on the material before it, whether then or following any adjournment to permit the PCC Representative to adduce further evidence and/or to make further representations to the Tribunal on this issue. If the Tribunal is so satisfied it may direct payment of such sum by way of compensation as it sees fit up to the amount of such loss or £2,000, whichever is the less. Further in determining whether any sum is to be paid under paragraph (iii) hereof, or in fixing the amount of such sum, the Tribunal shall in particular have regard to the availability to the complainant of other forms of redress, to the gravity of the conduct complained of and to the fee claimed by the barrister for the inadequate service.

(c)   In any case where a charge of professional misconduct or inadequate professional service has been found proved, the Tribunal may decide that no action should be taken against the defendant.

(3)   Sections 41 and 42 of the Administration of Justice Act 1985 (as substituted by Section 33 of the Legal Aid Act 1988) confer certain powers (relating to the reduction or cancellation of legal aid fees and to exclusion from legal aid work) on a Disciplinary Tribunal in the cases to which those Sections apply. Accordingly:-

(a)   Any Disciplinary Tribunal which hears a charge consisting of a legal aid complaint relating to the conduct of a barrister may if it thinks fit (and whether or not it sentences the barrister in accordance with paragraph (2) of this Regulation in respect of any conduct arising out of the same legal aid complaint) order that any such fees as are referred to in Section 41(2) of the Act of 1985 shall be reduced or cancelled.

(b)   Where a Disciplinary Tribunal hears a charge of professional misconduct against a barrister it may (in addition to or instead of sentencing that barrister in accordance with Paragraph (2) of this Regulation) order that he shall be excluded from legal aid work either temporarily or for a specified period if it determines that there is good reason for the exclusion arising out of (i) his conduct in connection with any such services as are mentioned in Section 40(1) of the Act of 1985; or (ii) his professional conduct generally.

(4)   Whether or not a Disciplinary Tribunal shall have found any charge proved, if the Disciplinary Tribunal considers that the circumstances of the complaint are relevant to the barrister in his capacity as a pupilmaster, it may notify the barrister's Inn of its concerns in such manner as it sees fit.

20   Sentence of Suspension

(1)   Any sentence of suspension may apply to the whole of a barrister's practice or to such part only as the Disciplinary Tribunal may determine.

(2)   The conditions to which a sentence of suspension may be made subject include a requirement that the barrister shall undergo such further pupillage or training or attain such standard of competence as the Tribunal may determine.

21   Wording of the Sentence

The sentence determined by a Disciplinary Tribunal if a charge of professional misconduct has been found proved shall be recorded as follows:

(1)   Disbarment

'That . . . . . be disbarred and expelled from the Honourable Society of . . . . .'

(2)   Suspension

'That . . . . . be suspended from practice as a barrister and from enjoyment of all rights and privileges as a member of the Honourable Society of . . . . . and be prohibited from holding himself out as being a barrister without disclosing his suspension for (stating the length of the prescribed period)'. (Note: If the Tribunal decides that the sentence of suspension shall apply to part only of the barrister's practice or shall be subject to conditions, such part or such conditions (as the case may be) shall be specified in the wording of the sentence.)

(3)   Payment of Fine

'That . . . . . pay a fine of £ . . . . . to the Bar Council.'

(4)   Repayment or Foregoing of Fees

'That . . . . . shall repay all fees (fees amounting to £ . . . . .) received by him (shall forego all fees (fees amounting to £ . . . . .) due to be paid to him) in connection with . . . . .'

(5)   Reprimand

'That . . . . . be reprimanded by the Treasurer of the Honourable Society of . . . . .'

(6)   Admonishment

'That . . . . . is hereby admonished'; or 'That . . . . . is hereby ordered to attend . . . . . to be admonished'.

(7)   Advice as to Future Conduct

'That . . . . . has been advised by the Tribunal as to his future conduct in regard to . . . . .' or 'That . . . . . is hereby ordered to attend on . . . . . to be given advice as to his future conduct in regard to . . . . .'.

(8)   Order for Reduction of Legal Aid Fees

'That the fees payable to . . . . . in connection with his services under or in accordance with the Legal Aid Act 1988 or otherwise chargeable in connection with his services in respect of advice or assistance made available under Part III of that Act in relation to the items or matters specified in the first column of the Schedule hereto be reduced to the sum or sums specified in the second column of that Schedule'.

The record of the sentence shall then contain a Schedule setting out the matters referred to above.

(9)   Order for Cancellation of Legal Aid Fees

'That the fees payable to . . . . . in connection with his services under or in accordance with the Legal Aid Act 1988 or otherwise chargeable in connection with his services in respect of advice or assistance made available under Part III of that Act in relation to the items or matters specified in the Schedule hereto be cancelled'.

The record of the sentence shall then contain a Schedule identifying the items or matters referred to above.

(10)   Exclusion from Legal Aid Work

'That . . . . . be excluded from legal aid work (as explained in Section 42(4)(b) of the Administration of Justice Act 1985 as substituted by Section 33 of the Legal Aid Act 1988 (until . . . . .) (for a period . . . . . of beginning on . . . . .)

(11)   Membership of More than One Inn

If the barrister is a member of more than one Inn, each Inn of which he is a member shall be mentioned in the sentence.

(12)   Absence of the Barrister Charged

If the barrister charged has not been present throughout the proceedings, the sentence shall include one of the following two statements:

(i)   If the relevant procedure under Regulation 14(1) has been complied with, that the finding and sentence were made in the absence of the barrister in accordance with Regulation 14(1).

(ii)   If the procedure under Regulation 14(2) has been complied with, that the finding and the sentence were made in the absence of the barrister and that he has the right to apply to the Directions Judge for an order that there should be a new hearing before a fresh Disciplinary Tribunal.

22   Report of Finding and Sentence

(1)   As soon as practicable after the conclusion of the proceedings of a Disciplinary Tribunal, the chairman of the Tribunal shall prepare a report in writing of the finding on the charges of professional misconduct and, where applicable, the sentence. At the discretion of the chairman of the Tribunal, the report may also refer to matters which, in the light of the evidence given to the Tribunal, appear to require investigation or comment. He shall send copies of the report to the following:

(2)   In all cases

(i)   The Lord Chancellor

(ii)   The Lord Chief Justice

(iii)   The Attorney General

(iv)   The President

(v)   The Chairman of the Bar Council

(vi)   The Chairman of the Professional Conduct and Complaints Committee

(vii)   The barrister charged

(viii)   The Treasurer of the barrister's Inn of Call

(ix)   The Treasurer of any other Inn of which the barrister is a member.

(3)   In cases where one or more charges of professional misconduct have been found proved and any such charge constitutes or arises out of a legal aid complaint, and/or the sentence includes an order under Regulation 20(8), (9) or (10), the Legal Aid Board.

23   Appeal to the Visitors

(1)   In cases where one or more charges of professional misconduct have been proved, an appeal may be lodged with the Visitors against the conviction and/or sentence (including any finding of inadequate professional service) in accordance with the Hearings Before the Visitors Rules.

(2)   In cases where no professional misconduct has been proved, but one or more charges of inadequate professional service have been proved, an appeal shall lie at the instance of the barrister from any such finding, and against any decision as to the remedy to be granted to the complainant for such service in the same manner as an appeal lies from a decision of an Adjudication Panel in respect of the same matters.

24   Appeal: Sum Payable

Where an appeal is lodged with the Visitors, the Notice of Appeal must be accompanied by the sum of £250 payable to the General Council of the Bar to defray expenses, such sum to be refunded in the discretion of the Visitors in the event of an appeal which is successful wholly or in part.

25   Action by the Barrister's Inn

(1)   On receipt of the report prepared in accordance with Regulation 22, the Treasurer of the barrister's Inn of Call shall not less than 21 days after the conclusion of the Tribunal's proceedings pronounce the sentence decided on by the Tribunal, and take such further action as may be required to carry the sentence into effect. The Treasurer shall inform the persons specified in Paragraph (2) of Regulation 22 of the date on which the sentence is to take effect.

(2)   Similar action shall be taken by the Treasurer of any other Inn of which the barrister is a member in conjunction with the Treasurer of the barrister's Inn of Call.

(3)   In any case in which the barrister has given notice of appeal to the visitors against the finding and/or sentence of the Tribunal on the charges of professional misconduct, the action set out in paragraphs (1) and (2) of this Regulation shall be deferred until the appeal has been heard by the Visitors or otherwise disposed of without a hearing.

26   Publication of Finding and Sentence

(1)   The following procedures are to be observed in regard to publication of the finding and sentence of a Disciplinary Tribunal:

(i)   When the Tribunal has found one or more charges of professional misconduct have been proved the President shall publish the charges found proved and the sentence as soon as he has been informed by the Treasurer(s) of the barrister's Inn(s) of the date from which the sentence is to take effect.

(ii)   When the Tribunal has found that one or more charges of inadequate professional service have been proved, the President shall not publish the charges found proved and the finding unless the barrister charged so requests.

(iii)   When the Tribunal has found that any charge whether of professional misconduct or of inadequate professional service has not been proved the President shall not publish that charge and the finding unless the barrister charged so requests.

(2)   When publishing any finding, sentence or decision in accordance with sub-paragraph (1) of this Regulation, the President shall communicate the same in writing to:-

(i)   the Lord Chancellor;

(ii)   the Lord Chief Justice;

(iii)   the Attorney General;

(iv)   the Director of Public Prosecutions;

(v)   the Treasurer of each Inn for screening in the Hall, Benchers' Room and Treasurer's Office of the Inn;

(vi)   the Leaders of the six circuits;

(vii)   the barrister concerned

(viii) such one or more press agencies or other publications as the President may decide.

27   Deferment of Sentence pending Appeal

In any case where the carrying into effect of the sentence of the Disciplinary Tribunal has been deferred in accordance with Regulation 25(3), the Chairman of the Tribunal may, on application by the PCC, impose such terms on or require such undertaking from the barrister charged as he may think fit, including an undertaking not to practise pending the hearing of the barrister's appeal, provided always that the barrister may apply in writing to the President for a variation of such terms or undertaking (provided that the barrister sends a copy of his application on the same day to the PCC), and the President shall have power to vary the Chairman's decision.

28   Costs

(1)   A Disciplinary Tribunal shall have power to make such Orders for costs, whether against or in favour of a defendant, as it shall think fit.

(2)   Upon making such an Order a Disciplinary Tribunal shall either itself determine the amount of such costs or appoint a suitably qualified person to do so on its behalf.

(3)   Any costs ordered to be paid by or to a defendant shall be paid to or by the Bar Council.

(4)   Subject as aforesaid, all costs and expenses incurred by a Disciplinary Tribunal or by the PCC in connection with or preparatory to the hearing before the Tribunal shall be borne by the Bar Council.

29   Service of Documents

Any documents required to be served on a barrister arising out of or in connection with disciplinary proceedings shall be deemed to have been validly served:-

(1)   If sent by registered post, or recorded delivery post, or receipted hand delivery to:

(a)   the address notified by such barrister pursuant to Paragraphs 304(a)(i) or 402(a) of the Code of Conduct of the Bar of England and Wales (or any provisions amending or replacing the same); or

(b)   an address to which the barrister may request in writing that such documents be sent; or

(c)   in the absence of any such request, to his last known address;

and such service shall be deemed to have been made on the fifth working day after the date of posting or on the next working day after receipted hand delivery;

(2)   If actually served;

(3)   If served in any way which may be directed by the Directions Judge or the Chairman of the Disciplinary Tribunal.

For the purpose of this regulation 'receipted hand delivery' means by a delivery by hand which is acknowledged by a receipt signed by the barrister or his clerk.

30   Miscellaneous Provisions

(1)   Any duty or function or step which, pursuant to the provisions of these regulations, is to be discharged or carried out by the President may, if he is unable to act due to absence or any other reason, be discharged or carried out by any other member of the Inns Council, the Treasurer of any Inn or by any other person nominated in writing by the President for any specific purpose.

(2)   When the Treasurer of an Inn is a Royal Bencher, references in these Regulations to such Treasurer shall be read as references to his deputy.

31   Exclusion from Legal Aid Work - Application for Termination

(1)   A barrister who has been excluded from legal aid work under Section 42 of the Act of 1985 may apply for an order terminating his exclusion from legal aid work in accordance with this Regulation.

(2)   Any such application shall be in writing and shall be addressed to the President.

(3)   On considering any such application the President may dismiss the application or may determine that the barrister's exclusion from legal aid work be terminated forthwith or on a specified future date.

(4)   The President shall give notification of his decision in writing to the same persons as received copies of the report of the Disciplinary Tribunal which ordered that the barrister be excluded from legal aid work.

(5)   Upon the receipt of any such report the Treasurer of the applicant's Inn of Call and of any other Inn of which he is a member shall take action equivalent to that which it took in respect of the report of the Disciplinary Tribunal which sentenced the barrister to be excluded from legal aid work.

(6)   The procedures to be observed in regard to the publication of the decision of the President on any such application as is referred to in this Regulation shall be those which were applicable to the publication of the finding and sentence whereby the applicant was excluded from legal aid work.

(7)   The President shall have power to make such order for costs as he thinks fit and Regulation 28 shall apply with all necessary modifications.

32   Citation, Commencement, Revocations and Transitional Provisions

(1)   These Regulations may be cited as 'The Disciplinary Tribunals Regulations 1996' and shall come into operation on 14th April 1997 save that no finding of inadequate professional service may be made against a barrister in respect of any conduct of his which took place before 13th July 1996.

(2)   Subject to Paragraph (3) below, the Disciplinary Tribunals Regulations of the Council of the Inns of Court and any other rules or regulations relating to Disciplinary Tribunals made prior to the commencement of these Regulations shall cease to have effect on 13th April 1997.

(3)   In relation to any case in which a barrister was served with the charge or charges before 14th April 1997 these Regulations shall not apply and the matter shall continue to be dealt with pursuant to the Disciplinary Tribunals Regulations 1993.

ANNEXE M

THE HEARINGS BEFORE THE VISITORS RULES

THE HEARINGS BEFORE THE VISITORS RULES 1990

We, the Judges of Her Majesty's High Court of Justice, in the exercise of our powers as Visitors to the Inns of Court, hereby make the following Rules for the purpose of appeals to the Visitors from Disciplinary Tribunals of the Council of the Inns of Court and certain other appeals to the Visitors:

Citation and Commencement

1   These Rules may be cited as the Hearings before the Visitors Rules 1997 and shall come into operation on 14 April 1997, save that paragraph 13 of these Rules shall not come into effect until 1 September 1997.

Interpretation

2   (1)   The Interpretation Act 1978 shall apply for the interpretation of these Rules as it applies for the interpretation of an Act of Parliament.

        (2)   In these Rules, unless the context otherwise requires, the following expressions have the meanings hereby respectively assigned to them, namely:

        'appellant' means an appellant from an order of a tribunal;

        'appellant student' means a student disciplined by or expelled from an Inn of Court, or a person refused admission to an Inn of Court as a student, who is appealing to the Visitors;

        'appellant legal practitioner' means a legal practitioner wishing to appeal to the Visitors from a decision, on review, by the JRC under Part IV of the Consolidated Regulations of the Inns of Court;

        'JRC' means the Joint Consolidated Regulations and Transfer Committee of the Inns' Council and the Bar Council;

        'Bar Council' means The General Council of the Bar;

        'the Directions Judge' means a Judge of the High Court or the Court of Appeal nominated pursuant to Rule 3;

        'the Inns' Council' means the Council of the Inns of Court;

        'the tribunal' means a Disciplinary Tribunal of the Council of the Inns of Court and includes a panel appointed to hear a summary case under the

Summary Procedure Rules at Annex P to the Code of Conduct of the Bar of England and Wales;

'the Visitors' means the Judge or Judges of the High Court or the Court of Appeal nominated to hear the appeal pursuant to Rule 10(1).

Directions Judge

3   The Lord Chief Justice may, at any time before the nomination of the Visitors, nominate a single Judge of the High Court or the Court of Appeal ('the Directions Judge') to consider the course of an appeal and give all such directions as appear to him necessary or desirable for securing the just, expeditious and economical disposal of the appeal.

Service of Documents

4   Service of any documents required by these Rules shall be made:-

(1)   on the Lord Chief Justice, by service on the Clerk to the Visitors, Royal Courts of Justice, Strand, London WC2A 2LL;

(2)   on the President of the Inns' Council, by service on the Secretary to the Council of the Inns of Court, The Treasury, Middle Temple, London EC4Y 9AT;

(3)   on the Chairman of the Bar Council, by service on the Chief Executive of the General Council of the Bar, 3 Bedford Row, London WC1R 4DB;

(4)   on the JRC, by service on the Chief Executive of the General Council of the Bar at the address set out in paragraph (3) of this Rule;

(5)   on the Treasurer of an Inn, by service on the Sub-Treasurer or Under-Treasurer of that Inn;

(6)   on the appellant, appellant student or appellant legal practitioner by service on him at the address submitted by him with the notice of appeal.

Service shall be made either by recorded delivery post, or by hand delivery against a receipt, or by facsimile confirmed by return facsimile message.

Notice of Appeal

5   Within 21 days from the date on which the order of the tribunal was made or within such further time as may be allowed by the Lord Chief Justice or the Directions Judge, written notice of

appeal against the finding or sentence of the tribunal must be served by the appellant on the Lord Chief Justice, the Chairman of the Bar Council, the President of the Inns' Council and the Treasurer of the Inn of which the appellant is a member. The appellant shall submit with the notice of appeal an address at which service is to be made on the appellant.

Service of Petition

6   Within 42 days from the date on which the order of the tribunal was made or within such further time as may be allowed by the Lord Chief Justice or the Directions Judge, the appellant shall serve a petition of appeal on the Lord Chief Justice, the Chairman of the Bar Council, the President of the Inns' Council and the Treasurer of the Inn of which the appellant is a member. Failure either to serve the petition or to apply for an extension of time within the period of 42 days specified above will invalidate the appeal, unless the Lord Chief Justice or the Directions Judge otherwise directs.

Petition

7   (1)   The petition shall state whether the appeal is against the finding or sentence of the tribunal, or both.

        (2)   The petition shall contain the following particulars:

            (a)   the charges;

            (b)   a summary of the facts on which the charges were based;

            (c)   the findings of the tribunal;

            (d)   the sentence;

            (e)   the grounds for appeal, including specific reference to the evidence on each charge on which reliance is placed;

            (f)   the relief sought.

        (3)   In an appeal against sentence the petition may refer to any factors which it is contended make the sentence unduly severe in relation to the appellant's record or to sentences in other similar cases.

        (4)   Failure to submit a petition in accordance with this Rule will invalidate the appeal, unless the Lord Chief Justice or the Directions Judge otherwise directs.

Documents

8   (1)   Subject to the following paragraph of this Rule the appellant shall serve on the Lord Chief Justice with the petition three copies of the transcript of the proceedings before the tribunal (three copies of the note of proceedings and statement of sentence, if the tribunal was a panel appointed to hear a summary matter), save that five copies shall be served if the Chairman of the tribunal was a Judge of the High Court, or the proceedings before the tribunal resulted in an order for disbarment.

    (2)   If the transcript is not available when the petition is submitted, the copies shall be served on the Lord Chief Justice as soon as practicable thereafter.

    (3)   A copy of every document intended to be produced at the hearing by any party shall be served on the other party or parties and copies shall be served on the Lord Chief Justice not less than 14 days before the hearing in the same numbers as laid down in paragraph (1) of this Rule.

Answer

9   (1)   The Bar Council may serve on the Lord Chief Justice an answer to the petition, with a copy to the appellant, within 28 days of service of the petition or within such further time as may be allowed by the Lord Chief Justice or the Directions Judge.

    (2)   The answer shall follow the form of the petition and shall state which points in the petition are accepted and which are rejected.

The Hearing of the Appeal

10   (1)   The appeal shall be heard by a single Judge of the High Court or the Court of Appeal nominated by the Lord Chief Justice, save that where an appeal

        (i)   relates to an order for disbarment or

        (ii)   is from a tribunal presided over by a Judge of the High Court

    the appeal shall be heard by three Judges of the High Court or the Court of Appeal so nominated.

    (2)   Subject to the following paragraphs of this Rule, the Visitors may give all such directions with regard to the conduct of, and procedure at, the hearings as they may consider appropriate.

(3) Pending the hearing, any direction incidental thereto may be given by the Judge, or one of three Judges, nominated pursuant to paragraph (1) of this Rule.

(4) The hearing shall be in private unless the appellant has made an application that the hearing shall be in public and the public interest does not require that it shall be in private.

(5) A hearing may proceed in the absence of an appellant, but not without a representative of the Bar Council.

(6) No witness may be called at the hearing without the consent of the Visitors.

(7) Fresh evidence shall not be admissible save in exceptional circumstances and with the consent of the Visitors.

(8) In an appeal which involves the decision of a Court the Visitors may, but only in exceptional circumstances, allow the appellant to challenge that decision.

(9) Counsel may appear at a hearing without the intervention of a solicitor.

The Visitors' Findings

11   (1) The Visitors shall pronounce their findings in a single decision.

(2) The Visitors may pronounce their findings in public or in private, and will do so in public if the appellant so requests otherwise and the public interest does not require a public pronouncement.

(3) The Visitors may allow an appeal in whole or in part, or confirm or vary an order of the tribunal or order a re-hearing on such terms as they may deem appropriate in the circumstances.

(4) The Visitors may order, in the event of an appeal which is successful wholly or in part, a refund to the appellant of any sum paid to the General Council of the Bar in accordance with the Disciplinary Tribunal Regulations of the Inns' Council.

Barrister's Exclusion from Legal Aid Work

12   These Rules shall apply in relation to an appeal against an order of the tribunal that a barrister's exclusion from legal aid work pursuant to Section 42(3) of the Administration of Justice Act 1985 (as substituted by Section 33 of the Legal Aid Act 1988) is not to be terminated subject to the following modifications:-

(1)   The petition shall contain the following particulars

(a)   the date of the order of the tribunal excluding the appellant from legal aid work;

(b)   the charges in respect of which that order was made, a summary of the facts on which those charges were based and the finding of the tribunal in respect of those charges;

(c)   the findings of the tribunal on which the order under appeal was based;

(d)   the grounds for appeal;

(e)   the relief sought.

(2)   An order of the tribunal to terminate a barrister's exclusion from legal aid work only from a date which is subsequent to that order shall for the purposes of appeal be treated as an order that the barrister's exclusion from legal aid work is not to be terminated.

Appeals by an appellant student against a decision of an Inn

13   In an appeal by an appellant student against a decision of an Inn, all these Rules shall apply subject to the following modifications:-

(1)   In Rules 5 and 6 the decision of the Inn shall be substituted for the order, finding or sentence of the tribunal, and service shall be made on the Lord Chief Justice, the Chairman of the Bar Council, the President of the Inns' Council, and the Treasurer of the Inn of which the appellant student is a member or the Treasurer of the Inn which has refused to admit the appellant student.

(2)   Paragraphs (1), (2) and (3) of Rule 7 shall not apply. Paragraph (4) of Rule 7 shall apply to this Rule as it applies to Rule 7. The petition shall contain the following particulars:

(a)   the decision of the Inn appealed from;

(b)   a summary of the facts giving rise to the decision of the Inn;

(c)   the grounds for appeal;

(d)   the relief sought.

(3)   Paragraphs (1) and (2) of Rule 8 shall not apply. The appellant student shall serve on the Lord Chief Justice with the petition copies of relevant documents including any complaint in respect of the appellant and the decision of the Inn. Paragraph (3) of Rule 8 shall apply, save that

copies of documents shall be served on the persons specified in paragraph (1) of this Rule.

(4) In paragraph (1) of Rule 9 and paragraph (5) of Rule 10 the Inn shall be substituted for the Bar Council.

(5) Paragraphs (3) and (4) of Rule 11 shall not apply. The Visitors may allow an appeal in whole or in part or confirm or vary the decision of the Inn or order the Inn to reconsider the decision on such terms as the Visitors may determine to be appropriate in the circumstances.

(6) Rules 12 and 14 shall not apply.

No appeal to the Visitors under these Rules shall lie from a decision of an educational institution (other than an Inn) or any officer or committee thereof in respect of any matter relating to a course recognised by the Bar Council as satisfying the requirements of the Academic Stage of Training for the Bar (including Common Professional Examination requirements), the Vocational Stage of Training for the Bar, or the Stage of Continuing Education and Training at the Bar, or any examination or assessment in connection with any such course. Any such appeal shall be made through the appropriate appeal procedures of the institution concerned.

Appeals by an appellant legal practitioner

14   In an appeal by an appellant legal practitioner, all these Rules shall apply subject to the following modifications:-

(1) In Rules 5 and 6 the decision, on review, of the JRC shall be substituted for the order, finding or sentence of the tribunal, and service shall be made on the JRC, and also on the Lord Chief Justice, the Chairman of the Bar Council and the President of the Inns' Council.

(2) Paragraphs (1), (2), and (3) of Rule 7 shall not apply. Paragraph (4) of Rule 7 shall apply to this Rule as it applies to Rule 7. The petition shall contain the following particulars:-

    (a)   the decision, on review, of the JRC appealed from;

    (b)   a summary of the facts giving rise to the decision, on review, of the JRC;

    (c)   the grounds for appeal;

    (d)   the relief sought.

(3) Paragraphs (1) and (2) of Rule 8 shall not apply. The appellant legal practitioner shall serve on the Lord Chief Justice with the petition copies of relevant documents including the decision, on review, of the JRC. Paragraph (3) of Rule 8 shall apply, save that copies of documents

shall be served on the persons specified in paragraph (1) of this Rule.

(4) In paragraph (1) of Rule 9 and paragraph (5) of Rule 10 the JRC shall be substituted for the Bar Council.

(5) Paragraphs (3) and (4) of Rule 11 shall not apply. The Visitors may allow an appeal in whole or in part or confirm or vary the decision, on review, of the JRC or order the JRC to reconsider its decision on review on such terms as the Visitors may determine to be appropriate in the circumstances.

(6) Rules 12 and 13 shall not apply.

Costs

15   The Visitors may make such order for costs of the appeal as they consider appropriate. Any order for costs made by the Visitors may include an order for payment of the cost of any transcript required for the purposes of the appeal.

Transition

16   These Rules shall apply to all appeals in being on 14 April 1997 notwithstanding that notice of appeal was served before that date, save that appeals shall continue to be heard under Rule 13 of the Hearings before the Visitors Rules 1991 in respect of appeals by students registered at the Inns of Court School of Law before 1 September 1997.

Revocation

17   The Hearings before the Visitors Rules 1991 are hereby revoked.

On behalf of the Judges of Her Majesty's
High Court of Justice

Lord Chancellor
Lord Chief Justice
President
Vice-Chancellor

THE SUMMARY PROCEDURE RULES

THE SUMMARY PROCEDURE RULES

1   Definitions

In these Rules:

(a) 'The Act of 1985' shall mean the Administration of Justice Act 1985 as amended by the Legal Aid Act 1988.

(b) 'Disciplinary Tribunal' shall mean a Disciplinary Tribunal of the Council of the Inns of Court.

(c) 'Disciplinary Tribunal Regulations' shall mean those Regulations appended by way of schedule, as amended from time to time, to the Constitution of the Council of the Inns of Court.

(d) 'The defendant' shall mean counsel against whom complaint has been made.

(e) 'Legal aid complaint' shall have the meaning ascribed to it by Section 40 of the Act of 1985.

(f) 'The PCC' shall mean the Professional Conduct and Complaints Committee of the Bar Council or the Professional Conduct Committee established under the rules in effect immediately before the coming into effect of these Rules.

(g) 'The PSC' shall mean the Professional Standards Committee of the Bar Council.

(h) 'Lay representative' shall mean one of the lay persons appointed by the Bar Council to attend PSC or PCC meetings or to serve on Disciplinary Tribunals.

(i) 'Sponsor member' shall mean the member of the PCC to whom the file was originally or subsequently assigned and who reported to the PCC on the complaint.

(j) 'Summary case' shall mean a complaint referred by the PCC for summary determination under these Rules.

(k) 'Summary hearing' shall mean the hearing of a summary case by a panel appointed under these Rules.

(l) 'Inadequate professional service' shall have the meaning ascribed to it in Annex K of the Code of Conduct of the Bar of England and Wales.

2   Composition of Summary Hearing Panels

A panel shall consist of not more than five, and not less than three, past or present members of the PSC or the PCC nominated by the Chairman of the PCC which number shall include at least:

    (a)   One Queen's Counsel as chairman of the panel

    (b)   One Junior over five years call

    (c)   One lay representative

    Provided that:

    (i)   No barrister shall be nominated to serve on a panel who has acted as sponsor member in relation to the summary case to be dealt with.

    (ii)   The proceedings of a summary hearing shall be valid notwithstanding that one or more of the members other than the chairman or lay representative becomes unable to continue to act or disqualified from continuing to act, so long as the number of members present throughout the substantive hearing of the charge(s) is not reduced below three and continues to include the chairman and the lay representative.

3   Timetable

(a)   As soon as possible after referral of a case to summary procedure, the Secretary of the PCC shall write to the defendant notifying him of the PCC's decision and enclosing a copy of the Summary Procedure Rules.

(b)   The defendant shall receive as soon as possible thereafter, the documents to be served upon him together with a letter laying down a fixed time and date (normally 5 pm on a working day within 60 calendar days or less from the date of the letter) for the hearing to take place. One alternative shall be given.

(c)   The defendant shall be invited to accept one or other of the dates proposed or to provide a written representation to the Chairman of the PCC, objecting to both dates with reasons and providing two further alternative dates. The Chairman of the PCC shall consider this representation and either confirm one of the original dates or re-fix the hearing. His decision shall be final.

(d)   Once fixed, a hearing date shall be vacated only in exceptional circumstances and with the agreement of the Chairman of the PCC.

4   Documents to be Served

On referral of a complaint to summary procedure, the Secretary of the PCC shall prepare and serve the following documents on the defendant:

(a)   Notification of the PCC's decision to refer the matter to summary procedure.

(b)   Statement of the charges made against the barrister which may include charges of inadequate professional service provided that:

(i)   the complainant is the barrister's lay client or his duly authorised representative or in the case of an employed barrister the person to whom he has supplied the professional service in question, and

(ii)   the subject-matter of the complaint is something in respect of which the barrister would not be entitled to immunity from suit as an advocate in civil law.

(c)   Statement of facts upon which the charge(s) is or are founded and upon which the PCC proposes to rely.

(d)   Copies of any documents which will be available to the summary hearing and which have not previously been served on the defendant. Any document shall be deemed to have been validly served in the circumstances laid down in Paragraph 29 of Disciplinary Tribunal Regulations 1996 or as later amended.

5   Acceptance of the Statement of Facts and of Summary Procedure

(a)   In the letter of notification, the defendant shall be required to state in writing whether or not he admits the charge(s) and, if he does not, whether or not he challenges any of the facts detailed in the statement of facts. If he admits the charge(s) or if he does not challenge any of the facts detailed in the statement of facts, he shall also be asked to say whether he is prepared to agree that the charge(s) should be dealt with by summary procedure.

(b)   If the defendant admits the charge(s) or does not challenge any significant facts and, in either case, if he agrees that his case should be dealt with by summary procedure, the case shall proceed to a summary hearing, failing which it shall proceed to a Disciplinary Tribunal.

(c)   Failure of the defendant to respond to these questions within 30 days of the date of the Secretary's letter shall be construed as refusal to admit the charge(s), to agree the statement of facts and to accept summary procedure.

6   Submission of Further Documents

(a)   If, following service of and agreement to the statement of facts and of documents relevant to summary procedure, the defendant seeks to submit further proofs of evidence, representations or other material for consideration at the summary hearing, he must do so not later than 21 days before the date fixed for the hearing.

(b)   If either before or at the summary hearing, it becomes apparent that the material submitted amounts to a denial of any significant fact in the statement of facts, the Chairman of the PCC or the panel shall refer the matter to a Disciplinary Tribunal.

7   Procedure

(a) Procedure at summary hearings shall be informal, the details being at the discretion of the chairman of the panel.

(b) The defendant shall be entitled to be represented by counsel of his choice, by a solicitor or by any other representative he may wish. The PCC should be represented by counsel (normally the sponsor member) only in particularly complex cases and subject to the prior agreement of the chairman of the panel in each case.

(c) No witnesses may be called at a summary hearing without the prior consent of the chairman of the panel and without the submission of a proof of evidence.

(d) The attendance of the defendant shall be required. Should he nevertheless fail to attend, the summary hearing may proceed in his absence, subject to the panel being satisfied that this course is appropriate, that all relevant procedures requiring the defendant's attendance have been complied with and that no acceptable explanation for the defendant's absence has been provided. Should the panel not be so satisfied, they shall have the power to adjourn the matter, to a specific date or sine die, or to refer the matter back to the PCC, as they may think fit.

(e) A record of each summary hearing shall be taken electronically and the tape retained under the arrangements of the Secretary of the PCC for two years, until the expiry of the period allowed for notification of intention to appeal or until the conclusion of any appeal, whichever period is longest.

8   Finding

At the conclusion of a summary hearing, the finding on each charge shall be set down in writing and signed by the chairman of the panel. If the members of the panel are not unanimous as to the finding on any charge, the finding to be recorded on that charge shall be of the majority. If the members of the panel are equally divided as to the finding on any charge, then, the burden of proof being on the complainant, the finding to be recorded on that charge shall be that which is most favourable to the defendant. The chairman of the panel shall then announce the panel's decisions as to finding.

9   Sentence

(a) If the panel shall have found any charge proved, the Secretary of the PCC shall lay before the panel details of any previous finding of professional misconduct, or of breach of proper professional standards or of inadequate professional service or any finding of guilt on a charge consisting of a legal aid complaint against the defendant. After hearing any representations by or on behalf of the defendant, the panel's decision as to sentence shall be set down in writing and signed by the chairman. If the members of the panel are not unanimous as to the sentence, the sentence to be recorded shall be of the majority. If the members of the panel are equally divided as to the sentence the sentence to be recorded shall be that which is most favourable to the defendant. The chairman of the panel shall then announce the panel's decision as to sentence.

(b) A barrister against whom a charge of professional misconduct has been found proved may be sentenced by the summary hearing to be:

(i)   Suspended from practice for up to three months, either unconditionally or subject to conditions;

(ii)   Ordered to pay a fine of up to £500 to the Bar Council;

(iii) Ordered to forego or repay all or part of his fees;

(iv) Reprimanded;

(v)   Admonished;

(vi) Advised as to his future conduct.

(c) A barrister against whom a charge of inadequate professional service has been found proved may be

(i)   directed to make a formal apology to the complainant for the conduct in relation to which the finding was made;

(ii)   directed to repay or remit all or part of any fee rendered in respect of the inadequate service; or

(iii) directed to pay compensation to the complainant in such sum as the Tribunal shall direct not exceeding £2,000.

Save that no order under paragraph (iii) shall be made unless the summary hearing is satisfied that the complainant has established on the balance of probabilities that he has suffered loss recoverable at law caused by the inadequate professional service and further the summary hearing is satisfied that no issue of law or fact arises in relation to such loss which cannot fairly be resolved on the material before it. If the summary hearing is so satisfied it may direct payment of such sum by way of compensation as it sees fit up to the amount of such loss or £2,000, whichever is the less. Further in determining whether any sum is to be paid under paragraph (iii) hereof, or in fixing the amount of such sum, the summary hearing shall have regard in particular to the availability to the complainant of other forms of redress, to the gravity of the conduct complained of and to the fee claimed by the barrister for the inadequate service.

(d)   In any case where a charge of professional misconduct or inadequate professional service has been found proved, the summary hearing may decide that no action should be taken against the barrister.

(e)   Under the powers conferred by Sections 41 and 42 of the Act of 1985 any summary hearing which hears a charge consisting of a legal aid complaint relating to the conduct of a barrister may if it thinks fit (and whether or not it sentences the barrister in accordance with paragraph 9(b) or (c) of these Rules in respect of any conduct arising out of the same legal aid complaint) order that any such fees as are referred to in Section 41(2) of the Act of 1985 shall be reduced or cancelled.

(f)   Where a summary hearing deals with a charge of professional misconduct against a barrister it may (in addition to or instead of sentencing that barrister in accordance with paragraph 9(b) of these Rules), if it determines that there is good reason for the exclusion arising out of:

(i)   His conduct in connection with any such services as are maintained in Section 40(c) of the Act of 1985, or:

(ii)   His professional conduct generally:

order that he shall be excluded from legal aid work for a period of up to six months.

(g)   The sentence determined by a summary hearing if a charge of professional misconduct has been proved shall be recorded as follows:

(i)   Suspension

'That . . . be suspended from practice as a barrister and from enjoyment of all rights and privileges as a member of the Honourable Society of . . . and be prohibited from holding himself out as being a barrister without disclosing his suspension for (stating the length of the prescribed period)'.

(Note: If the panel decides that the sentence of suspension shall apply to part only of the barrister's practice or shall be subject to conditions, such part or such conditions (as the case may be) shall be specified in the wording of the sentence.)

(ii)   Payment of Fine

'That . . . pay a fine of £ . . . to the Bar Council.'

(iii) Repayment or Foregoing of Fees

'That . . . shall repay all fees (fees amounting to £ . . .) received by him (shall forego all fees (fees amounting to £ . . .) due to be paid to him) in connection with . . .'

(iv) Reprimand

'That . . . is hereby reprimanded' or 'That . . . is hereby ordered to attend on . . . to be reprimanded'.

(v) Admonishment

'That . . . is hereby admonished' or 'That . . . is hereby ordered to attend on . . . to be admonished'.

(vi) Advice as to Future Conduct

'That . . . has been advised by the panel as to his future conduct in regard to . . .' or 'That . . . is hereby ordered to attend on . . . to be given advice as to his future conduct in regard to . . .'.

(vii) Order for Reduction of Legal Aid Fees

'That the fees payable to . . . in connection with his services under or in accordance with the Legal Aid Act 1988 or otherwise chargeable in connection with his services in respect of advice or assistance made available under Part III of that Act in relation to the items or matters specified in the first column of the Schedule hereto be reduced to the sum or sums specified in the second column of that Schedule.'

The record of the sentence shall then contain a Schedule setting out the matters referred to above.

(viii) Order for Cancellation of Legal Aid Fees

'That the fees payable to . . . in connection with his services under or in accordance with the Legal Aid Act 1988 or otherwise chargeable in connection with his services in respect of advice or assistance made available under Part III of that Act in relation to the items or matters specified in the Schedule hereto be cancelled'.

The record of the sentence shall then contain a Schedule identifying the items or matters referred to above.

(ix) Exclusion from Legal Aid Work

'That . . . be excluded from legal aid work (as explained in Section 42(4)(b) of the Administration of Justice Act 1985 as substituted by Section 33 of the Legal Aid Act 1988 (until . . .) (for a period of . . . beginning on . . .)

(x)   Absence of the Defendant

If the defendant has not been present throughout the proceedings, the sentence shall include the statement that the finding and sentence were made in the absence of the barrister in accordance with paragraph 7(d) of these Rules.

(h)   Sentences under paragraphs 9(b)(i), (ii) & (iii), 9(d) and 9(e) shall not be put into effect until expiry of the period allowed for service of Notice of Appeal under Hearings before the Visitors Rules or until the conclusion of any appeal, whichever period is the longer.

(i)   Sentences under paragraphs 9(b)(iv), (v) and (vi) may be put into effect at and by the summary hearing or by directing the defendant to attend on a person or persons to be nominated by the panel, as the panel may think fit. Any sentence of suspension may apply to the whole of the defendant's practice or to such part only as may be determined. The conditions to which a sentence of suspension may be made subject include a requirement that the barrister shall undergo such further pupillage or training or attain such standard of competence as the panel may determine.

(j)   Whether or not the panel shall have found any charge proved, if it considers that the circumstances of the complaint are relevant to the barrister's capacity as a pupilmaster, it may notify the barrister's Inn of its concerns in such manner as it sees fit.

10   Costs

A summary hearing shall have no power to award costs.

11   Report of Finding and Sentence

(a)   As soon as practicable after the conclusion of a summary hearing, the Secretary of the PCC shall confirm the finding and sentence to the defendant in writing.

(b)   In cases where one or more charges of professional misconduct have been found proved and on expiry of the period allowed for service of Notice of Appeal under Hearings Before the Visitors Rules or on the conclusion of any appeal, whichever period is the longer, the Secretary of the PCC shall communicate the finding and sentence (as varied on appeal) and, where the latter includes orders under paragraphs 9(b)(i), (ii), (iii), 9(c) or 9(d), the date on which these were carried into effect, in writing to the following:

(i)   The Lord Chancellor

(ii)   The Lord Chief Justice

(iii)   The Attorney General

(iv)   The President of the Council of the Inns of Court

(v)   The Chairman of the Bar Council

(vi)   The Chairman of the PCC

(vii)   The defendant

(viii) The Treasurers of the defendant's Inn of Call and of any other Inns of which he is a member.

Provided that the Lord Chancellor, the Lord Chief Justice, the Attorney General and the President shall be informed only when a charge constituting or arising out of a legal aid complaint has been found proved or the sentence includes an order of suspension for any period.

12   Appeals

(1)   In cases where one or more charges of professional misconduct have been proved, an Appeal may be lodged with the Visitors against finding and/or sentence (including any finding of inadequate professional service) in accordance with the Hearings Before the Visitors Rules in force. Notice of appeal must be accompanied by the sum of £250 payable to the Bar Council to defray expenses, a sum to be refunded in the discretion of the Visitors in the event of an appeal which is successful wholly or in part.

(2)   In cases where no professional misconduct has been proved, but one or more charges of inadequate professional service have been proved, an appeal shall lie at the instance of the barrister from any such finding, and against any decision as to the remedy to be granted to the complainant for such service in the same manner as an appeal lies from a decision of an Adjudication Panel in respect of the same matters.

13   Action by the Defendant's Inn

In a case where the sentence, where applicable as confirmed on appeal, includes an order under paragraph 9(b)(i) and on expiry of the period allowed for service of Notice of Appeal under Hearings before the Visitors Rules or on the conclusion of any appeal, whichever period is the longer, the Secretary of the PCC shall invite the Treasurers of the defendant's Inn of Call and of any other Inns of which he is a member to pronounce the sentence of suspension as at paragraph 9(g)(i) and to take such further action as may be required to carry it into effect. As seems to them fit, the Treasurer(s) will then pronounce the sentence and inform the Secretary of the PCC of the date on which it is to take effect.

14   Publication of Finding and Sentence

(a) The finding and sentence of a summary hearing on any charge or charges of professional misconduct shall be published.

(b) When publishing any finding and sentence in accordance with sub-paragraph (a) above, the Secretary of the PCC shall communicate the same in writing to those listed in paragraph 11(b) of these Rules, together with the following:

    (i)   The Director of Public Prosecutions.

    (ii)   The Treasurers of all four Inns for screening.

(iii)   The Leaders of the six circuits.

(iv)   One or more press agencies or other publications, as the Chairman of the PCC may direct.

(c)   When the summary hearing has found that one or more charges of inadequate professional service have been proved, the charge and finding shall not be published unless the barrister charged so requests.

(d)   When the Tribunal has found that any charge whether of professional misconduct or of inadequate professional service has not been proved the President shall not publish that charge and the finding unless the barrister charged so requests.

Commencement and Transitional Provisions

15   In relation to any summary hearing arising out of a complaint which had been raised in the records of the Professional Conduct Committee before the date fixed by the Bar Council for these Rules to come into effect ('the Commencement Date'), these Rules shall not apply but the Summary Procedure Rules in force immediately before that date shall apply to that summary hearing. In relation to summary hearings arising out of complaints raised after the Commencement Date, the procedure set out in these Rules shall apply save that no finding of inadequate professional service may be made against a barrister in respect of any conduct of his which took place before 13th July 1996.

ANNEXE O

SUMMARY OF THE EQUALITY CODE FOR THE BAR

SUMMARY OF THE EQUALITY CODE FOR THE BAR

Explanatory Note:

Mandatory requirements in the Equality Code are those which are direct requirements of legislation or the Code of Conduct of the Bar. These are indicated by use of underlined bold in the summary. The remaining bold text indicates those recommendations which are considered essential in order that chambers/barristers avoid direct, indirect and unintentional discrimination and monitor their performance. 'Should' in the text indicates best advice on the steps chambers should take to avoid discriminating either unlawfully or contrary to the Code of Conduct of the Bar. The remaining advice is recommendations for the development of good equal opportunity practice by chambers. The Equality Code for the Bar includes explanation of the legislation and case law and refers to findings of relevant research conducted for the Bar.

CHAPTER 1 — Regulatory and Legislative Framework

1. **Para. 204 of the Code of Conduct of the Bar of England and Wales prohibits a practising barrister from discriminating directly or indirectly against or victimising anyone on the grounds of their race, colour, ethnic or national origin, nationality, citizenship, sex, sexual orientation, marital status, disability, religion or political persuasion.** A barrister who is able to prove, on the balance of probabilities, that indirect discrimination was unintentional, will not be found guilty of professional misconduct.

2. **Under Para. 304 of the Code of Conduct barristers in independent practice must have regard to the Equality Code for the Bar.**

3. **The Sex Discrimination Act 1975 and the Race Relations Act 1976, as amended by section 64 of the Courts of Legal Services Act 1990, place a duty on barristers (and barristers' clerks) not to discriminate on the grounds of race or sex.** Individuals may bring complaints that they have suffered discrimination to a county court within six months of the alleged act of discrimination.

4. The Disability (Discrimination) Bill is currently before Parliament and information will be provided to chambers when it becomes law.

CHAPTER 2 — Unlawful and Prohibited Discrimination[1]

1. Unlawful direct discrimination consists of treating a person on grounds of race, colour, ethnic or national origin, nationality or citizenship, sex or marital status less favourably than others are or would be treated in the same or similar circumstances. Less favourable treatment is regarded as being on grounds of sex,

---

[1] All references to 'discrimination' unless specifically qualified in the text include both unlawful discrimination and discrimination prohibited by the Code of Conduct.

race, etc if but for that person's race or sex he or she would not have been subjected to the less favourable treatment.

2.   Indirect discrimination occurs where:

(a) a requirement or condition is applied equally to everyone but a considerably smaller proportion of one sex or racial group than of the other persons to whom it applies can comply with it;

(b) the particular individual cannot comply with the requirement;

(c) it results in a detriment to them; and

(d) the requirement cannot be shown to be objectively justifiable in spite of its discriminatory effect.

3.   **It is unlawful to victimise persons by treating them less favourably because they have brought proceedings under the Race Relations or Sex Discrimination Act, have given evidence or information relating to proceedings or have alleged that discrimination has occurred. Such treatment will also breach Para. 204 of the Code of Conduct.**

4.   **It is unlawful for a person to instruct induce or attempt to induce another person to discriminate on grounds of race, colour, ethnic or national origin, nationality, citizenship, sex or marital status. Equally, it is unlawful to act on such instructions or inducement.**

5.   **Employers or principals are vicariously liable for any unlawfully discriminatory act of their employees or agents in the course of their work, unless they can demonstrate that they have taken all reasonable steps to prevent such acts.** This is relevant to barristers' responsibility for their clerks and other staff in chambers.

6.   Positive action is the term used for lawful measures taken under the provisions of the Race Relations or Sex Discrimination Acts where one sex or particular racial or ethnic group is under-represented in particular areas of work, or to meet the special needs of particular ethnic groups.

7.   The above guidance on unlawful direct or indirect discrimination applies mutatis mutandis to discrimination on other grounds prohibited under Para. 204 of the Code of Conduct (including disability and sexual orientation).

8.   Sexual orientation — a Bar Lesbian and Gay Group was formed in 1994 and is represented on the Bar Council's Sex Discrimination Committee. Chambers should adopt an equal opportunity policy making it clear that chambers will not discriminate on the grounds of sexual orientation and will offer equal opportunity to potential and actual members of chambers, whatever their sexual orientation. They should also ensure that all members, staff and applicants of chambers are aware of this policy.

9.   Discrimination on the grounds of disability — the Bar Council has a Disability Panel whose members will advise on disability issues. Chambers are advised to ensure, as far as is reasonably possible, that the working environment is both safe and accessible. At interviews with people who have disabilities questions should focus on the interviewee's ability, experience and job-related qualifications. Interview panels should not make assumptions about candidates' ability to perform certain tasks but, where relevant, candidates should be asked to state how they would perform certain tasks.

CHAPTER 3 — Guidance on Harassment

1.   **Harassment which would not have occurred but for the race or sex of the recipient may constitute unlawful direct discrimination. Both formal and informal grievance procedures should be available and be operated sensitively by chambers.** Harassment is unwelcome conduct which is offensive to the recipient, whatever the motive or intention of the perpetrator.

2.   The European Commission's Code of Practice on sexual harassment, which may be taken into account by courts and tribunals in deciding what amounts to sexual harassment, defines it as 'unwanted contact of a sexual nature or other conduct based on sex affecting the dignity of women and men at work'. It also notes that 'harassment on grounds of sexual orientation undermines the dignity at work of those affected and it is impossible to regard such harassment as appropriate workplace behaviour.'

3.   Avenues of redress for individuals suffering harassment include chambers grievance procedures, complaint to the relevant Students' Officer about a sponsor or pupil master/mistress, complaints to the PCC where the harasser is a barrister, complaint to a county court or industrial tribunal alleging harassment as a form of direct discrimination, referral to the police when an act of harassment is a criminal offence. A recipient may also raise the matter informally with Inns Students Officers, the Bar's equal opportunities officers, CLE welfare staff, members of chambers, and sympathetic organisations such as the Association of Women Barristers.

4.   The Bar Council's procedures on sexual harassment include a separate confidential telephone line to the equal opportunities officer, encouragement to chambers to adopt formal and informal procedures for handling complaints of harassment, a panel of mediators to advise the complainant and, with his or her permission, to seek to mediate between the complainant and the alleged harasser, and 'safe haven' chambers who, on the recommendation of the Chairman of the Bar or the Secretary of the PCC or the equal opportunities officers, will provide pupillage or an opportunity to squat to pupils or junior tenants who are unable to remain in their chambers as a result of harassment. A streamlined PCC procedure for handling

complaints of harassment including measures to protect the anonymity of complainants, is under consideration.

CHAPTER 4 — Fair Selection of Pupils and Tenants

1. **Chambers must have selection procedures for pupils and tenants in which all applications are considered on an equal and non-discriminatory footing.** Here good practice may be evidence of what is lawful.

2. **The Code of Conduct requires sets of chambers to ensure that proper arrangements are made in chambers for dealing with pupils and pupillage. The guidelines to the Code of Conduct Annex A require that each set of chambers should have a document which sets out its policies in relation to the selection of pupils. There should also be a written policy for the selection of tenants.**

3. **No pupils should be accepted in chambers who have not come through the chambers selection procedure.**

4. **Before any consideration of applications for pupillage or for tenancy takes place, a decision should be made about the number and type of vacancies to be filled.**

5. **No decision about an applicant's suitability at any stage of the process should be taken by an individual member of chambers.** Selection decisions should be taken by a committee which should include as diverse a group of members of chambers as possible. All selectors should be familiar with the content of The Equality Code and with chambers procedures and selection criteria.

6. **The timetable for processing applications should be well publicised and chambers should adhere to it.** Chambers are recommended to join the Bar Council's pupillage admissions and clearing house scheme (PACH).

7. **All applicants should be assessed in competition with each other against objective and explicit selection criteria which relate to the demands of the work. The criteria should identify the knowledge, skills and other abilities required of a barrister doing such work. They should not be changed during the selection process.** Criteria should be checked for potentially discriminatory assumptions about the mobility, lifestyle, social background, financial resources, race or sex of applicants.

8. Many people come to the Bar later in life, having pursued a different career, or for other reasons. Traditionally, seniority in chambers has reflected age. There is a perception that young junior tenants may fear competition from older pupils and junior tenants. They may also fear that older pupils and junior tenants might be reluctant to conform to chambers' expectations of junior members. These assumptions should not feature in selection decisions concerning the skills and experience of mature

applicants for pupillage and tenancy. Such skills and experience should be assessed according to the agreed selection criteria.

9. Chambers should publicise all vacancies including administrative vacancies as widely as possible, unless a tenancy vacancy is only to be filled from current or former pupils. Pupillage vacancies should be advertised in the Bar Council's Chambers Pupillage and Awards Handbook. Advertisements should contain clear and accurate information about the areas of work undertaken by chambers, the selection procedures and timetables to be followed, guidance on the selection criteria to be applied and information about any awards or financial arrangements made for pupils.

10. It is recommended that chambers use an application form in preference to a CV. The questions on the application form should invite applicants to demonstrate how their knowledge, skills and abilities meet the selection criteria. Where application forms are used it is recommended that CVs are not accepted. Chambers should not request photographs of applicants.

11. **Chambers should either include separate forms for monitoring ethnic origin and the sex of applicants, or include a monitoring question on their application form.** Monitoring data should not be passed on to shortlisters or members of selection panels until the selection process has been completed.

12. Chambers should acknowledge all applications in writing and notify applicants of any decision taken upon their applications as soon as reasonably practicable.

13. **In shortlisting for interview, members of the selection committee should assess each candidate's application against the selection criteria and make their judgments independently on the basis of the information provided in the application form.** An agreed rating scale should be used and assessments should be recorded using an agreed format.

14. **Interviews should be structured to ensure that similar areas related to the selection criteria are covered in questions to all candidates in order to ensure comparability between interviews. The interview schedule and the guidelines for scoring and decision-making should be discussed and agreed between the committee members before the round of interviews begins.**

15. Questions to all applicants should cover similar areas, should give applicants similar opportunities to demonstrate the skills required by chambers and should be closely related to the seleciton criteria. Interview questions should be formulated so as to ensure that they elicit relevant and reliable information for the assessment of applicants with diverse backgrounds and abilities.

    Interviewers should take care to ensure that any differences between applicants in the quality of their answers are not merely a reflection of differences in the way questions are asked. Key questions should be planned in advance and written down, be clear and unambiguous and reviewed for potential bias and hence unlawful discrimination. Any follow up questions should be relevant to the selection criteria. Interviewers should avoid questions about personal relationships and family composition which are irrelevant to the applicants' professional performance. Interviewers should avoid asking any question which carries the implication that disabled applicants have not thought through the practical consequences of their particular disability and of the ways in which this is likely to affect their working and social lives.

16. Case studies or test exercises can be used in selection procedures and provide applicants with the opportunity to demonstrate their ability in an area of work in chambers. Questions used in case studies, should be related to the type of work which the barrister in that set of chambers will be expected to do. Applicants should be advised in advance that this will form part of the interview.

17. **When references are requested the referee should be asked to supply information that relates strictly to the selection criteria.** There is considerable variation in the quality of the references that candidates can obtain, particularly in the case of students, and it is recommended that references should be used only in the final check on the selected candidates and should not be introduced into the selection process.

18. **The terms of the offer should be set out in writing to pupils and tenants; they must not be directly or indirectly discriminatory; nor should they differ without good cause between one pupil or tenant and another.** Chambers should only take the final decision on pupillages or tenancies after the round of interviews has been completed.

19. **All documentation relating to selection decisions should be retained for 12 months.** Chambers should respond positively to requests for feedback from candidates.

20. **Where chambers have vacancies for experienced tenants, these should be advertised as widely as possible and notices should indicate the area of practice and number of years' call sought. Selection should be made in accordance with the principles set out above.** There are two situations which may be dealt with outside the recommended selection procedures. These are:

    (i) the approach by a set of chambers to a particular barrister or barristers whom the chambers want to recruit because of their skills or area of practice and

    (ii) the approach by a particular barrister or barristers to a set of chambers who are not looking to recruit but who may be prepared to make an offer because of the barrister(s) skiffs or area of practice.

Chambers should take care that such recruitment can be justified both in terms of the needs of chambers and the skills of the barrister(s) being recruited. Chambers should check where barristers recruited in this way are invariably of the same sex or racial group that discrimination is not occurring.

21.   **When selecting tenants from pupils, chambers should take care to avoid subjective judgments in the assessment of the performance of pupils. An explicit framework for the assessment of pupils' work should be agreed by the selection committee. The decision about the offer of a tenancy to a former pupil should be made by more than one member of chambers. The pupil master/mistress and at least one other member of chambers with whom the pupil has worked should independently assess the pupil against the pre-determined criteria and record their assessments in writing before they are discussed. Chambers should record all opinions on the suitability of a pupil. The right of an unexplained veto should not be granted to any member of chambers.**

22.   Chambers should recognise the value of mini-pupillages both to potential applicants and to chambers themselves and should try to ensure fairness in the grant of mini pupillages each year.

CHAPTER 5 — Equality of Opportunity in Chambers

1.   Every set of chambers should be in a position to state its commitment to equality of opportunity by reference to the Equality Code. Reference should be made to the statement in all material sent out to prospective applicants for mini-pupillages, pupillages, tenancy or employment in chambers.

2.   **In accordance with Annexe C of the Bar's Code of Conduct, Chambers should specify in writing the role and duties of pupils in chambers, the role and duties of pupil masters/mistresses, the pattern of pupillage, the method for fairly distributing briefs and other work amongst working pupils, the checklists which apply, procedures for providing pupils with an objective assessment of their progress at regular intervals during pupillage, policy and procedures for the recruitment of tenants, policy and procedures in relation to pupils not taken on as tenants (including third-six months pupillages and squatting) and chambers complaints and grievance procedures.**

3.   Barristers should be encouraged by their heads of chambers to discuss their career development individually with the clerk. They should tell the clerk their views of their past allocation of work in relation to the development of their practices. Heads of chambers should provide the opportunity for consultation on practice development and **should ensure that clerks know and observe the advice in this Code.**

4.   **Heads of chambers are required by the Code of Conduct's Pupillage Guidelines to ensure that the distribution of work to all members of chambers, working pupils and squatters is carried out in a manner that is fair to all and without discrimination.** All pupils in chambers are entitled to experience the range of training that a pupillage in that set of chambers offers.

5.   Heads of chambers should ensure that the distribution of work to working pupils is reviewed every two months and to junior tenants at least every six months.

6.   **The distribution of unnamed work[2] received by chambers and the re-distribution of work between members of chambers to pupils and junior tenants should be systematically monitored.**

7.   **Heads of chambers should make clear to chambers' clerks that they must not accede to discriminatory instructions from professional clients, whether solicitors or other instructing agents. Counsel may be selected only on the basis of the skills and experience required for a particular case.**

8.   **If a solicitor or instructing agent refuses to withdraw a discriminatory instruction the Code of Conduct (Annexe A) requires that it should be reported at once to the head of chambers who must report it forthwith to the relevant Bar Council committee chairman.** It should be noted that solicitors are bound by their practice rule and their statutory obligations not to practise discrimination.

9.   The Bar Council's maternity leave guidelines recommend that a woman tenant's seat in chambers should remain open for up to one year while she takes maternity leave. Chambers should offer a period of 3 months maternity leave free of rent and chambers expenses.

10.   **Heads of chambers should ensure that there is open and objective recruitment for all chambers' staff vacancies. Recruitment and selection procedures for clerks and other staff employed by chambers should follow the approach set out in chapter 4 for the selection of pupils and tenants.** Chambers should have a written staff grievance policy and a maternity leave and pay policy for female staff.

CHAPTER 6 — Monitoring

The purpose of monitoring is to check on the effectiveness of equal opportunities policies and procedures.

1.   **Chambers should monitor all selection decisions and the distribution of work to junior tenants and pupils by race and sex. Selection monitoring data should be analysed after each major recruitment exercise or at least annually. A senior member of chambers should have specific responsibility for monitoring procedures.**

2.   **Chambers should collect monitoring data by race and sex from a question on the application form or a separate monitoring form.** Categories consistent with the census ethnic classifications are recommended. These are: white, Black—African, Black—Caribbean, Black—other (please specify), Indian, Pakistani, Bangladeshi, Chinese, and other (please specify).

---

[2] Unnamed work — work that comes into a chambers with no name or work that comes into chambers for a named barrister selected by a solicitor on the advice of the clerk, or returned work reallocated by the clerk.

3. **The following stages of the selection process should be monitored: applications received, candidates shortlisted, candidates successful at interviews, terms and amounts of pupillage awards offered.**

4. Where under-representation of a particular group is identified in the applicant monitoring data, chambers should consider the use of the positive action provisions of the Race Relations and Sex Discrimination Acts to increase the rate of applications from under-represented groups.

5. Where equality targets are used they should be based on the existing situation in chambers and need to take into account available information on the representation of particular groups in the relevant populations (such as students seeking pupillage). Quotas should not be used and are unlawful.

6. **Where work for second six months pupils or junior tenants is allocated by the clerk, or on the clerk's suggestion, this allocation should be systematically monitored.** The ACE fees program, if available to chambers, can assist in this. Reasons for any differences in the quantity or type of work done or fees earned, or in the potential of the work for career development, between men, women, or different minority ethnic groups within chambers should be investigated and corrective action taken if necessary. The same principles apply to the allocation of work to pupils and barristers in chambers who are known to have a disability or who are openly gay, lesbian or bisexual.

7. Chambers which are measuring the effectiveness of their equal opportunities policy may wish to monitor the number of disabled applicants for pupillage, tenancy or employment. Questions about registration will not be appropriate as the majority of disabled people do not register.

8. The collection of data on sexual orientation is impractical because many lesbians, gay men and bisexuals conceal their sexual orientation.

9. Chambers should check at regular intervals that the advice in this Code has been observed by staff and members of chambers.

CHAPTER 7 — Complaints

1. **Chambers should have written grievance procedures as part of general chambers management which should include procedures for handling complaints of discrimination and harassment. They should be brought to the attention of every new pupil, tenant and chambers' employee.**

2. **There should be procedures to deal with complaints that concern selection of pupils, tenants and staff from external and internal applicants (including pupils not offered tenancies), conduct of pupillage, distribution of work in chambers, pressure or instructions to discriminate, the distribution of work, and harassment or other discrimination originating within or outside chambers.**

3.   **Chambers should nominate one or two senior members of chambers to act as informal advisors to potential complainants and to assist in the informal resolution of grievances.**

4.   **When a complaint is made confidentiality should be maintained throughout any investigatory process as far as possible and appropriate in the circumstances. Names of complainants should not be released (save to those conducting the investigation and to the person complained against) without their consent.**

5.   The written procedure should indicate the allocation of responsibility for investigating complaints to at least two members of chambers, names of chambers' informal advisors, an undertaking that complainants will not be victimised nor will suffer detriment because of a complaint made in good faith, an undertaking regarding confidentiality, a requirement for the complaint to be made in writing, a time limit within which a written response should be delivered, the range of remedial actions where complaints are substantiated, identification of the relevant Bar Council committees to which the complaints may be addressed and an indication of opportunities for supportive counselling provided by the associations and groups of women lawyers, members of minority ethnic groups, disabled people and lesbians or gay men. Confidential assistance may also be sought from the equal opportunities officers.

6.   Complainants of unlawful racial or sex discrimination should be informed of their legal right to apply within six months of the incident to the county court (or within three months to an industrial tribunal for chambers' employees) and their right to consult the Commission for Racial Equality or the Equal Opportunities Commission.

7.   **Where actual or potential discrimination has been identified, remedial action should be taken by chambers.**

8.   A report on all complaints and findings should be made to the head of chambers. Chambers should maintain confidential records of all complaints and records of meetings. These should be reviewed annually to ensure that procedures are working effectively.

ANNEXE P

ADJUDICATION PANEL AND APPEALS RULES

ADJUDICATION PANEL AND APPEALS RULES

Introduction

1.   Adjudication Panels ('Panels') shall be appointed by the Professional Conduct and Complaints Committee ('the Committee') to determine complaints considered by the Committee not to raise a *prima facie* case of professional misconduct, but to raise a *prima facie* case that the barrister concerned has provided inadequate professional service to the complainant.

2.   Panels shall consist of the Complaints Commissioner ('the Commissioner') as chairman, one lay member of the Committee and two barrister members of the Committee, at least one of whom shall be a Queen's Counsel.

3.   Anything required by these Rules to be done or any discretion required to be exercised by, and any notice required to be given to, the Complaints Commissioner ('the Commissioner') or the Secretary of the Committee ('the Secretary'), may be done or exercised by, or given to, any person authorised by the Complaints Commissioner to act in his stead or by the Chief Executive of the Bar Council to act instead of the Secretary of the Committee (either prospectively or retrospectively and either generally or for a particular purpose).

Powers of Panels

4.   The powers of a Panel shall be:

(a)   to consider any complaint referred to it pursuant to paragraph 28(e) of the Complaints Rules and to direct such investigations as they see fit in respect thereof

(b)   to dismiss any complaint without making a finding as to the existence or otherwise of inadequate professional service if they conclude that due to lapse of time, disputes of fact which cannot fairly be resolved by the Panel, or for any other reason it cannot fairly be determined

(c)   to determine whether the barrister concerned has provided inadequate professional service in respect of the matter complained of

(d)   to determine what remedy should be granted to the complainant in respect of such inadequate service.

Investigation and Procedure

5.   When a complaint is referred to a Panel as set out in paragraph 4(a) above the Commissioner shall consider what, if any, further

investigation is required to be made in order for the panel to deal fairly with the matters falling to it for decision, and the Secretary shall make such investigations as the Commissioner or the Panel direct, having regard so far as he thinks appropriate to the following provisions.

6.   Where the complaint is received more than six months after the date of the conduct complained of, the Panel shall dismiss the complaint unless, having regard to the nature of the complaint, the extent of the delay and any reason put forward by the complainant for such delay, it is satisfied that the complaint can nevertheless be considered fairly both to the complainant and to the barrister. If the Panel is so satisfied, it may, notwithstanding the delay, proceed to consider the complaint.

7.   Investigations may include an invitation to the complainant to provide in writing any further information as to the service provided by the barrister which he alleges were inadequate, and any evidence sought to be relied upon by the complainant in support of such allegation. Further, the complainant may be invited to specify whether he claims that he has suffered financial loss arising out of the conduct complained of, and the amount of such loss, and to provide any evidence sought to be relied on in support of that allegation.

8.   The complainant's reply to such invitation may be sent to the barrister concerned together with a letter inviting him to comment in writing on the further information provided by the complainant, and the barrister may in addition be required to provide details of the work he carried out for the complainant out of which the complaint arose, the fee claimed by him for such work, and whether or not such fee has been paid.

9.   The information received from the barrister under the foregoing paragraph will normally be sent to the complainant for his further comments, and any further or other investigations or enquiries that the Commissioner thinks appropriate may be made.

10.   The Panel may consider complaints and the results of any investigations in whatever manner they think fit, and may adjourn consideration of any complaint at any time, and for any reason.

11.   Following such consideration, the Panel may decide:

    (a)   that for any reason the complaint cannot fairly be determined by them, whereupon it shall dismiss the complaint and shall give notice in writing of its decision and the reasons for it to the barrister and the complainant

    (b)   that the complainant has not established on the balance of probabilities that the barrister concerned has provided inadequate professional service to the complainant, whereupon it shall dismiss the complaint and shall give notice in writing of its decision and the reasons for it to the barrister and the complainant

(c) that the complainant has so established, whereupon it shall consider what remedy should be granted to the complainant in respect of the service which it has found to have been inadequate.

12. Following a finding under paragraph 11(c) above, the Panel may:

(a) determine that it is not appropriate to take any action in respect of the inadequate service,

(b) direct the barrister to make a formal apology to the complainant for the inadequate service provided,

(c) direct the barrister to repay or remit all or part of any fee rendered in respect of the inadequate service,

(d) direct the barrister to pay compensation to the complainant in such sum as the panel shall direct not exceeding £2,000

Save that no order under paragraph (d) shall be made unless the panel are satisfied that the complainant has established on the balance of probabilities that he has suffered loss recoverable at law caused by the inadequate professional service and further that the panel are satisfied that no issue of law or fact arises in relation to such loss which cannot fairly be resolved on the material then before them. If the panel is so satisfied, it may direct payment of such sum by way of compensation as it sees fit up to the amount of such loss or £2,000, whichever is the less. Further in determining whether any sum is to be paid under paragraph (d) hereof, or in fixing the amount of such sum, the panel shall in particular have regard to the availability to the complainant of other forms of redress, to the gravity of the conduct complained of, and to the fee claimed by the barrister for the inadequate service.

13. Following any such finding as is mentioned in paragraph 11(c) hereof, the Panel shall give notice in writing to the barrister and to the complainant of the respects in which they have found the barrister to have provided inadequate professional service, and the reasons for such finding, and of the remedy to be granted to the complainant under paragraph 12 above.

14. If the panel is not unanimous on any issue, the finding made shall be that of the majority of them. If the panel is equally divided, the burden of proof being on the complainant, the finding shall be that most favourable to the barrister.

15. The panel may reopen or reconsider a complaint which has been disposed of under the provisions of these Rules;

(a) following a recommendation of the Legal Services Ombudsman that they do so, or

(b) where new evidence becomes available to the panel which leads them to conclude that they should do so, or

(c) for some other good reason.

16. Following such reopening or reconsideration, the panel may take any further or different action it thinks fit, as if the former decision had not been made.

17. No finding of an Adjudication Panel shall be publishable except:

(a) by the Commissioner in any annual or other report on his work, in which case the identities of the parties shall so far as possible be concealed, unless the barrister concerned seeks that any finding be published. In that case the manner and extent of publication shall be at the discretion of the Commissioner; or

(b) if the Adjudication Panel considers that the circumstances of the complaint are relevant to the barrister's capacity as a pupilmaster, it may notify the barrister's Inn of its concern in such manner as it sees fit.

Appeals

18. An appeal shall lie at the instance of a barrister against a finding that he has provided inadequate professional service, and against any decision as to the remedy to be granted to the complainant in respect of such inadequate service.

19. Any such appeal shall be heard and determined by a panel ('the Appeal Panel') consisting of not less than three or more than five past or present members of the Committee (or of the Professional Conduct Committee established under the rules in effect immediately before the coming into effect of these Rules) of whom at least one shall be a Queen's Counsel and shall chair the panel, at least one shall be a junior of more than five years' call and at least one shall be a lay representative. None of the members of the Appeal panel shall have been members of the tribunal which made any finding appealed against.

20. An appeal shall be made by the barrister sending to the Secretary within 28 days of being notified of the decision appealed against a notice stating the findings to be appealed against, the decision the barrister contends for, and the grounds of such appeal, accompanied by the sum of £100 payable to the Bar Council to defray expenses.

21. Service of notice of an appeal by a barrister shall operate as a stay of any order made in favour of the complainant.

22. On receipt of such a notice, the Secretary shall notify the Commissioner of the intended appeal, and shall afford him an opportunity to respond to the grounds of appeal stated in the notice. For the purpose of so responding the Commissioner may seek information or assistance from such persons and in such manner as he sees fit.

23.   On such an appeal,

(a)   the procedure shall be informal, the details being at the discretion of the chairman of the Appeal Panel including whether or not there should be an oral hearing in relation to the appeal

(b)   the barrister, the complainant and the Commissioner may attend or be represented

(c)   the Appeal Panel may make such order as they think fit in relation to the complaint, including any order which the tribunal appealed from had the power to make, save that they may not make any order in relation to the costs of the appeal

(d)   the Appeal Panel shall not allow the appeal unless they are satisfied that the tribunal appealed from reached a wrong decision on any question of law, made a finding of fact which was against the weight of the evidence or exercised any discretion granted to it on a wrong basis

(e)   if the Appeal Panel allows an appeal, in whole or in part, it may in its discretion direct the refund to the barrister of the sum deposited under paragraph 20 above.

Definitions

24.   In these Rules unless the context otherwise requires

(a)   Any term defined in the Code of Conduct shall carry the same meaning as it does in the Code of Conduct.

(b)   'The Complaints Rules' shall mean the rules prescribing the manner in which complaints are to be considered set out in Annexe K to the Code of Conduct and any term defined in the Complaints Rules shall carry the same meaning as it does in those Rules.

(c)   Any reference to a person includes any natural person, legal person and/or firm. Any reference to the masculine gender includes the feminine and the neuter, and any reference to the singular includes the plural, and in each case *vice versa*.

ANNEXE 9

THE CONTINUING EDUCATION SCHEME RULES

THE CONTINUING EDUCATION SCHEME RULES

Application

1   These Rules apply;

(a)   to all barristers who commence independent practice on or after the 1st October 1997 and

(b)   to all barristers who first commence employed practice on or after the 1st October 1998 and who exercise or intend to exercise rights of audience not having previously done so.

Save that a barrister who satisfies the requirements of these Rules whilst in independent practice and subsequently enters into employment is not required to undertake any further training under these Rules and vice versa.

The Mandatory Continuing Education Requirements

(a)   The practising barrister to whom these Rules apply shall complete a minimum number of 42 hours of approved continuing education within a period of three years the commencement of which shall be determined as follows:-

(i)   for those commencing practice between 1st October and 31st December – the three-year period shall run from the following 1st January;

(ii)   for those commencing practice between 1st January and 31st March – the three-year period will run from the following 1st April;

(iii)   for those commencing practice between 1st April and 30th June – the three-year period will run from the following 1st July;

(iv)   for those commencing practice between 1st July and 30th September – the three-year period will run from the following 1st October.

(b)   The Bar Council may, by resolution, specify the nature, content and format of courses and other activities which must be undertaken in order to satisfy these Requirements, and these Requirements may be varied to take account of the nature of the instructions barristers may receive within practice.

(c)   The Bar Council may, by resolution, increase the minimum number of hours following consultation with the Inns, Circuits and other providers as appropriate.

Approved Courses

3   For the purposes of these Rules continuing education training courses and/or providers shall be approved by the Bar Council according to criteria which the Bar Council shall from time to time determine, set down and publish.

4   The Bar Council shall maintain a register of courses approved for the purposes of these Rules ('approved courses') which shall contain the following information in relation to each course entered thereon:

    (a)   the title of the course;

    (b)   the name of the course provider;

    (c)   the date or dates on which the course is being held;

    (d)   the duration of the course;

    (e)   the subject matter of the course;

    (f)   the number of hours that the course represents;

    (g)   whether the course is one in advocacy, case preparation and procedure, or ethics.

Failure to comply with the Mandatory Continuing Education Requirement

5   Where a practising barrister to whom these Rules apply fails to comply with the Mandatory Continuing Education Requirement his/her Practising Certificate shall be suspended until such time as the said requirement has been met.

6   Notwithstanding Paragraph 5 above, a practising barrister to whom these Rules apply may apply to the Bar Council for an extension of the time within which they must comply with the said requirement. Such a request must be upon the grounds of mitigating circumstances and shall be supported as appropriate by all relevant documentary evidence. Where notified to the Bar Council, periods within which the barrister does not practise shall be added by way of extension to the three-year period contained within the Mandatory Continuing Education Requirement.

7   As they may apply to an individual practising barrister, the Bar Council shall have the power to waive any or all of the requirements of these Rules in whole or in part or to extend any or all of the time limits provided for by these Rules.

Refusal of Practising Certificates

8   The suspension of a Practising Certificate may be revoked by the Bar Council, or by a Disciplinary Tribunal before whom charges of professional misconduct under paragraph 301(a)(ii) or 403.3 of the Code of Conduct have been preferred.

INDEX

not a legal service 901

SECTION 3

Miscellaneous Guidance

This section contains miscellaneous guidance, advice and information issued by the Bar Council. It does not form part of the Code of Conduct

INDEX

Legal Aid Guidelines

Conditional Fees — guidance (further guidance will be issued shortly)

Guidance on Preparation of Witness Statements

Guidance on Preparation of Defence Case Statements

Service Standard on Returned Briefs agreed with the CPS

Approved List of Direct Professional Access Bodies

Joint Tribunal Standing Orders for Fee Disputes with Solicitors (see Annexe B, para 14)

Waiver of paragraph 212 for Non-Practising Barristers

LEGAL AID GUIDELINES

1.   Introduction

1.1   These Guidelines are intended to assist barristers to comply with the provisions of the Legal Aid Act 1988 (and regulations made under the Act) when advising the Legal Aid Board on merits on behalf of an applicant for civil legal aid, or when acting on an assisted person's behalf.

1.2   They are derived in part from the Legal Aid Handbook (published annually) which every barrister instructed under the terms of a civil legal aid certificate should consult.

1.3   They are essentially statements of good practice and should not be rigidly applied. They may, however, be taken into account when a wasted costs order is being considered against a barrister on the ground of his non-compliance with the Act, or in deciding whether or not a barrister has committed a disciplinary offence. They should be read in conjunction with the Code of Conduct (see especially paragraphs 203(b), 506(c)(d) and 802.1(d).

2   The Statutory test

2.1   The statutory test for the grant of civil legal aid to an applicant who is financially eligible is twofold:

(1)   The applicant must satisfy the Board that he has reasonable grounds for taking, defending or being a party to the proceedings (section 15(2) — the 'legal merits' test); and

(2)   Representation may be refused if it is unreasonable for him to be granted representation in the particular circumstances of the case (section 15(3)(a) — the 'reasonableness test').

2.2   The test does not apply to certain public law proceedings under the Children Act 1989 (section 15 as amended).

'Legal merits'

2.3   Reasonable grounds for taking, defending or being a party to proceedings may be said to exist if (a) assuming the facts alleged are proved, there is a case which has reasonable prospects of success in law; (b) assuming he had the means to pay the likely costs, the applicant would be advised to take or defend the proceedings privately.

2.4   When considering merits, it is important to remember that there is almost always an opposing point of view and that litigation is notoriously uncertain. Whilst it is no part of a barrister's duty to be over-cautious, he should not advise that legal aid be granted when the prospects of success are no more than slight.

2.5   A barrister should estimate the prospects of a successful outcome by reference to one of the following categories, namely: A. Very good (80 per cent); B. Good (60–80 per cent); C. Reasonable (50–60 per cent); D. Less than evens; or E. Impossible to say.

2.6   The means of the hypothetical private client being considered should be taken as moderate but not excessive. In other words, he would be able to meet the likely costs, albeit with some difficulty or as something of a sacrifice.

Reasonableness

2.7   Even if his case has legal merits, an applicant may be refused legal aid if it would not be reasonable for him to be granted it.

2.8   A common example of proceedings which it would be unreasonable for the Legal Aid Board to fund are those which are not likely to be cost effective, i.e. any benefit to be achieved does not justify the cost. Another example is where the applicant reveals some illegal motive or conduct on the part of the applicant or abuse of the legal aid.

2.9   More specific examples are where:

(a)   the applicant has other rights or facilities (such as trade union or insurance cover) making it unnecessary for him to apply for legal aid;

(b)   the applicant is a victim of a crime of violence who could obtain compensation from the Criminal Injuries Compensation Board;

(c)   the proceedings should be taken in a different court where the costs are likely to be lower; or

(d)   the arguments on which the applicant relies will be put forward on behalf of another party whose interests in the proceedings are substantially the same.

3   Contents of a barrister's opinion on merits

3.1   A barrister's written opinion on merits should:

(i)   show that both (a) the legal merits and (b) the reasonableness tests (as outlined above) have been specifically and separately addressed by him before reaching a conclusion — a general statement that legal aid should be granted is not sufficient; it should estimate the prospects of a successful outcome by reference to one of the categories A to E mentioned in paragraph 2.5 above; in a case falling within category D or E, more explanation must be given if the Board are to be satisfied that legal aid should be granted;

(ii)   where factual issues are involved (a) set out in sufficient detail, (although not necessarily at great length) the rival factual versions to enable the Board to assess their relative strengths, and (b) express a clear opinion as to whether the applicant's version has a reasonable prospect of being accepted by a court and why;

(iii)   in a case where the applicant's own evidence is likely to be contested, and a conference would assist the barrister to form a view of his reliability as a witness, state whether a conference has been held and what emerged from it, or if none was held, indicate briefly why;

(iv)   where legal issues or difficulties of law are involved (a) summarise those issues or difficulties in sufficient detail to enable the Board to come to a view about them without looking outside the opinion, and (b) express a clear view as to whether the applicant's case on the law has a reasonable prospect of being accepted by a court and why;

(v)   draw attention to (a) any lack or incompleteness of material which in his opinion might bear on the reliability or otherwise of the applicant's version, and (b) any other factor which in his opinion could — whether now or in the future — materially affect his assessment of the outcome of the case;

(vi)   in a case where damages are claimed, quantify at least the likely bracket for an award;

(vii)   draw attention to the need for the legal representatives between them to quantify the costs likely to be incurred by the Fund in the light of the barrister's opinion (if favourable) assuming the proceedings are fully contested;

(viii)   suggest or formulate for the Board any limitation or condition (whether as to the scope of the work that should be covered or as to the costs which should be expended) which in his opinion ought to be imposed on the grant of legal aid in order to safeguard the Fund;

(ix)   confirm that the proceedings are in his view cost-effective, i.e. that the estimated costs of the proceedings are likely to be justified by the benefit to the client, have regard in particular to the statutory charge which may be created by virtue of section 16 of the Act.

4 **A Barrister's continuing duty to the Fund**

4.1   A barrister is under a specific duty to comply with the provisions of the Legal Aid Acts 1974 and 1988 or any regulations made for giving effect to or preventing abuses of those Acts: para 802.1(d) of the Code of Conduct. Since these are directed at ensuring that legal aid is granted and continued only in justifiable cases, it follows that a barrister acting under a legal aid certificate is under a duty to bring to the attention of the Legal Aid Board any matter which in his view might affect the assisted person's entitlement to legal aid, or the terms of his certificate, at whatever stage of the proceedings that might occur.

4.2   An example of when the duty may arise is whenever proposals for settlement are made by the other side. He should report to the Board any decisions of the client which may cast doubt on the reasonableness of legal aid being continued contrary to his advice.

4.3   A further example is where a barrister finds that his legally assisted client has an interest in the proceedings which is or may become substantially the same as that of another party (see paragraph 2.9(d) above). A barrister should in those circumstances, after discussing the matter with his client, report it to the Board and advise whether in his opinion it is reasonable for legal aid to be continued.

CONDITIONAL FEES — INTERIM MEASURES
FOLLOWING 'THAI TRADING'
(Further guidance to follow pending approval)

At its meeting on 4 July 1998, the Bar Council approved the following amendments to the Code of Conduct.

1.   Delete paragraph 211

2.   Amend para 309 to read:

'Subject to paragraphs 205 and 207 a barrister in independent practice may charge for any work undertaken by him (whether or not it involves an appearance in court) on any basis or by any method he thinks fit provided that such basis or method is:

(a)   permitted by law; and

(b)   does not involve the payment of a wage or salary.'

The Bar Council also resolved that:

'It is inappropriate for a barrister acting in a criminal or public law child case to accept a fee which is dependent upon the outcome.'

Effect

The amendment:

(a)   will allow barristers to enter into fee agreements of the type considered in *Thai Trading Co.* v *Taylor* [1998] 2 WLR 893 and in *Bevan Ashford* v *Geoff Yeandle (Contractors) Ltd* (1998) April 8;

(b)   abolishes the existing prohibition against acting over a fixed period for a fixed fee irrespective of the amount of work done.

Subject to the guidance below, the amendment will permit at least the following arrangements:

(a)   'no win, no fee' — i.e. counsel agrees to forgo the whole fee if the case is lost;

(b)   'no win, reduced fee' — i.e. counsel agrees to forgo part of his normal fee if the case is lost; and

(c)   some 'conditional fee' arrangements outside the scope of those permitted under s. 58 of the Courts and Legal Services Act 1990 as shown by *Bevan Ashford* v *Geoff Yeandle (Contractors) Ltd* (1998) April 8.

The amendment does **not** permit 'contingency fee' arrangements — i.e. counsel takes a percentage of the monies recovered by the client if the case is won.

Guidance

1.   The full extent of the law in this area is unclear and members of the Bar are advised to consider the two decided cases in particular before entering into such agreements.

2.   It seems likely that such agreements in criminal and in *all* child care cases are likely to remain unlawful on grounds of public policy and, if this is the case, members of the Bar entering into such agreements in those cases will be guilty of professional misconduct, as well as finding that their fees are unenforceable.

3.   The cab-rank rule does not apply to such agreements.

4.   Members of the Bar entering into such agreements are advised to do so in writing before undertaking the case. The agreements should set out their terms clearly.

6th July 1998

PREPARING WITNESS STATEMENTS
FOR USE IN CIVIL PROCEEDINGS

DEALINGS WITH WITNESSES

GUIDANCE FOR MEMBERS OF THE BAR

Introduction

1   The purpose of this paper, which has the approval of the Professional Standards Committee of the General Council of the Bar, is to offer guidance to members of the Bar instructed to prepare or settle a witness statement and as to dealings with witnesses. Guidance already exists for practice in some Courts, notably paragraph 3.7 of the Chancery Guide, Part XIV of the Guide to Commercial Court Practice and the Notes to RSC Order 38 Rule 2A in the White Book, to which attention is drawn. The intention is that this paper should be consistent with that guidance.

2   This guidance is not applicable to criminal proceedings. Attention is drawn to Annex F to the Code of Conduct.

Witness statements

3   The cardinal principle that needs to be kept in mind when drafting or settling a witness statement is that, when the maker enters the witness box, he or she will swear or affirm that the evidence to be given will be the truth, the *whole truth* and nothing but the truth. In most civil trials almost the first question in chief (and not infrequently the last) will be to ask the witness to confirm, to the best of his belief, the accuracy of the witness statement. It is therefore critical that the statement is one that accurately reflects, to the best of Counsel's ability, the witness's evidence.

4   Witnesses often misunderstand the function of those drafting and settling witness statements. The function of Counsel is to understand the relevant evidence that a witness can give and to assist the witness to express that evidence in writing. It is important it is made clear to the witness (by reminder to the professional client or the witness, if seen by Counsel) that the statement once approved is *the witness's* statement. Ultimately it is the witness's responsibility to ensure that the evidence he gives is truthful. It is good practice to remind witnesses expressly of this from time to time, especially where Counsel is putting forward a particular piece of drafting for the witness' consideration (which is expressly permitted by the proviso to Rule 606 of the Code of Conduct).

5   It is not Counsel's duty to vet the accuracy of a witness's evidence[1]. We all may doubt the veracity of our clients and

---

[1] If para 3.6(7) of the Chancery Guide suggests otherwise, the PSC respectfully disagrees.

witnesses occasionally. Counsel is, of course, entitled and it may often be appropriate to draw to the witness's attention to other evidence which appears to conflict with what the witness is saying and is entitled to indicate that a Court may find a particular piece of evidence difficult to accept. But if the witness maintains the evidence, it should be recorded in the witness statement. If it is decided to call the witness, it will be for the Court to judge the correctness of the witness's evidence.

6   It follows that the statement:

(i)   Must accurately reflect the witness's evidence. Rule 606(d) of the Code of Conduct states:

'A practising barrister must not devise facts which will assist in advancing his lay client's case and must not draft any . . . affidavit [or] witness statement . . . containing:
. . .
(d)   in the case of an affidavit or witness statement any statement of fact other than the evidence which in substance according to his instructions the barrister reasonably believes the witness would give if the evidence contained in the affidavit or witness statement were being given *viva voce*;

Provided that nothing in this paragraph shall prevent a barrister drafting a[n] . . . affidavit or witness statement containing specific facts matters or contentions included by the barrister subject to the lay client's confirmation as to their accuracy.'

(ii)   Must not contain any statement which Counsel knows the witness does not believe to be true. Nor should the witness be placed under any pressure to provide other than a truthful account of his evidence.

(iii)   Must contain all the evidence which a witness could reasonably be expected to give in answer to those questions which would be asked of him in examination in chief. The witness statement should not be drafted or edited so that it no longer fairly reflects the answers which the witness would be expected to give in response to *viva voce* examination-in-chief in accordance with the witness's oath or affirmation. Although it is not the function of a witness statement to answer such questions as might be put in cross-examination, great care should be exercised when excluding any material which is thought to be unhelpful to the party calling the witness and no material should be excluded which might render the statement anything other than the truth, the whole truth and nothing but the truth. While it is permissible to confine the scope of examination-in-chief to part only of the evidence which a witness could give, that is always subject to Counsel's overriding duty to assist the Court in the administration of justice and not to deceive or knowingly or recklessly to mislead the Court (Rule 202 of the Code of Conduct). Consequently, it would be improper to exclude material whose omission would render untrue or misleading anything which remains in the statement. It would also be improper to include fact A while excluding fact B, if evidence-in-chief containing fact A but excluding, fact B could not have been given consistently with the witness's promise to tell the truth, the whole truth and nothing but the truth. Whether it is wise and in the client's interest in any given case to exclude unfavourable material which can properly be excluded is a matter of judgment.

(iv) Save for formal matters and uncontroversial facts, should be expressed as far as reasonably practical in the witness's own words. This is especially important when the statement is dealing with the critical factual issues in the case — e.g. the accident or the disputed conversation. Thus the statement should reflect the witness's own description of events. It should not be drafted or edited so as to massage or obscure the witness' real evidence.

(v) Must be confined to admissible evidence that the witness can give, including permissible hearsay. Inadmissible hearsay, comment and argument should be excluded.

(vi) Should be succinct and exclude irrelevant material. Unnecessary elaboration is to be avoided. It is not the function of witness statements to serve as a commentary on the documents in the trial bundles. Nor are they intended to serve as another form of written argument.

7   Sometimes it becomes apparent, after a witness statement has been served, that the witness's recollection has altered. This may happen when the witness sees how another witness puts the facts in a witness statement served by another party. Where Counsel learns that the witness has had a material change of recollection this should be recorded in an additional witness statement to be served on the other parties. Where this is not possible because it occurs very shortly before the witness is to be called, the other parties should be informed and the statement corrected in chief before the truth of its contents is established. It would be improper for the other side to be kept in the dark as to a material change in the witness's evidence especially when settlement negotiations are taking place.

Formalities

8   A witness statement:

(i)   Should be expressed in the first person;

(ii)   Must state the full name of the witness and, unless there is a good reason for omitting it, the witness's residential address or, where the statement is made in a professional, business or other occupational capacity, the address at which he works, the position held and the name of the firm or employer. Where there is said to be a reason for omitting the witness's address, the reason should be given;

(iii)   Must state the witness's occupation (if any);

(iv)   Must state if the witness is a party to the proceedings or has a connection with any party — e.g. is an employee or a relative;

(v)   Should be in chronological sequence divided into consecutively numbered paragraphs;

(vi)   Must include a statement by the witness that the contents are true to the best of his/her knowledge and belief;

(vii)   Except for good reason (which must be stated) must be signed by the witness;

(viii)   Must be dated.

Dealings with Witnesses

Counsel seeing witnesses[2].

9   The old rules preventing Counsel from seeing a witness, other than the client, have been progressively relaxed over recent years. The current position in civil proceedings can be summarised as follows:

(i)   There is no longer any rule which prevents a barrister from having contact with any witness. Indeed, in taking witness statements and generally, it is the responsibility of a barrister, especially when the witness is nervous, vulnerable or apparently the victim of criminal or similar conduct, to ensure that those facing unfamiliar court procedures are put as much at ease as possible.

(ii)   Although there is no longer any rule which prevents a barrister from having contact with witnesses, a barrister should exercise his discretion and consider very carefully whether and to what extent such contact is appropriate, bearing in mind in particular that it is not the barrister's function (but that of his professional client) to investigate and collect evidence.

(iii)   The guiding principle must be the obligation of Counsel to promote and protect his lay client's best interests so far as that is consistent with the law and with Counsel's overriding duty to the Court (Code of Conduct paragraphs 202, 203). Often it will be in the client's best interests that Counsel should meet witnesses whose evidence will be of critical importance in the case, so as to be able to form a view as to the credibility of their evidence and to advise the lay client properly;

---

[2] This is largely taken from Annexe F as recently amended by the Bar Council and approved by the Lord Chancellor's Advisory Committee on Legal Education and Conduct and the designated judges.

(iv) A barrister should be alert to the risks that any discussion of the substance of a case with a witness may lead to suspicions of coaching, and thus tend to diminish the value of the witness's evidence in the eyes of the court, or may place a barrister in a position of professional embarrassment, for example, if he thereby becomes himself a witness in the case. These dangers are most likely to occur if such discussion takes place:

(a) before the barrister has been supplied with a proof of the witness's evidence; or

(b) in the absence of the barrister's professional client or his representative.

(v) Rule 607 of the Code of Conduct provides that a barrister must not rehearse practise or coach a witness in relation to his evidence or the way in which he should give it. This does not prevent Counsel giving general advice to a witness about giving evidence e.g. speak up, speak slowly, answer the question, keep answers as short as possible, ask if a question is not understood, say if you cannot remember and do not guess or speculate. Nor is there any objection to testing a witness's recollection robustly to ascertain the quality of his evidence or to discussing the issues that may arise in cross-examination. By contrast, mock cross-examinations or rehearsals of particular lines of questioning that Counsel proposes to follow are not permitted. What should be borne in mind is that there is a distinction, when interviewing a witness, between questioning him closely in order to enable him to present his evidence fully and accurately or in order to test the reliability of his evidence (which is permissible) and questioning him with a view to encouraging the witness to alter, massage or obscure his real recollection (which is not). The distinction was neatly drawn by Judge Francis Finch in *In Re Eldridge*[3] in 1880, where he said:

'While a discreet and prudent attorney may very properly ascertain from witnesses in advance of the trial what they in fact do know and the extent and limitations of their memory, as guide for his own examinations, he has no right legal or moral, to go further. His duty is to extract the facts from the witness, not to pour them into him; to learn what the witness does know, not to teach him what he ought to know.'

At the risk of stating the obvious, this is a difficult area calling for the exercise of careful judgment.

(vi) A barrister should also be alert to the fact that, even in the absence of any wish or intention to do so, authority figures do subconsciously influence lay witnesses.

---

[3] New York Court of Appeals; 37 NY 161, 171

Discussion of the substance of the case may unwittingly contaminate the witness's evidence.

(vii)   There is particular danger where such discussions:

(a)   take place in the presence of more than one witness of fact; or

(b)   involve the disclosure to one witness of fact of the factual evidence of another witness.

These practices have been strongly deprecated by the courts as tending inevitably to encourage the rehearsal or coaching of witnesses and to increase the risk of fabrication or contamination of evidence: *R* v *Arif* (1993) May 26; *Smith New Court Securities Ltd* v *Scrimgeour Vickers (Asset Management) Ltd* [1994] 1 WLR 1271.

(viii)   That is not to suggest that it is always inappropriate to disclose one witness's evidence to another. If conflicting witness statements have been obtained from different witnesses or served by the other side, it is almost inevitable that a witness's attention must be drawn to discrepancies between statements. Discretion is, however, required, especially where the evidence of independent witnesses is involved.

(ix)   Whilst there is no rule that any longer prevents a barrister from taking a witness statement in civil cases, there is a distinction between the settling of a witness statement and taking a witness statement. Save in exceptional circumstances, it is not appropriate for a barrister who has taken witness statements, as opposed to settling witness statements prepared by others, to act as Counsel in that case because it risks undermining the independence of the barrister as an advocate. Exceptional circumstances would include:

(a)   The witness is a minor one;

(b)   Counsel has no choice but to take the proof and this is the only practical course in the interests of justice — this would apply, for instance, where a witness appears unexpectedly at Court and there is no one else competent to take the statement;

(c)   Counsel is a junior member of a team of Counsel and will not be examining the witness.

The Cab Rank rule does not require a barrister to agree to undertake the task of taking witness statements.

(x)   A barrister should be prepared to exchange common courtesies with the other side's witnesses. However, a barrister should only discuss the substance of the case or any evidence with the other side's witnesses in rare and exceptional circumstances and then only with the prior knowledge of his opponent.

21 February 1997
J.H.Q.C

THE PREPARATION OF DEFENCE CASE STATEMENTS
PURSUANT TO THE CRIMINAL PROCEDURE
AND INVESTIGATIONS ACT 1996

GUIDANCE ON THE DUTIES OF COUNSEL
(As approved by the PCCC on 24 September 1997)

1 It is becoming increasingly common for solicitors to instruct counsel to draft or settle Defence Case Statements, required under section 5 of the Criminal Procedure and Investigations Act 1996. Often these instructions are given to counsel with no or little previous involvement in the case shortly before the expiry of the time limit.

2 The relevant legislation is set out at §12–82 et seq. of the 1997 edition of Archbold. In summary, however:

(i) The time limit for compliance is short — 14 days from service of prosecution material or a statement that there is none. The permitted grounds for an extension of time are limited[1];

(ii) The contents of the Defence Case Statement are obviously of great importance to the defendant. An inaccurate or inadequate statement of the defence could have serious repercussions for the defendant, if the trial judge permits 'appropriate' comment;

(iii) Whilst it will be the natural instinct of most defence counsel to keep the Defence Case Statement short, a short and anodyne statement may be insufficient to trigger any obligation on the prosecution to give secondary disclosure of prosecution material.

3 Normally it will be more appropriate for instructing solicitors to draft the Defence Case Statement, since typically counsel will have had little involvement at this stage.

4 However, there is nothing unprofessional about counsel drafting or settling a Defence Case Statement, although it must be appreciated that there is no provision in the current regulations for graduated fees allowing for counsel to be paid a separate fee for his work. This most unsatisfactory situation (which has arisen, as a result of the 1996 Act, since the graduated fees regulations were negotiated) is being addressed urgently by the Fees and Legal Aid Committee. A barrister has no obligation to accept work for which he will not be paid. The absence of a fee will justify refusal of the instructions of counsel who are not to be retained for the trial and are simply asked to do no more than draft or settle the Defence Case Statement. Where counsel is retained for the trial, Rule 502(b) of the Code of Conduct deems instructions in a legally aided matter to be at a proper fee and

---

[1] See the Defence Disclosure Time Limit Regulations 1997 made pursuant to the Act: Archbold Supplement §12–93.

counsel would not be justified in refusing to draft or settle a Defence Case Statement on the sole ground that there is no separate fee payable for this work.

5   Many members of the Bar will nevertheless feel that, in the interests of their lay client and or of good relations with instructing solicitors, they cannot refuse work, even where they would otherwise be entitled to do so. Those who do so need to recognise the crucial importance of:

(i)   Obtaining all prosecution statements and documentary exhibits;

(ii)   Getting instructions from the lay client, from a properly signed proof and preferably a conference. Those instructions need to explain the general nature of the defence, to indicate the matters on which issue is taken with the prosecution and to give an explanation of the reason for taking issue. They must also give details of any alibi defence, sufficient to give the information required by Section 5(7) of the 1996 Act;

(iii) Getting statements from other material witnesses;

(iv)   Ensuring that the client realises the importance of the Defence Case Statement and the potential adverse consequences of an inaccurate or inadequate statement;

(v)   Getting proper informed approval for the draft from the client. This is particularly important, given the risks of professional embarrassment if the client seeks to disown the statement during the course of the trial, perhaps when the trial is not going well or when under severe pressure in cross-examination. Counsel ought to insist on getting written acknowledgement from the lay client that:

(a)   he understands the importance of the accuracy and adequacy of the Defence Case Statement for his case;

(b)   he has had the opportunity of considering the contents of the statement carefully and approves it.

This may often mean having a conference with the lay client to explain the Defence Case Statement and to get informed approval, although in straightforward cases where counsel has confidence in the instructing solicitor, this could be left to the solicitor. Where the latter course is taken, a short written advice (which can be in a standard form) as to the importance of obtaining the written acknowledgement before service of the statement should accompany the draft Defence Case Statement. A careful record should be kept of work done and advice given.

(vi)   If there is inadequate time, counsel should ask the instructing solicitor to apply for an extension of time. This needs to be considered at a very early stage, since the application must be made before the expiry of the time limit.

6   It follows that counsel ought not to accept any instructions to draft or settle a Defence Case Statement unless given the opportunity and adequate time to gain proper familiarity with the case and to comply with the fundamental requirements set out above. In short, there is no halfway house. If instructions are accepted, then the professional obligations on counsel are considerable.

SERVICE STANDARD ON RETURNED BRIEFS

1   **PRINCIPLE**

1.1   This Standard applies to all advocates instructed to prosecute on behalf of the CPS.

1.2   The fundamental principle upon which the Standard is based is that the advocate initially instructed should conduct the case.

1.3   This applies to all cases irrespective of whether or not they are contested.

1.4   For the purpose of this Standard a return means a brief which is passed to another advocate because the advocate instructed is unable to appear to represent the prosecution at any hearing, subject to the exceptions for interlocutory hearings referred to in paragraphs 1.13–1.15 below.

1.5   There is a need for positive action to be taken by all advocates, acting in conjunction with the CPS, to minimise the level of returns in order to ensure that the best possible service is provided. Such action will include ensuring that the advocate's availability is considered when cases are being fixed and that efforts are made to take this into account.

1.6   Whatever positive action is taken to reduce the level of returns, it is recognised that there will always be some briefs which are returned.

1.7   The impact of a return is dependent upon the nature of the case and the timing of its return.

1.8   There will be some degree of flexibility in uncontested cases in that the acceptability of the return will be influenced by the nature, complexity and seriousness of the case and the degree of involvement of the advocate before committal or transfer.

1.9   Where a return is unavoidable, the advocate will be responsible for ensuring that immediate notice is given to enable the CPS to choose and instruct another advocate and for that advocate fully to prepare the case.

1.10   Special attention must be paid to retrials, sensitive cases or those involving vulnerable witnesses, especially children, and those cases in which the advocate has settled the indictment, provided a substantive advice, attended a conference or been present at an ex parte hearing.

1.11   The advocate prosecuting a case in which the brief has been returned should not, without good reason and prior consultation with the CPS, reverse a decision previously taken by the advocate originally instructed. This is especially important in cases involving child witnesses and video evidence.

1.12   Whenever a brief is returned, the choice of an alternative advocate will always be a matter for the CPS. Where counsel has been instructed, the availability of alternative counsel in the chambers holding the brief will not be the determining factor in selecting a new advocate. Counsel's clerk will be expected to make realistic proposals as to an alternative advocate, whether or not within the same chambers, and consideration will be given to them.

1.13   When the CPS instructs an advocate to appear at an interlocutory hearing, including plea and directions hearings (PDH), bail applications, applications to make or break fixtures and mentions, the advocate instructed in the case will, wherever practicable, be expected to attend. If the advocate instructed is not available, an alternative advocate may be instructed provided that advocate is acceptable to the CPS and following consultation with the CPS.

1.14   If an advocate is unable to attend a PDH as a result of work commitments elsewhere, a returned brief will not be treated as a return for the purpose of monitoring compliance with this Standard, unless the advocate's clerk was consulted about, and had confirmed, the advocate's availability for the PDH before the brief was delivered.

1.15   In the case of other interlocutory hearings, which may be potentially difficult or sensitive, the CPS will, whenever possible, consult the advocate's clerk about the advocate's availability before the date of hearing is arranged. Unless such consultation has taken place, a returned brief will not be counted as a return for the purpose of monitoring compliance with this Standard.

1.16   Following any interlocutory hearing, the brief will revert to the advocate originally instructed, subject to the CPS exercising its discretion to depart from this practice in any particular case.

1.17   In any case in which a brief is returned, and whatever the nature of the hearing, it will be the responsibility of the advocate holding the brief to ensure that the advocate to whom the brief is returned is fully informed of all matters relating to that hearing and, *where practicable*, to endorse the brief accordingly.

1.18   Notwithstanding the responsibility resting with the advocate returning the brief, the advocate accepting the brief also has a duty to be fully prepared to deal with any matter likely to arise at the hearing.

1.19   Subject to any other agreement negotiated with the CPS on the transfer of papers between advocates, whenever a brief is returned it will be the responsibility of the advocate or the advocate's clerk holding the brief to make arrangements to transfer the brief promptly to the agreed alternative advocate.

1.20   Neither the advocate nor the advocate's clerk should permit the number of briefs held by a single advocate to reach a point where returns are inevitable. The CPS must be informed if it appears that this situation might arise.

1.21   The CPS will make arrangements for the distribution of work to individual advocates so as to minimise the possibility of this happening.

2.   GUIDANCE

2.1   Recommendations and guidance on counsel's responsibilities in relation to returned briefs have been given in the following reports:

Seabrook Report on the Efficient Disposal of Business in the Crown Court — June 1992.

- Counsel should ensure that the CPS is notified as soon as he or his clerk knows he might have to return a brief due to other professional commitments.

- Counsel should ensure that immediate steps are taken to return a brief to another barrister acceptable to the CPS as soon as he or his clerk becomes aware that he will not be able to conduct the case.

Bar Standards Review Body Report — Blueprint for the Bar — September 1994.

- Counsel should provide written reasons upon request as to why a brief is returned.

- Counsel returning a brief should do so with as little disruption to the conduct of the case as practicable. This involves the provision of information to counsel taking on the case.

2.2   It is against this background that the procedures which follow have been developed.

3.   PROCEDURE

Categorisation of cases

3.1   For the purpose of setting standards aimed at reducing the level of returns cases will fall within 3 categories.

3.2   **Category A** will comprise the following:

- cases in which the fees will be assessed ex post facto;

- pre-marked cases in which a Grade 4 Advocate or Special List Advocate (London and South Eastern Circuit) is instructed;

- cases in which Leading Counsel (including a Leading Junior) has been instructed by the CPS;

- cases falling within classes 1 and 2 of the Lord Chief Justice's Practice Direction classifying business within the Crown Court.

3.3 In category A cases no return of the brief is acceptable save where the following applies:

- the advocate is unable to attend court because of illness, accident, childbirth or unexpected incapacity;

- attending court would cause the advocate grave personal hardship as, for example, following a bereavement;

- subject to paragraph 3.8 below, circumstances have arisen outside the advocate's, or the advocate's clerk's, control which are such as to make a return inevitable;

- the case has been fixed for trial by the court in the knowledge that the advocate instructed will not be available.

3.4 Where a case has been so fixed, the CPS will decide whether to apply to the court to change the fixed date or to instruct a different advocate.

3.5 **Category B** will comprise cases in which the brief has been pre-marked and which do not fall within category A, and standard fee cases in which a fixed trial date has been allocated.

3.6 If a trial date has been fixed, no return of the trial brief is acceptable except as in 3.3 above.

3.7 If a trial date has been fixed before the brief is delivered, or has been fixed regardless of the advocate's availability, immediate steps will be taken by the CPS in liaison with the advocate or the advocate's clerk, to identify an appropriate advocate who will be available on the fixed date. Once the brief has been delivered or reallocated, no return is acceptable.

3.8 The advocate's involvement in a part-heard trial will not in itself justify a return in a category A or B case, unless the part-heard trial has been prolonged by unforeseeable circumstances. Where the advocate is involved in a part-heard trial, the position must be kept under constant review, and the CPS kept fully informed, so that an early decision can be made by the CPS as to whether to require a brief to be returned.

3.9 If a brief in a category A or B case is returned, the advocate will, upon CPS request, provide a written explanation as to why the return was unavoidable.

3.10 **Category C** will comprise standard fee cases which have not been given fixed trial dates.

3.11 It is recognised that, for cases which attract standard fees, a higher return rate is more difficult to avoid.

3.12 Subject to the requirements of Bar/CPS Standard 2 on pre-trial preparation having been carried out, if the advocate originally instructed in a category C case is not available, the CPS will agree to the brief being returned to another advocate of appropriate experience, who has adequate time to prepare for the hearing.

General procedural matters

3.13 If a case appears in a warned list or firm date list and the advocate instructed will not be available, the advocate or the advocate's clerk must notify the CPS immediately.

3.14 The CPS will then decide whether to make representations to the court to take the case out of the list, or to allow the brief to be returned to another advocate.

3.15 Where a case has appeared in a reserve list, or where a system of overnight listing operates within the warned list, it is accepted that some returns will be inevitable.

3.16 The advocate or the advocate's clerk should give as much notice as possible of returns in these instances and should aim to give the CPS **two working days notice**. This situation could apply, for example, when an advocate becomes committed part way through the week to a case expected to last several days.

3.17 Where a system of firm dates operates within the warned list period, the CPS must be notified if it appears likely that the advocate may be unavailable, so that an early decision can be made on whether to instruct another advocate or whether to defer the decision.

3.18 The timing of the decision whether to instruct another advocate will always be a matter for the CPS and will be influenced by the nature of the case as well as the information provided by the advocate or the advocate's clerk.

August 1996

APPROVED LIST OF DPA BODIES

Registrar
The Architects Registration Council of the UK
73 Hallam Street
London
W1N 6EE

APPROVED
November 1989

Chief Executive
The Architects and Surveyors Institute
St Mary House
15 St Mary Street
Chippenham
Wiltshire
SN15 3WD

APPROVED
September 1995

Executive Secretary
The Association of Authorised Public Accountants
10 Cornfield Road
Eastbourne
East Sussex
BN21 4QE

APPROVED
September 1989

Joint Secretary
The Association of Average Adjusters
H.Q.S. 'Wellington'
Temple Stairs
Victoria Embankment
London
WC2R 2PN

APPROVED
June 1989

General Secretary
Association of Consultant Architects
7 Park Street
Bristol
BS1 5NF

APPROVED
November 1989

Association of Taxation Technicians
12 Upper Belgrave Street
London
SW1X 8BB

APPROVED
September 1996

Banking Ombudsman
70 Gray's Inn Road
London
WC1X 8NB

APPROVED
March 1990

Building Society Ombudsman
Grosvenor Gardens House
35–37 Grosvenor Gardens
London SW1

APPROVED
March 1990

Secretary
The Chartered Association of Certified Accountants
29 Lincoln's Inn Fields
London
WC2A 3EE

APPROVED
April 1989

The Chartered Institute of Loss Adjusters   **APPROVED**
Mansfield House   **July 1990**
376 Strand
London
WC2R 0LR

Secretary
The Chartered Institute of Management Accountants **APPROVED**
63 Portland Place   **September 1989**
London
W1N 4AB

Secretary
The Chartered Insurance Institute   **APPROVED**
20 Aldermanbury   **May 1990**
London
EC2V 7HY

Commissioner for Local Administration   **APPROVED**
21 Queen Annes Gate   **March 1990**
London SW1

Commissioner for Local Administration   **APPROVED**
Derwen House   **March 1990**
Bridge End
Mid Glamorgan

Health Service Commissioner   **APPROVED**
Church House   **March 1990**
Great Smith Street
London
SW1P 3BW

Secretary
The Faculty of Actuaries   **APPROVED**
23 St Andrews Square   **November 1989**
Edinburgh
EH2 1AQ

Chief Executive
The Incorporated Society of Valuers & Auctioneers **APPROVED**
3 Cadogan Gate   **July 1989**
London
SW1X 0AS

President
Insolvency Practitioners Association   **APPROVED**
Buchlet Phillips & Co   **September 1989**
43/44 Albermarie Street
Mayfair
London
W1N 4AB

Secretary General
Institute of Actuaries
Staple Inn Hall
High Holborn
London
WC1V 7QJ

**APPROVED
November 1989**

Secretary, Management Committee
Institute of Chartered Accountants
PO Box 433
Chartered Accountants Hall
London
EC2P 2BY

**APPROVED
April 1989**

Director
The Institute of Chartered Accountants in Ireland
Chartered Accountants House
87/89 Pembroke Road
Dublin 4
Ireland

**APPROVED
July 1989**

Secretary
Institute of Chartered Accountants in Scotland
27 Queen Street
Edinburgh
EH2 1LA

**APPROVED
July 1989**

Under Secretary
The Institute of Chartered Secretaries and Administrators
19 Park Crescent
London
W1N 4AH

**APPROVED
July 1989**

Secretary
The Chartered Institute of Taxation
12 Upper Belgrave Street
London
SW1X 8BB

**APPROVED
July 1989**

Administration Manager
The Institution of Chemical Engineers
George E Davis Building
165–171 Railway Terrace
Rugby
CV21 3HQ

**APPROVED
July 1989**

Executive Director
The Institution of Civil Engineering Surveyors
26 Market Street
Altrincham
Cheshire
WA14 1PF

**APPROVED
November 1989**

The Institute of Civil Engineers
Great George Street
Westminster
London SW1P 3AA

APPROVED
November 1989

Director, Technical Affairs
The Institute of Electrical Engineers
Savoy Place
London
WC2R 0BL

APPROVED
November 1991

Chief Executive
The Institute of Financial Accountants
Burford House
44 London Road
Sevenoaks
Kent

APPROVED
January 1995

Secretary
Institution of Mechanical Engineers
1 Birdcage Walk
London
SW1H 9JJ

APPROVED
July 1989

Assistant Director, Administration & Finance
The Institution of Structural Engineers
11 Upper Belgrave Street
London
SW1X 8BH

APPROVED
July 1991

Insurance Ombudsman Bureau
City Gate One
135 Park Street
London
SE1

APPROVED
July 1990

Parliamentary Commissioner for Administration
Church House
Great Smith Street
London
SW1P 3BW

APPROVED
March 1990

Senior Legal Officer
The Personal Investment Authority
Ombudsman Bureau Ltd
Hertsmere House
Hertsmere Road
London
E14 4AB

APPROVED
January 1998

Director General
The Royal Institute of British Architects
66 Portland Place
London
W1N 4AD

APPROVED
September 1989

President
The Royal Institution of Chartered Surveyors   **APPROVED**
12 Great George Street   **April 1989**
Parliament Square
London
SW1P 3AD

Director, Public Affairs
The Royal Town Planning Institute   **APPROVED**
26 Portland Place   **April 1989**
London
W1N 4BE

JOINT TRIBUNAL STANDING ORDERS

Standard Time Scale Proposed

(1)   The Applicant shall within 28 days of submitting written agreement to be bound by the decision of the Joint Tribunal send:

   (a)   direct to the OSS;

      i)   two further copies of the agreement,

      ii)   two copies of the Statement of Case with any supporting documents which must include relevant fee notes and correspondence (one set for the OSS and one for the Joint Tribunal Law Society member) and,

   (b)   i)   direct to the Bar Council two further copies of the Statement of Case and supporting documents; (one set for the Bar Council and one for the Joint Tribunal Bar Council member), and,

   (c)   direct to the Respondent;

      i)   a Statement of Case, together with all documents relied upon, which must include relevant fee notes and correspondence.

(2)   The Respondent shall, within 28 days of receipt of the Applicant s Statement of Case, supply:

   a)   two copies of their Statement of Response direct to the OSS (as in (1) above) and,

   b)   two copies to the Bar Council (as in (1) above), and,

   c)   supply to the Applicant a Statement of Response, together with all documents relied upon.

(3)   All documents which are submitted shall be indexed and paginated consecutively in the top right hand corner.

(4)   If either party relies upon the evidence of another person a statement of such evidence shall be signed and dated by the witness.

(5)   The Joint Tribunal shall be appointed within 14 days of the receipt by the OSS and the Bar Council of the Statement of Case. The members of the Joint Tribunal shall be supplied with copies of the Statements, by the OSS and the Bar Council respectively. Upon receipt of the Statements by the Joint Tribunal, it shall notify the parties of a date for the determination of the dispute which is not later than 56 days after the date provided above for the supply of the Statement of Response.

(6)   If, in exceptional circumstances, the Applicant wishes to submit a Statement of Reply, or either party wishes to submit additional material to the Joint Tribunal, they shall request permission to do so within 14 days of the receipt by the Applicant of the Statement of Response. Such requests shall be accompanied by a draft Statement of Reply and/or any material sought to be relied upon. The Tribunal shall rule upon the admissibility of such documents and its ruling shall be final.

(7)   Any applications by either party in respect of the conduct of the dispute shall be included within the Statement of Case/Response. The Joint Tribunal shall determine the dispute on the basis of the written submissions of the parties unless in the opinion of the Joint Tribunal an oral hearing is appropriate.

(8)   If an oral hearing has been requested the Joint Tribunal shall, when fixing the date for the determination of the dispute, inform the parties, the OSS and the Bar Council, whether or not a hearing is considered to be appropriate, of the date, time and venue for the hearing.

(9)   The Joint Tribunal shall rule upon any application by either party in respect of the conduct of the dispute, and shall notify the parties, the OSS and the Bar Council, of any consequential directions when giving notice of the date for the determination of the dispute.

(10)   Payment of any sum found to be due shall be made within 14 days of the date of notification of any determination by the Joint Tribunal.

(11)   Non compliance with these directions shall entitle the Joint Tribunal to dismiss any case or response and to determine the dispute as the Tribunal thinks fit.

(12)   The Joint Tribunal shall have power in its absolute discretion to award interest upon unpaid fees for such period and at such rate as it deems appropriate in the circumstances.

(13)   The Joint Tribunal shall have power to direct payment of undisputed sums forthwith and payment shall be made within 14 days of any interim determination.

(14)   In the event of non-payment within the due time of any determination or interim determination the Joint Tribunal shall refer the matter as professional misconduct to the Office for the Supervision of Solicitors or to The General Council of the Bar.

Implemented 1 May 1998

NON-PRACTISING BARRISTERS

**WAIVER APPROVED
BY THE PROFESSIONAL STANDARDS COMMITTEE
ON 22 APRIL 1998**

(Revised at the PSC's June 1998 meeting)

Pursuant to Rule 212 of the Code of Conduct, the Professional Standards Committee grants the following exemptions in respect of non-practising barristers offering legal services to the public or any section of the public:

(1)   From the prohibitions on advocacy under (a):

(a)   barristers working in firms of solicitors and exercising rights of audience pursuant to section 27(2)(b) – (e) or section 27(7) of the Courts and Legal Services Act 1990;

(b)   barristers working in firms of Chartered or Certified Accountants appearing before statutory tax tribunals;

(c)   barristers working in firms of

     (i)   patent or trade mark agents and exercising rights of audience pursuant to section 102A of the Patents Act 1977 or section 292 of the Copyright, Designs and Patents Act 1988 or in relation to intellectual property work ordinarily carried out by patent or trade mark agents;

     (ii) European Patent Attorneys and exercising rights of audience before the European Patent Office pursuant to Article 134 of the European Patent Convention;

(d)   barristers qualified as Chartered Surveyors in relation to work ordinarily conducted by Chartered Surveyors;

(e)   barristers qualified as Chartered Quantity Surveyors in relation to work ordinarily conducted by Chartered Quantity Surveyors;

(f)   barristers qualified as Chartered Engineers in relation to work ordinarily conducted by Chartered Engineers;

(g)   barristers working outside England and Wales, exercising rights of audience not derived from or dependant on their currently being members of the English Bar.

(2)   From the insurance requirements under (b)(i) and (b)(ii)(b) and from the notification requirements under (b)(ii)(a):

(a)   barristers working in firms of solicitors or Chartered or Certified Accountants, who are insured in respect of their legal work in accordance with the requirements of the Law Society or the relevant Accountant's professional body respectively;

(b)   barristers working in firms of actuaries who are insured in respect of their legal work in accordance with the requirements of the Institute or Faculty of Actuaries;

(c)   barristers working in firms of patent agents or trade mark agents who are insured in respect of their legal work in accordance with the requirements of the Chartered Institute of Patent Agents or the Institute of Trade Mark Agents.

(d)   barristers working as Chartered Surveyors who are insured in respect of their legal work in accordance with the requirements of the Royal Institution of Chartered Surveyors;

(e)   barristers working as Civil Engineers who are insured in respect of their legal work in accordance with the recommendations of the Institute of Civil Engineers;

(f)   barristers offering legal services to Government Departments and Agencies;

(g)   barristers acting pro bono where the client is not being charged directly or indirectly for the barrister's services, conditional upon the lay client being informed in advance and in writing that the barrister is not required by the Code of Conduct to be insured;

(h)   barristers working outside England and Wales in so far as they provide legal services as members of another Bar[1];

(i)   barristers working as Architects who are insured in respect of their legal work in accordance with the recommendations of the Code of Professional Conduct and Practice of the Architects Registration Board.

(3)   From the prohibition on handling client money:

(a)   barristers working in firms of solicitors, including multi-disciplinary practices registered with the Law Society or other professions listed in 1(b) – (f) above, entitled to hold or handle client money, securities, or other assets by the rules of that professional body and acting in accordance with those rules;

(b)   barristers working in institutions authorised by Statute or Statutory Regulation to handle client money and acting in accordance with that Statute or Statutory Regulation;

(c)   barristers who work outside England and Wales and who are subject to professional or statutory rules in the jurisdiction where they work in relation to the handling

---

[1] N.B. this only applies to *non*-practising barristers. Moreover the International Practice Rules require barristers to comply with local requirements.

of client money, securities or other assets and acting in accordance with those rules[2].

(4)   From the prohibition in (e):

barristers who are members of foreign Bars and entitled in that capacity to describe themselves as barristers or Queen's Counsel. Nevertheless, those barristers who wish, in addition, to describe themselves as members of the English Bar must make it clear that they are non-practising members of the English Bar and the capacity in which they are acting.

---

[2] Again, this only applies to *non*-practising barristers. Moreover the International Practice Rules require barristers to comply with local requirements.

THE
CONSOLIDATED REGULATIONS
OF THE
HONOURABLE SOCIETIES
OF
LINCOLN'S INN
INNER TEMPLE
MIDDLE TEMPLE
and
GRAY'S INN

(1st October 1998 to 30th September 1999)

(extracts)

PART V — PUPILLAGE AND ENTRY INTO PRACTICE

42   **Obligation to Undertake Pupillage**

42.1   A person who intends to practise as a barrister in accordance with paragraphs 301 or 403.2 of the Code of Conduct is required:

(i)   to read as a pupil for an aggregate period of not less than 12 months in the chambers of one or more Pupil Masters who are barristers in independent practice except as provided for in Regulation 47 ('alternative service'); and

(ii)   to complete such further training after completion of the Vocational Stage as may be required from time to time by the Bar Council.

42.2   Pupillage shall be divided into two parts:

(i)   the non-practising six months, which, save with the approval in writing of the designated body, shall be undertaken in a continuous period of 6 months in chambers in England and Wales; and

(ii)   the practising six months

(1)   which, save with the approval in writing of the designated body, shall be undertaken in a continuous period of six months or with only such intervals (each not exceeding one month) as to ensure that the practising six months is completed within an overall period of nine months;

(2)   which, save with the approval in writing of the designated body, shall commence not later than 12 months after the completion of the non-practising six months;

(3)   all of which in the case of those undertaking pupillage both in independent and employed practice shall be undertaken after Call; and

(4)   which may be undertaken in any country of the EU.

42.3   The approval of the designated body under Regulation 42.2(ii)(3) may be subject to such conditions, including conditions as to additional training, as the designated body deems appropriate having regard to the particular circumstances of the person concerned.

43   Registration of Pupils

43.1   On arranging any period of pupillage, or any period of service under Regulation 47 ('alternative service'), a pupil shall notify the Masters of the Bench and the Bar Council of the name of the Pupil Master, or of the person with whom he is to serve alternative service ('alternative Pupil Master'), and of the commencement date and proposed duration of the pupillage or alternative service.

43.2   It is the duty of each pupil to notify the Masters of the Bench and the Bar Council of all material changes in the arrangements for pupillage or alternative service of such pupil.

44   Commencement of Pupillage

Subject to the transitional arrangements set out in Part A, B or C as appropriate of Schedule 14, and subject to Regulation 46, a person who is required by Regulation 42 to read as a pupil may not commence pupillage unless and until either:

(i)   he has attended a Vocational Course and has been certified as having completed such Course; or

(ii)   in the case of a qualified legal practitioner admitted under Part IV (or in the case of a legal academic admitted under Regulation 55A), he has been exempted from the Aptitude Test, or has sat and has been certified as having completed the Aptitude Test or such section or sections or part or parts of any sections of the Aptitude Test as he is required to take.

45   The Vocational Stage – Stale Qualifications

45.1   A person may not commence pupillage after the expiration of a period of five years from the date when that person was certified as having completed a Vocational Course or a Vocational Conversion Course or the Aptitude Test or any section or sections or part or parts of any sections of the Aptitude Test as he was required to take, or such other period as the Bar Council may from time to time specify.

45.2   Such period may be extended by the Bar Council in an individual case for such period and on such terms as it thinks fit including the requirements as to further courses of study or training to be undertaken by the person seeking the extension.

45.3   This regulation shall not apply to persons who registered for the Vocational Course or Vocational Conversion Course or were required to take the Aptitude Test or any section or sections or part or parts thereof before 1st September 1998.
Note: This regulation is subject to the approval of the Lord Chancellor under Schedule 4 of the Courts and Legal Services Act 1990.

46   Exceptions and Dispensations from Pupillage

46.1   A qualified legal practitioner may be exempted wholly or in part from the obligations in Regulations 42 and 44.

46.2   Subject to the transitional arrangements set out in Parts A, B and C (as appropriate) of Schedule 14, if a person who is required to read as a pupil under Regulation 42 satisfies the designated body:

(i)   that he intends and has reasonable grounds to expect to practise as a member of the Bar of England and Wales or of one of the Channel Islands either in any of these countries or, being a national of a Member State of the EU, in the territory of any member state of the EU, and at the date of application for admission has such qualification or permissions as are required by law to enable him to do so; and

(ii)   either

(a)   that at the time when he entered for the Bar Examination, he did not have the intention specified in Regulation 18(b), and that his subsequent change of intention was *bona fide*; or

(b)   that other exceptional circumstances exist by reason of which his failure to satisfy the condition specified in Regulation 44 ought to be excused;

then the designated body may either

(1)   grant him exemption from all or any of such conditions; or

(2)   grant him permission to commence pupillage by undertaking such part of the Vocational Conversion Course and reaching such standards in the formal assessments as the Bar Council may require.

47   Alternative Service in lieu of Part of Pupillage

47.1   Subject to the prior approval of the designated body and as mentioned in Regulation 47.3 below, and in addition to Regulation 42.3(ii), alternative service with an alternative Pupil Master may take the place of part of pupillage as follows:

(i)   3 months pupillage may be satisfied by an equivalent period of pupillage spent with a solicitor who is either employed or who is in private practice in England and Wales or in another member country of the EU.

(ii)   3 months pupillage may be satisfied by an equivalent period of pupillage spent with a lawyer qualified and in private practice in one of the

Member States of the EU (other than England and Wales);

(iii)   6 months pupillage may be satisfied by undertaking a 'stage' of 5 months duration or more, in the legal departments of the European Commission in Brussels or Luxembourg, or a 'placement' at the European Commission in London;

(iv)   up to 6 weeks pupillage may be satisfied by an equivalent period as a marshal with a Judge of the High Court of Justice or with a Circuit Judge;

(v)   up to 6 months pupillage may be satisfied by an equivalent period of pupillage with a Pupil Master who is an employed barrister;

(vi)   up to four weeks pupillage may be satisfied by a pupil, with the permission of his Pupil Master, working for the equivalent period with a solicitor or other professional person whose work is relevant to his Pupil Master's practice.

47.2   Subject to Regulation 42.2, alternative modes of satisfying pupillage may be served at any time.

47.3   Alternative modes of satisfying pupillage may be aggregated in any combination, but in no case shall count towards the non-practising 6 months.

47.4   Except for Regulation 47.1 (iv) and (v) above (service as a marshal or with a relevant professional person for the purposes of which the actual period served will count), no alternative service of less than the periods respectively prescribed shall count, proportionately or at all, towards pupillage.

48   **Registration of Pupil Masters**

48.1   'Pupil Master' means a practising barrister who is for the time being on the register of approved pupil masters kept by the Bar Council.

48.2   Each Inn shall, from time to time, provide the Bar Council with a list of approved Pupil Masters.

48.3   In order to be eligible for entry on the register of approved Pupil Masters kept by the Bar Council, an eligible barrister must satisfy the conditions set out in Regulation 49 and be approved as a Pupil Master by his Inn (or in accordance with the requirements in force prior to 1st January 1988).

49   **Eligibility to Seek Approval as a Pupil Master**

49.1   A barrister is eligible to seek approval as a Pupil Master if, for not less than 6 years in a period of 8 years immediately preceding the date of his application:

(i)   as a barrister in independent practice he has practised in England and Wales from a date calculated not earlier than the date on which he commenced independent practice as a tenant in chambers; or

(ii)   as an employed barrister in England and Wales he has been engaged in that capacity from a date calculated as not earlier than the day after the commencement of his employment, or the day after the conclusion of 12 months' pupillage if his employment commenced earlier; and

(iii)   in either case, he has practised or been so engaged continuously during the 2 years immediately preceding the date of the application.

49.2   For the purpose of this Regulation, a person shall be deemed to practise in England and Wales if he practises as a barrister in independent or employed practice within any state in the EU.

49.3   The Masters of the Bench may approve a person as a Pupil Master even though that person who does not satisfy the conditions set out in 49.1 and 49.2 above provided they are satisfied that he has the necessary experience to be so approved.

49.4   In the case of a barrister in independent practice, only those practising in chambers of which they are not the sole member are eligible to seek approval as Pupil Masters.

49.5   No Queen's Counsel other than an employed barrister may be a Pupil Master.

49.6   A Pupil Master may not be responsible for more than one pupil at a time save with the approval in writing of the designated body.

49.7   The Bar Council, in consultation with the Inns' Council, shall prescribe what training, if any, shall be undertaken by persons either before or after such persons have been entered on the register of approved Pupil Masters.

49.8   A Pupil Master who fails to undertake the training prescribed by Regulation 49.7 above, within the time prescribed by the Masters of the Bench, shall have his name removed from the Register of approved Pupil Masters held by the Bar Council. An application for Pupil Master status will only be approved if the applicant undertakes the training prescribed by Regulation 49.7 above within the prescribed time.

49.9   An appeal against removal under 49.8 shall lie to the designated body under Regulation 52.

50   **Application for Approval and Registration as Pupil Master**

50.1   The procedure as regards applications by barristers in independent practice for approval and registration as a Pupil Master is as follows:

(i)   An eligible barrister (not being an employed barrister) who wishes to be a Pupil Master must submit to the Masters of the Bench an application in the form specified in Schedule 8, Part 1;

(ii)   The application must be supported by

(a)   the applicant's Head of Chambers (being a Queen's Counsel, a Master of the Bench, a Recorder or Treasury Counsel) or, if for any reason such support is unavailable, by a Master of the Bench of any Inn;

(b)   an independent person who is a Master of the Bench of any Inn, a Queen's Counsel, a Recorder, a Judge or Treasury Counsel. If the applicant's Head of Chambers is not a Master of the Bench of one of the Inns, a Queen's Counsel, a Recorder, or Treasury Counsel the applicant should arrange for the provision of references from his Head of Chambers and from two independent persons falling within one of the aforementioned categories. If the applicant himself is a Head of Chambers, he should arrange for the provision of references from two such independent persons.

(iii)   If the Masters of the Bench approve the application, they shall notify the applicant and the Bar Council, which shall cause the applicant to be entered on the register of approved Pupil Masters accordingly;

(iv)   Any approval may be provisional and subject to such terms as the Masters of the Bench may at any time in their discretion impose to ensure that the Pupil Master is qualified and able to discharge his responsibilities;

(v)   If the Masters of the Bench refuse the application they shall notify the applicant accordingly;

(vi)   An appeal shall lie from such a refusal to the designated body in accordance with Regulation 52.

50.2   The procedure as regards applications by employed barristers for approval and registration as a Pupil Master is as follows:

(i)   An eligible barrister who wishes to be an employed Pupil Master must submit to the Masters of the Bench an application in the form specified in Schedule 8, Part 2;

(ii)   The application must be supported by the applicant's immediate superior, or if for any reason such support is unavailable, by a Master of the Bench of any Inn;

(iii)   If the Masters of the Bench approve the application, they shall notify the applicant, and shall cause the applicant to be entered on the register of approved Pupil Masters accordingly;

(iv)   Any approval may be provisional and subject to such terms as the Masters of the Bench may at any time in their discretion impose to ensure that the Pupil Master is qualified and able to discharge his responsibilities;

(v)   If the Masters of the Bench refuses the application the applicant should be notified accordingly;

(vi)   An appeal shall lie from such a refusal to the designated body in accordance with Regulation 52.

51   Removal of Pupil Masters from the Register

51.1   Any complaint or other matter which appears to affect the fitness of a barrister to continue as a Pupil Master or the desirability of his continued registration as such, should be referred to the Masters of the Bench who shall investigate the same, and if thought necessary or desirable, invite the barrister concerned to comment thereon in writing or in person.

51.2   The Masters of the Bench may pending the outcome of such enquiries resolve that a Pupil Master's registration be suspended, and shall notify the barrister accordingly.

51.3   Having considered any such case, the Masters of the Bench may:

(i)   dismiss the complaint (if any);

(ii)   take no action;

(iii) refer the case to the Professional Conduct Committee of the Bar Council;

(iv)   if in the opinion of the Masters of the Bench the case is such as to require informal treatment, draw it to the barrister's attention in writing and, if thought necessary, direct him to attend upon the Treasurer or some other person nominated by the Treasurer;

(v)   in any case where the conduct disclosed is such as, in the opinion of the Masters of the Bench, to render the barrister unfit to continue as a Pupil Master, resolve that the barrister be removed from the register or suspended for such period as they may determine.

51.4   The Masters of the Bench may, in any case where the Pupil Master has not taken a pupil for a period of five years or more, resolve to remove the barrister's name from the register of approved Pupil Masters.

51.5   Any approved Pupil Master becoming a sole practitioner or being appointed as Queen's Counsel shall automatically have their name removed from the register.

51.6   Where a resolution is passed for the removal or suspension of a barrister from the register, the Masters of the Bench shall notify the barrister accordingly.

51.7   An appeal shall lie from any resolution for the removal or suspension from the register under Regulation 51 to the designated body in accordance with Regulation 52.

52   **Appeal to the Designated Body**

(a)   An appeal under Regulations 49.6, 50.1, 50.2, 51.6 or 53.6 shall be by way of a rehearing.

(b)   Notice of appeal shall be given in writing to the Secretary of the designated body.

(c)   Notice of appeal must be served on the said Secretary within 28 days from the date on which notification of the decision or the resolution of the Inn was given to the appellant, provided always that the designated body may, on such terms as it thinks fit, extend the period for appeal.

(d)   For the purposes of determining an appeal under this Regulation the quorum shall be 3 members of the designated body.

(e)   The appellant shall be entitled to appear in person or be represented before the designated body and (in addition or as an alternative) to submit a written statement of his case.

(f)   Having considered the appeal the designated body may:

(i)   dismiss it;

(ii)   allow it unconditionally or subject to conditions.

53   Certification for Entry into Practice

53.1   On completion of the non-practising 6 months of pupillage, a pupil shall obtain from his Pupil Master a certificate for submission both to the Masters of the Bench and to the Bar Council certifying that he has satisfactorily completed this period. Provided that the pupil has completed such further training as is referred to in Regulation 42.1(11), on receipt of such certificate, the Bar Council shall forthwith register the same and, if the pupil has been called to the Bar, issue the pupil with a Provisional Practising Certificate.

53.2   On completion of the practising 6 months of pupillage, a pupil shall obtain from his Pupil Master and from any relevant alternative Pupil Master a certificate for submission both to the Masters of the Bench and to the Bar Council certifying that he has satisfactorily completed this period. Provided that the pupil has completed such further training as is referred to in Regulation 42.1(ii), on receipt of such certificate, the Bar Council shall forthwith register the same and issue the pupil with a Full Practising Certificate.

53.3   If a pupil is unable to obtain a relevant certificate from his Pupil Master or from any relevant alternative Pupil Master, the Masters of the Bench and the Bar Council may accept a certificate from the Pupil Master's Head of Chambers, or from the member of those chambers designated by the Head of Chambers as the person in charge of pupillage, or such other person as is acceptable to the Masters of the Bench and the Bar Council, that the pupil has satisfactorily completed the periods specified in Regulation 42.2, provided that the certificate contains an explanation of the reason why the Pupil Master or any relevant alternative Pupil Master has not provided such a certificate which is satisfactory to the Masters of the Bench and the Bar Council.

53.4   If a Pupil Master or any other person mentioned in Regulations 53.1, 53.2 or 53.3 refuses to sign a relevant certificate for any reason, the pupil may ask the Masters of the Bench, on the grounds that the signature has been wrongfully withheld, to grant a certificate themselves and to request the Bar Council

(i)   to register the same; and

(ii)   to issue the pupil with a Provisional Practising Certificate or a Full Practising Certificate as the case may be.

53.5   On receipt of a certificate under Regulation 53.3 above, or on the grant of a certificate by the Masters of the Bench under Regulation 53.4 above, the Masters of the Bench will request the Bar Council to issue the pupil forthwith with a Provisional Practising Certificate or a Full Practising Certificate as the case may be.

53.6   A pupil may appeal to the designated body against any refusal by the Masters of the Bench to take any of the steps set out in Regulations 53.3, 53.4 or 53.5.

54   **Duties of a Pupil**

54.1   During each pupillage or period of alternative service it is the duty of the pupil to be conscientious in receiving the instruction given, to apply himself full time thereto, to preserve the confidentiality of every client's affairs, and to comply with such other rules or guidelines relating to pupillage as may be approved from time to time by the Bar Council in consultation with the Inns' Council (including the Code of Conduct).

54.2   Where on the conclusion of a period of pupillage or a period of alternative service a pupil does not intend to serve another pupillage or period of alternative service he shall notify the Records Office of the Bar Council and the Under Treasurer in writing:

(i)   of any tenancy he has secured, giving details of the chambers; or

(ii)   if he has not secured a tenancy, whether he is seeking a tenancy in England and Wales, whether he intends to practise abroad, or whether he is seeking employment in England or Wales, and in each case shall give all relevant details.

54A   **Duties of a Pupil Master**

The duties of a Pupil Master are set out in Part II of Annex A to the Code of Conduct, or such other rules or guidelines relating to pupillage as may be approved from time to time by the Bar Council in consultation with the Inns Council.

54B   **Acceptance of Instructions**

A person (not being a barrister who was Called before June 1965 and who was in independent practice at 1st October 1988) may not as a barrister in independent practice accept instructions in England or Wales or conduct any case or any part of a case unless and until:

(i)   he has completed 6 months non-practising pupillage prior to 1st October 1988; or

(ii)   he has completed the non-practising 6 months' pupillage in accordance with these Regulations and obtained a Provisional Practising Certificate under Regulation 53, and is then undertaking the practising six months pupillage specified in Regulation 42.2(ii) which has been duly registered under Regulation 43 prior to the receipt of the Full Practising Certificate specified in Regulation 53.2; and

(iii)   in the case of a barrister called after March 1979 who has been required by the Masters of the Bench to take a test in oral English, he has obtained a certificate of competence after testing by an oral English examination board;

Save that:

(1) a pupil may accept a noting brief during the non-practising six months' pupillage in a case in which is Pupil Master is instructed and would normally be expected to be present in court;

(2) a pupil commencing the practising six months' pupillage may accept instructions or conduct any part of a case if he is qualified to hold a Provisional Practising Certificate under Regulation 53.1 and is awaiting its receipt from the Bar Council.

55   Status during Pupillage

55.1   Every person who commences a pupillage shall be deemed to remain in pupillage until the satisfactory completion of 12 months pupillage in accordance with these Regulations and (in relation to any part of pupillage which ends after 1st October 1988) the consequential grant of a Full Practising Certificate under Regulation 53.

55.2   So long as he is or is deemed to remain in pupillage no barrister may become or hold himself out as a member of chambers or permit his name to appear anywhere as such a member.

APPENDIX TWO

THE TAX POSITION OF BARRISTERS

INTRODUCTION

A barrister carries on a profession, and therefore is taxed under Schedule D Case II. He or she is also potentially liable to register for VAT. The taxes are outlined in **Chapter 21** of the *Remedies Manual*.

As a barrister is self-employed, he or she will have a personal responsibility for keeping full records of income and expenses from which annual accounts can be drawn up — accounts can only be drawn up accurately from clear records! Since April 1996 there is a specific legal duty to keep proper records, and to retain them for five years after the last date for filing the tax return for the year in question. This duty includes setting up and running an adequate system, and retaining back-up records such as bank statements and invoices.

It is important to be generally aware of the tax position of the barrister well before starting practice, for example, because sums you spend before starting practice may be deductible in appropriate circumstances.

Other members of the Bar or your clerk may be of great assistance in giving advice on tax liability, keeping records and drawing up accounts. Many chambers have systems to assist you in doing this.

INCOME

All income from briefs, and from other work performed by an individual carrying on a profession as a barrister, will be taxable under Sch. D Case II. All such sums are currently taxable on a cash basis. The position of paid pupillage was not clear, but an informal agreement was reached between the Inland Revenue and the Bar Council in 1992 and a copy of the wording of this agreement is attached at the end of this chapter.

Barristers have traditionally been taxed on the cash basis because they could not sue for their fees, and therefore it was appropriate to tax money only when it was actually received. However, the cash basis for barristers is an anomaly because most income under Sch. D is taxed on an earnings basis, that is it is taxed when earned even if it is not actually received until some time later. The Finance Act 1998 provides for barristers to move from the cash to the earnings basis. The Bar Council made representations regarding the difficulties that might be caused by the change, especially due to the burden of having to pay tax on fees earned but not yet paid and some of the details were modified. The first tax year that will be affected for existing practitioners is 1999–2000, and the change from the cash to the earnings basis will be phased over ten years. Newly-qualified barristers will be able to remain on the cash basis for the first seven years of practice as they might otherwise suffer unduly at a time when many suffer some financial difficulty. On 10 March 1999 the Bar Council issued guidance (not reproduced here) for the computation of profits for tax purposes. This and related guidance is subject to regular revision.

The taxable income of a barrister can include sums for legal writing or teaching which can be seen as ancillary to practice. However, this does not mean that all income from such sources will necessarily be taxable under Sch. D Case II and will go into the same accounts. If teaching or writing is carried out under a contract on a regular basis, especially if there are detailed terms as to when and where work is done, then it is possible that income from it will be taxable under Sch. E. This means that it will be subject to PAYE tax, and should not be entered on Bar accounts but separately entered on a tax return. On this point see *Sidey* v *Phillips* [1987] STC 87, where a qualified barrister gave up practice to lecture, and it was held that he was clearly taxable under Sch. E. On the relevant test see also *Hall* v *Lorimer* [1994] 1 All ER 250. Taxation under Sch. E is not so favourable because of PAYE and because rules for deductions are less favourable, but it may not be possible to avoid this. It seems that a barrister is not taxable on notional receipts and does not have to value work in progress.

Any prizes or awards from Inns and the like should be free of tax: ICTA 1988, s. 331.

If a barrister takes up employment rather than practising, income from the employment will be taxed under Sch. E. If a barrister is appointed a judge he or she will be taking up an office, and will therefore be taxable under Sch. E.

DEDUCTIONS

Deductions will be available under Sch. D, Case II. However, it is stressed that it is important to keep detailed records of money spent, and to keep receipts whenever possible. You cannot 'invent' accounts at the end of the year, but must base your figures firmly on proper records. If the expense is capital rather than income, a capital allowance may be available.

Note that sums spent in the seven years before commencing practice may be deductible, provided they are spent for the purpose of practising as a barrister, e.g., buying practitioner books. This will not include the cost of the Bar Vocational Course, or the cost of dining, as these expenses are incurred as a student rather than as a practitioner.

The following topics give some guidance on main areas where tax relief may be claimed:

(a) *Chambers expenses*. These will in general terms be deductible, so long as they are clearly spent for the purpose of being a barrister. Note that expenses can only be deducted when they are actually paid by the individual.

(b) *Clothes*. The difficulty of seeking to deduct the cost of clothing is illustrated in *Mallalieu* v *Drummond* [1983] 2 All ER 1095, HL, where it was held that a female barrister could not deduct the cost of buying black clothing and having it cleaned, because the personal need for clothing was fatal to a claim that it was purchased wholly and exclusively for work. There should be no difficulty in deducting the cost of a wig and gown, subject to the possible technical argument that such items might be a capital expense.

(c) *Travel*. The cost of travelling from home to work each day is clearly not tax deductible: *Newsom* v *Robertson* [1953] Ch 7. However, the costs of travelling to court, either from chambers or from home, are deductible. A list of the cost of tickets should be kept for this purpose. If the barrister runs a car and uses it to go to court, an appropriate part of the costs of running the car may be deducted. A barrister who is appointed a recorder cannot deduct the costs of travelling to the town at which he or she is a recorder from the income received as a recorder: *Ricketts* v *Colquhoun* [1926] AC 1, HL.

(d) *Books*. The cost of law reports and periodicals relevant to the barrister's practice is deductible. Books that are regularly bought and replaced as they become out of date are also deductible. Note, however, that buying a substantial body of books at one time, such as a complete set of *Halsbury*, will normally attract a capital allowance rather than be deductible: *Munby* v *Furlong* [1977] 2 All ER 953. Books purchased as a Bar student will only be deductible if they are practitioner works rather than being written primarily for students.

(e) *Other items.* It is increasingly common for barristers to buy word-processors and personal computers. If these are purchased by chambers, the cost should be deductible as part of chambers expenses in the normal way. If the barrister buys one personally to use for work, the cost may be deductible, but it is also possible, depending on the circumstances, that the Inland Revenue might argue that a capital allowance is more appropriate. The cost of disks and paper used for work should be deductible.

DRAWING UP ACCOUNTS

The first question is to decide the date when you commence practice as a barrister. This cannot be a date before you qualify, but must be a date before you start to do work and be paid for it. It is not necessarily best to put the date off as long as possible, as you can start to claim deductions, as well as being taxed on income. It may well be logical to start your first accounting period when you start your second six months of pupillage and you can be paid for work on briefs.

From the date you start practice, accounts of income and deductions must be drawn up on an annual basis and submitted to the Inland Revenue, whether you draw up the accounts personally or employ an accountant to do it. These accounts are currently drawn up on the cash basis, though this will change in the future as outlined above. It is not difficult to draw up accounts consisting of a simple summary of income and deductions, and many starting practice should be able to do this for themselves, though note that an accountant should be able to suggest deductions you may not have thought of personally. A sample format for a profit and loss account appears later in this chapter.

In the past barristers have been taxed on the preceding-year basis and have been subject to special opening-year rules for the first three years of practice. However, those going into practice now will be assessed on the simpler current-year basis, and will also be subject to the new self-assessment system. You will need to investigate the full details of this personally (the Inland Revenue provides without charge some useful pamphlets which describe the system).

In outline, for someone qualifying as a barrister in July 1999 the system might work as follows:

Sepember 1999	Start pupillage.
March 2000	Start second six and start taking cases.
March 2001	Draw up first set of annual accounts. This set of accounts will be drawn up in the income tax year 2000–2001, and will be charged to tax in that tax year.

An annual set of accounts for 2000–2001 would basically be taxed as follows:

January 2001	First payment on account of tax for 2000–2001 due. (Once you are established in practice this will be half of the tax you paid for the previous year.)
April 2001	New-style tax return sent out for the year 2000–2001.
July 2001	Second payment on account of tax for 2000–2001 due. (Again once you are established in practice this will be half of the tax you paid for the previous year.)

| September 2001 | Send in the completed tax return for 2000–2001 if you want the Inland Revenue to compute the tax due. |
| January 2002 | Deadline for sending in the tax return if you compute the tax due, and for paying any additional tax that is due for 2000–2001. |

Where income is below a certain level (not yet set) it will not be necessary for payments on account to be made. You should clarify the position when it becomes relevant for you.

Any income from sources other than being a barrister, e.g., from part-time employment, must be entered separately from your income as a barrister on the tax return. Your income from all sources will be taken into account in computing your tax liability, and personal allowances etc. will be deducted from your total income for the tax year. A simple example of this is provided at the end of this chapter.

It is quite possible that in your first year you will make a loss, for which you can claim tax relief against other income for the same year or against your income as a barrister in later years. Note that a barrister taking silk is continuing an existing profession, not starting a new one (*Seldon v Croom-Johnson* [1932] 1 KB 759).

VALUE ADDED TAX

In addition to income tax, a barrister is liable for VAT as the supplier of a service. However, there is the benefit that VAT paid for professional purposes can be reclaimed.

You do not need to register for VAT immediately on starting practice as it is not necessary to register until your annual income reaches £48,000 a year. However, it is possible to register voluntarily while your income is below this figure, and it is worth seeking advice from other practitioners and from your clerk about this. The possible advantages are that the VAT you expend for professional purposes can be reclaimed once you are registered, and the fact that you are registered may enhance your professional image. On the other hand once you are registered for VAT you not only have to pay it but also complete quite substantial quarterly returns.

TAXATION OF CHAMBERS AWARDS

Guidance for pupils

The following guidance has been issued by the Bar Council.

In the past, the Inland Revenue has accepted that all pupillage awards (whether from the Inns or from the pupils' Chambers) have been exempt from income tax in the pupils' hands as 'scholarships'.

The Inland Revenue still accepts this as far as awards from the Inns are concerned: nothing in this note affects such awards, which are still tax free. However, now that it has become effectively part of the Code of Conduct that a pupil should receive an award from the Chambers in which he or she does pupillage, the Inland Revenue has pointed out that the treatment of such awards as 'scholarships' can no longer be maintained, and that they fall to be taxed as income in the hands of the pupil.

Exactly *how* they should be taxed is, however, as a matter of strict law, debatable. A case can be made out for saying that they are receipts of the pupil's new profession (at least once the pupil has done six months' pupillage and is thus able to accept briefs) and are thus chargeable under Sch. D Case II; alternatively it can be argued that they are income chargeable under the general sweep-up provision, Sch. D Case VI. Rather than risk a test case going all the way to the House of Lords on this point, the Bar Council has agreed with the Inland Revenue that each pupil may *choose* in which of the two ways he or she should be taxed. The choice is as follows:

Either

    (i)   The pupillage award in respect of the pupil's first six months will continue to be tax free, but the award in respect of the second (or subsequent) six months will be included as an income receipt in the Sch. D Case II computation for the year of receipt;

    (ii)   Both the 'first six' and 'second six' awards will be taxable in the fiscal year of receipt under Sch. D Case VI. In computing Case VI income, for this purpose, expenses incurred by the pupil (for example, the cost of travelling) will be deductible in exactly the same way as they are under Sch. D Case II rules (the 'wholly and exclusively' test).

Notes

(1)   At first sight, Choice (i) may look more advantageous; but it must be remembered that under the Sch. D Case II commencement rules, any profit for the first period of account can form the basis of assessment for the first three years of assessment; so a pupil who gets off to a good start may effectively be paying tax three times on the 'second six' award under Choice (i). Under the Sch. D Case VI rules which apply to Choice (ii), income only gets taken into account once, in the year of assessment in which it is received.

(2)   The arrangements outlined above are to apply to all *genuine* pupillage awards irrespective of amount and exact date of payment. Payments made by Chambers in return for services provided by pupils are not covered by the arrangements but will be taxable in the normal and appropriate manner.

(3)   The above arrangements came into force on 6 April 1992, and apply to all pupils who commence their *first* pupillage on or after that date.

(The first period of account can now form the basis for assessment for only two years, not three.)

Basic profit and loss account for a barrister

Barrister-at-Law

Profit and Loss Account   Year ended 30th April 19

Fees
Expenses

    Chambers rent and expenses

    Use of own flat

    Travelling

    Books and periodicals

    Subscriptions

    Printing, stationery etc.

    Professional indemnity insurance

    Accountancy

    Bank charges and interest

    Sundries

Net profit

Accountants' Report

We have prepared the above profit and loss account from the books and records of Mr   and from information and explanations received and we certify that it agrees therewith.

& Co.,
Chartered Accountants

London WC1

October, 19

Barrister-at-Law

Schedules to Accounts   Year ended 30th April 19 ____

Fees

    Chambers receipts
    Private tutoring   ———

                                                ═══

Chambers rent and expenses

    Share of chambers rent and expenses
    Clerk's fees   ———
                              £
                              ═══

Travelling

    Public transport
    Car expenses
        Tax
        Garage repairs and maintenance
        AA subscription
        Insurance
        Petrol   miles @   m.p.g.
                   = gallons @   ———

        Private use   miles, i.e.   ———

        Parking   ———   ———
                                        £
                                      ═══

Subscriptions

    Bar Council
    N. London Bar Mess
    Society of Public Teachers of Law   ———
                              £
                              ═══

Printing, stationery etc.

Notebooks, pens, folders, computer supplies, photocopying   £
                                                       ═══

Sundries

    Laundry
    Gratuities
    Telephone
    Postage

    £

Tax computation and assessments

Profit for tax for year to 5 April 19   £

Capital allowances for year to 5 April 19

    Motor vehicle purchased

    W.D.A.   less private use   £

    Carried forward   £

Exercise

EXERCISE 4

Problem

You qualified as a barrister in 1997 and started pupillage in October 1997. You started your second six months of pupillage in April 1998 and started earning money from briefs then. It is now April 1999 and you need to draw up your first annual account. Your records show the following sources of income and expenses paid. Draw up a basic set of accounts showing taxable income and allowable deductions to show what your taxable income will be.

You have had income from the following sources:

(a) You have completed work on briefs marked at £5,000, but you have only been paid £3,000.

(b) You have received a chambers award of £6,000, payable in respect of your whole 12 months of pupillage.

(c) You were awarded a prize of £300 by your Inn.

(d) You have given a course of lectures on advocacy to a group of solicitors. The lectures were arranged by a large college and run over 10 weeks in the evenings on the college premises. The gross pay for these lectures is £1,000.

(e) You have given private tuition in A-level law at your own home. For this you have been paid £800.

(f) You have written a variety of articles on environmental law, a subject you specialise in, for a variety of legal journals. For these you have been paid £500.

(g) An aunt is giving you £100 a month until you have established your practice as a barrister.

You have spent the following sums in connection with your practice:

(a) £600 to pay chambers expenses.

(b) £220 as an annual subscription to the Weekly Law Reports. You have also bought a set of Law Reports for the last 15 years at a cost of £2,000.

(c) £300 to buy practitioner textbooks. You also spent £200 on a White Book and £150 on student books while you were studying to become a barrister.

(d) £1,600 on running your car. Your records show that about one-quarter of your annual mileage has been used in journeys to court, and another one-quarter to travel from home to Chambers each day. You have also spent £1,000 on a parking space in your Inn.

(e) £2,000 for a word processor which you keep at home but use for work connected with your practice and teaching.

(f) £200 on a gown and £250 on a second-hand wig, this money being spent while you were completing the Bar Vocational Course.

(g) £150 on a course to update your knowledge of environmental law, and £750 to attend a conference on European Community law held in Rome. Your chambers has also paid £200 for you to go on an advocacy course.

Once you have drawn up your accounts, on what basis will tax be calculated and payable? Should you register for VAT?

Solution

Taxable income

- The income from the work on briefs will be £3,000 as you are taxed on a cash basis.

- The chambers award is payable for the whole 12 months. It would appear that half of this would be regarded as paid for the first six months and would therefore be tax-free. The other half, £3,000, will be taxable. (That is, you elect for the award to be taxed under Schedule D Case II.)

- The prize is tax exempt as scholarship income (ICTA 1988, s. 331).

- In the circumstances described, the course of lectures is probably a separate employment taxable under Schedule E. If the lectures were not organised by a large college and delivered in such a structured way, the income from giving them might be seen as a natural extension of your professional activities, and would therefore go into your accounts as income as a barrister. (Note that the latter is preferable. Schedule E is subject to the PAYE system so tax would be deducted at source from the £1,000, and rules for deductions under Schedule E are much more limited than for Schedule D Case II.)

- The money from private tuition in law should probably go into your Bar accounts as coming from a natural extension of your profession as a barrister. (Note that if you were giving private tuition in something wholly unconnected with law you should draw up separate accounts for that activity.)

- The money from the legal writing should probably go into your Bar accounts as a natural extension of your profession. (Note that a contract to write regularly for a particular legal publication might amount to an employment taxable under Schedule E. Also note that if your writing were wholly unconnected with law you should draw up separate accounts for it.)

- The income from your relative appears to be a gift that does not come from a taxable source.

405

Deductions

● Chambers expenses are deductible when paid.

● Annual subscriptions to publications relevant to your work are deductible. However, buying a set of law reports would be a capital expenditure attracting a capital allowance (*Munby* v *Furlong* [1977] 2 All ER 953). Here there would be a first-year allowance of 40%, that is, of £800.

● The cost of purchasing practitioner textbooks is deductible, even if they are purchased before you start practice. The cost of student textbooks is not deductible. (Note also that the cost of studying to qualify as a barrister is not deductible.)

● The cost of travel from home to chambers is not deductible. The cost of travel to court is deductible, and here this would be calculated as 25% of the cost of running your car, that is £400. Although there are technical arguments over whether the cost of a parking space is deductible it seems that in practice such a cost is allowed.

● Almost certainly the cost of the word processor is a capital expense rather than an income expense. It would therefore attract a capital allowance, with a 40% first-year allowance of £800.

● The wig and gown are technically capital items attracting a capital allowance, but in practice are normally allowed as a deduction because the cost is relatively low. Again it does not matter that the items are purchased before you start practice so long as they are purchased with a view to practice.

● The cost of going on a course connected with your work is allowable. This is the case wherever the course is held, as long as the purpose of your travel is to attend the course rather than to have a holiday. The cost is only deductible if paid by you and not if it is paid by someone else.

PROFIT AND LOSS ACCOUNT

These answers would result in the following profit and loss account:

Income	*Deductions*
£	£
3,000	600
3,000	220
	200
800	400
500	400
	1,000
	450
	900
———	———
7,300	4,170

Net profit £3,130

Capital allowances

£800
£800

Taxable profit under Schedule D Case II	£1,530
Add Schedule E income of	£1,000
Total taxable profit	£2,530
Deduct personal allowance	£3,765

No tax payable (note also the PAYE paid on the lecturing income could in these circumstances be reclaimed).

APPENDIX THREE

ANSWERS TO PROBLEMS

The following are the answers to the problems set in the course of **Chapter 2** and **Chapter 5**. The problems in **Chapter 7** will be dealt with in tutorials with practitioners.

2.1 Relationship with the Court

2.1.1 DUTIES AND RESPONSIBILITIES OWED TO THE COURT

(1) Para. 610(c) makes it clear that you have no choice (in civil or criminal proceedings) but to bring the authority to the attention of the court, whether or not you believe that you can distinguish it by argument.

(2) It would be impolite and embarrassing to interrupt counsel for the claimant or stand up and address the court on the point. Inform counsel for the claimant of his error as soon as practicable, either by passing a note or speaking to him or her as he or she is leaving or just outside the court. It is then for him or her, knowing his or her duty, to return to the court, apologise and put the matter right.

(3) Accept his or her ruling with good grace, carry on as best you can and, if your client is convicted, appeal. Once the judge has ruled you must accept it. Do not argue with the tribunal, whatever your feelings; remember your duty to be courteous to the court.

2.1.3 FURTHER DUTIES

(1) Your views on the reason for the jump are largely irrelevant! The defence are entitled to see the note. You remain under a continuing duty to review questions of disclosure (s. 9 of the Criminal Procedure and Investigations Act 1996). If you, at any time before the accused is acquitted or convicted, form the opinion that there is material that might undermine the prosecution case, or be reasonably expected to assist the accused's defence, then it must be disclosed to the accused as soon as reasonably practicable (subject to the court's ruling to the contrary). In these circumstances your duty would probably be to get the witness back to court if requested. If the note were very much older then it would be better for defence counsel to apply to reopen cross-examination and satisfy the judge that the information was relevant (para. 11.2, Annexe F of Standards Applicable to Criminal Cases).

(2) The principle is the same as that involved where the judge makes an error in summing-up (para. 11.7, Annexe F of Standards Applicable to Criminal Cases). You are bound to draw the error to his or her attention. If he or she does not correct it, consider carefully whether you still want to adduce the evidence or otherwise take advantage of the ruling. What is the point of securing a conviction which will be overturned on appeal?

(3) It would be quite wrong for you not to tell your opponent. Even if, having taken instructions from the defendant, no objection is raised you should think very carefully before continuing to act. You might well feel inhibited in the conduct of your case. More importantly, you risk a possible complaint if the defendant is convicted.

2.1.4   SPECIFIC RESPONSIBILITIES OF DEFENCE COUNSEL

(1)   From a practical point of view, it is to be hoped that you kept a careful note of what your client told you. Ideally that should have been copied to your instructing solicitor, or the account at least communicated to him or her at the time. In that way, the account should be in the defendant's proof of evidence in any event. If it was not in the proof when the brief was delivered you should have spotted and rectified the omission prior to the trial. Prior to the Criminal Justice and Public Order Act 1994, guidance was given in the case of *R* v *Jaquith*; *R* v *Emode* [1989] Crim LR 508 and 563, CA. The basic rule is still the same: you should not give evidence unless it is absolutely necessary. It is necessary if your client will suffer if you do not and there is no other way. In this case your client may not be able to avoid the statutory inferences deriving from his silence **in interview**, but the suggestion of recent fabrication is obviously unfair. Your first move is to tell your opponent of the position (by interrupting him or her, if necessary), as discreetly as you can. If you have conducted yourself properly thus far, he or she will probably accept your word and withdraw the specific suggestion after you have agreed a formula about the date. Showing him or her your client's proof should be avoided if possible. If no agreement can be reached you must explain the situation to your clients (lay and professional) and withdraw (para. 3.4, Annexe F, General Standards). The trial will have to restart with fresh counsel so that you can give evidence. If you have a leader the trial can continue without you. If you are sure that withdrawal is the only proper course, do not be put off by any unsatisfactory compromise whether suggested by your opponent or the judge, merely to avoid a threat of wasted costs orders.

(2)   Obviously if you have simply not put your case properly, you should immediately make that clear in front of the jury. Your client must not be prejudiced by your mistake and cannot be prejudiced by its correction. However, in the circumstances described here much will depend on what the judge has said. Most judges would realize what has happened and simply smile to themselves or at prosecution counsel. If, however, the judge asks you: 'That is not how it was put, was it Mr or Ms Smith?' or 'You did not challenge the evidence of your client's presence, did you Mr or Ms Smith?', you can simply agree. If the judge asks, 'Mr or Ms Smith, what on earth is going on?', you can simply state that you have put the case according to your instructions. Do not engage in or rise to comments about whose 'fault' it is. If there is some explicit demand to know your client's instructions, you should politely but firmly refuse to answer such a question: 'Your Honour, should not ask me such a question . . .' or 'Your Honour, it is not appropriate for me to answer that question . . .' If the judge presses the matter then ask him or her to send the jury out. In the absence of the jury you should point out that you cannot under any circumstances reveal your client's instructions and waive privilege without your client's consent (para. 603). For the same reason you should not show your instructions to the judge.

(3)   Paragraph 603 applies here. With regard to the first part of the problem, you are under no obligation to volunteer the information, but **you must not** refer to the defendant's character in any way which suggests that he or she has no previous convictions. In other words, you must never mislead the court. This is bound severely to restrict what may be said in mitigation and may have the effect of preventing any reference at all to character. You may then be faced by a penetrating question from the court, in which case (subject to your client's instructions, as to which see below) you would use a formula such as 'There is nothing further I can add.'. If you have not got clear instructions from your client, then ask for time to take some. From a practical point of view, as soon as you realize the police antecedents are incomplete (which ought to be before you go into court) you should explain the position to your client and obtain from him or her clear instructions as to whether he or she wishes you to disclose straight away, or only if asked, or not at all. Tactics will play a part in any advice you give. If the court puts the case over for reports then the information is likely to come out anyway. A virtue can be made in mitigation of the fact that disclosure has been made.

The answer to the second part of the question is the same, although your advice will almost inevitably be to make disclosure. The original sentencing court is likely to find out about the breach and may take the view, if the defendant is called back to that court, that the instant court imposed too lenient a sentence because it was not in possession of all the pertinent information.

2.2 Relationship with the Lay Client

(1) Distinguish between your duty and his or her rights. You must put in cross-examination all those instructions which are relevant and material to the defence. You are the arbiter of that. He or she is entitled to give evidence himself or herself and call witnesses who can give material evidence. You can only advise him or her. If he or she rejects your advice you must still pursue his or her case with vigour. (See paras. 610(a) and 5.10 Annexe F, General Standards and 12.4, Annexe F, Standards Applicable to Criminal Cases.)

(2) The first step is to obtain instructions from the client as to what really happened. Write this down and invite him or her to sign your note. This is to guard against him or her subsequently alleging that you acted improperly or contrary to his or her instructions. Explain to the client the consequences, if any, of this new information upon the conduct or likely outcome of his or her case. It may be you are now unable to pursue part of his or her claim/defence. If this is so, inform your opponent and the court as soon as possible. You do not need to say why. Alternatively, it may be necessary to apply to amend your statement of case. Inform your opponent of your intention to do so and the extent of the amendment you will seek. Explain to the client the likely implications upon the question of costs. Ensure he or she understands the nature of the oath he or she will take in court and the necessity to give evidence in accordance with the truth of what he or she says actually happened. After the case, telephone your instructing solicitor and inform him or her of what took place. This may affect the future relationship between him or her and the lay client.

(3) Clients frequently react in emotional terms to losing in court, both in civil and criminal proceedings. They may threaten harm to others or even to themselves. Do not 'disappear' without speaking to your client after the case. Poor communication is often the cause of dissatisfied clients lodging a complaint with the Professional Conduct Committee. It is important to spend some time with the client after the hearing of the case, explaining precisely what has happened, why it has happened and whether there are any grounds of appeal. Warn the client of the consequences both to him and others (in this example, his children and the nature of his future relationship with them) of either making or carrying out such threats. Do not repeat to any third party what the client has said (see para. 603).

2.3 Relationship with the Professional Client

2.3.1 DUTIES AND RESPONSIBILITIES OWED TO THE PROFESSIONAL CLIENT

(1) You should not agree to supply such an opinion. It is a breach of the Code (para. 205) if you compromise your professional standards in order to please your client or permit your absolute independence to be compromised.

It is a clear abuse of your position, and it is tantamount to fraud, to supply an opinion for publication to others which is at odds with your true opinion. In various individual situations it may be proper for you to write an opinion for your client which will be shown to a third party, in which you deal with the matter differently from an opinion given to the client for the client's consumption only, e.g. by omission of reference to privileged matters or to considerations or qualifications which do not ultimately alter the effect or emphasis of your conclusions, but it is an area fraught with technical difficulty and one in which you will always be wise to discuss the points of concern with your colleagues in chambers.

Note: In any case where a solicitor asks for your advice in general terms, or on a particular basis without sufficient details for the giving of definitive advice governing an individual case, if you have any reason to suspect that the opinion is for circulation to others than an individual client, you should carefully state the assumed facts or other basis on which you advise in the body of the opinion itself.

(2)   Remember your duty to act fearlessly on behalf of your lay client without regard to any consequences to yourself (para. 203(a)). You should make an application for the 'costs thrown away' to be paid by the defendant's solicitors irrespective of the extent of your personal or professional relationship with them. Otherwise your client will suffer loss through no fault of his or her own. It is for the court to determine the merits of your application.

2.3.3   PROSECUTING COUNSEL AND THE CROWN PROSECUTION SERV=ICE

Whilst para. 11.6, Annexe F (Standards Applicable to Criminal Cases) gives some guidance, the problem is one of communication. You have given weight to factors which you consider important. The solicitor may have others, including the need to adopt a consistent approach to all cases. You should listen to his or her arguments and explain yours clearly to him or her. If you are unable to persuade him or her and you maintain your original opinion, you should withdraw.

2.4   Relationship with Other Members of the Profession

(1)   Almost certainly no, particularly if there is an issue on liability. Your knowledge of the view taken by your colleague of the strength of the claimant's case gives you an unfair advantage, particularly if, on the papers before you, the claimant's case does not strike you as being so weak. It is only if liability is not in dispute that you could consider continuing. Even if you do not feel embarrassed you should disclose to your colleague what has happened and ensure that he or she feels that his or her case is not unfairly disadvantaged by your earlier discussion.

(2)   The first step is to speak to your senior clerk. It is courteous to ask for a word with him or her in private, as it is likely to embarrass him or her if you question him or her in front of the junior clerks. Ask him or her for an explanation as to why this particular brief was given to the pupil when you have advised on the case previously. There may be a good reason, for example, the solicitor may have asked for a pupil to do the case for reasons of cost or he or she may have indicated to the clerk that the client was not happy with your previous advice and did not feel confident about you conducting his or her case. If no satisfactory explanation is forthcoming, ask your clerk what reason the solicitor was given for your unavailability. If you are satisfied that the clerk has deliberately lied to the professional client in order to stop your work, speak to the head of chambers about the matter. You should not 'retrieve' the brief from the pupil for the next day when the solicitor has already been informed that he or she is doing the case. At the very least, however, you should ensure that the situation does not recur.

5.7   Court Etiquette: Problems

(1)   Don't panic. The first step is to telephone your clerk. Instruct him or her to contact the court and your solicitors to inform them of your delay and your expected time of arrival at court. On arrival at court, you must apologise to your client, instructing solicitor and opponent. If you have kept the judge (and jury) waiting, it will be necessary to apologise in open court. Do not make excuses which are untrue such as 'my car broke down'. You have a duty to be candid no matter how embarrassed or concerned you are about the consequences. Punctuality is vital so do not make a habit of being late. Having said that, most members of the Bar have had one experience of this!

(2)   Unfortunately, this situation is a not uncommon one to face members of the criminal Bar, known as 'double-courting'. Once the first case has finished you have no

option but to hasten to the second court and make your apologies to the judge. Expect a reprimand from the judge, and possibly the consideration of a wasted costs order. This is a situation that ought not to have arisen: Annexe F of the Code of Conduct provides at para 4.1 that 'When a barrister has accepted a brief for the defence of a person charged with a serious criminal offence, he should so far as reasonably practicable ensure that the risk of a conflicting professional engagement does not arise'. Both cases ought not to have been accepted. You should have discussed the matter with your clerk before going to court. It is sometimes difficult to have a discussion in which you are asking the clerk to alter something he or she has put into the diary. Remember, however, that you are responsible for the proper administration of your practice, and you will get the flak from the judge, not your clerk.

Speak to your clerk on your return to chambers. Tell him or her what has occurred and try to ensure that it never happens again. In the event of a dispute with your clerk which cannot be resolved between you, consult your head of chambers.

INDEX

Notes